Folklore and Fascism

FOLKLORE STUDIES IN TRANSLATION

General Editor, Dan Ben-Amos

ADVISORY BOARD

German Volkskunde: *A Decade of Theoretical Confrontation, Debate, and Reorientation (1967–1977)*, translated and edited by James R. Dow and Hannjost Lixfeld.

The European Folktale: Form and Nature by Max Lüthi, translated by John D. Niles.

The Fairytale as Art Form and Portrait of Man by Max Lüthi, translated by John Erickson.

Nordic Folklore: Recent Studies, edited by Reimund Kvideland and Henning K. Sehmsdorf (in collaboration with Elizabeth Simpson).

Kalevala Mythology by Juha Y. Pentikäinen, translated and edited by Ritva Poom.

Folk Culture in a World of Technology by Hermann Bausinger, translated by Elke Dettmer.

Folktales and Reality by Lutz Röhrich, translated by Peter Tokofsky.

Principles for Oral Narrative Research, translated by Kirsten Wolf and Jody Jensen.

Folklore and Fascism

The Reich Institute for German *Volkskunde*

Hannjost Lixfeld

**Edited and translated by
James R. Dow**

Indiana University Press

Bloomington & Indianapolis

The generous support of the L. J. Skaggs and Mary C. Skaggs
Foundation has made the Folklore Studies in Translation series possible.

Publication of this volume was made possible in part by grants from the
Sophie and Hermann Freyling Stiftung and the Liberal Arts and Sciences
College of Iowa State University.

The paper used in this publication meets the minimum requirements of
American National Standard for Information Sciences—Permanence of
Paper for Printed Library Materials, ANSI Z39.48-1984.

∞™

Manufactured in the United States of America

Library of Congress Cataloging-in-Publication Data

Lixfeld, Hannjost.
  Folklore and fascism : the Reich Institute for German Volkskunde /
Hannjost Lixfeld ; edited and translated by James R. Dow.
    p. cm. — (Folklore studies in translation)
  Includes bibliographical references and index.
  ISBN 0-253-33512-4 (cloth : alk. paper)
    1. Folklore—Germany—History—20th century. 2. Folklore—
Political aspects—Germany. 3. National socialism—Germany—
History. 4. Germany—Politics and government—1933–1945. I. Dow,
James R. II. Title. III. Series.
GR166.L59 1994
398'.0943'0904—dc20   93-10014

1 2 3 4 5 99 98 97 96 95 94

With gratitude to Wolfgang Jacobeit

Contents

Foreword
Dan Ben-Amos

THIS IS A book about a grim chapter in the history of German folklore. Hannjost Lixfeld approaches his task with clinical precision, recounting the ways folklore fell prey to Nazi politicians, ideologues, and sham scholars. He deliberately concentrates on individual personalities, establishing dates, noting locations, documenting memoranda, and citing sources with exacting care. This historical methodology, which he follows with an orthodox dedication, also serves a psychological function. It enables him, and other modern German intellectuals who share his approach, to relieve themselves of the burden of collective guilt. In such a narration the blame is individual rather than social or cultural. The careful documentation also enables him to separate the guilty from the innocent. Under National Socialism some German folklorists took a firm stand against the regime, and some paid with their lives for their struggle to maintain their personal and scholarly integrity.

While such a careful exposition is necessary, the detailed narration could easily hide a lesson which goes far beyond the boundaries of Germany, then and now, and which touches upon the very nature of human society as a whole. The very historical occurrence of National Socialism evidences humankind's potential to sink to the lowest moral depths. Unfortunately, historical events since that period confirm a continuing willingness to use ideas as a reason for murder. The killing fields of Cambodia and the ethnic cleansing in the former Yugoslavia may be smaller in scale but are no different in nature from the Nazi crimes. In the name of imagined communities and imagined utopias, people committed unimaginable atrocities. Therefore the testimony of this book does not implicate just German scholars and German society during the Third Reich, but the entire community of our species. Its relevance is current and global as a constant reminder of the potential culpability of humankind.

Paradoxically the eeriness of Lixfeld's narrative grows tenfold because its principal players are not the customary set of characters we have learned to associate with the rise of National Socialism and the holocaust. They are not the gas chamber operators or the SS officers; they are not the scientists who performed experiments on human beings, not the bureaucrats who managed the entire Nazi machine of destruction. Rather, Lixfeld tells the story of people who believed, like Voltaire, that the pen is mightier than the sword—people who provided the scholarly and ideological basis for genocide. He describes their surrender to political totalitarianism, reducing the abstractness of evil to minute actions, conversations, meetings, notes, and memoranda. The shameful picture that emerges from these details shows scholars crossing from the domain of academic freedom to political servitude, not because of coercion, but following the seductive lure of financial support, promotions, prestigious positions, and public recognition. And as they made this passage, neither naive nor innocent, and well understanding the nature of the pact they signed, they lulled themselves into self-deception, believing they could continue to pursue truth in the household of the totalitarians.

Such self-deception could occur whenever the boundaries between the state and the university erode and the politicians, of whatever persuasion, take control of science. Research becomes prescriptive rather than open-ended. By accepting these conditions the folklore scholars might have thought that they were adjusting to a new political situation. But with their decision to adapt to new realities rather than to fight, they entered into the prison-house of political thought, where they served ruling dictators rather than scholarly ideals.

Lixfeld refers to them as bourgeois-national scholars. Name-calling notwithstanding, the fact of the matter is that most scholarship around the world is carried out by the bourgeois. Even intellectuals of Marxist persuasion share in the relative comfort of the middle-class. The scholars who collaborated with the Nazis and abdicated their moral and scholarly principles, started their careers following a set of values common to most intellectuals. Their story would therefore serve all of us as a constant reminder that excellence in scholarship without a firm moral foundation is a vacuous achievement.

The troubling fact for modern-day folklorists is that their predecessors' crossover was also made easier by the very proximity between folklore ideas and Nazi ideology. Nationalism was an idea that motivated folklore research in Germany and many other countries; it is also one of the principles of fascism. For them, a transition from analysis to advocacy of these ideas did not conflict with their fundamental disciplinary assumptions. Folklore theory and Nazi ideology drew upon the shared intellectual resources of German romantic-nationalism. The concept of folk (*Volk*) and folklore (*Volkskunde*) were fundamental both to the discipline of folklore and to National Socialist ideology. The notions of nationalism and primitivism, the idealization of the peasantry, the "fatherland," and the community, have been motivating ideas for both discipline and party. Scholars constituted these ideas as subjects of research, while politicians used them as rally slogans for action. But the proximity between them allows no room for comfort.

Therefore modern German folklore scholars take great care to distance themselves from the aberrant use of romantic ideas and seek to reconstitute their discipline on the basis of social-scientific and humanistic concepts and terms. Lixfeld's historical analysis is part of the effort to reformulate the purposes of folklore scholarship and to establish the discipline of folklore—in Germany in particular and in the academies of the world in general—in scholarly terms and in such a way that it will never again become a political tool.

Foreword
James R. Dow

> I find it correct to investigate philologically the texts of researchers who had to work during the Nazi period. I also find it correct to identify with them a little bit—let him who is sure how he would have reacted at that time cast the first stone. I find it wrong, however, to try to clean up those brown spots that did exist.
>
> Utz Jeggle [1]

IN THE YEARS after the Second World War the problem of German and Austrian folklorists' involvement with National Socialism was pushed aside with the argument that there had been two *Volkskunden* (folklores) during the Third Reich: a rather small and opportunistic group of avid Nazis who had abandoned serious scholarly work and disseminated instead their ideological nonsense and a larger number of respectable scholars who had continued their work in an unobtrusive manner. Recent research suggests, however, that even "respectable" German folklorists were bound to a bourgeois and nationalist attitude and that their arrangement with Nazi postulates and expectations paved the way for a militant and inhuman concept of the folk and the nation. This alliance became clear as early as 1933, when a group of over fifty German folklorists put out a call to found a Union for German Folklore (Bund für deutsche Volkskunde) and stated: "Precisely the worldview foundations for National Socialism and the national movement have been prepared in the past through folklore research, as the names of Jahn, Riehl, etc. prove" (see text of the call, appendix III.1).

In 1986, when the Deutsche Gesellschaft für Volkskunde (German Folklore Society) finally devoted an entire working session to the question of *Volkskunde und Nationalsozialismus*,[2] the matter of *zwei Volkskunden* was very much a subtext. Except for a historian who was invited as a special referent,[3] no one specifically addressed what is now referred to as the "legend of two *Volkskunden*," but virtually all participants were dealing with the topic.

When I attempted to transmit some of this debate to American colleagues at the 1987 meetings of the American Folklore Society and the Modern Language

Association, I realized that some members of these audiences also accepted the premise of the German "legend." It would of course be presumptuous for me to assume that my presentations in the United States caused an uproar which soon arose in Germany, but there can be little doubt that they contributed. During much of 1988 there was a shrill tone in the air when the question of *Volkskunde* and National Socialism was under discussion, causing members of the Executive Board of the German Folklore Society to make reference to a *neue Streitkultur* (new combative culture) which was developing.[4] German and Austrian folklorists were clearly beginning to try once again to deal with their past history.

Since that time a rather predictable sequence of events has come about. Many more articles have been published on *Volkskunde* and National Socialism, a few dissertations have been written, and there have been discussions at many of the folklore meetings in the German-speaking world. Much more important, scholars in Germany and Austria who are interested in this topic have gone into the archives and libraries and have begun to supply more complete documentation on the activities of *Volkskundler* (folklorists) during the Third Reich.

Studies from the early years of the 1980s have become models and pioneer studies, but now it has become necessary to begin to fill in the details with well-documented research. Hannjost Lixfeld, with whom I have worked for the past fifteen years, is clearly the strongest voice in the German-speaking world in rejecting the notion of two *Volkskunden*. This volume, a translation of his study of the Reichsinstitut für deutsche Volkskunde based on extensive work in the archives, is an outstanding example of how one may counter the notion of two *Volkskunden* through a detailed investigation of individuals and institutions of the period.

When Lixfeld presented his paper on the umbrella organizations of German *Volkskunde* at the 1986 Munich meeting, it was obvious to most of us in attendance that we were dealing with an early attempt at a detailed study of various organizations of the Third Reich that supported *Volkskunde* so energetically.[5] He specifically treated the Deutsche Forschungsgemeinschaft (German Research Council), the primary source of research funds for German scholars, including folklorists, both then and now. Because he was limited to a brief time for his presentation, he could do little more than outline his ideas on this one umbrella organization.

While he and I were working on the companion to this volume, *The Nazification of an Academic Discipline: German* Volkskunde *of the Third Reich*,[6] Lixfeld continued his archival work in Germany and started to fill in details to which he had only referred in his Munich paper. What has resulted is this seminal study of the Reichsinstitut für deutsche Volkskunde. Details found in this work will certainly contrast with what we have both come to call an apologetic and revisionist interpretation of German and Austrian folklorists' activities and their mind-set during those terrible years 1933–1945.

Lixfeld's study is a primary piece of contemporary German scholarship which draws its special strength from detailed and archival research in the Bundesarchiv in Koblenz and the Berlin Document Center in West Berlin. This unique archival work was then greatly enhanced by Lixfeld's access to East German archives through our mutual friend and colleague, Wolfgang Jacobeit. Jacobeit, as *Ordinarius* for *Volkskunde* at the Humboldt University in East Berlin in the former German Democratic Republic, was also able to acquire materials for Lixfeld from other East German archives through his friends, professional colleagues, and students.

Some of the materials presented in this volume and some of the insights which Lixfeld gained are just now becoming available to scholars in the West, i.e., now that Germany is reunited and there is freer access to these archives and files. This book is thus of great significance, not only because it rejects the "legend" concept but also because it reveals what a storehouse of information is waiting to be extracted and examined by scholars, including of course materials on the role of *Volkskunde* during the National Socialist period.

For some time Lixfeld has devoted most of his research energy to the frequently planned but never realized Reichsinstitut für deutsche Volkskunde as the essence of what virtually all of the umbrella organizations were striving toward. Like most German scholars, Lixfeld has done his historical homework, and thus he devotes the early portions of his study to the plan, before there was any attempt to establish such an institute in reality. He next delves deeply into the "seedbed" for a Reich institute during the war year 1917, which later (1927–1928) led to the *Atlas der deutschen Volkskunde*, then traces other futile attempts to bring about a pan-German institute during the short-lived Weimar Republic.

When the National Socialists came to power in January 1933, they found the concept of a Reich institute very much in agreement with their own plans for *Gleichschaltung* (political coordination) of the political and social order, which was to function according to the rapidly emerging *Führerprinzip*. It should come as no surprise, then, that respected folklorists would be swept up by the new regime. For many the stimulus was the promise of finally being able to realize their dream of a pan-German Reich institute. Lixfeld treats numerous folklorists in this volume, but special attention is paid to those who assumed an ambiguous stance in their dealings with the fascists (John Meier, Adolf Spamer, etc.), and it is precisely these individuals who had long nurtured and promoted the idea of a Reich institute (see Appendices III.1–III.3).

By the time the National Socialist regime held full sway in Germany, it was easy to see the advantages this planned institute would offer. The two most powerful National Socialist ideologists literally seized on the idea and made detailed plans to implement it. Alfred Rosenberg, the Führer's Commissioner for the Supervision of all Intellectual and World-View Schooling and Education of the NSDAP, worked toward a *Hohe Schule* (Advanced School) which would serve to implement the Reich institute according to ideas laid out in his *Mythus des 20. Jahrhunderts* (see appendices I.1–9). Heinrich Himmler, who ran the rival SS Office of Ancestral Inheritance, also planned implementation of such an institute (see appendices II.1–

2). Rosenberg and Himmler continually competed for dominance in the struggle to establish a *völkisch* (pure German) ideology. Their purpose was always clear: to create a vehicle for complete dissemination of the new National Socialist world-view.

What finally emerged was a fledgling Reich institute, one which almost never came into being even though an expansive infrastructure was prepared. Like every other portion of the Third Reich, the institute was doomed to fail, and little has been heard of it since it died in a beautiful monastery in southeastern Austria in early 1945.

The core of Lixfeld's study, I suggest, answers the question about the existence of two *Volkskunden*. Throughout his investigation of the Reichsinstitut für deutsche Volkskunde, Lixfeld works with what we might refer to as an underlying presence of bourgeois-national elements in National Socialist *Volkskunde*. Through his many examples he makes it clear that fascist *Volkskunde* drew heavily from bourgeois-national sources. In spite of the blatant anti-Semitic statements found in the call for a Union for German Folklore, it would be possible to interpret this call as an attempt to provoke a conservative mass movement which would not owe complete allegiance to the general party line. But Lixfeld, in his treatment of the call in chapter 1, clearly does not choose this interpretation.

Even within Nazi *Volkskunde* there is a major cleavage, though it is often difficult to fix real differences. Rosenberg's *Volkskunde* is allegedly different from that of Himmler, but here the differences would seem to amount to only relatively small issues concerning specific formulations of the Rosenberg *Mythus*. Often these were predetermined or fictitious differences, if one can trust the publications of that period and the sources found in the archives. That is also the case with differences within the bourgeois-national disciplines.

It is thus of great importance to ascertain the relative relationships which existed when Nazi folklorists took over the preliminary plans of John Meier and other bourgeois-national professionals and tried to implement them according to the *Mythus* or the objectives of the Office of Ancestral Inheritance. What resulted was a program of folk-national cultivation, or "folk renewal," as applied *Volkskunde*, and this became a rather obvious common point between the two (or more) *Volkskunden*. The primary difference lay in the fact that bourgeois-national *Volkskunde*, which was also faithful to a pure German ideology and pursued folk renewal as a utopia, unlike National Socialist *Volkskunde*, was never able to formulate its goals clearly or carry them out because of inadequate institutional opportunities and financial support. Nazi *Volkskunde*, which profited from more than adequate funds supplied by the Reich leadership of the party, tried to implement what it had borrowed from the bourgeois-nationals and make it fit its own world-view. If the war and the regime had ended successfully for the Nazis, there is every indication that they would have achieved their goals.

That is where *Volkskunde* stood in 1945—i.e., just where it had been in 1933—

and nobody wanted to address this problem or come to terms with it. The process of *Vergangenheitsbewältigung* (dealing with the past) was not engaged.

And so the problem remained. Was there in fact during the Third Reich a reputable, quasi-bourgeois *Volkskunde* which resisted the onslaughts and came through unscathed, in contrast to a militant and National Socialist *Volkskunde?* Lixfeld clearly maintains that such a division is not legitimate, that all folklorists were more or less ideologically and institutionally so involved that one cannot talk about an unscathed *Volkskunde*. All of us who are conducting research on this topic are aware, of course, that it is impossible to throw the bourgeois-national John Meier and the Nazi Matthes Ziegler into the same pot, but we must also be willing to see that they were both in the same oven and that the upright senator's son, Meier, was thoroughly roasted. It must, however, be added that Meier threw himself into the pot for German national reasons, whether good or questionable.

These few thoughts should suggest the complexity of trying to unravel the involvement of respectable individuals and institutions with the strong-armed powers of the National Socialists. In the postwar years the German-speaking world had good opportunities to engage in the process of *Vergangenheitsbewältigung*, but for the most part it was avoided by *Volkskundler*. In the first meeting of folklorists after the war, in Jugenheim an der Bergstraße in 1951, German scholars could have begun the process, but alas it was not to be.[7] The topic was basically suppressed by a conspiracy of silence, and when it did surface in 1965 and 1968[8] it was soon once again moved back from a position of central focus. Even today there is still great difficulty in dealing with the topic, but there is every reason to believe that German and Austrian scholars no longer have the sense of taboo which was previously associated with the theme.

Translating this work into English was done for three reasons. First, the idea of two *Volkskunden* is of such importance that Lixfeld and I felt it necessary to try to expand the debate surrounding it beyond the German-speaking world. The book needed to be translated into English so that others might be equipped to join the debate. The second objective of this book is to keep the matter of *Vergangenheitsbewältigung* in focus, even though specific portions of the study will likely divide critics into those who accept the notion of two *Volkskunden* and those who will not or cannot. Third, even good folklore scholars in contemporary Germany and Austria have not been aware of just how insistently this idea of a Reich institute was promoted in the German world. They too will be able to see how individual after individual jumped onto a bandwagon that never really got under way. Interesting for all will be the continuity of this institute concept through such a long period as well as the continuity of an ideological concept which ennobled the simple folk.

Following the text we have included a set of appendices which were chosen to give the reader specific references for better understanding of the various methods by which the Reichsinstitut für deutsche Volkskunde was to be implemented. All come from the various archives mentioned above and below. They are divided into three parts: those which deal with the Rosenberg Bureau, those which deal with the SS Office of Ancestral Inheritance, and those which come from folklorists whom we would designate as bourgeois-national in their focus.

The section "Translations, Terminology, and Abbreviations" is basically the same as the one that appears in the companion volume. It is intended to aid the reader who knows no German, and to clarify to those who do, just how a number of the difficult translations were carried out. The bibliography is drawn directly from materials cited in the text.

It only remains for us to attempt to thank all those individuals, universities, departments, archives, foundations, societies, and publishers who have assisted us in the preparation of the material in this volume and the companion volume. Such a list is never adequate, but one will have to suffice.

We are particularly indebted to all of the following in Germany: Archiv der Landesstelle für Volkskunde Freiburg im Breisgau (FRG), Archiv der Philosophischen Fakultäten der Universität Freiburg im Breisgau (FRG), Bundesarchiv Koblenz (FRG), Berlin Document Center, United States Mission Berlin-West, Deutsche Gesellschaft für Volkskunde. Akten im Deutschen Volksliedarchiv Freiburg im Breisgau (FRG), Deutsches Volksliedarchiv Freiburg im Breisgau (FRG), Institut für Zeitgeschichte München (FRG), Staatsarchiv Schwerin (GDR), Universitätsarchiv der Humboldt-Universität zu Berlin (GDR), Universitätsarchiv Freiburg im Breisgau (FRG), Universitätsarchiv Greifswald (GDR), Universitätsarchiv Halle-Wittenberg (GDR), Universitätsarchiv Jena (GDR), Zentrales Staatsarchiv der Deutschen Demokratischen Republik Potsdam (GDR), Zentrales Staatsarchiv der Deutschen Demokratischen Republik Abteilung Merseburg (GDR).

We want to thank the directors and their co-workers in the archives mentioned above for their helpful assistance and their support, without which this study would not have been possible. We want to express our gratitude especially to the Deputy Director of the Staatliche Archivverwaltung der Deutschen Demokratischen Republik, Martin Seckendorf of Berlin, Wolfgang Jacobeit of Berlin/Birkenwerder, and Reinhard Schmook of Bad Freienwalde, all of whom helped us gain admittance to the state and university archives of the former German Democratic Republic.

In the United States we would like to thank the National Endowment for the Humanities for a Summer Stipend for James R. Dow (1987). Several students helped process the manuscript: Michele Bents as a work-study student, Stefanie Buck who just found the topic so interesting that she volunteered her help, and Fred Schwink who made the first translation of the Ziegler article which appears as appendix I.9. In addition, expressions of gratitude go to Iowa State University for various kinds of help with processing of the manuscript, particularly the Graduate College and the College of Liberal Arts and Sciences, but also to many of the members of my own department who listened to me talk about the project for several years. We are particularly grateful to Dean David Glenn-Lewin and Associate Dean Kim Smith of the College of Liberal Arts and Sciences at Iowa State University and to the Sophie and Hermann Freyling Stiftung in Germany for finding subvention funds to help defray the cost of publication.

Finally we would like to thank the series editor Dan Ben-Amos for his continuing interest in our work. We also would like to thank Hermann Bausinger in Germany and Linda Dégh in the United States for their advice and interest. We are particularly indebted to Professor Bausinger for his careful reading of this manuscript and his many suggestions, some of which are included in this foreword. In addition we want to thank Susan Christiansen and Gisela Lixfeld for their personal interest and support during the years of work on this book. All of the above deserve our warmest thanks.

Introduction

THE INSTITUTIONAL HISTORY of the discipline of German *Volkskunde* during the Third Reich is concerned with both ideology and personality. It is a history of ideas, of organizations and individuals, of strong-armed political objectives with theoretical prerequisites for the discipline, of economic bases, and of cultural, political, and social developments. Such a complex history cannot be treated without considering the time before and after the "Thousand Year Reich."[1] On one hand, the very short (twelve-year) epoch of *Volkskunde* under National Socialism remains incomprehensible for the most part when its preliminary stages are not considered, and on the other hand it is exactly this period which lays a foundation for the institutional establishment of the discipline of *Volkskunde* at universities and research institutes in those states which came from the German Reich: the Federal Republic of Germany, the German Democratic Republic, and the Republic of Austria.

It is a fact that most of the scholarly folklore institutions in the three German-speaking countries of contemporary central Europe did not exist before the beginning of the Third Reich. Many were founded during this time and were then reestablished in the postwar years. Several questions arise, however. What was the eventual effect on scholarly theory of establishing contemporary German-language *Volkskunde* in institutions during National Socialism? Which scholars who were influential or worked in these institutions during the Third Reich were then reemployed after the war and which ones were not, and what were the justifications by which these distinctions were made? Which objectives of the discipline or attitudes and behavioral patterns of the scholars of our discipline that we now consider historically perverted were continued through these institutions and individuals during the postwar years; and when, in what way, and by what means could they be removed? Why did the iconoclastic analysis of National Socialist folk ideology by Hermann Bausinger not appear until twenty years after the end of the war?[2] Why could the first meeting on *Volkskunde und Nationalsozialismus* not take place until twenty years after that, in 1986 in Munich?[3] Why does a broad spectrum of established professional colleagues continue to make taboo, to suppress and hide, now as before, the National Socialist past of *Volkskunde*, and why does it project its accusation of a nest-dirtying syndrome paradoxically onto those who do not conform, on those who find it necessary to work up this past history of the discipline in the interest of self-understanding?

To give answers to these and related questions is the task of German-language *Volkskunde*. Nearly fifty years after the fall of the Third Reich the time has come to put this work at the center of our scholarly endeavors, not to exercise in some limited way a judgment on the historical happening and those who took part in it but rather to do justice, in the final analysis, to ourselves, to the past, and thus also to the present and to the future of our discipline.

The period from 1933 to 1945 represents one of the most important eras in the history of German *Volkskunde* during this century, but few research conclusions are available. For the most part it has been younger scholars who have dealt with it, since those scholars who lived and conducted their scholarly works during the Third Reich followed the trend after the Second World War and came to a conspiracy of silence on what had happened, thus hiding and thereby trivializing it. Those who had participated in National Socialism were of course quiet. However, those folklorists who had stood in opposition were also quiet, even though such behavior was actually not to be expected from them. It has thus become even more difficult to treat the institutional foundations of this epoch of our discipline, foundations that now lie half a century in the past.

The scholarly history of German *Volkskunde* from 1933 to 1945 is concentrated in the history of its umbrella leagues, of which there were several. Soon after the seizure of power by the fascist regime on January 30, 1933, with the naming of Adolf Hitler to the chancellorship of the German Reich, interested parties and groups from the "leading circles"[4] of the National Socialist German Workers Party (NSDAP) joined the only folkloric umbrella organization which had existed up to that time, the bourgeois-national Verband deutscher Vereine für Volkskunde (League of German Societies for Folklore), chaired by Professor John Meier. With their help, further umbrella leagues arose: the Abteilung Volkskunde (Department of Folklore) of the Reichsgemeinschaft für deutsche Volksforschung (Reich Community for German Folk Research) under Professor Adolf Spamer; the Forschungs- und Lehrgemeinschaft "Das Ahnenerbe" (Research and Teaching Community "Ancestral Inheritance") of the Reichsführer-SS Heinrich Himmler with its folkloric subdepartments; and the Dienststelle des Beauftragten des Führers für die Überwachung der gesamten geistigen und wèltanschaulichen Schulung und Erziehung der Nationalsozialistischen Deutschen Arbeiterpartei (Service Branch of the Führer's Commissioner for the Supervision of All Intellectual and World-View Schooling and Education of the NSDAP) of the Reich Leader Alfred Rosenberg, also called the Amt Rosenberg (Rosenberg Bureau) or the Reichsüberwachungsamt (Reich Overview Office) with various folklore programs.

All of these large scholarly organizations conceived of themselves as pan-German umbrella leagues for a *Volkskunde* applied to the cultivation of the folk-nation. Common to all such offices of the Third Reich was the usual internal hierarchical structure based on the autocratic "Führer principle" and the attempt to win absolute control of all *Volkskunde* in the entire Reich, and later, after the annexation of Austria in 1938, all of Great German *(Großdeutsche) Volkskunde*.

In the interest of this objective—which, however, was not accomplished by the end of the fascist regime by any single umbrella league—all participated in the establishment, alignment, or "political coordination"[5] of disciplinary institutes, associations, leagues, journals, series, publishers, etc., and all tried to present insofar as possible the results of their impressive research works. These were then to be applied and indeed were applied utilizing the concept "folk-national cultivation" to the broad masses of the populace. This folk education was for everyone concerned an integral part of scholarly *Volkskunde*.

These umbrella leagues were in vigorous competition with each other in carrying out their own specific German *Volkskunde*, hoping to lend it their respective ideas and to defeat their adversaries in the field. As was so often the case in the "Thousand Year Reich," there was no kind of unified *Volkskunde* scholarship but rather, if one chooses to believe the scholars of that time, several disciplines which were quite different from one another and which were engaged in battle with the others for supremacy.

Virtually all scholars of the discipline were a part of these confrontations, so that almost everyone was damaged by opponents or personally persecuted. In the period after the Second World War this disadvantage brought on by the system could be used as proof of one's opposition to National Socialism. This documents indirectly, even though not always absolutely, the affinity of the vast majority of the so-called bourgeois-national German folklorists with National Socialist ideology or with the National Socialist world-view and the behavioral principles which resulted from it.

In the beginning this battle was intended to help secure the economic basis of those *Volkskunde* leagues and interest groups which participated. The easiest means was to assume influence over the scholarly foundation that had been started in 1920, after Germany's loss of the First World War, as the Notgemeinschaft der deutschen Wissenschaft (Cooperative Council for Aid to German Research) and later assumed the name Deutsche Forschungsgemeinschaft, or DFG (German Research Council). An important source of funds for all umbrella leagues, the DFG developed into an "economic central office" for folklore scholarship. All umbrella leagues subsequently participated in controlling the distribution of funds from this central German scholarly foundation. If an umbrella league was not successful in maintaining its influence over the DFG because it had been suppressed by its competitors, then other means of financing scholarly research work had to be undertaken. The battle for power among rivals continued, occasionally interrupted by fortuitous agreements.

The intent of this study is to investigate the prehistory, background, and objectives of this scholarly ideological confrontation in the discipline of *Volkskunde*. In the final analysis, this confrontation was nothing less than strong-armed power politics.

Folklore and Fascism

1

Bourgeois-National *Volkskunde* between the Monarchy and Fascism

THE PRESIDENT OF the Notgemeinschaft der deutschen Wissenschaft (Cooperative Council for Aid to German Research), or Deutsche Forschungsgemeinschaft (DFG, the German Research Council), during the Weimar Republic was the former Regal-Prussian cultural minister, His Excellency Dr. Friedrich Schmidt-Ott. During the first year of fascist rule in Germany he felt called upon to present a statement of accounts for the DFG, in which he rejected the fallen democratic state. He then offered himself in a statement of submission to the National Socialists, i.e., to continue to be of use in his office.

To convince the parliament and the government prior to 1933 of the necessity of the Cooperative Council and to familiarize them with the large sums being requested, Schmidt-Ott had conducted negotiations with the representatives of the most varied parties and had established closer contacts with the members of the appropriate governmental offices. As Schmidt-Ott wrote,

> If one wanted to deduce from this that the Cooperative Council or its president, through such alliances, had been estranged even in the least from its *national orientation*, then one might raise a very serious objection. Even personal relationships have had to help carry out our requirements for scholarship, and they have found herein and everywhere their limitations and their conclusions. I personally feel completely free of the former regime and its supporters, and I confess that I am filled with *extreme amazement for the Führer*, who has succeeded in rescuing us from the hundreds of years of miserable party politics and has brought us together as one folk. It is my inmost wish that he succeed in freeing our people and making us happy.[1]

This attempt to remain president of the DFG even under fascist rule was destined to failure. Schmidt-Ott was removed from office in 1934.[2]

THE *ATLAS DER DEUTSCHEN VOLKSKUNDE* AS A SEEDBED FOR THE REICH INSTITUTE

According to Schmidt-Ott's statement of accounts, the Cooperative Council had from the very beginning placed those branches of scholarship in the foreground "which demanded adherence to the fatherland viewpoint."[3] In this way the discipline of *Volkskunde* had also been promoted financially prior to 1933. John Meier, who was chairman of the League of German Societies for Folklore and was for many years the sole folklore referee for the Cooperative Council, had agreed with Schmidt-Ott that this foundation should "not only support but even take on the responsibility itself" for the *Atlas der deutschen Volkskunde*, in recognition of the entire scholarly and national importance of the planned work.[4] This work had first been promoted in 1926 by Wilhelm Peßler.[5]

This agreement was carried out by Schmidt-Ott himself from 1928 until the last years of the Weimar Republic. The *Atlas* was thus directly under the DFG Presidium in the Reich capital, Berlin. Its work space was for the time being in the Berlin palace of the Hohenzollern kaisers. In this Berlin central office a staff of folklore collaborators was assembled and supported by a financial subvention from DFG funds. From here *Atlas* questionnaires were sent out and were then filled in with the help of over thirty regional offices of the *Atlas* throughout the German-speaking world.

Work on the *Atlas* was supported by a plan to collect both the spiritual property and the material elements of German folk culture, if at all possible throughout the German-speaking world. That which belonged together was to be recorded on a special map showing its distribution, and it was to be interpreted or explained through scholarly comparisons and then published.[6] The choice of folk material worthy to be collected was the result of a presentation and an evaluation of folk culture that had been conclusively predecided in a discussion of the plan of the *Atlas* in 1928. The decision was controversial and continued to be debated again and again.[7] This is, of course, quite obvious today from what we know about the project's methodological procedures. The collecting and presenting of elements of folk culture were associated with a "concept of salvaging."[8] That part of folk culture which was viewed as valuable, most often traditional relics, not only was preserved in the form of a scholarly archive and through publication so that it would not be forgotten but also was returned automatically and intentionally to the folk.[9] Now it was filtered through scholarship and folk-national cultivation, given new life, and preserved from extinction. What was not collected was pushed aside, for the most part.

Added to this leadership function of *Volkskunde* for the folk and for folk culture was an expansion of the network of collectors, or the network of localities which were investigated. It now included those German "speech islands" which existed outside the German state. The unity of these ethnic Germans to all people who spoke German was emphasized, a viewpoint with eminent political importance. It must be emphasized that in addition to conclusions which were methodologically questionable, which were intended to cultivate the folk-nation, and which were politically misused, there were also scholarly conclusions which reflected reality and were worth knowing. All things considered in this calculation were typical for the age; there was "the entire scholarly and national importance of the planned work,"[10] which, according to its claims, was supposed to work out "the cultural structure, the cultural-morphological face of our fatherland."[11]

For implementing this *Atlas* work, there were plans for questions (i.e., outlines and suggestions for questions to be asked) from, among others, Professors John Meier, Adolf Helbok, Friedrich Panzer, Otto Lehmann, Otto Lauffer, Georg Schreiber, Adolf Spamer, and Dr. Eduard Wildhagen.[12] Originally it was thought that one thousand questions were necessary; then for financial reasons three hundred were viewed as sufficient.[13] After a regionally limited test probe, "to a certain extent as a general test of the undertaking,"[14] workers began early in 1930 sending out the first questionnaire, 40,000 copies to the regional offices. It contained fifty questions,[15] asking among other things about the kinds of grain being planted and their names, farm draft animals and their harnesses, children's cradles and their forms, funeral colors, greetings and forms of address, public festivals, customary games and sports competition, musical instruments, Christian saints and related customs, and various demonic legendary figures.

This questionnaire and the five which followed had, for the most part, fifty items and were distributed from the regional offices to the local workers to be filled out. In 1933 workers totaled about 20,000 teachers, clerics, farmers, etc., all of whom were associated with the community in which they lived so that they were familiar with the local situation. (The informant principle is still troublesome today, especially the problem of inadequate representation, a problem which raises questions about this empirical fieldwork methodology.)

Atlas results came from thirty-seven regional offices and included all Reich German provinces, states, and regions. With Grenzmark Posen–West Prussia, Danzig, and Upper Silesia they clearly moved beyond state boundaries. With the Burgenland, Carinthia, Lower and Upper Austria, Salzburg, Styria, Tyrol, and Vorarlberg, all of the Republic of Austria was included, and the sovereign state of Luxembourg was added in.[16] For those ethnic Germans of Czechoslovakia and Romania as well as for the Germans of Hungary and Bessarabia,[17] there were regional offices in Prague, Temeschwar, and Hermannstadt.[18] The directors of these regional offices were for the most part educated people with names well known in the discipline. Frequently they were university professors,[19] and even though there were occasional changes of directors, still there were about fifty scholars.

To establish this network of regional offices, there was in addition to the German-language *Atlas* in Marburg a similarly structured Deutsches Volksliedarchiv (Folk Song Archive) in Freiburg im Breisgau which utilized the same collecting principle and which, like the *Atlas*, conformed to the Berlin Central Office. The founder and director of the Folk Song Archive was John Meier, who was also chairman of the League of German Societies for Folklore and with whom the vast

majority of the regional directors of the *Atlas* were in contact. The monumental
scholarly undertaking of the *Atlas*, its conceptualization and its structure as well
as its implementation during the earliest and the most decisive years, must be
looked upon as the work of this outstanding scholar and scholarly organizer.

Meier was also chairman of the Folklore Board of the German Research Council, which administered the scholarly portion of the Berlin Central Office of the
Atlas. This board was made up of nine scholars. During the fiscal year 1929–1930
there were, in addition to Meier, Germanists, historians, theologians, and folklorists
such as Hermann Aubin, Hanns Bächthold-Stäubli, Theodor Frings, Arthur Hübner,
Georg Schreiber, Adolf Helbok, Wilhelm Peßler. Fritz Boehm was director of the
Berlin Central Office; its business director was Eduard Wildhagen.[20] For carrying
out the collecting activity there were state boards in all Reich German states and
provinces which had been set up with the aid of churches, appropriate adminis-
trators, and large professional leagues.[21]

The unique model developed by the *Atlas* for foreign colleagues of the discipline
led to the development of similar plans in Denmark, Sweden, France, Belgium,
the Netherlands, and Switzerland, or at least it brought about the beginning of
cooperation with scholars in these countries.[22] A certain comparison can be made
with international cooperative work in continuing appeals by the directorship of
the *Atlas* for scholarship and openness, since the German work on the *Atlas* had
eminent national significance. Such appeals are found throughout the reports of
the Cooperative Council; they reach a high point in 1933 after seizure of power
by the National Socialists.[23]

Meier wrote the *Atlas* reports of the DFG anonymously during the time he
worked for the *Atlas*, or at least they were under his direct supervision and thus
he was equally responsible for them. Their pan-German national intentions certainly
corresponded to Meier's "fatherland" ideas.

John Daniel Florens Meier came from the German grand bourgeoisie. He was
the youngest of nine children, born June 14, 1864, in Horn by Bremen, where his
family had an estate. His father was Dr. John Daniel Meier, who was born in 1804
in New York and died in 1871. He was a senator and the officiating mayor of
Bremen, and was thus the chief political figure of a small German state. The son
chose a scholarly career, finished his study of Germanistics in 1888 in Freiburg
im Breisgau with a doctorate, completed his *Habilitation* in 1891 in Halle an der
Saale, and was named full professor for German language and literature at the
University of Basel in Switzerland. His career reached a first high point in 1907
with his election to the rectorship of the university.[24]

Shortly before the outbreak of the First World War Meier gave up his Basel
professorial position since, as a well-to-do man, he did not need the salary and
moved into the nearby southwest German city of Freiburg im Breisgau, where he
had studied earlier. In Freiburg he was named in 1913 by the still-ruling Baden

Grand Duke to an honorary full professorship for German language, literature, and *Volkskunde*. This was an honorary university position without regular salary. With a subvention by the German Kaiser in the sum of 100,000 Reichmarks in 1914, Meier founded the Deutsches Volksliedarchiv (DVA). It is still housed in his former private home.

Meier made a name for himself with pioneering folklore publications, especially on folk song research.[25] Shortly before his return to Germany in 1911, the League of German Societies for Folklore elected him as its chairman. He kept this position until he stepped down for reasons of age in 1949. He relinquished the directorship of his folk song archive only in 1953 with his death, at age eighty-nine.

The presidency of the League represented a second high point in Meier's professional career. Through scholarly accomplishments and professional organizational services for the League, he became the highest-ranking representative of German *Volkskunde*. His most urgent task was the building up of folklore scholarship, which before and after the First World War was hardly established institutionally, into a self-sufficient discipline represented equally at universities and research centers. He did it through enormous work and with highly developed diplomatic and tactical skills, but his relationships to the ruling social circles, which he came by due to his heritage, certainly aided him.

It can be assumed that Meier identified himself with the discipline and with the League. It can also be assumed that he directed the League much as he did his folk song archive, in a most "authoritarian" way.[26] He was, so to speak, the embodiment of German *Volkskunde*.

The disciplinary and strong-armed political importance of this monumental *Atlas* undertaking must not be underestimated. The *Atlas* formed the "seedbed"[27] for a Reich institute for German folklore, which Meier had talked about a decade earlier. He obviously thought about taking over the *Atlas* directorship, since it represented not only his disciplinary but also his personal inclination.

A 1917 PROPOSAL FOR A CENTRAL INSTITUTE FOR GERMAN FOLKLORE

During the First World War, around 1917, while there was euphoria over the apparent victories of the Kaiser's German army, John Meier drew up a seven-page undated manuscript entitled "Creation of an Institute for German Folklore" (see partial text in appendix III.3).[28] Even though it was marked "Strictly Confidential!" the proposal was known to other scholars and ministerial officers and served as a model for the umbrella organizations of *Volkskunde* and their competing objectives at the beginning of the Third Reich.[29]

The proposal was not in any way new. The creation of a folkloric central office had been planned as early as 1906 by the Würzburg professor Oskar Brenner,[30] and a similar plan can be found an entire century earlier. Meier refers in his manuscript to the Prussian state minister Freiherr von Stein, the brothers Wilhelm and Jacob Grimm, the historian Karl Friedrich Eichhorn, the teacher of the Grimms Carl Friedrich von Savigny and his Berlin Proposal of 1816,[31] as well as to a letter recommending it which was written by Wilhelm Grimm to Johann Wolfgang von Goethe at the latter's request. So it was not only Wilhelm and Jacob Grimm, the fathers of *Volkskunde*, and their circle of professorial friends who were at the beginning point; there was also the statesman and prince of poets (Goethe), who was for Meier at "the head of spiritual Germanism."

But it was also the conditions of their times, the wars against Napoleon, which represented a parallel to the First World War. As Meier's plan states, "Germany had freed itself in a battle a hundred years ago from the oppressive rule of foreign conquerors, through a similar and unheard of sacrifice in goods and blood. And in spite of the limitations of the available means being competed for by state and private concerns, it employed its most meaningful forces for the spiritual establishment and renewal of its own folk type." And with those models the "best of our folk . . . found their way toward a common work . . . they wanted to unite all friends of the German folk type and of the German folk-nation into a broad, part state and part private society which was then supposed to bring together in large collections both the sources and the materials for a history of Germandom and its culture and thus make possible later presentations." Meier's plan is thus equated with the Berlin Proposal of 1816, and the sought-after founders and financiers are likewise equated with the "best of our folk." That certainly included Meier himself.

In addition to the ideal, there are some concrete thoughts in Meier's plan concerning the material bases of the institute. The important founding or beginning capital is supposed to "be brought together from voluntary gifts. Once the necessary requirements of the undertaking are secured through voluntary gifts from the private sector, then the German federal states and the German Reich will not be able to neglect their duty to promote the institute and its objectives by means of financial subventions, but an initial step from private sources will be absolutely necessary for the present time [during the war]."[32] State funds are thus supposed to follow private contributions. "The establishment of an institute for German folklore must be a voluntary creation by members of the folk . . . ,"[33] i.e., it must not be founded by the state, since the "procedure" or the prior inauguration by private founders assured an independent directorship in the person of the chairman of the institute. The contributors are offered acceptance into a ruling advisory council for the institute, but the "general overall direction" is to "be decided more exactly at a later date."[34]

The task of the institute was to be, for the present, the collecting and salvaging of folk goods and relics which were threatened with extinction. Here the League, with its list of sixty allied societies,[35] had already accomplished considerable preliminary work, all of which had appeared in an annotated series:[36] a collection of blessings and exorcism formulas (I), German folk songs (II), military folklore (III), and bell sayings and customs and legends associated with bells (V). A history of German costumes (IV) was in preparation as well as the first volume of the *Bibliographie der Volkskunde*, for 1917 (VI). Also stimulated and influenced by the League were statistics on German farmhouses (VI/I), a collection of German place names (VI/II), and German letters and diaries from the world war (VI/III).

With this advantage in the area of collecting, Meier's plan indicates, it is no longer questionable whether the League will decisively influence the work of the institute, which now will receive additional collecting areas reflecting the folklore canon.[37] The division of the institute into a central office and regional organizations is planned. Through the expansion of the already existing corporate members of the League, the associations, the museums, etc., collections are to be carried out and all of Germany is to be covered by means of this net, with no gaps. The central office, "the institute itself," is to be divided into an archive, a library, and a research institute. It will receive all of the collected folk material, work it up in a scholarly fashion, publish the results, and direct the entire undertaking.

This structure for the planned institute draws heavily on the model set up by Meier's Folk Song Archive in Freiburg im Breisgau.[38] In regard to the regional organizations, the institute and the League or its associations are to be united through the leadership of one person (and, as we have seen, Meier was certainly striving toward this position). The primary structure of the *Atlas der deutschen Volkskunde* which followed a decade later was clearly the same as that of the institute, and the deeper intentions of both large proposals by Meier were clearly related.

Meier's emphatic style—directed toward the presumed money giver, hardly the man on the street—calls in tireless repetition for the creation of an institute. It also addresses the core idea of *Volkskunde* as it is to be employed: the concept of a collecting and salvaging scholarship closely associated with active folk-national cultivation.[39] That which is questionable in regard to Meier's folk educational calling comes to the fore:

> . . . more and more old things are disappearing and are washed away by the leavening and changing stream of modern life.
>
> In addition to collecting, the preservation of living and valuable folk possessions is to be represented. With the disappearance of customs and practices we are, insofar as they are of value, to save them by filling them with a new sense and life.
>
> More and more of the old possessions which the folk inherited from our ancestors have been lost, weaker and weaker are the life forces of the materials still in existence, because its maternal and nourishing soil has been drawn out by foreigners and by things unreal. Thus it is a national duty for us, which we must not shirk, to collect not only with a holy zeal that which is still alive but

also, and here quite consciously going beyond the breadth of former plans [Savigny's and others], to strengthen what has become weak, to reshape in a homeland-oriented way that which is still useful but which has outlived its form.

Modern life and foreign influence—or, expressed somewhat differently, economic and social advances during the industrial age and the international cultural exchange as well as generally everything which leads to a supposed "inauthenticity" in folk culture—are declared to be the enemies of the folk and folk goods. The impression arises that the folk being described here has become spiritually sick and much in need of salvation and the help of scholarship. Possessing knowledge of that which is "authentic" and of those healing forces are in fact the folklorists who, like subversive agents of a foreign power, "listen to our folk during its life, . . . who know precisely its essence and the soil on which it grows, and also know the path to its feelings, opinions, and beliefs." Folk goods thus become purified, in their opinion; when necessary they are reshaped, given a new sense, and enlivened by placing them at the disposal of the folk, but only after this specialized control. Out of these relics or survivals are created intentional revivals.

Censured in this way, a new body of scholarly work will come into existence which begins with presumptions concerning the transmission process, folk-national preservation, and folk education: "For only he can work as an educator who has researched the spiritual organism of those who are to be educated, and knows: this is valid for the cleric, the teacher, the doctor, the civil servant and in general for all personalities who lead the folk spiritually."

In this "attempt at an inner renewal of our folk," which is so distant from any realistic understanding and reveals a bourgeois educational arrogance and absolutist thought process, the Institut für deutsche Volkskunde to be directed by Meier will play a dominant role. It forms the "middle point . . . from which all attempts of a scholarly and folklike nature emanate, for recognizing, preserving, and developing the German race [Art] and the German essence, and it awakens and warms those affected." For its establishment, the time of the world war, according to Meier's calculations, was "singularly favorable," since it has on one hand cleansed the folk-nation "in a fire which cleansed away the degenerative smut and the sudden appearance of that which is fundamentally foreign." On the other hand, "national sensitivities have been newly enlivened." The contributors on whom they are depending are supposed to be won over through this nationalistic appeal; the institute to be founded is a gift to the German folk, "born out of a warm sense of gratitude for the accomplishments of the German folk-nation during the war, a most noble deed of German patriotism."[40]

These thoughts, which can only be called devious, and this spiritual position exemplify the deep rift which existed between the folklorist Meier, who came from a grand bourgeois family, and the broad strata of the populace, who were suffering in 1917 in an especially hard way from the world war. The rift could not be bridged. The revolution which broke out in 1918 among people who had been senselessly sent into a battle which could not be won, the final military defeat, the downfall of the monarchy, and the rise of the Weimar Republic devastated the founding of Meier's institute.

A 1926 PLEA FOR A RESEARCH INSTITUTE FOR GERMAN FOLKLORE

In the new democratic state the *Primus* of German *Volkskunde* presented a reworked and somewhat different concept for his institute to a broad range of professionals. Meier published it in 1926 in the Notes of the Akademie zur wissenschaftlichen Erforschung und zur Pflege des Deutschtums, or Deutsche Akademie (Academy for Scholarly Research and for the Cultivation of Germanness, or German Academy),[41] part of the cultural and political institution for ethnic Germans founded one year earlier.[42] After a detailed presentation of the Berlin Plan of 1816, Meier concluded that the tasks assigned back then to German philology and to art history had in the meantime been worked up, and only the area of German *Volkskunde* had been left aside without any attention; its treatment had been left to the chance interest of individuals.[43]

Meier thus called for a Forschungsinstitut für deutsche Volkskunde (Research Institute for German Folklore)[44] which was, as in 1917, not to be financed by the state but rather by private funds. As a source of funds he saw the German Academy, which had already established a Section for German Language, Literature, and Folklore and within which there was to be an Abteilung für Volks- und Altertumskunde (Department for Folk and Antiquity Studies). The members of this department were Johannes Bolte (the Prussian Academy of Sciences, Berlin), Erich Gierach (University of Prague), Arthur Hübner (University of Münster in Westphalia), Friedrich Panzer (University of Heidelberg), Edward Schröder (University of Göttingen), and John Meier.[45]

Quite logically the League of German Societies for Folklore was presented as exemplary for the structure of the research institute being called for.[46] It was supposed to form a necessary central point for everything collected by the regional offices and to present for research work all of the German material, i.e., "the literary creations of the German folk and its tribes, inside and outside of the German political boundaries, through copies and partially through phonographic records and cylinders," the "objects of folklore" in a "picture and photo archive." In addition, "a professional library was to be established . . . which places the material for research activities at the disposal of German and foreign scholars."[47] The "salvation idea" was brought into play because any further delay of an extensive scholarly collection of the material and its treatment "seriously threatens the recognition of important portions of the German folk-nation" and endangers "vital interests."[48]

This was the preamble for the political objectives of the central research institute being called for and thus also of German *Volkskunde* during the postwar period. The disappearance of traditional research objects under the influence of the modern age was not only a danger for scholarship; "what is more important and more meaningful is that the solving by the German folk-nation of meaningful sociopolitical and national-political problems is being made impossible." The "construction and expansion of our nation" necessary for future development can only be carried out successfully if it is understood that "our folk" will be listened to at its life sources, its essence and the soil on which it grows will be known exactly, and the path to its feelings, opinions, and beliefs is known. "Only this deeper knowledge of German essence and of the German race can protect us from errors in the attempt at an inner renewal of our folk. . . . "[49]

Meier's intention, which he had already stated in his plan of 1917, for an "inner renewal" or ideological-reactionary education of the folk with the help of *Volkskunde* is also found in his 1926 concept.

A further "most important sociopolitical objective" of the research institute could, according to Meier's concept, "be accomplished almost exclusively by means of German *Volkskunde*, and it must be accomplished if important national interests are not to be destroyed." It was "one of the most necessary requirements of our age that the landed populace which has been frivolous, especially the rural youth, be reunited once again with the land and the rural homeland." It was not only the purely material interest which the state had for preserving the widespread rural work force; it was also the knowledge that the landed populace represented the healthiest and the freshest kernel of the folk, i.e., the organic concept of the socially unchangeable folk personality.

Measured against the actual social developments of the German industrial nation during the period, this call to and assignment of objectives for the discipline of *Volkskunde* is not only reactionary but even anachronistic. Meier tried to justify it with many ideological truisms, as for example "love of the homeland," the "inner alliance with parents and ancestors and their inheritance," the "insight into that which is special and necessary" of a "life-style related to the home and the hearth, but also to the customs and character," etc. In reality it was directed toward the "state and national feeling"[50] which ostensibly grew out of the previously mentioned truisms. More clearly stated, it was the political well-being of the rural folk which was always preferred by bourgeois-national *Volkskunde* as an element of traditional preservation, much more so than that of the industrial folk, who were looked upon as an element of social movement and change, especially in the urban areas.

Meier's concept of folk education with the goal of stopping the flight from the land degrades the discipline into an instrument of sociopolitical control. The conservative scholar and theoretician Wilhelm Heinrich Riehl as early as 1858 thought that this was "indeed one of the most meaningful callings of *Volkskunde*."[51]

A third national-political objective of the research institute was closely related. It corresponded to one of the main goals of the German Academy, which Wolfgang Schlicker has called an "institution for imperialistic foreign politics during the time of the Weimar Republic and of fascism."[52] According to Meier, "proving that all creations of the folk-nation in the spiritual and material realms" among both domestic and ethnic Germans were "most closely related" was a task which was to be accomplished by *Volkskunde*, and in this way "the spiritual union of all German folk elements abroad and in the great German tribal lands, . . . can be brought to a clear consciousness among the entire ethnic German folk."[53] The creations of the folk-nation and, at the same time, the research areas for folklore were to be the type of village layout, the uniqueness of buildings and the arrangement of the house, belief and opinions, names and personalities, regional and place names, customs and practices, folk song, legend and fairy tale, and finally the language itself.

The verification of foreign-born Germans as an inseparable part of the German folk-nation living within its state boundaries was completely suited to lending a necessary "scholarly" emphasis to national-political expansionist demands. Meier's plea of 1926 concludes with this offer, one which considerably expands the national and political objectives of the institute plan of 1917 and one which is now prescribed for German *Volkskunde* as an applied science.

Even though Meier proposed the establishment of his pan-German institute as "one of the most important and most worthy tasks" for clarifying and presenting "that 'honorable part of the nation which one calls the folk,' "[54] the German Academy apparently was not ready to promote this ambitious undertaking. The dream was nevertheless not at an end. Continuity was also part of Meier's political definition of German *Volkskunde*, as a self-sustaining folk-national cultivation with a nationalistic and social reactionary character.

GERMAN *VOLKSKUNDE* AS FOLK-NATIONAL CULTIVATION DURING THE WEIMAR REPUBLIC AND AT THE BEGINNING OF THE THIRD REICH

If one looks at the names of the professional institutions which Meier chaired, founded, or planned, whether it was the League, the Folk Song Archive, the *Atlas,* or the Reich institute, they all bore the designation "German." This was not just a simple designation for their area of work; it was much more a national commitment to "German" *Volkskunde*. This *Volkskunde* was a "splendid national scholarship,"[55] and its representatives, especially the university scholars, thus took an active part in the cultural and political confrontations of this period of crisis after the loss of the First World War.

The political scientist Wolfgang Abendroth has emphasized that the mentality of German university professors during the Weimar Republic "was clearly shaped by their position in the monarchical authoritarian state."[56] With few exceptions, Abendroth has written, the ranks of professors remained

> essentially politically homogeneous. They opposed the Weimar constitution and its democratic norms even though they did not refer to this as a political opposition as such but still held onto the ideology that they were "unpolitical" and thus "scholarly objective" and were only committed to "German culture." They perpetuated themselves for the most part through the *Habilitation* of young scholars who brought with them from their backgrounds and their studies similar biases or who admitted quite openly that they were "conservative-revolutionary." They rejected every attempt to analyze this preregulation of their thinking by sociopolitical, socioscientific, and psychological means, and viewed it as an apparent attack on the principle of scholarly objectivity. They thus closed off for themselves all paths for escaping this self-limitation of their scholarly and political accomplishments or even to come to terms with democracy.[57] . . . The "normal" professor of the Weimar period was thus an opponent of democracy and also of the Weimar Reich Constitution. He was not a fascist nor a National Socialist, but he passed his biases on to a student body which then transposed them into active deeds.[58]

The discipline of *Volkskunde* had at the universities of the German Reich only one full professorship, which had been established between 1919 and 1925 in Hamburg.[59] Until the end of the Weimar Republic this was essentially the only position. *Volkskunde* was, however (as was the case with Meier in Basel), treated by several dozen university professors in various disciplines, such as Germanistics, theology, music, etc., both in their teaching and in their research. The attitudes and behavior of the majority of these scholars probably was traditional and conservative.

As the Germanist Klaus von See has pointed out in his study of *Deutsche Germanenideologie* (German Germanic ideology),

> from this confrontation there arose the defeat of 1918 and from the opposition to the apparently mechanistic, arithmetical, leveling principle of the new democracy, a significant Germanic renaissance was growing, a *Germanenideologie* which, in light of the political isolation, was striving for a "pure German renewal" out of its own strengths. The so-called continuity problem begins now, as a part of the attempt for a new national self-understanding, to move into scholarly awareness. What is meant by this is the question of whether the continuity of culture comes from the transmission of cultural goods from one folk to another, from international exchange, that is, from translation and reception, or from an isolationist steadfastness to pure German uniqueness? Expressed differently, should the *acquiring that which is foreign* have precedence or should it be the *preservation of that which is indigenous*?[60]

The comments by von See are in reference to scholarship, that is, intellectual scholarship in general, but they also apply to a great extent to German *Volkskunde*, which was dealing with the cultural goods of the broad strata of the populace, with so-called folk material.

This German *Germanenideologie* reaches far back beyond 1918, and it was actively employed in the decade and a half of the Weimar democracy, only to fall prey after 1933 to a very real political perversion. In 1926 the seven-hundred-page *Germanische Wiedererstehung* (Germanic Rebirth) appeared, and von See has pointed to it as a good example.[61] It is a collection which intended to present a scientifically true picture of "old Germanic customs" through summaries of the various areas of ancient Germanic spiritual life. It attempted "to present the reformation and the suppression of old Germanic customary values during the time when foreign education penetrated into Germany, and finally to lay out the recent reawakening of such ancient Germanic values."[62]

To create "noble values" was required of the German folk. A "new ascent" could come from the "*indigenous* strength of the folk soul . . . not through the stimulus of accepting educational values from foreigners, but rather only through the awakening of strengths, which means the most original and most ancient contents of the soul of our people, through a stronger emphasis on the Germanic basis of our customs."[63] The "folk soul" which was called upon here as the savior from the spiritual and economic postwar misery had already served during Romanticism as a nebulous objective.

Eight scholars from Germanistics, law, religious history, musicology, art history, and *Volkskunde* devoted themselves to the "scientifically accurate" illumination of the roots of ancient Germanic spiritual life in order to elevate the contemporary "Germanic" folk custom. They were for the most part well-known professors who were also doing research in *Volkskunde*.

It can be seen from the titles of some of the articles that a contrast was being made between that which was "indigenous," i.e., Germanic-German, and that which was "foreign." The contrast was either specifically pointed out or briefly described. Andreas Heusler (University of Basel, Switzerland) wrote about "Altgermanische Sittenlehre und Lebensweisheit" (Ancient Germanic Customary Teachings and Life Wisdom). Klaudius Bojunga (gymnasium director, Frankfurt am Main) wrote on "Werden und Wesen der deutschen Sprache in alter Zeit. Die Fremdsprachenherrschaft und der Freiheitskampf der Deutschen Sprache" (The Development and the Essence of German during Antiquity: Foreign Language Domination and the Battle for Freedom of the German Language). Friedrich von der Leyen (University of Cologne) wrote on "Altgermanische Dichtung, ihre Umbildung im Mittelalter und ihre Belebung in neuerer Zeit" (Ancient Germanic Poetry, Its Reformation during the Middle Ages and Its Recent Awakening), Claudius Freiherr von Schwerin (University of Freiburg im Breisgau) on "Der Geist des altgermanischen Rechts, das Eindringen fremden Rechts, und die neuerliche Wiedererstarkung germanischer Rechtsgrundsätze" (The Spirit of Ancient Germanic Law, the Penetration by Foreign Law, and the Recent Strengthening of Germanic Legal Principles), Karl Helm (University of Marburg/Lahn) on "Die Entwicklung der Germanischen Religion; ihr Nachleben in uns neben dem Christentum" (The Development of Germanic Religion: Its Survival in Us alongside Christianity), Josef Maria Müller-Blattau (University of Königsberg) on "Die Tonkunst in altgermanischer Zeit; Wandel und Wiederbelebung germanischer Eigenart in der geschichtlichen Entwicklung der deutschen Tonkunst" (Sound Art in Ancient Germanic Times: Change and Reawakening of Germanic Uniqueness in the Historical Development of German Sound Art), Albrecht Haupt (Technical University of Hannover) on "Die Altgermanische bildende Kunst, ihr Nachleben in den Jahrhunderten der Herrschaft fremder Kunst und ihre neuerliche Wiederaufdeckung. Altgermanisches in der neueren bildenden Kunst" (Ancient Germanic Art, Its Survival during the Centuries of Foreign Art Dominance and Its Recent Rediscovery: Ancient Germanic Elements in Recent Art).

The first study of about 130 pages, "Die Entwicklungsstufen der germanischen Kultur. Umwelt und Volksbrauch in altgermanischer Zeit" (Developmental Stages of Germanic Culture: Environment and Folk Custom in Ancient Germanic Times), was written by Otto Lauffer.[64] He had been director of the Museum for Hamburg History since 1908, and since 1919/1925[65] he had been full professor for German antiquities and *Volkskunde* at the University of Hamburg, the only possessor of a chair for German *Volkskunde* in Germany. From 1911 on he was vice-chair of the League of German Societies for Folklore, the deputy of John Meier.

Lauffer too distinguished between that which was indigenous and that which was foreign. In one subheading, "Germanic Life and the Effect of Neighboring Peoples,"[66] he defined "Germanic culture" as "the uniformity of the folk-nation and *race*" and the "uniformity of life-style," as the "totality of a series of traits which remain constant in their outer form and in their spiritual contents." According to Lauffer, they "have come down through Germanic life unchanged *for thousands of years*."[67] On the basis of this astonishing continuity, i.e., ever since the development and the fulfillment of "heathen-Germanic culture," down past the "history of Christian nations with German blood," down to the present, "German blood" still flowed in German arteries after the First World War. This racial "Germanic inheritance" formed the basis of that which was essential to Germanness. "Hail to us that we all have reason to be proud of this inheritance a thousandfold!"[68]

Just what does this thousand-year-old "Germanic inheritance" of the Germans mean? What constitutes that "foreignness" which is in opposition to German essence? Clearly committed to the cultivation of the German folk-nation, Lauffer had published six years earlier a popular little book with several of his research conclusions or convictions on Germanic continuity in German customs.[69] These briefly stated comments were lacking in the kind of caution required in a scholarly treatment. They thus might express the unguarded viewpoints of their writer.

In four sections with significant headings, Lauffer treated "The Essence of

Custom" (I), "Germanic Inheritance in Custom and Usage" (II), "Foreign Effects on German Custom" (III), and "The Old and the New Age" (IV). Lauffer's conclusions were according to his understanding "scientifically objective," and portions were even progressive for that age, for example in the first chapter, where he presumed that economic effects on customs and practices were self-evident.[70] But in the chapter on Germanic inheritance in custom and practice,[71] he touched on many of the Germanic continuity commonplaces which later were to be raised into hypertrophy by National Socialist *Volkskunde*: the entire picture of the Germanic folk character in the *Germania* of Tacitus;[72] tribal characteristics; the lasting effects of god cults; demonic and death beliefs in lower mythology; heathen-Germanic cults during festivals; superstitious interpretations of omens, blessings, and magical charms; and symbolic protective signs (symbols), including the swastika, the sacred fire (Notfeuer), and law.

Toward the end Lauffer elucidated German and Germanic heroism, which "found its most convincing expression in the Nordic concept of the end of the world, in the *Götterdämmerung*." "Felix Dahn justifiably designated it as 'the outstanding magnificent traditional deed of Germandom,' when Odin, even though he foresees the end of the world and with it his own downfall, heroically and decisively goes forth with the rest of the gods and the *Einherier* [the warriors in Valhalla], and when they all proudly and without fear seal their own greatness through their death on the battlefield. This same spirit speaks which was expressed most recently, during the world war, when it was said to all of the peoples of the earth that 'Germany must live, even if we must die!' "[73] The ideology of the Nordic *Götterdämmerung* was carried out by German fascists during the Second World War in a most fatal way.

In "Foreign Effects on German Custom" Lauffer presented the role of medieval courtly culture, of Roman law, and especially of Christianity, i.e., the effect of the proselytizing church on heathen Germanic tribesmen, on changes of Germanic customs and Germanic practices. From the standpoint of the history of customs, it was not so much that the ecclesiastical form of the Christian church was now transferred into the German lands. "The decisive point lies much more in the fact that all of extra-ecclesiastical private and public life is slowly penetrated by the spirit of Christianity and that thereby the entire realm of custom and practice was gradually completely changed in its innermost essence. New Christian concepts penetrated, as for example that of *charity* . . . , others reshaped existing concepts, by filling the newly acquired Germanic verbal repertoire with new contents in order to make these easily fit the folk."[74] With the Christian "foreign effect" on the German folk and the historical destruction of ancient Germanic "high culture," National Socialist *Volkskunde* was later able to lay a foundation for its plan to destroy the German Christian churches and to undertake its uncharitable persecution of religious folklorists.[75]

Lauffer was not a National Socialist when he wrote this article, and he was certainly not the only scholar and folklorist who wrote down these kinds of thoughts, but he did it in an exemplary way in the service of a folk education directed toward ancient Germanic customary practices. Just how ideological in the sense of "false consciousness,"[76] how politically misusable this Germanophilia was, can be seen in Lauffer's concluding statements. They clearly reflect the strong-armed policies of a folk ideology and folk-national cultivation employed by the National Socialist ideologists Alfred Rosenberg and Heinrich Himmler, who were most interested in *Volkskunde*:

> As long as the German folk has the ability to create from its own essence new customs and practices which are equal to the ancient ones in their living strength and in the beauty of their form, in the depth of their feeling and in their poetic contents, and even to outdo them in their purity and consistency, in other words as long as the German folk remains faithful to the innermost essence of its fathers, in its belief and in the core of its external life, it will remain strong, it will fulfill its tasks which have been imparted to it, and to it alone, by fate for the development of humanity. Whether the other people will love us or hate us in this matter, that must be for us only of secondary importance. If we just preserve our special race, purely and unfalsified, then we will keep our place in the sun.[77]

If we compare Lauffer's folk-national cultivation sketched here or his folk renewal concept with that which Meier recorded three years earlier in his *Reichs-institutsplan*, the connections become quite clear. Both scholars were concerned with the creation and preservation of customs and practices with a so-called "ennobling" content. Even though these novations apparently corresponded to ancient German ancestral inheritance, which was supposed to preserve the "indigenous" over the "foreign," they did not arise from the creative forces of the broad strata of the populace but were transmitted to the German people in their entirety through their preceptors or guardians, i.e., bourgeois-national scholars. At the same time the revivals created in this way had a highly practical function: to help fulfill the fate of the German folk, to secure for it its predestined and unique position within the folk community. That was what it was striving for in the First World War.

The planned ethical novations in customs, practices, or revivals possess a life-giving meaning, and they were certainly intended to influence the behavior and thinking of their bearers. Lauffer in particular associated these "behavioral suggestions" for the broad strata of the populace with a presumed ancient German-Germanic blood and spiritual inheritance, which peaked in the fatal ending of the heroic *Götterdämmerung*. He then contrasted this with the "foreign effect" brought on by historically documented cultural influences such as Christianity. As was the case with Meier, essential portions of occidental cultural development were subject to question or were intentionally put aside.

This Germanophilic racial thinking scheme in fact formed one of the most effective ideological and practical bases for subsequent fascist *Volkskunde*, which was transformed into a power policy by the Rosenberg Bureau as well as the SS Office of Ancestral Inheritance. Their scholarly collaborators and official protectors in the National Socialist party wanted, as did Lauffer, to maintain the German folk "as peculiarly pure and unfalsified," i.e., to secure its racial uniqueness and its "place in the sun." Whether the other peoples would love or hate the Germans for this was for them, in contrast to Lauffer, completely immaterial.

The "preservation of that which was indigenous," in contrast to "acquiring of that which was foreign," was also one of the goals of racial studies with which *Volkskunde* was supposed to work closely and in an interdisciplinary way during the Third Reich. Racial studies had not been initially introduced into the discipline under fascism, as we can document with the key terms used by Lauffer in regard to Germanic race and Germanic blood. A unique, even though exponentially racist, journal, *Volk und Rasse. Illustrierte Vierteljahrsschrift für Deutsches Volkstum* (Folk and Race: Illustrated Quarterly for the German Folk-Nation), issued by the Munich publisher J. F. Lehmann, listed in the first issue of the first volume in 1926 twelve scholars as co-editors who came from folklore studies,[78] mostly professors from Germany, some few from Austria and Switzerland.[79] From 1926 to 1933 there appeared some thirty folkloric, racial studies on themes such as the *Atlas*, ethnic Germans, peasantry, custom, narration, house and settlement, costume, music, and mythological folklore. The majority of the authors were editors who did folklore research, as well as other well-known folklorists.[80] In addition, well-known exponents of the NSDAP published there, such as R. Walther Darré, who later became Reich food minister and farm leader. In 1933 the folklorists, with the exception of Eugen Fehrle, stepped down from the editorial positions and Himmler stepped in. The organ, now led exclusively by racial studies scholars, was, however, still available for pertinent folklore studies.

Racial studies by folklorists are also to be found in other publications, and there was an abundance of them during the Third Reich. In the journal of the German Academy, Meier himself declared that the ultimate goal of literary-folkloristic as well as musical folk song research must be "to isolate the national uniqueness of one's own folk as well as to distill out the pure German elements and wherever possible to lay bare where and in how far race has been a determining factor."[81]

Hans Naumann, the most important folklore theorist during the Weimar Republic, was devoted to research on the "indigenous" in German folklore and Germanic antiquity studies, as well as on the acquisition of that which is "foreign," utilizing methodological suggestions taken from ethnology. His innovative and hotly debated attempt to develop through his 1922 book *Grundzüge der Deutschen Volkskunde* (Basic Principles of German Folklore) "a kind of system of *Volkskunde*"[82] includes the concept of reception theory. His teaching of *gesunkenes Kulturgut* contains the key sentence "folk goods are made in the upper stratum,"[83] only to sink down from there to a primitive communal culture. This teaching corresponds, *cum grano salis*, unintentionally to the reality of everyday folk-national cultivation in *Volkskunde*, but it was applied generally to an educated upper stratum of the populace and its exemplary culture.

Naumann borrowed this concept from ethnology, which investigated "primitive societies" as "nature peoples" from the standpoint of the educated bourgeoisie and combined it with others which were common in Germanic antiquity studies under the influence of a *Germanenideologie*. The unusual culture-stage model which resulted could only be accepted with great difficulty by traditional folklorists. The stage of absolute primitiveness, in which humans were still an almost unconscious piece of nature, was hardly known among the German folk at the beginning of the twentieth century. Naumann thus postulated three developmental cultural stages in history: the agrarian society, the heroic or Germanic aristocratic upper stratum and warrior caste, and the educated upper stratum with a clear character of individualism. The peasant society formed "of necessity the main object of German *Volkskunde*, but remains and rudiments of primitive communal culture live on a hundredfold in the urban and educated upper strata of the nation."[84]

If traces of this primitive communal culture were still to be found in the upper stratum, they must be found in far greater measure in the peasant stratum. Naumann analyzed the folkloric canonical objects with very convincing arguments and according to their areas of origin, but he was not at all afraid of equating the peasants with primitive society. It was not for his educated, bourgeois arrogance over against the broad folk strata but rather for his ideological equating of that which cannot be united that this theoretician was to reap severe consequences after 1933.

The upper stratum as an exemplary culture bearer ran counter to the prevailing concept of the creative strength of the folk. This is not found for the first time during the Third Reich. On the other hand, the heroic stage of the Germanic aristocratic upper stratum and the warrior caste could be accepted as a randomly assembled culture-stage model, and it was spiritually related to Friedrich Nietzsche's later popularized concept of the *Herrenmensch* (master race).[85]

Naumann shared completely the need in *Volkskunde* for a folk-national cultivation with a basic tendency which was antiprogressive, and thus he made known his intention to protect the "indigenous" from the "foreign":

And, if we simply leave the movies, the gramophone, the operetta, and the department store to be the field for applied and practical *Volkskunde*, we cannot be surprised if the character of new folk goods is not particularly pleasant. It has not disappeared, it has only become worse; but the guilt for this is born by the upper stratum. The culture of knighthood once left behind the ennobling and beautiful folk dances, the upper stratum of our day is leaving behind those shoving dances. *Volkskunde* shows a very earnest countenance to the upper stratum and teaches it to know the immense responsibility which rests in it.[86]

Naumann singled out peasant society as the primary research object of *Volkskunde*. In this he was in complete agreement with traditional folkloric practice, a fact which becomes clearer through the example of the two large collecting projects by John Meier. The German Folk Song Archive and the *Atlas der deutschen Volks-kunde* drew their materials primarily from the countryside, where folk goods were selected in a one-sided way, i.e., mostly relics, and where they were still to be found in contrast to the large cities and industrial districts. It was not the workers[87] but rather the peasants who were equated in an industrially developing Germany with the real folk of *Volkskunde*. National Socialist *Volkskunde*, of course, accepted this anachronism.

Meier was quite skeptical about Naumann's theory of *gesunkenes Kulturgut*. In his programmatic essay "Wege und Ziele der deutschen Volkskundeforschung" (Paths and Goals of German Folklore Research), he stated that

> the transfer mentioned almost exclusively by Naumann and which has now taken a primary position, i.e., from the upper stratum to the lower stratum in the same folk circles, is only *one* isolated case. We have, in addition to this, the transfer between two regionally separated areas of the same folk as well as the acceptance of folk goods from a foreign folk.[88]

A reference follows to an example of taking folk goods from among Germans and Slavs, concerning the origin of which "the recordings of the folklore *Atlas* are supposed to offer a final decision."

Meier treats here the "relationship between reception of that which is foreign and autogenetic creation," for him "*the most important problem of folklore research work*,"[89] i.e., the well-known theme of the preservation of that which was indigenous and the acquiring of that which was foreign. In the final analysis this theme seems to be the primary goal of the *Atlas der deutschen Volkskunde*. Meier's programmatic essay of 1928 was part of a "propaganda piece"[90] of the Cooperative Council for Aid to German Research for the *Atlas*, with contributions by several of the most important interdisciplinary promoters and collaborators of this undertaking. Arthur Hübner, Kurt Wagner, and Richard Wossidlo wrote generally about the *Atlas* or the principles of collecting and presentation, Georg Schreiber about religious folk-lore, Fritz Boehm about folklore and schools, Theodor Frings about folklore and language geography, Walther Mitzka about folklore and ethnic Germans.[91] Boehm, Frings, and Wagner, like Meier, rejected Naumann's theory about *gesunkenes Kul-turgut*.[92] Especially in Mitzka's contribution the theme of the separation between that which is indigenous and that which is foreign was addressed again, supporting the folklore *Atlas*.

Just how readily this theme was taken up can be seen in the person of the ethnic German Bruno Schier from Czechoslovakia and in his 1932 *Habilitation* publication *Hauslandschaften und Kulturbewegungen im östlichen Mitteleuropa* (House Landscapes and Cultural Movements in East-Central Europe). For him the Slavs were in many ways the preservers and developers of so-called eastern Ger-manic cultural goods. Many individual traits of this eastern Germanic world of expression would be revealed by detailed investigations of Slavic traditions. Schier thus called for expanding the research work of the *Atlas der deutschen Volkskunde* in east-central Europe into a "*Grenzsaum*" (boundary strip) three hundred kilometers long, where the Slavs had settled and which now belonged to Slavic countries.[93]

Soon after the seizure of power by the fascist regime in Germany, the aggressive nationalistic tendencies of German *Volkskunde* were expressed in direct terms. The collaborator from Austria in the Berlin Central Office, Richard Beitl, wrote concerning the political function of the *Atlas der deutschen Volkskunde*:

> The maps of the *Atlas* show us not only the living richness, the manifold connections, and the intertwining of pure German life but also its points of danger. We see where a foreign folk-nation since time immemorial has influenced that which is German and has perhaps even overshadowed it. We see where implements, words, attitudes, and customs appear in recent times to overcome very slowly the advanced outpost of Germandom. One look at such maps suggests the necessity of spiritual and, as far as it is possible, the spatial unification of those separated and weakened areas with the strong fatherland. This is more convincing than are long treatments and speeches.
>
> On the other hand, however, strong weapons for us arise out of the *Atlas der deutschen Volkskunde*, against attempts to separate the German folk-nation through lines which have never indicated folk boundaries. If there are today, unfortunately, speakers and writers who want to separate Austria racially and as a people from the German folk league and to represent it in this way, then there is nothing more important than to point out the cartographic results of the questionnaires which have come in great numbers from the valleys of the Austrian Alps. Just as settlement types and house forms, food ways and costumes, and especially the language in the Alemannic and Bavarian-Austrian dialects, know no boundaries between Austria and Germany, it is the same for custom and folk belief.[94]

Beitl was certainly not the only one who employed the *Atlas* for political objectives and misused it. There were other folklorists interested in the *Atlas*, for example the vice-president of the League of German Societies for Folklore, Lauffer. For him the discipline of *Volkskunde* was, according to his journal article of 1934, "Volkskunde und der deutsche Osten" (Folklore and the German East), a "splendid national scholarship" which offers scholarly assistance when "the National Socialist state under its great Führer Adolf Hitler devotes itself anew to the task of cultivating the traditions of the German folk-nation and keeping them alive."[95] This greeting to the new regime is no mere word play, for Lauffer explains concretely just where the scholarly help of the discipline is found:

> In the battle between the oppositional claims of the nations for folk and cultural soil, *Volkskunde* is the inscrutable judge. . . . Here the folklorist stands as a reliable secondary figure to the politician. He does not judge according to the various conditions of political power relationships. He is interested only in establishing the truth, and so his work is especially of the highest significance

there where his own folk finds itself in a defensive battle against unjustified foreign claims.[96]

The claims of the German nation for folk and cultural soil were directed for the most part toward the states on the eastern boundary, where former German or Austrian regions with Slavic and German peoples had been claimed after the First World War. Groups of ethnic Germans, however, occupied so-called speech islands still farther east, in the Russian area. They were in regions settled in earlier centuries that had never belonged to the German homeland. Entire Germanic ethnic groups had settled in several of these regions prior to the Middle Ages, but they had already moved out during these early times. In contrast, the medieval German "eastern colonization" had subjugated the Slavic peoples and assimilated them, only stopping near the later boundaries of the German Reich with some few incursions beyond this.

Lauffer directed attention in his essay to this ostensible "German East," to the reciprocal cultural exchange between Germans and Slavs. He began, however, with the assumption that it was the higher standing culture which essentially prevailed. Immediately following this he added: "The Slavic world does not come out in this comparison very favorably." Thus the defaming presumption of the "West-East cultural decline" was touched upon, one which maintained a cultural melioration continuing in an eastern direction. For Lauffer there was an a priori assumption that, seen historically, "German culture was the superior one."[97]

As proof of the ideology of German cultural superiority and of the helpful role of *Volkskunde* for the politician, Lauffer treated a few "folk-national traits" at the end of his essay which were similar between Germans and Slavs, i.e., common cultural folk goods of the two groups. He made use of "the laudable work of the German folklore *Atlas*"[98] and came to the conclusion that corn demons, because they were feminine, were of Slavic origin. The white color of the folk mourning dress was in contrast to other concepts hardly sad; the *Rundling* (round) village was not of Slavic origin even though it was formerly attributed to the Slavs.[99] The *Ostdeutsches Laubenhaus* (East German trellis house) was German, since it could be traced back to the eastern Germanic tribes (Ostrogoths, who lived in the east before the great folk migrations). Thus "this house form, which still appears today in Poland, represents an example of the old Germanic culture in this region."[100] Five years later the fascists, for whom Lauffer indeed had been a "reliable secondary," had the "old Germanic cultural areas" of the state of Poland brought back by means of German troops *"heim ins Reich"* (home to the Reich), and thus started the Second World War.

It is not this short summary of ideas by Lauffer in a journal article which causes us to doubt the reality of his conclusions; it is the lack of exact research methods. His methods are, instead, based on an ideological bias. The real interethnic cultural exchange did not take place in such a clear way, but rather through essentially more complicated ones. To explain what happened through hundreds of years and in such a large region, other and more scholarly presuppositions are necessary.[101]

Folklore research of this type had scarcely been recognized by scholars of a higher theoretical and methodological niveau during the Weimar Republic. John Meier, in his statement of accounts of 1947, admitted this indirectly. The activity which served to elevate *Volkskunde* to the level of an independent scholarship by the League of German Societies for Folklore had encountered "only very limited understanding during the first decades and in the authoritative circles of scholarship, as well as with the government" of the Reich and of the German states. "It was in the beginning a foolish scholarship and annoyance to the ruling political parties."[102] There is little to be added to this accurate estimation.

During the Weimar Republic this scholarship had found recognition more among ideologically like-minded people, among the laity and the dilettantes, for example, who have always played an important role in the realm of *Volkskunde*. They met out of general interest in the cultivation of the folk-nation, for awakening and strengthening of pure German sensitivity, "for edifying the German folk through the spirit of the German folk-nation,"[103] i.e., in a reactionary sense for its "inner renewal." Among the most active sympathizers of *Volkskunde*, especially during the Third Reich, were the "leading circles of the party," of the NSDAP, for which many folklorists had worked ideologically even before 1933. After 1933 these same "leading circles" brought about the institutional establishment of the discipline, and Meier openly expressed his gratitude to them in 1947 for their support during the fascist regime.[104]

German *Volkskunde* of the Weimar period, based on its conservative-reactionary, national, and sociopolitical objectives, was highly disposed if not even predestined[105] to be employed under fascist rule as a systemically stabilizing state science and, as we must conclude, to be misused. The specific politicization of the discipline, however, grew directly out of its scholarly history and the scholarly practice toward which it was striving. It was manifest long before the beginning of the Third Reich and did not come about initially through the National Socialists. The latter simply seized from the discipline some eminent ideological tendencies, such as "nation," "Nordic race," "Germandom," "peasantry," "organism," "super individual," "symbolic world," "personal belief," "revival,"[106] and used them for their purposes, developing them further into a "National Socialist *Volkskunde*." Its predecessor was, in the final analysis, a bourgeois-national *Volkskunde*, and many of the representatives of the discipline were able to ally themselves during the Third Reich with *National Socialist Volkskunde* with no particular reservations.

Also from this symbiosis, latent even before 1933, between bourgeois-national *Volkskunde* and the adherents of a pure German spiritual position, among them the fascists, there resulted a widespread low opinion of the discipline during the Weimar democracy. That was documented by Meier among the authoritative circles of scholarship and throughout the democratic government. It resulted in a stigmatization as "foolish" and an "annoyance"[107] of those attempts by the League of German Societies for Folklore to create a representative validity for the scholarly discipline. Nevertheless the democratic form of state allowed folklorists to present their traditional objectives again and again in public and to make propaganda in this way for the discipline. That was also the case during the last years of the Republic when the German Research Council or the Cooperative Council lent financial support to the *Atlas,* the seedbed of the *Reichsinstitut,*[108] and thus brought about a new impetus for the discipline and its umbrella organization. It did not, however, bring about a change in scholarly ideology or in scholarly politics.

"That is the beautiful part of our work, that both pure scholarship and applied scholarship are valid for our folk and rest with them: in one's own folk it sees its materials and can, according to its scholarly work, have an effect again directly on the essence and development of the folk."[109] Meier's words document the unbroken continuity of his disciplinary understanding of *Volkskunde* and folk-national cultivation. He spoke these words in 1929 at a Delegate Assembly in Berlin, at the celebration of the twenty-fifth anniversary of the League of German Societies for Folklore. One year later the League converted its representative assemblies into congresses, or *Deutsche Volkskundetage* (German Folklore Meetings), and thus appeared through its lectures before a much larger scholarly public. The first Folklore Meeting took place in September 1930 in Würzburg,[110] the second in October 1933 in Weimar.

By that time the German political situation had changed fundamentally. The Republic, named after the city in Thüringen where its national assembly convened, had died on January 30 of that year, and the new regime had been in power for about seven months. The program of the German Folklore Meeting had also changed. The lecture planned for Hans Naumann on *Nationalsozialismus und Volkskunde* had to be dropped, since the speaker had declared that it was impossible for him to give the lecture assigned.[111] Other speakers with appropriate themes were waiting in the wings:[112] Julius Schwietering (Frankfurt am Main) with "Die sozialpolitische Aufgabe der Volkskunde" (The Social-Political Task of Folklore)[113] and Herbert Freudenthal (Halle/Saale) with "Volkskunde und Nationalerziehung. Zur Geschichte ihrer Beziehungen" (Folklore and National Education: Concerning the History of Their Relationships).[114]

At the Weimar meeting, representatives of the new regime took part in the primary session in great numbers. Meier was thus able to greet representatives of the Foreign Office, the Reich State Keeper, and the state officials of Thüringen; the cultural ministries of Thüringen, Baden, and Prussia; the Reich military; the German Research Council; the state university and the scholarly institutions of Thüringen; and the senior mayor of Weimar. Still, before his scholarly lecture "Uraltes in unserer Zeit" (The Most Ancient Things in our Times) he made the most meaningful political speech of the meeting, although it appears to be only a few insignificant lines in the official proceedings of the League of German Societies for Folklore.[115]

It was a programmatic speech about German *Volkskunde* and its meaning for the "pure German" state,[116] with the central theme, "inner folk renewal," directed by Meier toward his bourgeois-national scholarship and the National Socialists:

> The new age has also knocked with a heavy pounding on our gates, but—with proud modesty we may say—we were able to open the gates wide for it, and we did not have to cast our eyes down, but were able to look directly into the eye of this new day. For we have, insofar as it was within our strength, contributed during our lifetime and through our work to the creation of the German essence.

A harking back to Wilhelm von Humboldt's statement that "the state must replace by moral strength what it has lost materially" was followed by an appeal to German folklore scholars:

> We must join ranks in order to remove the rubbish which has clogged the holy springs of our innermost being; we must press on to the innermost realms of this being in order to lead all of our folk comrades to a fresh and refreshing drink, so that they can draw health from it.

Meier went on to say that the Führer, Hitler, had placed insightfully and consciously a social demand alongside this internal national renewal. The growing healing process needed "such a knowledgeable and patient doctor who knows that continuing health is only possible through purification and reenlivening of the innermost fluids." In regard to these healing measures, *Volkskunde* was receiving significant assignments and great responsibility. A "reorientation" (that is, political coordination) of *Volkskunde* had not been necessary in a formal or personal way, for, according to Meier, "Our goals are the goals of the national movement." This equation of *Volkskunde* and National Socialism reflected no doubt a tactical calculation, but it also reflected a very deep truth.

Meier stated further that through the feeling for national values which had recently been awakened everywhere by those ruling and those ruled, the work of *Volkskunde* fortunately had received the strongest kind of impetus, whereas in the past it had been "for the most part foolishness and an annoyance to those in power." As proof of the previous contribution by *Volkskunde* to the "inner folk renewal," Meier reached back to the contents of his Reich institute concepts of 1917 and 1926, to sociopolitical hindering of the flight from the land and to the deepening of state and national feelings as well as to the cultural cooperation which had been promoted for such a long time with ethnic Germans. In conclusion, the obedient, submissive, and happy alignment of folklorists "into the ranks of warriors for Germany's rebirth out of the spirit of the German folk-nation" was promised, "in the consciousness that willpower and a *unified leadership* in this most difficult of battles will win out and can create anew the truly German man. One folk, one path, one goal!"[117]

Meier's speech before the representatives of the state, the party, and the assembled scholars utilized the linguistic intentionality of the National Socialists, which was also to a large degree that of *Volkskunde*. It was simultaneously changed, however, to represent the interests of the political objectives of the League to continue to provide its own independent leadership for German *Volkskunde*. The League wanted to promote *Volkskunde* with the support of the regime, not to surrender it, and to turn it into an independent science and folk-national cultivation.

Also at the Delegate Assembly in Weimar, the League chairman greeted the "National Socialist revolution" and put his German *Volkskunde* "in the service of this fatherland movement."[118] Meier was further able to inform the delegates of the societies that the governments of the German states planned a general development of professorships for *Volkskunde* and called for a careful choice by the ministerial officers of appropriate people to occupy these chairs. Representatives who indeed possessed the necessary enthusiasm but not the scholarly preparation had to be kept at a distance, since they would discredit *Volkskunde* as a scholarly discipline.[119] This requirement was intended to counter the influence of dilettantes from the ranks of the "fatherland movement" and thus also from the NSDAP.

The League thus also matched up with the existing norms of the Weimar Delegate Assembly. After changes in the bylaws were accomplished, it was unanimously decided to employ the *Führerprinzip* with Meier as Führer, and thus also an "autonomous political coordination"[120] was carried out. To "strengthen South German and the National Socialist elements," the influential Baden ministerial officer, party functionary, and folklorist Eugen Fehrle was taken into the council of the Executive Board.[121] This was also for security purposes.

This unanimous conclusion was not carried out through political force. The mood of the folklorists was generally euphoric, as one can see from sources of that period of transition. They could be sure now of full recognition of the national and political importance of the discipline, even though it had been plagued until then with much resistance. Thus this was also the beginning of its establishment and spread at the universities and teacher training schools. Public education also meant institutionalized security for scholarly research as well as expansion of folk-national cultivation by folklore into adult education and especially into the schools. Expressions of this attitude are the greetings and addresses of submission to the new state leadership of Germany which are to be found in virtually all German folklore journals of 1933 and 1934.[122] These journals were published by the regional or local associations, all of which were members of the League.

FAILURE OF THE UNION FOR GERMAN FOLKLORE OF 1933

During the Third Reich Meier undertook all kinds of tactical maneuvers to maintain and expand the primary influence of his own umbrella organization for German *Volkskunde* which existed prior to 1933.[123] The most spectacular of these was the founding in 1933 of the Bund für deutsche Volkskunde (Union for German Folklore). According to Meier's comments in 1947, that is, after the end of fascist rule, such a union had been discussed at the beginning of the 1930s. In spite of the primary organization of the League, the central point for scholarly research work, there was still missing a place to "promote an understanding for folklore work among the broad circles of the folk and to stimulate them for work which they could do and which was necessary for research. . . . This Union was to have the primary task of uniting the friends of German *Volkskunde* within the Reich and within the German realm beyond the state boundaries, to awaken and enliven folkloric interest through writings and lectures."[124]

In a call by the Union for German Folklore in 1933 (see appendix III.1), we read something a little different. Here the founding takes place at that moment "when the great pure German and National Socialist renewal has made *Volkskunde* into a public affair of the German nation as research and instruction of the folk-national thought and life forms in the past and the present."[125] Of highest priority is the financing of the Union (or rather the League which supported it). It was planned with the help of the desired "not hundreds, no: thousands" of "warriors for *Volkskunde*" or the members of the Union. Publications of scholarly works in the realm of folklore were to be supported, "valuable" folklore books were to be delivered at no cost to the libraries of schools and scholarly institutes, a folklore correspondent position was to be established to provide newspapers and magazines with "perfect" contributions, lectures about *Volkskunde* with verified scholarly significance were to be held according to an exactly prescribed plan, the work of individual folklore associations was to be promoted, new scholarly tasks were to be assigned. In addition, the presumed members were promised a yearly folklore publication at no cost.

Such splendid folkloric and folk cultivating activity by the Union and the League could only be carried out by the establishment of a central institute which directed everything. It can thus be assumed that the Union for German Folklore was intended to result in Meier's Reich institute of 1917 and 1926 in modified form. It was called for once again and most urgently at the beginning of the Third Reich, in the festschrift for Meier's seventieth birthday.[126] There are further indications to strengthen this assumption. It was pointed out in the call by the Union, as well as in Meier's conceptualization of 1917 and 1926, that there had been prior to this great accomplishments by bourgeois-national *Volkskunde* and its umbrella organization:

> The associations and institutes which have promoted German *Volkskunde* through collections and research have joined together in a League; the German Folk Song Archive has collected German folk songs throughout the entire German area since 1914; the great German folklore *Atlas* is in process; folk art is promoted throughout the widest area; handbooks which bring together synoptically the ma-

terials of superstition, fairy tales, etc., and numerous other works have had a far-reaching effect.[127]

But the capitalistic strengths of private individuals from the past are now, at the time of the "great pure German and National Socialist renewal," being replaced by the broad strata of the populace, by those who belong to the middle and lower stratum throughout the entire German-language area. They are to be stimulated "for the work which is possible for them and necessary for research." This means they are to finance everything and participate in the folklore and folk-national cultivation. The planned undertaking could "only take place, however, if in fact thousands contribute, if it is all of Germany, indeed all *Deutschtum* [Germandom], wherever our language is spoken, wherever it has validity."[128]

The founding of the Union for German Folklore, as Meier himself said after the war, failed because of insufficient membership and "because of the most varied reasons which cannot be explained here."[129] Unfortunately, the idea had to be given up again. In reality the League for German Folklore worked regularly at all of the following Folklore Meetings for the lagging development of the Union. It only died out completely with the Second World War.[130]

It would be most informative to learn more details about the "most varied reasons" which hindered the Union and blocked its path. There seemed to be no lack of agreement among the rulers of the new regime. The Prussian minister for scholarship, art, and folk education, Bernhard Rust, the subsequent Reich education minister, had made himself available as a patron, which was sufficient for Meier to express his "thankful gratitude" in 1947.[131] Very clear statements of committal addressed to the fascist party were also not forgotten in the initial call by the Union. The scholars of the discipline, who were established during the Weimar Republic and were ostensibly unpolitical, were also represented on a list of nearly fifty charter members of the Union. It reads like a pantheon of German folklore scholarship of that era. They all had been drawn in by the significant statement which the call carried, not just for tactical reasons, but were deceived and misunderstood the real character of the fascist regime:[132]

> Precisely the world-view foundations for National Socialism and the national movement have been prepared in the past through folklore research, as the names Jahn, Riehl, etc. prove.[133]

This is the official admission by bourgeois-national German *Volkskunde* that it was not unimportant strands of their scholarly ideology which helped prepare for National Socialism. It conformed to the fascist ideology and the ruling practice and can be seen in the call through the "Aryan paragraph" and the "political co-ordination" which were requirements for acceptance: "Every German of Aryan heritage and every politically coordinated association can become a member of the *Bund*."[134] Foreigners, Jews, Gypsies, and every association which was not "Nazi-fied" were thus excluded from personal or corporate membership.

It may well be that the director of the Berlin De Gruyter publishing house, Gerhard Lüdtke, worked on this unbelievably "loyal" and racist text "in a significant way."[135] Meier, however, also bears some responsibility for the text, since he was without a doubt the *spiritus rector* of the entire undertaking. As is known from other situations, he regularly made all such decisions as the chairman. He of course signed it as the first of three members of the chartering committee. The second and third Union officers were Lauffer and Naumann. The secretaries of the Union were Adolf Spamer, Herbert Freudenthal, and Ernst Bargheer.[136] With the exception of Gerhard Lüdtke the Executive Board consisted of professors, the first three being full professors. The parallel functions of Meier and Lauffer in the Union and in the League document the close alliance of the two organizations.

It can be assumed that the autonomous political coordination of the League and the founding of the Union—with the support of a high National Socialist functionary, Rust—present attempts by bourgeois-national representatives of the discipline and their Führer, the organizationally very skilled Meier, to cozy up to the National Socialists. It was also an attempt to participate successfully or even to steal the march on the battle to divide up the spoils of German *Volkskunde*, which began in 1933 and was continued until the very end of the regime. It is precisely the overall structural—and ideological—identification between the *Reichsinstitutsplan*, which Meier had wanted to carry out in 1917 in the Kaiser's Germany and again in 1926 during the Weimar Republic, with the Union for German Folklore that supports this assumption.

The plan of 1933 projected a spread of the operational base of the scholarly league by winning over thousands of participants, not only "in every city" but also "in every village,"[137] among the broad strata of the populace. The League wanted to make skillful use of the widespread euphoria of a "national revolution" in 1933 by presenting a "*levée en masse*" and to distance itself from the isolation of the "Scholars' Republic," for this Republic had become very shaky soon after the fascist seizure of power. For the League, as we can easily see, it was important to mobilize the masses as well as the Reichsinstitut für Volkskunde, the primary organization for the discipline in Germany, in order to acquire useful disciplinary and political influence. To get this economic security, which was to be guaranteed by the membership, it was necessary for the League and its applied *Volkskunde* to submit to influence, to be both the promoter and the promoted.

In this most unusual calculation, however, very decisive mistakes were made that perhaps brought about the Union's downfall. Instead of the expected tens of thousands of members, there were only about two thousand.[138] This in itself would not have been the worst situation, for what German folklore association has ever accomplished on its first attempt such a high membership list? But the fees for personal membership were for the most part one Reichsmark and for corporate membership three Reichsmarks per year. With a gross yearly income of about two thousand Reichsmarks, this grandiose undertaking was difficult to finance. On the other hand, there was certainly no lack in organizational plans to increase the membership list in the course of time. The decisive cause for the failure must thus be sought in the "most varied reasons" which Meier did not want to discuss in 1947. Meier and his followers had not realized that the National Socialist party apparatus was not at all bound by Rust's agreement. In the Reich leadership of the NSDAP there were, at the uppermost levels, opponents to the Union who were also interested in *Volkskunde*. Ever since the seizure of power they had politically coordinated cultural associations and leagues in great numbers and had incorporated them into their own party organizations. These opponents probably blocked out the competition by the professorial camp. Their own totalitarian needs hindered this attempt at a broadly based and massively supported dominance by representatives of German *Volkskunde* through the Union and the League.

In the festschrift given to Meier in 1934 there is, in addition to many eulogies to Adolf Hitler and the fascist regime, favorable mention once again of a Reich institute. Harry Schewe, Meier's collaborator in the German Folk Song Archive, takes up in his opening words the decades-old and pressing call by the celebrant for an Institut für deutsche Volkskunde. Schewe declares in the name of the congratulators that we "join with you in the wish that this might soon be realized, that there will not be further waiting, and that it is not too different from your own design. We praise this early warrior and organizer of German folklore research!"[139]

The "early warrior" and above all this early thinker of scholarly and folk-national cultivation of applied German *Volkskunde* had been passed over, not so much for reasons of age, in his attempt to realize his central project for the discipline. He was a traditional bourgeois-national scholar and was thus for the National Socialists quite obviously not one of their own. He stubbornly defended his own position of power as chairman of the League of German Societies for Folklore and represented a clear personal concept of the discipline. Thus he could not be integrated into a special fascist *Volkskunde* as it was being developed—which, however, does not change the fact that Meier had worked for fascism in Germany in many ways and for its ideological conglomerate and continued this spiritual collaboration until the end of the Third Reich.[140]

Meier's Union for German Folklore and the Reich institute which most likely would have arisen from it and which would have been under his direction, would have meant a third high point in the professional career of the *Meister*, as his contemporaries called him, one which could scarcely have been more impressive. His exclusion from all key positions in the German Research Council at the beginning of the Third Reich[141] clearly marked the first phase of his defrocking as the *Primus* of German *Volkskunde*. He did maintain his leadership position in the League and in his German Folk Song Archive, but his largest scholarly and organizational work, the *Atlas der deutschen Volkskunde*, was given away to scholars who were not favorably disposed toward him, and there was no further participation on his part. They were to become the German folklorists with authority in the later years of the Hitler regime. They took over the bourgeois-national inheritance, and in the final analysis they established the scholarly discipline at universities and research institutes and put themselves completely at the service of the fascist ideology and power politics.[142] The first stage of this official party representation in the discipline was carried out during a two-year transitional phase by the Reichs-gemeinschaft für deutsche Volksforschung, with its Department of Folklore. Here bourgeois-national and National Socialist researchers and dilettantes worked together.

2

The Reich Community for German Folk Research
Forerunner of Fascist Folklore Scholarship

THE GERMAN RESEARCH Council (DFG, the former Cooperative Council for Aid to German Research)[1] was subjected during the Third Reich to fascist "political co-ordination," which took place in several stages. In the first stage Reich Leader Alfred Rosenberg, who looked upon himself as the "chief ideologist" of the NSDAP, was clearly successful in placing his hand on the scholarly funds and thus was able to outdo all other interests within the leading circles of the party.

At the end of June 1934 Dr. Friedrich Schmidt-Ott had to submit his resignation as president of the DFG to Reich Educational Minister Bernhard Rust. Ostensibly at the wish of Adolf Hitler, Professor of Physics and Nobel Prize winner Johannes Stark took his place.[2] Stark was an "old warrior" of the NSDAP, and from the period prior to the seizure of power he was a personal acquaintance not only of Hitler but also of Rosenberg, whose Kampfbund für deutsche Kultur (Battle Union for German Culture) he had helped found.[3]

Dr. Eduard Wildhagen was named vice-president of the DFG on July 2, 1934.[4] According to Helmut Heiber, "Wildhagen at least had friendly contacts with the Nordic Ring, which had maintained close contacts with Rosenberg during the time of the struggle."[5] Soon after the seizure of power, on April 1, 1933, he became a member of the NSDAP.[6] He had belonged to the Cooperative Council or the DFG for several years during the Weimar Republic,[7] serving as business leader or technical director of what was then the Central Office of the *Atlas der deutschen Volkskunde*.[8] Now he returned as a "National Socialist of deed"[9] from a research referee position in the University Department of the Reich Educational Ministry[10] and became "the great National Socialist political coordinator,"[11] the "gray emi-nence"[12] of the DFG. President Stark was closely allied through his service as-signments as director of the Reich Physical-Technical Institute; he visited the research community daily only for short periods and otherwise "let Wildhagen do as he pleased."[13]

In reality Vice-President Wildhagen represented for Reich Leader Rosenberg and his National Socialist Service Branch the most important person on the Executive Board of the scholarly foundation. He was responsible for humanities scholarship and thus for *Volkskunde*. He was also clearly the dominant force during the planning by Stark and Wildhagen of five or six "Reich communities" for individual disciplines or disciplinary groups. Of these, however, only one could be brought to life, the Reichsgemeinschaft für deutsche Volksforschung (Reich Community for German Folk Research), not without resistance on the part of very powerful party and governmental offices and individuals.[14]

In 1966, Helmut Heiber, to whom the discipline of *Volkskunde* will long be grateful, published some long-neglected pieces of information. He documents that Wildhagen, "in order to realize his favorite idea of a central, overarching research institution," had, according to his own statement after the Second World War, "joined forces with the devil himself."[15] Stark and Wildhagen, who needed an influential protector from the former circles of the party, offered to Reich Leader Rosenberg the honorary presidency of the DFG. Rosenberg accepted "only too gladly" and thus gained influence over the foundation and simultaneously its financial assistance for scholarly projects in his service branch. In Rosenberg's house "the plans were conceived for a restructuring of the Council."[16]

As of April 1, 1934, the director of the "Main Office for World-View" of the Rosenberg Bureau was the folklorist, Germanist, and religious scholar Matthes Ziegler. From November 1, 1935, until December 1, 1936, as one of those who replaced John Meier, "he was given as an assignment from Reich Leader Rosenberg the office of referee for folk research in the German Research Council."[17] In this position Ziegler was the facilator, or "intermediary officer," between Rosenberg and the DFG or its vice-president, Wildhagen. Ziegler, the Reich leader's "commissioner for all folkloric questions,"[18] and Wildhagen were quite suited for close cooperation. They possessed both folkloric interests and knowledge and were allied through their pure German and National Socialist confession, with special attention being given to the Rosenberg Bureau. Among the collaborators of Rosenberg, in addition to the prehistorian Hans Reinerth, Ziegler was particularly blessed with DFG foundation money. Financial assistance for the research programs and research grants set up and distributed within the Rosenberg Bureau were very lucrative[19] and give evidence of the dominant influence on the foundation. This was viewed quite negatively by jealous competitors.

During the summer or early fall of 1934 the DFG founded the Reich Community for German Folk Research. It included five Departments, of pre- and early history, racial studies, folk speech, settlement (originally boundary and ethnic Germandom), and *Volkskunde*.[20]

The purpose of this Reich Community was "research of the German folk-nation, in the sense of a national arising, to be conducted with greater emphasis and to transmit in an appropriate way these newly acquired results to the German folk."[21]

This meant carrying out scholarly folk research and thereby having an effect on applied folk-national cultivation. The goal was to "work for the spread of our German folk-nation . . . in the sense of a national arising," which meant National Socialism. The departments named were "to work together in the closest personal and professional harmony."[22]

The concept of a connection, particularly of these five disciplines or of the core disciplines prehistory, racial studies, and *Volkskunde* for common scholarly work, reflects the ideological guiding image of a racial study of the Germanic tribes as it was being carried out in the Rosenberg Bureau and in other offices of the National Socialist state. Rosenberg, who seemed doctrinaire and was looked upon as such by his collaborators and those who depended on him, had created, however, a special form of the racist-Germanic world-view and had made this known in his seminal work published first in 1930, *Der Mythus des 20. Jahrhunderts*.[23]

Education was being carried out not only within Rosenberg's Service Branch in the Reich leadership of the NSDAP, within the so-called Rosenberg Bureau, but also within virtually all of the subdivisions of the party. It was called folk-national cultivation or folk education and was propagating "Rosenbergianism" manifestly or latently, completely or partially,[24] i.e., the ideology of the *Mythus des 20. Jahrhunderts*. Thus Rosenberg's title as "the Führer's commissioner for the supervision of all intellectual and world-view schooling and education of the NSDAP"— and, as Michael H. Kater adds, "of the folk"[25]—acquires a certain justification. Thus the title "Reich Overseeing Office" assumed by Rosenberg's Service Branch, in spite of its lack of executive rights,[26] is not an empty formula. These disciplines, which were united within the DFG and which conducted the folk-national cultivation, especially the core disciplines of racial studies, prehistory, and *Volkskunde*, were thus able to become part of the National Socialist Rosenbergian schooling and educational program.

The Reich Community of German Folk Research and its departments were no doubt subjected to constant ideological and political influence by the Rosenberg Bureau. A central position as mediator was assumed for more than a year by the intermediary officer and "faithful" Rosenbergianer, Ziegler. His position as referee for folk research in the DFG was in agreement with the disciplinary and work areas assigned to the Reich Community, and Ziegler "could thus gain a more complete overview of practical, personnel and organizational questions in the areas of *Volkskunde*, prehistory, and racial studies."[27] That he was also carrying out disciplinary politics in the Rosenbergian sense can be seen by his many publications.

A Rosenbergian presence can also be seen somewhat through placements made in departmental leadership positions, but this cannot be clearly proven. The professors chosen as Führers of the Departments of Folk Speech and Settlement, the Germanist Walther Mitzka (University of Marburg an der Lahn) and the geographer Friedrich Metz (University Erlangen, later Freiburg im Breisgau), were both considered respected professionals in their scholarly disciplines before and after 1945.

I have not yet examined their work in the Reich Community from the standpoint of Rosenbergianism. Professor Hans F. K. Günther (University of Berlin, later Freiburg im Breisgau) was for a long time recognized as the ideological and racist *Germanen* scholar in the Rosenberg Bureau and in addition was an NSDAP member as of May 1, 1932.[28] The Department of Racial Studies could not have found a better or more suited director in the entire German Reich.[29] However, the Führer of the Department of Pre- and Early History is to be singled out particularly as a follower of Rosenberg.

Professor Hans Reinerth (University of Berlin) was a student of the prehistorian Gustav Kossinna. The former was repeatedly praised in Rosenberg's *Nationalsozialistische Monatshefte* and was one of the first members of Rosenberg's Battle Union for German Culture.[30] In 1932 Reinerth had led the *Reichsfachgruppe für Vorgeschichte* (Reich Professional Group for Prehistory) within the Battle Union and had tried "to gather all German prehistorians around himself, including those who belonged to a counter direction."[31] He repeated this attempt three weeks after Hitler's seizure of power "by suggesting to Prussian Cultural Minister Bernhard Rust the founding of a Reichsinstitut für Vor- und Frühgeschichte (Reich Institute for Pre- and Early History), . . . which in fact was supposed to bear the stamp of a Rosenbergian Reich Bureau." As a preliminary stage for the Reichsinstitut, Reinerth founded in the same year his Reichsbund für deutsche Vorgeschichte (Reich Union for German Prehistory).[32] In 1934 he received the Department of Pre- and Early History in the Reich Community of the DFG and was named the deputy for pre- and early history in the Rosenberg Bureau.[33] His later confrontations with colleagues in the SS Office of Ancestral Inheritance on prehistory research caused him to emulate Reich Leader Rosenberg, who was now competing with Reichsführer-SS Heinrich Himmler.[34]

Reinerth's career and the history of his discipline during the National Socialist period which culminates in his person are of great significance because one of the personal bridges between the Rosenberg Bureau and the DFG Reich Community becomes clear. In addition, it was Reinerth who had developed a "plan for a totalitarian restructuring of German prehistory"[35] and had presented it for the first time in the *Nationalsozialistische Monatshefte*, the scholarly journal of the NSDAP, which was published by Hitler and edited by Rosenberg. This 1932 plan, published as "German Prehistory during the Third Reich,"[36] indicates that in one of the scholarly disciplines[37] which was to be of use for Rosenberg's racist-Germanic worldview, a fascist organizational structure was established long before the seizure of power. Thus, soon after January 30, 1933, the party ideologists of the Rosenberg Bureau could proceed to carry out this plan for prehistory. Reinerth then did this by attempting to win over Education Minister Rust for his Reich institute. The project described by Michael H. Kater as a "Rosenbergian Reich Bureau" allows us to see the intent to politically coordinate the entire scholarly discipline of pre- and early history during the Third Reich.

Even though it is not possible to conclude from the prehistory case that such special concepts of a totalitarian kind were in existence for other disciplines before 1933, the basic structure of the Rosenbergian scholarly organization was clear in the eyes of all of those who were initiated to the cause. The Reinerth concept probably served as an example for DFG chairmen Stark and Wildhagen and influenced their planning of the Reich communities. It also served as an example for the Reich Community for German Folk Research founded at that time, and for the four other disciplinary divisions found within it, i.e., divisions that suited Rosenberg's racist study of the *Germanen*. Soon prehistory became the fifth discipline to begin to realize this totalitarian plan.

Many of the clarifications of intent and the organizational objectives included in Reinerth's concept are found again in the Department of Folklore. Within the Reich Community, which had been in existence for about two years, in addition to prehistory only the Folklore Department developed institutionally and promised to be successful. The discipline of *Volkskunde* had also brought with it a plan for a central German Reich institute, which was certainly familiar to DFG Vice-President Wildhagen as part of the history of the discipline through its developmental stages of 1917, 1926, 1928, and 1933.

From 1929–1930 until 1932, the year of his departure from the Cooperative Council or DFG, Wildhagen had been able to immerse himself in his knowledge of and ability in folklore by means of his reliable collaboration in the Central Office of the *Atlas der deutschen Volkskunde*.[38] He was at this time, and prior to this, occasionally the righthand man of DFG President Schmidt-Ott and had become more familiar with the internal political situation of the discipline of *Volkskunde*. The *Atlas* itself, whose business director and technical leader he had been, represented, as we have seen, the "seedbed"[39] of the folklore Reich institute. This *Atlas* was in the possession of the DFG, which founded in the summer or fall of 1934 the Reich Community for German Folk Research. The exemplary plan by John Meier for a folkloric Reich institute as part of the new pan-Reich foundation by the DFG must be taken into account along with the prehistory concept of Reinerth. The Department of Folklore of the Reich Community also received a director who came from Meier's professional circle, who was his personal friend, and who was also supposed to work in the future with Reinerth.

THE DEPARTMENT OF FOLKLORE OF THE REICH COMMUNITY AS A PRELIMINARY STAGE OF THE REICH INSTITUTE FOR GERMAN FOLKLORE

On August 29, 1934, DFG President Stark named as Führer of the Department of Folklore the bourgeois-national folklore professor Adolf Spamer. At that time he was still full professor at the Technical University of Dresden. As of April 1, 1936, he became *Ordinarius* for *Volkskunde* and occupied the newly created chair at the Friedrich Wilhelms University in the Reich capital city of Berlin.[40] The new *Primus* of German *Volkskunde* represents one of the most problematic personalities of the discipline during the Third Reich. His scholarly fate during National Socialism was accompanied by personal tragedy and exemplifies in the crudest form the nature of the alliance between bourgeois-national and fascist scholarship.

Karl Emil Gustav Adolf Spamer was born on April 10, 1883, in Mainz as the only child of parents who died early. His father was a doctor who early on was most active in psychology research. He was a docent at the University of Giessen; later he was in state service and finally became the district doctor in Darmstadt. Adolf Spamer grew up in Darmstadt in Hessia, studied from 1902 to 1908 at the universities in Freiburg im Breisgau, Munich, Berlin, and Giessen, and completed his doctorate in Germanistics in 1912 with "Über die Zersetzung und Vererbung in den deutschen Mystikertexten" (Concerning Change and Inheritance in German Mystical Texts) under Otto Behagel at the University of Giessen. His doctoral minors were national economics and art history. In 1908 he went to Munich and built up a folklore archive as director of the Folklore Department of the Bayerischer Landesverein für Heimatschutz (Bavarian Regional Association for Homeland Protection) and was until 1920 secretary of the journal *Bayerische Hefte für Volkskunde*, which he helped found in 1914 and which was published by the Bayerischer Verein für Volkskunst und Volkskunde (Bavarian Association for Folk Art and Folklore). During the First World War he saw service in the military in the royal regiment of guards detached to Munich but was released early.

After a failed attempt in Munich, Spamer completed his *Habilitation* in 1921 with Karl Helm at the University of Frankfurt am Main in German philology and folklore and taught there as a private docent. On May 1, 1926, he was named a regular full professor of German philology and folklore in the Cultural Science Department of the Technical University of Dresden and was given as a special task the scholarly development of elementary education students in the disciplines of *Volkskunde* and Germanistics.[41] Particularly in Dresden the later *Primus* of German *Volkskunde* developed a very active scholarship, especially in the theory of the discipline, with both pedagogical and regional interests.

Spamer had come from traditional German *Volkskunde*. He had continued to develop during the Weimar Republic as a theoretician and most decisively through a critical confrontation with Hans Naumann's teachings on *gesunkenes Kulturgut*. According to Kristin Sokol, "Spamer's conception of *Volkskunde*, which he presented essentially unchanged in several articles over an entire decade, was supposed to contribute to the development of an independent folklore scholarship which unites its individual disciplines by means of a single unified theoretical and methodological construct."[42] In Wolfgang Jacobeit's estimation, Spamer's theory and methodology came down to "an attempt to ascertain the 'folk soul' " and found its high point "in the hypothetical fiction of a 'folk man.' " Spamer represented a "psychological questioning of the objects of *Volkskunde*,"[43] i.e., his questioning was limited to fictive, idealistic concepts concerning the "folk soul" and the "spiritual-soul,"[44] which were by their very nature splendid material for ideological manipulation.

Spamer's basic ideological positions made him somewhat appealing to the National Socialists, even though his ideas were quite distinct from their attitudes. According to Hermann Strobach's brief listing of the aspects of Spamer's scholarly thought constructs, these were, on one hand, a looking back to Wilhelm Heinrich Riehl[45] and his conservative concept, i.e., "the rejection of the historically realistic divisions of society into economic and socially determined classes and strata and of the social opposition between rulers and those ruled in a capitalistic system." According to Spamer these economic groups were to be contrasted with "types of spiritual groups." He represented a decidedly anti-Marxist position. On the other hand, "Spamer's scholarly thinking and his personal behavior were determined by a very decisive, repeated, and primary attitude which never forsook its bourgeois-humanism."[46]

An analysis which does justice to the reality of the role and fate of Spamer during the Third Reich has never been undertaken within folklore until recently. The first iconoclastic treatments were presented in 1986 at the Munich meeting on *Volkskunde und Nationalsozialismus* by the GDR scholars Strobach and Jacobeit, more than forty years after the end of the war.[47] All previous folklore publications about Spamer during the postwar years were influenced by a protective and silent cartel of his Third Reich friends, students, and comrades in the discipline, and critical points have been far from reality.

In Spamer's case an exemplary tragedy of the postwar historiography of *Volkskunde* was developed, especially concerning the real institutionalization of the discipline during National Socialism. There one can read in both West and East German publications about a highly intelligent, dear, and good but highly impractical Spamer who wanted the very best for *Volkskunde*, whose integrity and simplicity were horribly deceived, and who was cheated. He was a man who could no longer stop bad things from happening to the discipline and who was finally subjected himself to persecution by those who fell prey to the fascist dictatorship.[48] The understandable piety and respect for that kind of "innocent" fate of a *Primus* of German *Volkskunde* allowed critical and uncritical scholarly historians of folklore to discontinue further research and to join in the basic tendency toward an "apotheosis" of Spamer. This came about originally through a conscious deception in which he himself was not uninvolved.[49] The discipline of *Volkskunde*, as well as the scholar and the man Spamer himself, is better served, however, through objective, critical, and fundamental analyses wherever possible. Strobach and Jacobeit have made a beginning.

Spamer, a human and impressive personality to those around him, was during his time an outstanding individual for the discipline. He intended in the years 1934 to 1936–1937 to expand "his" German *Volkskunde* into a scholarly discipline, and not only as John Meier had recently tried to do, through financial support, but much more so through active collaboration with the fascist regime. His starting point was his own role as an important and dominant scholar in the discipline. What he did not consider and perhaps did not want to presume was that this undertaking would of necessity fail because of the impossibility of decisively uniting opposing primary positions.

Spamer incorrectly estimated the presumptions and the results of his intellectual and practical collaboration with fascism. He clearly believed that he could make this collaboration useful for the discipline and his own objectives, and he was apparently successful at this in the beginning. Fascism required, however, consistent with its own totalitarian needs, an absolute subjugation of scholarship and its representatives to its specific ideological and power political intentions, and it finally succeeded in this by means of its own power structure. The compromises which Spamer had made in the meantime, from whose results he later suffered his own downfall, turn his case into a most instructive lesson for the history of the discipline.

Particularly in light of the bourgeois-humanistic basic attitude which he promoted quite openly, the very critical question arises, as Strobach points out, whether Spamer really could "not recognize the true essence of German fascism, based on his own bourgeois class standpoint . . . and in spite of his differences with overt fascist ideology, as well as his own subsequent opposition to the politics of Hitler's fascism."[50] Here considerable doubt is fitting, because the "terroristic character of the Hitler regime," its inhuman domestic political rule, had already "appeared quite clearly" during the first two years when leading folklorists were greeting the "national" or "National Socialist revolution."[51]

In Spamer's personal life too there were existential crises brought on by the political situation. As a result of the fascist political coordination and the structural change of the Technical University of Dresden, four colleagues who had befriended Spamer in the Cultural Science Department lost their professorships and thus the material basis for their scholarly work. Among them was the Jewish Romance language scholar Victor Klemperer.[52] Professor Klemperer repeatedly recorded in his memoirs private conversations with Spamer which give information about the latter's personal estimation of the political situation:

> My colleague Spamer, the folklorist, who knows so much about the origins and the continuity of legends, said to me once during the first year of the Hitler regime, when I was in rage about the mental condition of the German folk: "If it were possible—(he considered it at the time still to be an unreal conditional sentence)—to reduce the entire press coverage, all publications and teaching to one single tone, and if it were taught everywhere that there was no World War between 1914 and 1918, all the world would believe after three years that it really did not happen." When I reminded Spamer about this during our first subsequent lengthy discussion, he corrected me: "Yes, I still remember; but you have remembered one thing incorrectly; I said then and still mean that today: after one year!"[53]

The untruthfulness of political propaganda during the Third Reich and the totalitarian political coordination of the opinions of the broad strata of the populace by fascism were well known to Spamer. The answer to the question is suspicious; just what did he think about this German folk which allowed itself to be so willingly manipulated, and just how did he view the real object of *Volkskunde* in everyday reality? Klemperer also gives information about this in his diaries in the form of a sharp judgment of Spamer. Klemperer writes on April 29 (apparently in the year 1936) to a friend:

> Do not forget in your *Vita* about those who were comfortable and careful in both directions! [Do not forget] the Biedermann Spamer who visited us and who called the *Stürmer* an insignificant scandal sheet such as we have always had, and who is a big folklore animal with the Nazis and is thus betraying his scholarship. It was he who spoke so openly about the stupidity of the folk who can be poured full of everything.[54]

Spamer's basically improper and tactless attempt to trivialize the importance of the well-known anti-Semitic journal *Der Stürmer*, published by Nürnberg *Gau* Leader Julius Streicher, and by means of this to silence the concerns of his Jewish colleague, brought on the latter's predictable emotional reaction which he recorded as a diary entry. This crass verdict about the *Primus* of German *Volkskunde*, who thought so little about the broad masses of the populace and was betraying his discipline through collaboration with the Nazis, must thus be evaluated with considerable care in regard to the realistic nature of its contents.

On the other hand, Spamer worked with the German fascists and was even promoted by them, at least in the beginning. From the viewpoint of his racially disadvantaged colleague Klemperer, who had been denied his profession by the Nazis and had reason to fear for his personal safety, even his life, Spamer was thus absolutely "a big folklore animal with the Nazis." Since he wanted to maintain his contact with Jewish friends at the same time, he was thus a dubious "Biedermann." Spamer had to attempt to justify this double standard for himself and his Jewish friend, and he did this in an illusionist way, i.e., for example by calling *Gau* Leader Streicher's *Stürmer* insignificant.

Klemperer no doubt saw the "actual essence of German fascism" and the involvement of his friend more clearly and with less illusion. His confused indignation concerning Spamer's basically unjustified behavior is understandable. There can be no diminution of his judgment, however, in regard to the "one who is careful in both directions," who made it illusionistically and opportunistically "comfortable" for himself in his personal attitude toward the inhuman political reality and in favor of an idealistically based voluntary cooperation with the National Socialist Party and the governmental offices at both the state and the Reich level.[55]

Spamer never joined the NSDAP.[56] He was also no adherent of National Socialism or of the fascist world-view. He conformed to a bourgeois spiritual ideology, considering himself to be "scholarly objective" and otherwise "unpolitical."[57] Scholarly objectivity, the mark of his folklore theory and methodology, separated it from the National Socialist work on the subject which he himself never accepted. The National Socialist folklore concept had, however, ultimately come from the bourgeois-national concept, and it had many common points with it. That which was its unique property, a specific fascist *Volkskunde* ideology, still must be clarified.

Spamer's scholarly positions and especially the concepts "scholarly objective" and "unpolitical" must also be evaluated from the standpoint of a false consciousness. The idea of finding oneself to be scholarly objective, which cannot be anything particularly great,[58] is added here to the generalization that politics is not the concern of scholars but rather exclusively that of those who are ruling, politicians.

In spite of this personal estimation, his work as a folklorist, as a scholarly theoretician and practitioner, was of eminent political importance, and at the beginning of the Third Reich, Spamer became the complete *homo politicus* who cultivated in many ways his connections with the *Real* politicians of the time, in the interest of establishing his discipline as an independent branch of scholarship. That he thus turned into an excellent connoisseur of the cultural and scholarly-political inner workings and then used this knowledge to promote his own career must not be left unanalyzed in such a critical evaluation as this. In any case the verdict by Klemperer of the "one who is careful in both directions" is fitting. For Spamer actively promoted bourgeois-national German *Volkskunde* and folk-national cultivation with the fascist powers. The latter, on the other hand, were greatly interested in a scholarly discipline which was excellently suited for their ideological and power political objectives and were not any less interested in this professional and scholarly leader who became during this three-year period of transition an intermediary, a sojourner on a perilous path between two mutually exclusive worlds.

Spamer's Dresden teaching period was very different from his time as a private docent in Frankfurt, where he taught only a few students, occasionally only one single student in his private apartment.[59] The number of elementary education students who took an elective course with him in *Volkskunde*, which was not yet a required course, climbed from year to year and reached 328 during the summer semester of 1932. In the ten years from 1926 to 1936 in the Cultural Science Department of the Technical University of Dresden, he directed almost 190 State Examination studies.[60] The Saxon pedagogy students who later became teachers formed a core of folklorists who were educated by him. He could employ them successfully for folk research and folk-national cultivation, which were being rapidly institutionalized in Saxony after the National Socialist seizure of power.

Under the political leadership of his student, the National Socialist functionary Karl Ewald Fritzsch, there developed around the middle of 1933 the Landesstelle für Volksforschung und Volkstumspflege im NS-Lehrerbund des Gauverbandes Sachsen (Regional Institute for Folk Research and Folk-National Cultivation in the NS Teachers Union of the *Gau* League Saxony). One year later, "two and a half thousand teachers" were added "as responsible folk-national warders in the service of collecting and observing"[61] and were directed by twenty-five selected regional folk-national warders.[62] Continual observation by these folk-national warders was devoted to the expressive forms of folk life in order to be able to compare, as Wilhelm Heinrich Riehl did, the " 'statistics of customs' with the 'statistics of economics.' "[63] The questionnaires sent to the teachers were processed and the results sent back to local and *Gau* archives.[64]

The themes of these official inquiries were part of a ten-year plan and dealt with traditional canonical realms: from life customs through calendrical customs and festivals, folk belief, folk medicine, narrative, speech, song, childrens' songs and games, and folk art from the house and the farmyard. The material collected was processed in the folklore seminars of the state universities of Dresden and Leipzig and was available there for all pedagogy students—at least this was the statement of intent.[65]

The folk-national assignment was added to the scholarly one. Every folk-national warder had to independently build up for his area of responsibility a *"Volkskunde"* with a local archive, a local history, a homeland room or a homeland museum. The questionnaires sent in were supposed to supply the impetus, i.e., the collection of material was not supposed to be an end in itself. The real meaning was given to the work by means of its interpretation and evaluation for instruction and education.

Since those who participated were without exception teachers, they could take part completely through their profession "in the task of German folk development" and, according to Fritzsch, could happily realize "that in the new Germany all education can be built only on an indigenously stable folk-nation and must lead to a nobler form of the German folk-nation."[66] The festivals and celebrations in Saxon schools, to mention only one example of this folk-national cultivation, were "in the service of a pure German education and German character building" and thus became "a clear avowal to the Third Reich."[67]

The scholarly director in 1934 of the Regional Institute for Folk Research and Folk-National Cultivation in the NS Teachers Union (NSLB) of Saxony, one of the subdivisions of the NSDAP, was Spamer, who had in the meantime risen in Berlin to the position of Reichsleiter für Volkskundeforschung (Reich director for folklore research), and who was as of January 1, 1934, himself a member of the NSLB.[68] The organizational plan of the Saxon regional party institution was based on Spamer's "need expressed for many years for state offices for folklore research."[69] This was apparently a preliminary stage of the Reich institute which was being attempted by him in the Reich Community for German Folk Research. The Regional Institute of the NSLB in the *Gau* of Saxony was united corporately with the Reichsbund Volkstum und Heimat (Reich Union Folk-Nation and Homeland) and the NS-Gemeinschaft "Kraft durch Freude" (NS Community "Strength through Joy"), both of which were under the National Socialist Reich organizational leader and head of the fascist Workers' Union, Dr. Robert Ley. Many of the folk-national warders of the Regional Institute carried out party functions through a personal union with the Reich Union[70] and shortly thereafter were in the Folk-Nation and Homeland Department of the National Socialist Cultural Community of Reich Leader Rosenberg.[71]

A chance developed through all this activity in Saxony for Spamer to become more closely aligned with cooperating but also with competing party figures, which he of course realized. Thus he became director of the Landesfachstelle für Volkskunde im Reichsbund Volkstum und Heimat (Research Office for Folklore in the Reich Union Folk-Nation and Homeland), which had been formed by means of the political coordination of the Sächsischer Verband für Volkskunde (Saxon League for Folklore), founded by him and Fritz Karg in 1931.[72] The Research Office was converted a little later into the Gaufachstelle für Volkskunde in der Abteilung "Volkstum und Heimat" der NS-Kulturgemeinde (Gau Sachsen) (*Gau* Research Office for Folklore in the Department "Folk-Nation and Homeland" of the NS Culture Community [*Gau* Saxony]), which was under Rosenberg.[73] Spamer thus became in 1934 the Führer of regional party organizations in Saxony which ultimately served the cultural politics and the folk-national cultivation of the Rosenberg Bureau. His party functions and his relationship to Rosenberg may well have helped him on his road to Berlin and into his central position at the Reich Community, even though, amazingly enough, he was not a member of the NSDAP.

Although the most decisive piece of evidence for this obvious conclusion is still lacking, it is clear from the series of events presented here that Spamer was not a scholar oblivious to the world, as he has been presented until now. The judgment by the Germanist Arthur Hübner, which is often cited and has often been taken for the final word, appears not to be completely accurate:

> He is the best theoretical mind among the folklorists and this is the first matter which one must consider if one were to think about creating in Berlin an *Ordinariat* specifically for *Volkskunde*. He is to be sure impractical and immovable and would certainly need assistance, which could be accomplished through a very skillful private docent.[74]

To call Spamer "immovable" and "impractical" conflicts with the fact that this "best theoretical mind" had, as of the middle of 1933, very consciously promoted the political career of his discipline as well as his own and had proved to a high degree to be a capable scholarly organizer. The judgment by Hübner, however, was dated May 22, 1933. It was being used in regard to the appointment of Spamer on April 1, 1936, to the Berlin *Volkskunde* chair and was intended to counter resistance by the Rosenberg Bureau and of those referents who were associated with him.[75]

In a preliminary study to diploma work directed by Wolfgang Jacobeit, Kristin Sokol documents her impressions of a worldly and well-informed Spamer. He was not simply a theoretician who was "politically incapable of evaluating what awaited him with the assumption of the Department of Folklore into the Reich Community for German Folk Research." He was "absolutely familiar with the ideas and the strategic plans of the collaborators in the Ministry who surrounded Bernhard Rust, and of the 'Cooperative Council . . . ,' where he regularly trafficked." "He knew in detail about the political expectations which had been passed on in writing by the president of the Cooperative Council of German Scholarship, Stark, to his 'Führer of the departments of the Reich Community.' "[76] And finally, "the decisions by Spamer to go to Berlin, as well as the scholarly organizational occurrences which were known to him through his ministerial contacts, had been influenced."[77]

It was the DFG vice-president, Wildhagen, who convinced Spamer as a "man with his trust"[78] to take over the directorship of the Department of Folklore in the Reich Community for German Folk Research. President Stark signed this appointment on August 29, 1934.[79] It could scarcely have come about without the approval of the men behind the scenes from the Rosenberg Bureau, whereas the Reich Educational Ministry had ostensibly "not been informed at all"[80] about the founding of the Reich Community and treated Spamer with fewer reservations toward the end of the year.[81]

Wildhagen and Spamer were friends, according to Helmut Heiber.[82] Together they had worked to complete the questionnaire of the *Atlas der deutschen Volkskunde*, making suggestions for almost 150 of the questions. Their work, published in 1933 by Friedrich Schmidt-Ott,[83] provided the basis for the fifth questionnaire of the *Atlas*.[84] Wildhagen and Spamer both devoted themselves in the Reich Community to the *Atlas*, which in the DFG was looked upon as the "rather curious hobbyhorse" of the Vice President.[85] Wildhagen had indeed promoted the *Atlas* work quite decisively. This can be seen in a book which he subsequently published about the *Atlas*.[86]

The *Atlas* specialist Wilhelm Peßler was named nominal director of the Berlin Central Office of the *Atlas* on August 29, 1934, and thus became a collaborator of Spamer's.[87] He was director of the Fatherland Museum of the city of Hannover. According to the document of appointment, he received a monthly research stipend in the sum of two hundred Reichsmarks for his administrative work and was supposed to travel to Berlin "about every four to six weeks, for one or two days." Peßler was scarcely able during these infrequent visits "to meet the necessary requirements and to exercise this complete control" which had been nominally assigned to him.[88] That was from the very beginning not the intent of the DFG Presidium nor of Spamer.

Spamer nevertheless made fun of Peßler's insufficient accomplishments for the *Atlas* in a letter to John Meier that emphasized Peßler's position as a "straw man": "That you wanted to let Peßler speak about the *Atlas* is both correct and malicious. He is indeed (*honoris causa*) the official director, but he has no sense of what has happened nor of what is going on (this however in confidence, since P. is otherwise a very nice fellow)."[89] Wildhagen once expressed ironically to Peßler his astonishment that "the apparent director of the undertaking" had once all by himself left a Regional Office directors' meeting of the ADV early and had not shown the "necessary seriousness" for *Atlas* matters.[90] Peßler's limited engagement could be traced back, however, to the fact that in reality the *Atlas* specialists Spamer and especially Wildhagen were carrying out his functions.

One predecessor of Peßler as director of the *Atlas* Central Office under President Schmidt-Ott had been Adolf Helbok, who now agitated against Wildhagen, much like Hübner and others who had been "excluded" from the *Atlas*.[91] The "showpiece" of the discipline of *Volkskunde*—which was being supported by the DFG and for which all of the folklore umbrella organizations competed with one another during the Third Reich (including the University of Berlin, the Germanist Hübner, and even the prehistorian Reinerth)[92]—had fallen in 1934 as "booty" into the hands of Wildhagen, who now had to defend it and who probably also for this reason had the famous scholars Spamer and Peßler called as his supporters.

Security measures were necessary in regard not only to the scholarly but also to the political competition. Thus Spamer and Wildhagen turned to the influential folklorist and National Socialist party functionary Eugen Fehrle.[93] Spamer invited him on September 8, 1934, to participate "in the leadership of the works of this Reich Community,"[94] and Wildhagen revealed to him on January 2, 1935, after conversations with the staff director of the Rosenberg Bureau, Gotthard Urban, his intention to call Fehrle as "a trusted man" of Alfred Rosenberg to the DFG. Perhaps it would be possible to use the opportunity of Fehrle's presence in Berlin for a discussion either with Herr Rosenberg himself or with Herr Urban.[95]

Wildhagen and Spamer unfortunately acquired a false friend in the person of Fehrle. He not only recommended a flattering dedication to President Stark in a folklore volume[96] and called for a DFG subvention for his *Oberdeutsche Zeitschrift für Volkskunde*,[97] but he also made overtures to Reich Leader Rosenberg, to whom he handed a hastily written memorandum on the occasion of his visit to Berlin on January 13, 1935. In a three-page typed outline titled "Der Ausbau der Volkskunde für die NS Erziehung" (The Expansion of Folklore for National Socialist Education),[98] Fehrle attacked those "homeless intellectuals" (he meant Spamer and Naumann) as well as the "worst enemies" of National Socialist folklorists, the Catholic popular piety researcher Georg Schreiber, and called for a Reichsinstitut für Volkskunde with the main office at his own university in Heidelberg. The League of German Societies for Folklore of the old master John Meier, "which was not at this point in any way being led National Socialistically," should also be attached to this Reich institute. Fehrle apparently wanted to become the Führer of this Heidelberg Reich institute.

Fehrle reported on January 22, 1935, to Wildhagen, to whom he had made his proposal available. He did not realize the interests of the vice-president, who was so enthusiastic about the *Atlas*. Fehrle wrote that he had not yet received an answer from Reich Leader Rosenberg.[99] It was also of little interest, since Fehrle most likely had not been viewed by the DFG Presidium as a "trustworthy man" and Spamer continued to direct his Department of Folklore, planned as a preliminary stage to the Reich institute, during the next years. Fehrle's power-hungry attempt to exclude Spamer and also John Meier by means of political denunciation and to assume at the same time for himself the most important positions in the discipline is most characteristic of fascist behavior. Other strategists simply started out more intelligently and thus had more possibility of success.

Wildhagen was completely capable of dealing with that kind of National Socialist "early warrior." He behaved congenially, not only during the less-than-dignified deposing of his former superior Schmidt-Ott[100] but also under other circumstances. Wildhagen had "numerous enemies,"[101] whom he treated, insofar as they were scholars, with certain sarcastic *bon mots* which came from years of experience in the scholarly foundation, e.g., "There is no scholarly honor; these fellows all just want money."[102] He had said at one time to Fritz Boehm, director of the *Atlas* Central Office, that professors and prostitutes stood at the same level; for money one could have everything from them. When Hübner excitedly called him on the carpet, he explained cynically that he had only repeated an expression made by the King of Hannover when the "Göttingen Seven"[103] were banished and that it was not his own opinion.[104] The behavior of Fehrle did not seem to him in any way abnormal.

Wildhagen is said by Heiber to have "commanded a certain clientele who were promoted by him; the rest he treated *en canaille*."[105] Spamer was his friend, the "man with his trust,"[106] and his protégé. Many others did battle with Wildhagen and had to expect bad treatment, including workers in the Berlin Central Office of the *Atlas*. Wildhagen had often disagreed with their work done under the aegis of Schmidt-Ott[107] and had fought arrogantly with many of the participating folklorists. Arrogance and irony betray his subsequent judgment of the period when he was business and technical director of the *Atlas*:

> After I had forced those lazy fellows in the *Atlas* to do their work, and with results, which in spite of all reticence advanced even further than my precalculations, there was in no way an inner peace, not to mention friendship or caring, to be found in this mausoleum of the German spirit.[108]

Under Vice-President Wildhagen ten scholarly collaborators[109] were removed in 1934 from this "mausoleum of the German spirit." Among them was Richard Beitl, whose scholarship represented counteropinions.[110] Beitl was guilty of obstinacy and continued to suffer in his career from damaging persecution by Wildhagen.[111] "Peace, friendship, and caring" were not found at all in the Central Office of the *Atlas*. In 1935 a further "undisciplined" scholar was moved out by means of a less-than-favorable report,[112] and Wildhagen conducted a legal process against Anneliese Bretschneider.[113] Beitl then designated him as the "usurper [of the *Atlas*] supported by the party."[114]

These damaging confrontations were used after the war as an alibi for apparent National Socialist opposition. It was, however, of no significance whether the opponents were National Socialists of conviction who entered the party early, as was the case with Bretschneider,[115] or, as was the case with Beitl, became members of Rosenberg's Battle Union for German Culture and as long as this existed were looked upon favorably in the Rosenberg Bureau.[116]

During the rule of German fascism, at all ideological levels influenced by the party, whether it was the DFG, the ministries, the Reich Directorship of the NSDAP, or others, it was a matter of power and not justice; it was actually the survival of the fittest. To prevail, the means to power had to be acquired, no matter how. Ethical norms were damaged in the process. It was completely immaterial if such behavior patterns spread into university society, as can be seen in the case of Fehrle. The fascists finally turned against the DFG Presidium itself, which was both a personnel and institutional part of this university and scholarly society. This brought about its collapse in 1936, and in the following year came the defeat of Wildhagen's "favorite idea,"[117] the Reich Community for German Folk Research.

In addition to his contribution to the organizational structure of the Department of Folklore, Wildhagen, much like Spamer, carried out folk research. At the very core of their common personal interest was their preoccupation with the *Atlas der deutschen Volkskunde*. Jacobeit has sharply criticized the scholarly objectives of Wildhagen,[118] who had seen in the *Atlas* the possibility of "solving many of the nebulous *Germanen* questions" by "penetrating into the area of the racial soul."[119] In this sense he interpreted the maps in his own way, to follow very realistic goals as a "National Socialist in deed," namely to draw conclusions "about the old Germanic settlement areas." We can see this clearly in the writings of Wildhagen.

> Then it will be easier to prove what other scholars have adduced with such difficulty, the indigenous stability of Germandom in those areas under question. A first glance reveals an almost complete failure on the part of Slavs to penetrate into the German folk-nation. This is still ascertainable in a few superstitious ideas and customs. . . . Extending the work of the *Atlas* beyond the western boundaries would result in better examples for the aftereffects of early Germanic influences![120]

Wildhagen's intent and his assignment at the *Atlas* were for "a conscious falsification of *Atlas* material and maps for the purpose of 'bringing home' those ostensible former Germanic settlement areas as an ideological aid in the creation of a 'Great Germany.' "[121] This meant the subjugation of the neighboring peoples by means of Hitler's war, the annexation of portions of their state regions, and the rule of the German "master race" in Europe. Tendentiously similar-sounding statements about the political function of the *Atlas* were made, as we have seen, by bourgeois-national folklorists such as Richard Beitl[122] and Otto Lauffer.[123] John Meier and his friends created the basis for this politicization by seeing the task of the *Atlas* as the most important problem of folkloric research work,[124] i.e., to protect their own from acquiring foreign elements.

Wildhagen, who expressly recognizes Meier's extensive service at least in the organizational structure of the *Atlas*,[125] is only following ideologically in the footsteps of his predecessors. *Volkskunde* and *Atlas* are supposed to reveal the pure German strengths of the German folk-nation. In his documentation of this he depends on Meier's Reich institute plans, portions of which he paraphrases.[126] He does this in connection with his views about the helpful role of the *Atlas* in the removal of foreign elements from Germanic and German uniqueness, e.g., Christianity, especially the Catholic Church.[127] What is new from him is that he is completely in agreement with the special ideology of Rosenberg.

The pan-Germanic ideology of folk research and of the folklore *Atlas* of the Reich Community, which could be politically misused so easily, led to the founding of a short-lived scholarly society. With the active participation of Wildhagen, Spamer, representatives of the Department of Folklore, and of the Rosenberg Bureau, including Matthes Ziegler, the Internationaler Verband für Volksforschung (International Association for Folklore and Ethnology)[128] was founded in 1935 and was promoted by the journal *Folk*. Its Executive Board was invited in April 1936 to a meeting in the DFG office in Berlin.[129] The International Association included professional scholars from the countries of middle and northern Europe which were viewed as "Germanic." One of its purposes was to expand the questionnaire research by the *Atlas* to these "Germanic-Nordic" peoples, including the Baltic states.[130] These plans for expansion by the *Atlas* never came about, since at the demise of the Reich Community the International Association for Folklore and Ethnology, at least the journal *Folk*, also disappeared from sight. We must bear in mind that many of the foreign members appeared during the Second World War as collaborators of the SS Office of Ancestral Inheritance.

There has until now been little talk about Spamer's participation in the *Atlas* work of his friend Wildhagen, work which supported a special Germanophilia as well as fascist foreign policies. His willing collaboration has not been proved; however, his scholarly theoretical intentions found expression in the fifth questionnaire of the *Atlas*. This questionnaire presents a reworked selection of the 1933 Wildhagen-Spamer suggestions for almost 150 questions.[131] The questionnaire was published in January 1935 by the DFG, with comments on the founding of the Reich Community, on the ADV, on contemporary *Volkskunde*, and on how to answer the questions.[132] Even though the individual contributions were not signed, the thought processes of Spamer cannot be overlooked. It can also be assumed that there was collaboration by Wildhagen.

The research team had finally prevailed at the *Atlas* and now promoted its "psychological questioning concerning the objects of folklore" and its "hypothesizing of the fiction of a 'folk man.' "[133] The research goal of Spamer's contemporary folklore was "everyday man," folk man "in sober reality" and his contemporary customs, which are "common to all folk comrades, which form to a certain extent their spiritual possessions," and are "folklorically meaningful."[134] "This obvious element in daily life" was to be researched. It reached "from the present back to the beginnings of the history of the folk" and let "that which was unchangeable in our folk soul, through all times and through all changes of the times, be both recognized and sensed."[135]

The questions in the first block dealt with "Traits and Helpful Means of the Simplest Kind for Direct Acquisition of True Human Knowledge."[136] Here there were questions about the opinions of the folk which associated the shape of a person's nose with certain character traits, and an exemplary answer was included: "pointed nose and pointed chin, a living devil sits therein!" It is clear that this compelling agreement of the external with the inner human image was and is to be interpreted racially.

The character of people was also of interest in question complexes,[137] e.g., proverbs and adages about the judgment of a person after a first impression. "A splendid gift for observing and a priceless folk humor" are expressed in numerous short expressions about the character of humans, e.g., in "scaredy cat," "old fish wife," "schnapps nose," "babbling cousin," "slut." The writers add: "The brevity and accuracy of these judgments are so appropriate that no poet can say them better."

There were questions with exemplary answers added "according to firmly established judgments about individual human characteristics" ("smart as a fox," "dumb as a hoe handle").[138] There were questions about interpretations of the future: "If someone is in a bad mood, one says he got out of bed on his left leg"; "if a cat runs from the left across the path, this is supposed to bring luck"; "someone stumbles over a stone (or something similar) . . . what does one say about this? (e.g., here a Jew is buried)."[139] There were questions about derogatory names for professionals such as "a herring tamer" for a merchant's apprentice.[140] And there were a few questions about marriage customs.[141]

With this fifth questionnaire Spamer and Wildhagen were not simply collecting harmless curiosities which might cause an enlightened person to smile[142] but were looking primarily for primitive prejudices which could be interpreted racially, were usable in everyday human interaction, and could be raised all the way to inhuman aggression. They were carrying out this prejudicial study, however, not with the enlightened intention of improving the prevailing behavior patterns. The folk materials being collected reflected what they positively evaluated as the "unchangeable nature of our folk soul." As part of an applied *Volkskunde* and folk-national cultivation, it was supposed to be returned to the "pure German community" after being collected in more than twenty thousand localities of the German region and after being interpreted by scholars.[143] These objectivizations of "subintellectual"[144] prejudicial behavior were supposed to become revivals and from then on, after receiving scholarly sanction, they were to continue to function.

This contemporary folklore of Spamer and Wildhagen was intended to stabilize that which already existed. It represented an antienlightenment ploy for stupefying the German folk. It was open to all kinds of consciousness manipulation and was thus excellently suited for the fascist propaganda machine.

To do justice to the scholar and the man Spamer, we must of course try to evaluate whether he was even aware of the irrational core of his psychological *Volkskunde*. Use of the social scientific methodology of his time would have helped him to an understanding of this. Then Klemperer's contention that Spamer had spoken to him so unguardedly about the stupidity of the folk, whom one could convince of anything,[145] would be completely believable. It is clear, however, that, as Fritzsch stated, Spamer rejected "the sociological method of viewing the German folk-nation"[146] and did not apply social scientific concepts and methods which were foreign to his psychological concept of *Volkskunde*. For this reason also we will have to start in all likelihood from the principle that he was biased toward the folk ideology of his age, which thus denied him an objective and realistic recognition of his research field and of his scholarly undertakings. But this does not change our judgment of his illusionist attitude toward the political reality of the Third Reich and of his opportunistic collaboration with fascism.

Spamer went repeatedly on lecture tours to explain to his friends in the discipline and to lay persons the project of the Department of Folklore of the Berlin Reich Community of German Folk Research and to request their help. In October 1934 he reported only a little bit about the organizational structure of this "gift of the state"[147] at the Leipzig meeting of the National Socialist Teachers Union (NSLB) in Saxony. The *Atlas* was praised, and so was the Regional Institute for Folk Research and Folk-National Cultivation in the NSLB of the *Gau* League Saxony.

In June 1934 in Plauen, at a meeting Spamer organized of the *Gau* Research Office for Folklore in the Department "Folk-Nation and Homeland" of the NS Culture Community (Gau Saxony), several interesting aspects were added. Spamer criticized among other things the Viennese Mythological School, which was being promoted by the Rosenberg Bureau and its National Socialist Culture Community, but he did not give the names of its representatives, such as Karl von Spieß and Edmund Mudrak.[148] He also devoted lengthy comments to the meaning of racial studies for *Volkskunde*. A "folklore on a racial basis" seemed to him only possible when "detailed racial maps within the German folk realm" were in hand, such as those the *Atlas* "possesses today for German customs and German beliefs." He accepted a "hand-in-hand collaboration" of the two disciplines of *Volkskunde* and racial studies, not however a blending of the two.[149]

Spamer was speaking not primarily about the Department of Racial Studies but about the racist *Volkskunde* of Rosenberg's chief branch leader, Ziegler. Spamer distinguished his own *Volkskunde* from that of Ziegler and from the latter's standard work "Folklore on a Racial Basis"[150] (see text in appendix I.9), which Spamer cited, once again however without naming names. His offer of "working hand-in-hand" was intended for the Department of Racial Studies under Hans F. K. Günther, scarcely for Ziegler, who was not educated in racial studies and whom the *Primus* of German *Volkskunde* believed he could treat with indifference.

Spamer welcomed "the close collaboration with prehistory"[151] under Reinerth. The Department of Folk Speech under Walther Mitzka belonged, according to Spamer's definition, to *Volkskunde* and was made independent for purely practical reasons, since it took care of the German speech atlas (University of Marburg an der Lahn) and the dialect dictionaries.[152] The Department of Settlement (formerly boundary and ethnic German studies) under Friedrich Metz, with its task of investigating folk tribes within the folk German realm, was not claimed as a part of *Volkskunde*.[153]

At the Fourth German Folklore Meeting of the League of German Societies for Folklore in Bremen in October 1936, Spamer spoke about the structure and the goals of his folklore umbrella organization, the Department of Folklore in the Reich Community.[154] Spamer's version of the concept of the DFG department comes out very clearly in this most interesting lecture. It had long since been bypassed, however, as a result of the political happenings of the preceding months, i.e., the removal from office of DFG Vice-President Wildhagen on August 15, 1936.[155] This was to become obvious only a little later. Spamer too had asked at the beginning of June 1936 to be relieved from carrying out his assignments in the Reich Community because the Rosenberg Bureau had discredited one of his scholarly articles.[156]

Spamer's "attempt at public justification" after "two years of work" leaves many gaps in our information in spite of the specificity of dates and numbers. It is thus not quite understandable why "this work station prior to this time appeared by design only occasionally before a broader public and thus its desires and activities were known through hearsay and for the most part by only a narrow circle of professional colleagues." Why were the five departments of the Reich Community blocked, for "external and internal reasons," from clarifying "in a narrow working community those questions concerning the essence and the development of the German folk-nation"?[157]

Except for such presentations, which were still somewhat nebulous, the subdivisions of the Department of Folklore were clearly described. They had reached their highest and at the same time their final point. They included the *Atlas der deutschen Volkskunde*, which in 1936 Spamer called "the greatest communal undertaking in the humanities which ever took place on German soil."[158] It was nominally under the direction of Wilhelm Peßler. Further, there were the regional offices, which also served the *Atlas*, the Regional Institute Kurmark for German Folk Research for the Provinces of Brandenburg and the Grenzmark Posen-West Prussia, the Regional Institute for Folk Research and Folk-National Cultivation in the NSLB (*Gau* Saxony),[159] and the Low German League for Folklore under the direction of

Otto Lauffer. Of these three regional offices the first was under the direction of Ernst Otto Thiele, who was closely allied with the Rosenberg Bureau,[160] the second under the Spamer student and National Socialist functionary Fritzsch.

Amazingly there were no other regional offices beyond the Middle German and Northwest German area, if one disregards those of the *Atlas*, which did not belong to the Reich Community. On the other hand, there existed a series of centralized projects, or they were in the process of being planned: the *Corpus der deutschen Hausinschriften* (Corpus of German House Inscriptions), for which preliminary work was being carried out in Hessia under the direction of Bernhard Martin, in Saxony, and in the "Kurmark." The National Socialist student body, the party offices, the SS Schule Haus Wewelsburg in Westfalen (SS Schoolhouse Wewelsburg in Westphalia), and the NS Frauenarbeitsdienst (NS Women's Work Service) participated or were supposed to participate. There was also the *Handwörterbuch der deutschen Sachkultur* (Handbook of German Material Culture), produced under the direction of Lauffer with the special collaboration of Herbert Freudenthal and Ernst Bargheer, and a Hauptstelle für deutsche Sachforschung (Central Office for German Material Culture Research). There was the "establishment of a Central Word and Picture Archive" and of a Zentralarchiv der deutschen Volkserzählung (Central Archive of German Folk Narrative) under the directorship of Gottfried Henßen. There was the Volkskundliche Bestandsaufnahme der deutschen Archive (Folkloric Stock-Taking of German Archives) under Hans Moser and Otto Gebhard; the Volkskundliche Bestandsaufnahme der deutschen Bildersammlungen (Folkloric Stock-Taking of German Picture Collections); and that "of German museums." There was the Hauptstelle für Sinnbildforschung (Central Office for Symbol Research), which was directed by the ally of Wildhagen and of the Rosenberg Bureau,[161] Karl Theodor Weigel,[162] as well as a film archive at the Central Office of the Department of Folklore in Berlin. Even though there were few regional offices, a large number of research projects associated through Spamer with the DFG department did not just exist on paper.[163]

The collaborators named above, who were primarily in leadership positions, came for the most part from bourgeois-national *Volkskunde*, or at least they felt they were part of it. Lauffer was in fact deputy chairman of the League of German Societies for Folklore. Lauffer, Herbert Freudenthal, Ernst Bargheer, and Spamer himself had belonged to the Executive Board of the unsuccessful Union for German Folklore in 1933, and Wilhelm Peßler had even belonged to the Advisory Council. Spamer presented Gottfried Henßen and Hans Moser as the best young professional people in the discipline. Freudenthal, Bargheer, Karl Ewald Fritzsch, and Ernst Otto Thiele had singled themselves out as scholars committed to National Socialism. The latter two, along with Karl Theodor Weigel, were close to the Rosenberg Bureau, which was weakly represented at the leadership level. This leadership was made up of collaborators who were scholars, party functionaries and dilettantes.

When one compares Reinerth's Department of Prehistory, which was situated together with Spamer's Department of Folklore for a time in a Berlin housing complex,[164] one finds several points of agreement. Like Spamer, Reinerth had fought for an applied scholarship in folk education. He had proclaimed even before 1933 that "a complete reshaping of our German educational system" was necessary during the Third Reich, one which would result from the happy and positive basic attitude of National Socialism toward the folk and the soil and of its battle against everything which was alien to the folk and unauthentic. In order to arm German youth by means of "weapons with indigenously stable and authentic roots in its culture," he called for an extensive expansion of the "scholarship on the German man," "of German racial studies, of prehistory, history, *Volkskunde*, and regional studies in the closest alliance with the cultivation of German art, German writing, German language and music." These scholarly undertakings, which were to be reduced to a common Germanic racist denominator, were even supposed to "become in the future the primary foundation in the educational process of our youth!"[165] Here we have quite clearly a Rosenbergian concept before our eyes, one which would only need to be enhanced by the political intent of the *Mythus* ideologist in order to be completely clear. At the same time there are here clear reflections of the objectives of the DFG Reich Community as well as of the Department of Folklore.

Spamer's organizational plan for folklore, just like Reinerth's, had a film and photo office, regional offices (with Reinerth these were "Regional Offices for the Preservation of Monuments"), and the National Socialist Workers' Service, which was supposed to participate in the work. Just like Reinerth, Spamer expected professorial positions for the discipline at all German universities,[166] as well as the professional collaboration of teachers in the schools. He thus started with the practical principle of the possibility of educationally evaluating "all folkloric work."[167] Even the call for a "Reich Institute for German Prehistory as a central office for prehistoric research"[168] can be found in Spamer's history of the discipline of folklore as a predetermined objective for a "strictly disciplined and well-balanced central research station, a 'Reichsinstitut für deutsche Volkskunde,' or however this work center for German *Volkskunde* will be called in the future (and we hope today in the near future)."[169]

Nothing ever came of this plan for a pan-German central folklore Reich institute which Spamer continued to pursue after the war and in the German Democratic Republic which followed.[170] One must ask today how Spamer, in October 1936 and in light of the changes in the Presidium of the DFG which were already under way, was able to be so completely optimistic to his assembled professional colleagues. Is it possible that he was establishing a kind of preliminary defense and really wanted to document through this public lecture his right to the possession of the Department of Folklore?

Among the professional colleagues sitting there was John Meier, chairman of the Bremen meeting conducted by the League of German Societies for Folklore. Three years earlier he had been put at considerable disadvantage by the National

Socialist competition. He was able to hear, on the occasion of the Spamer lecture, what kinds of financial means the DFG had put at the disposal of the Department of Folklore for its work. According to the scrupulous department leader, 85,000 Reichsmarks (RM) were available annually for the *Atlas*, and of that about 50,000 RM went as salary (stipends) and 7,000 RM for the regional offices, which were also enhanced by subventions from the individual states. The annual fund for the Regional Institute Kurmark consisted of 19,000 RM without subventions for specific tasks. The annual business expense of the Central Archive for German Folk Narrative consisted of about 35,000 RM without stipends (salaries). Even with this, not everything was calculated in, but the amounts listed here make up a rather large financial sum for the prewar period.

In his memorandum which was not intended for the public, "First Thoughts on the Tasks and the Possibility of Establishing a Reichsinstitut für deutsche Volkskunde" of 1936 (see text in appendix III.2),[171] Spamer gives specific information on the DFG funds and comes up with a yearly total sum of 158,000 RM. He does not take into account the cost of building a Central Folklore Library (planned is the purchase of the library of Johannes Bolte).[172] There is mention of the cartographic work of the *Atlas*, that its "first fascicles are now available," and that "the *Atlas* from the very beginning was conceived of as a one-time undertaking." In contrast to this, with the Regional Institute for Folk Research and Folk-National Cultivation in the NSLB (*Gau* Saxony), which was founded with Spamer's help, the first continuing regional organization for observing the expressive forms of folk life was created.[173]

The Reich institute is also supposed to become a continuing organization toward which, from the very beginning, the DFG Department of Folklore was working. For its founding, "no special difficulties should arise, since such a Reich institute can simply be created by assuming, gathering together, and developing further already existing institutes."[174] What is intended is a kind of "political coordination" of continuing research establishments which "in the beginning are in different places and are independently run." Among these are the collections of folk speech in the German speech atlas in Marburg an der Lahn and the German Folk Song Archive in Freiburg im Breisgau. Together with the Central Archive of German Folk Narrative in Berlin they represent "a considerable foundation of German archival collections."[175] The power political NS instrument of "political coordination" is also quite evident with Spamer.

Spamer calls the planned Reich institute "a homeland and a maternal household for German folk research that is spread throughout the entire land"[176] and for the subdivisions of the DFG Department of Folklore mentioned in his Bremen lecture. He adds also a Hauptstelle der deutschen Hausforschung (Central Office for German House Research), which was brought to life by Wildhagen and remained, according to Spamer, his "intellectual property."[177] Of course the Reich institute was only concerned with the cultivation of the "core areas of folkloric research" and was not concerned with the "ballast of real or assumed neighboring disciplines." It will be, at least in the beginning, "for the most part determined by already existing research holdings,"[178] i.e., by Spamer's disciplinary concept and by traditional *Volkskunde*.

"Leaving out the financial possibilities would not let such a beautiful plan grow beyond a useless memorandum which would end up in the wastepaper basket." With this sentence Spamer addresses his main concern, the search for a financier. The German Research Council seems to have gotten into financial difficulties, since "by all appearances" the annual funds which were to flow in the future for its undertakings "are not reaching previous levels." The Reich Educational Ministry, the Reich Propaganda Ministry, the Foreign Office, and the state governments are thus brought into play by Spamer as potentially new and additional financiers. We do not know to which or to how many recipients outside the University of Freiburg im Breisgau Spamer's memorandum was sent.[179]

The sociopolitical functions of Spamer's psychological *Volkskunde* and of the Reich institute are sketched out clearly by Spamer. His conviction of the "meaning of folkloric work for the cultivation and preservation of the folk-nation" is summarized in his claim: "No folk-national cultivation without *Volkskunde*, no *Volkskunde* without folk-national cultivation!"[180] On the part of folklorists as well as folk-national cultivators, Spamer asserts, there exists an agreement concerning "the service role of *Volkskunde* as a science," which has the task of delivering "the knowledge and theoretical bases for folk-national cultivation."[181]

With the presumption of the primacy of all theory before practice, scholarship would in reality determine folk-national cultivation, and we see now that the scholarly director of the Reich institute, Spamer, wanted to assume the dominant role in this collaboration. According to his intention, contemporary folklore research can only be "led to a direct and practical evaluative possibility of its conclusions"[182] by creating for itself that which remains the "steadfast goal," i.e., a "stable and helpful organization . . . which continues to monitor (simultaneously as spiritual statistics) the mental and soul-like life processes of our folk."[183] These stand as "stronger and more timeless powers of the spirit and of the soul . . . behind and above all economic life processes."[184]

In the Regional Institute for Folk Research and Folk-National Cultivation, directed by Spamer during his Dresden years, the members of the Saxon National Socialists Teachers Union discharged the tasks. For the Reich institute for German Folklore it was to be the National Socialist German Workers Party (NSDAP). Breaking it down into a large number of subdivisions which carried out folk-national cultivation caused Spamer difficulty and led him to a conclusion which was positive but which did not just become illusionist at the end of 1936:

> From all this subdividing at least one thing becomes clear, that the future folklore collecting and helping organizations (at least in the Reich) can be established

neither by a scholarly central institute nor by local homeland alliances, but only by the movement itself [the NSDAP], which must reach a clear division of assignments within its individual organizations.[185]

Spamer was certainly not the man to get rid of what Bollmus has termed the eminent "leadership chaos in the Führer's state."[186] He nevertheless demanded removal of this chaos illusionistically and made himself opportunistically available for further collaboration with the fascist powers, disregarding all negative experiences which he had had up to that point.

DESTRUCTION OF THE DEPARTMENT OF FOLKLORE AND PERSECUTION OF SPAMER

During the Third Reich, Spamer was the only bourgeois-national folklorist, i.e., non-National Socialist, to whom the party apparatus turned over a scholarly and leadership position in a Reichwide folklore umbrella organization being watched over by National Socialism, though this lasted for only a few years. The collaboration between the leading German folklore theoretician-organizer and those party functionaries who were implementing the special ideology of Alfred Rosenberg in applied scholarship brought disappointments for both sides. Since Spamer would not assume the world-view objectives of the Rosenberg Bureau,[187] as it was certainly hoped he would in the beginning, Rosenberg's followers gradually turned to a massive criticism. Spamer must have felt that this tactic was unjust and full of intrigue.

Hans Hagemeyer, as director of the Department of Writing in the Rosenberg Bureau and a member of the official Party Testing Commission which produced the National Socialist Bibliography,[188] singlehandedly designated one of Spamer's articles as "not worthy of being further advanced . . . since one could not appreciate his primary position in folklore."[189] At the beginning of June 1936 Spamer submitted his resignation to the DFG, i.e., still prior to his Bremen lecture, but he kept his leadership position. Spamer felt that Ziegler was behind this action; he was Rosenberg's star folklorist as well as the DFG referee for folk research.[190] Spamer expected that kind of attack and judgment from Ziegler.

Ziegler had begun in 1934 with somewhat more reserved attempts at disciplining. This is most apparent if we look at his otherwise rather aggressive style in dealing with the competition. At that time Spamer submitted to the Reich Community his important handbook *Die deutsche Volkskunde*,[191] which then appeared in a second edition in its series "Das deutsche Volk."[192] In his review of the first volume Ziegler found much to praise.[193] He heaped praise on the following contributors, Georg Fischer, Arthur Haberlandt, Adolf Helbok, Lutz Mackensen, Friedrich Maurer, Friedrich Panzer, Friedrich von der Leyen, Konrad Hahm, also on Wolfgang Schuchardt and Walther Bernt as well as Joseph Maria Ritz and Oswald A. Erich, both of whom later had to put up with his vicious attacks.

On the other hand, Friedrich Ranke, Friedrich Pfister, and Georg Koch were reprimanded because of their "spiritual attitude," their world-view, from the standpoint of which they had written their contributions *sub specie orientis* and thus did not follow the still-disguised Rosenbergian *Mythus*. Specifically this *sub specie orientis* or "compulsory dogma of *ex oriente lux*" meant deriving of folk goods from the orient. This was also ostensibly the disciplinary thrust of religious folklore and served as the basis for attacks on their scholarship. Still Ziegler showed patience. His teachings on "racial soul study views" for a folklore "based on racial thinking"[194] were very inclusive. The entire review took up four columns of the *NS-Monatshefte*, and the second volume of the handbook was reviewed by Ziegler one year later more or less positively.[195]

Along with the "compulsory dogma of *ex oriente lux*" Ziegler rejected a second point, which he called "a dogma of the primitive communal spirit." By this he meant Hans Naumann's theory of *gesunkenes Kulturgut*. Spamer, however, dealt with Naumann in his handbook contribution on "Wesen und Aufgaben der Volkskunde" (The Essence and the Tasks of Folklore), which was for Ziegler "a sober and successful judgment of Naumann's conceptual speech." "Unfortunately he cannot see," however, that Spamer has overcome this.[196] Spamer's definition, which was so vulnerable during the Third Reich and which was indeed pointedly attacked,[197] that the goal of *Volkskunde* was "the researching of the folk-national within folk rootedness (*Volkhaft*), the spiritual and soul substance and life view of folk man in the folk community," seemed to Ziegler to lie "still too much" on the "world-view level" of Naumann's dogma.[198] With the wording "still too much," Spamer was being challenged to line up on the "world-view level" with Rosenberg.

When one becomes familiar with Ziegler's style, it is clear that Spamer is being dealt with here carefully. This "compromise for the time being" became unnecessary later when Spamer did not align himself with the National Socialist *Volkskunde* of Ziegler and when he was no longer director of the Department of Folklore in the Reich Community. In the famous and notorious guidelines of the Rosenberg Bureau, "Deutsche Volkskunde im Schrifttum" (Index of German Folklore Publications),[199] for which Ziegler bears the primary responsibility, there is no compromising in 1938 on Spamer's 1937 study of "Weihnachten in alter und neuer Zeit" (Christmas in Olden and Recent Times). Spamer has assumed no clear world-view, and his interpretation and conceptual speech, in spite of attempts at more recent folkloric viewpoints, were still essentially allied with the old school.[200] In the little 1936 book on Shrovetide there is, according to the official party viewpoint, a "false" interpretation of Shrovetide, the demonological interpretations of numerous Shrovetide symbols are "untenable," and the Germanic-peasant bases of the custom are being "underestimated."[201] In the 1935 lead article on theory, "Volkskunde als Wissenschaft" (Folklore as Science), Spamer is admitting that he belongs to a liberal *Volkskunde* epoch which "calls for complete lack of values and lack of prejudice."[202] In regard to his handbook *Die deutsche Volkskunde*, after one positive sentence, there is the remark: "Unfortunately no unified world-view line can be recognized and this gives room for views which are lacking in all world-view intentions. In the picture volume [the second volume compiled by Spamer] the presentation of ecclesiastical viewpoints is obvious."[203]

For Spamer, as he said in his statement of accounts after the war, there began during the Third Reich "a battle which was carried out behind the scenes and often with the most base means, against all German university teachers of *Volkskunde* (with the exception of a very few), and especially against me, by means of which they obviously wanted to take away the Berlin professorship. It was carried out in the beginning by a group of young people in the Rosenberg Bureau who had joined together under the directorship of the Reich Office Leader Matthes Ziegler in a Working Community for German Folklore, and was being conducted not so much for scholarly but rather for political-propagandistic objectives."[204]

Spamer did not analyze the background of the situation of the time concretely and thus contributed to a concealing of the history of *Volkskunde* during the Third Reich. It is true that the "battle" of the Rosenberg Bureau and of Ziegler was carried out against many university teachers of *Volkskunde* and many other folklorists, that Spamer had to suffer especially because of his position as the well-known "theoretical head" and had to fear for his professorship at the University of Berlin. But the "very few" who were spared were those whose folklore research was carried out along the lines of Rosenberg's *Mythus* or fit directly into his ideological concept. They were adherents of Rosenberg's world-view or at least found favor in his office. All others came under fire by the doctrinaire ideologists who were under the direction of Ziegler, whether they were bourgeois-national folklorists, National Socialist "accomplices," National Socialists of conviction, or SS members and collaborators in Himmler's Office of Ancestral Inheritance. The latter were viewed by the Rosenbergians as opponents or worse, yet as sectarians of the "pure" teaching.

In his statement of accounts after 1945 Spamer himself delivers the key to the ideological background. Ziegler's "organization emphasized again and again in the *Völkischer Beobachter* and elsewhere, 'that the NSDAP had announced its sovereign rights to the research area of *Volkskunde* and had carried this out.' "[205] Behind Ziegler's "organization" stood the editor of the National Socialist newspaper *Völkischer Beobachter* and the Führer's commissioner for the supervision of all intellectual and world-view schooling and education of the NSDAP, Rosenberg. He wanted to transmit to the party and to the folk his special ideology, which he had recorded in his *Mythus*. In the final analysis, *Volkskunde* had to be of service to this objective. The scholarly concept of the Rosenberg Bureau was in agreement with the political-propagandistic objectives which Spamer had objected to, and it did not share the "false consciousness" of bourgeois-national intellectuals concerning "objective" and "unpolitical" research.

The intermediary between Rosenberg and the discipline of *Volkskunde* was

Ziegler. Just as Spamer knew and accepted Ziegler's concept of the subject, Ziegler had also accepted Rosenberg's conceptualization of the discipline. To bridge the gap between these two worlds was impossible, as we can see from Spamer's lack of understanding and Ziegler's ideological intolerance. Spamer claimed after 1945 that the Rosenbergians soon presented him, because of his interest in religious folklore, as a member of the *actio catholica*, and then as the "liberal professor type."[206] Both are true, and one can read about this in the judgment passed on in his writings in the guidelines of 1938.[207] The *Katholische Action* and the *Liberalismus* were two of the most obvious attack points for Rosenberg's and Ziegler's polemic, which still must be clarified. Spamer fell through both cracks in this ideological trap and was thus vehemently criticized and persecuted.

Spamer's removal from the DFG office and the disillusion of the Reich Community and the Department of Folklore were not caused by the Rosenberg Bureau. They were a result of the regular battles for power during fascism, with each against the other. One competitor of Reich Leader Rosenberg in the cultural, political, and world-view area, Reichsführer-SS Himmler, had understood how to put officials whom he trusted into appropriate positions in the Reich Educational Ministry of Bernhard Rust. Finally, from this circle of Himmler followers came the ministerial and SS officer and professor for military chemistry Rudolf Mentzel,[208] who participated in one of those not unusual political intrigues of the Third Reich. When it was set in motion it brought about the removal on August 15, 1936, of Wildhagen,[209] vice-president and "gray eminence" of the DFG and friend of Spamer. Following this, DFG President Stark stepped down on November 15, 1936.[210] On December 1, Rosenberg's connection, Ziegler, also lost his DFG referee position for folk research.[211] Stark's successor was Mentzel, who subsequently redirected the financial help of the foundation for the most part to the SS Office of Ancestral Inheritance.

Spamer submitted a new resignation in November 1936 but remained on and took over at the beginning of March 1937 the nominal directorship of the *Atlas* work from Wilhelm Peßler. Then, two months later, on May 4, he transferred everything to the new DFG president. "His final reason for resignation," Heiber has stated, "was that he had to appear at the signing of the contracts for the *Atlas* as a 'private person' and because the Research Community had refused any responsibility for financial debts. This was the pretense with which they had apparently wanted to scare off this man who had become excessive, and thus they wanted to get rid of him."[212] The same sham arguments of the intrigue concerning financial difficulties of the DFG were taken up by Spamer in his Reich institute memo of 1936.

It becomes clear how vigorously Spamer was clinging to his position even during this resignation procedure. It was the *Atlas* which he in vain believed that he had to continue and to "rescue." Spamer's dream of a Reich Institute for German Folklore had died. The position of director of the Department of Folklore was not filled again, and the Reich Community for German Folk Research was destroyed. Portions of the folklore research projects which had been promoted and were at an advanced stage of development, among them the *Atlas*, the Central Archive, and the Weigel Symbol Archive, were distributed for the most part by the DFG to those who were interested within the SS Ancestral Inheritance, especially to Mentzel's ministerial and SS colleague, folklore professor Heinrich Harmjanz. The collaborators in the Department of Folklore moved over to the SS Ancestral Inheritance, to the Rosenberg Bureau, or to other positions. Reichsführer-SS Himmler had assumed power in the DFG.

Spamer was certainly not left alone in his folklore professorship at the University of Berlin. He was now completely persona non grata with the fascists, with whom he egocentrically and blindly had wanted to carry out common work. In addition to the Rosenberg Bureau, the SS Ancestral Inheritance also exercised its psychic terror over this man who was now disliked by everyone. The man who persecuted him on the part of the SS was Harmjanz. From a psychological standpoint, he was compensated by usurping the *Atlas der deutschen Volkskunde* and the Central Archive of German Folk Narratives, and he wanted to make himself the *Primus* of German *Volkskunde*. In 1937 he had been made *Ordinarius* for *Volkskunde* at the University of Königsberg in East Prussia, and after 1938 he held the same position at the University of Frankfurt am Main. He was above all a fascist, and his behavior exemplified this.

In his 1936 *Habilitation* Harmjanz had opposed Spamer's folklore theory from his own contrary scholarly viewpoint[213] and had, so to speak, dethroned the leading German theoretician of the discipline up to that point. In 1938 the Reich Educational Ministry, in which Harmjanz assumed a leading position for the humanities, rejected Spamer's election as a regular member of the Prussian Academy of Sciences in Berlin.[214] Then Spamer was interrogated because of a report by the Rosenberg Bureau to the Gestapo that he was conducting communistic teachings and had contact with "infamous" people such as the folklorists Joseph Maria Ritz and Leopold Schmidt. The hearing was before a University of Berlin judge, and when nothing significant came of it Spamer was watched over by the Gestapo and the Security Service (SD).[215]

In 1942 the Reich Educational Ministry, under the signature of Harmjanz, blocked Spamer's call as ordinary professor for *Volkskunde* at the University of Freiburg im Breisgau, even though the ministry had made him number one on their list and kept him in that position.[216] A move to southwestern Germany, which Spamer was obviously prepared for, might have made Spamer's life and work somewhat less negative. He, however, could not stand the psychic terror which was intentionally instigated to remove one of the "great" men of the discipline, and in the fall of 1942 he fell into a deep psychosomatic sickness. He recovered in 1946, after the war, but remained until his death in 1953 merely a shadow of himself.[217]

Physical and psychic breakdown as well as loss of hope for a Reichwide career for the discipline under his directorship were the personal costs paid by Spamer for his illusionist and opportunistic collaboration with fascism. His fate raises questions about the "bourgeois-humanistic primary position" formerly attributed to him for his "personal behavior."[218] The National Socialists simply exploited the competence and the prestige of the bourgeois-national scholar during the first years of their rule, during which time they were not yet in a position to build for themselves a central German folklore institution. As soon as this had been done by Spamer and Wildhagen[219] and was in a promising developmental stage, they took over the direction of that which resulted from the systemically determined internal competitive battles. It is important to see that Spamer was not uninvolved in the "preparation of the path for a fascist *Volkskunde* science in Germany."[220]

The removal from office of Vice-President Wildhagen, the "great man"[221] of the German Research Council, as well as the replacement of the DFG Presidium in the interest of Himmler and his SS Ancestral Inheritance, also affected the Rosenberg Bureau, where this was felt to be "almost a catastrophe."[222] As a result the competitive battles between the two cultural-political National Socialist organizations of Himmler and Rosenberg became more heated. It was the question not only of "whether subventions which the Bureau owed to the good intentions of Wildhagen would continue to be paid in the future"[223] but also of who would receive the scholarly departments of the Reich Community for German Research, which was now being dissolved.

Until the change in power in the DFG Presidium, only two had prospered institutionally; the Department of Prehistory, led by the Rosenberg functionary Reinerth, was already de facto under the bureau. It was different, however, with the nominally independent Department of Folklore. Even though it was under the influence of Rosenberg and his "specialist for folklore and religious scholarship,"[224] Ziegler, the personnel connections with the Rosenberg Bureau were numerically weak at the level of the subdivision directors, and it had been further troubled by the decidedly independent disciplinary course of the departmental leader Spamer. Now some of the most desirable portions of the Folklore Department went to scholars of the discipline who did not belong to the Rosenberg Bureau but to competitors, who were in sympathy with the SS Ancestral Inheritance and who later belonged to it. As a result the Service Branch of the Reich leader had to accept a grave reduction in influence in the important cultural and political sector of *Volkskunde*, which perhaps may even have had the effect of being "nearly a catastrophe."[225]

3

Fascist *Volkskunde* and Folk Renewal during the Third Reich

APPLIED SCHOLARLY *Volkskunde* as part of folk-national cultivation or folk renewal was carried out during the Third Reich by several branches and related leagues of the National Socialist Workers Party (NSDAP).[1] However, the party Service Branch of the the Führer's commissioner for the supervision of all intellectual and world-view schooling and education of the NSDAP, Reich Leader Alfred Rosenberg,[2] which was also called the Rosenberg Bureau or the Reich Overseeing Office, stands out, as does the Research and Teaching Community "Ancestral Inheritance" of the Reichsführer-SS Heinrich Himmler."[3] Only these two large cultural organizations of the NSDAP, together with their disciplinary institutes, can claim validity as Reichwide folklore umbrella organizations.

The high party functionaries Rosenberg and Himmler, who were convinced of the usefulness of *Volkskunde* for their ideological and strong-armed political intentions, took over from this bourgeois-national discipline its research institutions as well as the results of its work in order to develop them further and to expand them for special fascist objectives. They also took over professionally trained leaders, collaborators, and temporary workers for their branch offices, as well as certain traditional theorems and ideologies which would fit the new concept of the discipline as it was being fundamentally changed.

The National Socialist *Volkskunde* of the Rosenberg Bureau and the Ancestral Inheritance had fundamental differences with bourgeois-national *Volkskunde* in ideology, methodology, and personnel. There were, however, common points. Clarifying these distinguishing and common criteria presents a problem for us still today, one which was discussed heatedly during the Third Reich as well as during the postwar years.

We can only agree with Utz Jeggle's conclusion that individual strands of the methodological discussion in the discipline[4] which was conducted prior to 1933 led "right into the world-view of National Socialism."[5] It is questionable in more than one sense, however, whether the other strands of the discussion which existed,[6] had they been continued in the period after 1933, "would have lent our discipline, perhaps several decades earlier, an independence and sovereignty for which we are still working today."[7] For one thing, the traditional and ideological encrustation[8] which grew out of the methodological discussions in the discipline would most likely have blocked far-reaching changes in disciplinary concepts even if the Weimar Republic had continued to exist after 1933. For another, the scholarly discipline *Volkskunde* owes its "independence," which was the political goal for the discipline of reputable bourgeois-national folklorists such as Adolf Spamer,[9] and its decisive establishment in institutions not to the Weimar Republic but to the fascist regime which came to power on January 30, 1933. Even the reinstitutionalization of *Volkskunde* in the postwar Federal Republic of Germany, German Democratic Republic, and Republic of Austria would not have been possible without its fundamental rise during the twelve years of the Third Reich.

The inheritance from National Socialism was a heavy mortgage that was placed by the Third Reich on the *Volkskunde* of the successor states, all the more so since during the Weimar Republic and in the years thereafter bourgeois-national *Volkskunde* and folklorists prepared the way for the National Socialist discipline. Based on broad agreements from the ideological and methodological sector, there were fluid transitions in regard to personnel, which means there were not just a few bourgeois-national scholars of the discipline from the younger generation who switched over to a National Socialist *Volkskunde* or worked for it intentionally. In this way we must differentiate between voluntary and involuntary, convinced National Socialists and unconvinced seekers; and after the institutionalization of a National Socialist *Volkskunde*, we must also differentiate between the engaged champions and representatives of National Socialism, the accomplices, the indifferent, and finally the opponents.

Professional folklore scholars became, consciously or unconsciously, pathfinders for a National Socialist *Volkskunde*. And yet not all were made into pioneers, as Jeggle has said. Still we must not forget those for whom "the ideological and personal compulsion which was exercised by National Socialism was so overpowering that it even defiled the biography of those who shied away from and tried to distance themselves from it."[10]

The ambitious attempts of many folklorists must not be overlooked. Under the fascist regime that was solidified soon after the seizure of power and seemed likely to last for an indeterminate time, professional careers were made, and the discipline of *Volkskunde* experienced for the first time a broad institutional upswing, receiving a considerable number of new positions at universities, teachers' colleges, and research institutes. To participate profitably, political confessions or opportunistic admissions to the state party, which controlled all areas of public life more and more, were unavoidable. From the early small steps of accommodation or compromise, very grave ones could rapidly come about; careerists could rapidly find themselves in total agreement with fascist attitudes and behavior patterns.

Relatively small is the group of researchers and teachers in the area of folklore who confessed a counterposition world-view, theoretical or individual and ethical, to National Socialist *Volkskunde* or to National Socialism itself. To them, based on their behavior and their fate, those of us who were born later owe a great debt of honor. There was the Münster professor of Catholic theology, Prelate Georg Schreiber, for whom there was unbroken and hateful terror and a life-threatening persecution by the fascist regime;[11] the mentor of the Munich resistance group the White Rose and bourgeois-national professor of philosophy, psychology, and folk song studies Kurt Huber, whom the National Socialists tried and executed before the folk court;[12] the Breslau private docent for *Volkskunde* and former Social Democrat Will-Erich Peuckert, who lost his teaching license and was threatened with removal to a concentration camp, and whom Christoph Daxelmüller praises as "an almost unique personality";[13] Rudolf Kriss, the Bavarian folk piety researcher and Viennese private docent, who was sentenced to death by the folk court and was freed from prison when the allies marched in;[14] Adolf Reichwein, the Social Democratic resistance fighter, professor of history and state civil studies, who was active as a schoolteacher after forced removal from his university career and later was a collaborator in the Berlin Folklore Museum and who as a result of the coup attempt on Adolf Hitler of July 20, 1944, was sentenced to death by the folk court.[15]

Analysis of this iridescent behavior of the majority of German folklorists under the National Socialist dictatorship remains difficult,[16] and for representatives of the discipline, the students and followers of those from the Third Reich, it is still a very emotional and hotly debated political issue. An "individualized observation of events," called for by Helge Gerndt, is however unavoidable, for "only in individuals and in the works which they created as individuals can an *abstraction* be made concrete. In this way a scholarly discipline like *Volkskunde* can be subjected to analysis."[17]

But to begin, with "the unsolvable problem of judging the behavior of folklore scholars during the time of National Socialism,"[18] as Ingeborg Weber-Kellermann does, runs counter to the principle of serious historical writing. It does not contribute to investigative conclusions by those historians who have been dealing individually and for a long time with scholarship under National Socialism,[19] and in the final analysis it does not help attempts by contemporary folklorists to clarify the history of their discipline during the period when its own institutions were founded.

The scholarship of German *Volkskunde* fell prey to perversion under the fascist regime, a perversion, as Gerndt writes, of the "primary scholarly principle that only better *arguments* count"[20] and of the ethical basic principle that the support of clearly inhuman behavior is to be avoided by individuals. For German folklorists, Gerndt continues, "became instruments for the scholarly legitimization of political demands and became the handmaidens of a cynical seizure of power"[21] whose ideological bases had been partially prepared by the academic discipline and in whose transformation into practice by the Third Reich it was only too willing to help out.

There is no way around a recognition by the discipline of this heavy encumbrance, and thus a critique of fascism[22] must also be directed toward those folklorists who participated. Assuming a position on ethical questions, to which we as scholars are obligated, as Gerndt says, "not just to accuse but rather as a reminder to be alert, to be self-critical, and to lament,"[23] will not find its definitive end today in a "dimension of illusionless insight into the possibilities and limitations of scholarly behavior," according to Jeggle. "It is illusionless because the need for heroes cannot be legitimized scientifically but only quasi-religiously."[24] It is necessary for us and other scholars to demand, with Bollmus, that the "establishment of a moral-political measure be recognized . . . since the ideal was not completely utopian: a series of folklorists has already met the requirement. . . . "[25] Bollmus refers to those who were tortured, removed from their profession, sentenced, and murdered as opponents of the fascist power. Even if their theoretical and ideological perspectives diverged and were occasionally split,[26] the forms of their resistance were heterogeneous. They nevertheless representatively document the existence of a group of scholars with personal behaviors which were primarily different from those who submitted to a National Socialist *Volkskunde* or who came forth as its active representatives and promoters.

If there were opponents and proponents among the folklorists, there could also be various conceptions of the discipline. The key slogan of "two *Volkskunden*," that of the National Socialists and that which differed from this because of its divergent principles and was thus not National Socialist, served the representatives of the discipline in the immediate postwar period as a protective statement, i.e., that during the Third Reich they had unhesitatingly conducted their own specific scholarly work separate from that of party *Volkskunde*.[27] Wolfgang Emmerich decisively rejected this undifferentiated and thus ominous attempt at justification. Instead he postulated quite simply a single *Volkskunde* which had a "primarily questionable scholarly concept" and was then subsumed in the blood-and-soil *Folklorismus* of the National Socialists.[28]

For the historian Reinhard Bollmus there were, "according to the contemporary research situation [1987] from an historical standpoint, two *Volkskunden* during the Third Reich."[29] Bollmus draws on Will-Erich Peuckert's concept[30] of a "scholarly *Volkskunde* . . . according to non-National Socialist standards," but he adds a limitation: "That means: if there were from an historical standpoint and in the experienced reality of the National Socialist period 'two *Volkskunden*,' then this finding may lose its meaning from the standpoint of errors by the discipline. To decide that is not the task of a political-historical questioning."[31] The history of "errors made by the discipline" verifies, however, the obvious closeness of the two *Volkskunden*, from which only a National Socialist discipline would have remained had the regime ended differently.

The postulating of several *Volkskunden* during the Third Reich actually goes back to the National Socialists themselves. It was particularly the folklorists of the Rosenberg Bureau, at whose pinnacle was Matthes Ziegler, the *Volkskundeprimus* of party ideologist Alfred Rosenberg, who promoted it without fail. Their claim was to secure absolute primacy for Rosenberg's ideologically based conception of the discipline, an official and party-sanctioned sole right of representation. Thus they excluded by definition all other *Volkskunden* and fought the bourgeois-national folklorists as well as the other branches and leagues of the NSDAP, especially that of the Office of Ancestral Inheritance of the SS. Based on the absolute intentions and the political power of its curator and later president, Heinrich Himmler, Ancestral Inheritance entered the bitter battle of the survival of the fittest.

This kind of battle, which was eminent in the fascist system,[32] had disciplinary and power political objectives and was based on a world-view ideology. Even though National Socialist ideology was of course utilized as a means or a disguise for conducting research according to existing requirements, this was not its primary function, i.e., to disguise or embellish research.[33] The disciplinary and power political prerequisites and objectives derived directly from National Socialism, as did the world-view perspectives and individual behavior patterns of those who participated, including the scholars. It certainly stamped its own behavior on them.

National Socialist ideology continued to serve with the help of those scholarly disciplines which had to systematize its contents and to prepare it for use in political practice, e.g., for folk education, folk-national cultivation, or folk renewal. Bourgeois-national *Volkskunde*, with its specific and agreeable folk-national ideology,[34] had long since sold out. Here especially is that which unites but also that which separates traditional *Volkskunde* and National Socialism. The latter took traditional folklore ideologies, raised them to hypertrophy, and by means of state-sanctioned changes adapted them into products of fascist scholarship and everyday practice.

National Socialist *Volkskunde* could thus view itself justifiably as a continuation of bourgeois-national *Volkskunde*, and the bourgeois-national was thereby a part of National Socialist *Volkskunde*. The two directions in the discipline were nevertheless separate from one another ideologically, and the National Socialist one was actually the most innovative.

WORLD-VIEW AND POLITICAL OBJECTIVES IN ROSENBERG'S *MYTHUS*

Alfred Rosenberg's *Mythus des 20. Jahrhunderts. Eine Wertung der seelisch-geistigen Gestaltenkämpfe unserer Zeit* (The Mythus of the Twentieth Century: An Evaluation of the Soul-Spiritual Struggles of Our Age),[35] published for the first time in 1930, had an eminent meaning for the ideology of National Socialism (see Rosenberg's summary of his *Mythus* in appendix I.3). After Adolf Hitler's *Mein Kampf*[36] it was "the second standard work of Nazi ideology," of which more than a million copies were printed and distributed. "Its author was considered to be 'the world-view authority' of the party" and "next to Hitler the leading Nazi ideologist," according to Petzold.[37]

In light of the decisive "fact that the ideology of National Socialism excellently fulfilled its *instrumental* function as a masterful technical aid," it seems useless to "calculate whether it is a matter here of a consistent ideological system or a mishmash, an 'idea soup.' " This general assertion by Wolfgang Emmerich[38] can also be made with justification in regard to the *Mythus des 20. Jahrhunderts*. Its randomly thrown together ideas concerning nineteenth- and twentieth-century forerunners are well known by researchers, and the vagueness of Rosenberg's philosophical autodidacticism has been pointed out.[39] The ideological conglomerate which developed in this way and which was committed to irrationalism and inhumanity should nevertheless be viewed, in accordance with the desire of its creator, as a complete work. With all of its individual parts it was in a position to give strict rules for action in creating a unique National Socialist world-view.

The developmental history and the contents of the *Mythus* verify that Rosenberg's abstruse ideology or world-view will not stand up to a logical test. Still, it exercised a strong fascination on many contemporaries. During the Third Reich there were even attempts, e.g., by folklorists, to develop from it a National Socialist scientific lesson which,[40] by expanding the *Mythus* into a masterful technological instrument, was supposed to aid everyday fascistic practice. However, this "science," as we can see with the example of *Volkskunde*, proceeded inductively. Together with the "ideology theoretician" Rosenberg and with his intuitively gained "insights," it rejected from the very beginning "the testing of hypotheses empirically or analytically"[41] and verified the theses of the *Mythus* which had been affirmed a priori, as an applied assignment of its scholarship. The methodological parallels to a bourgeois-national *Volkskunde* are inescapable, since it too set its folk-national ideology a priori and continued to verify it. They deviated on individual points but in much they agreed.

The contents and the expressions of the *Mythus* were looked upon as being absolutely true by Rosenberg, who according to Bollmus "really believed in his world-view,"[42] as well as by his collaborators and adherents from whom a strict loyalty toward the teaching of the *Mythus* and the "world-view authority" of its "genial creator" were demanded and accomplished. In this way the designation of Rosenbergian *Volkskunde* as a "scholarship of faith"[43] is completely justified. It is, however, necessary to ask whether the attitude of bourgeois-national *Volkskunde* to its folk-national ideology does not also represent an "attitude of faith."

The attempt to determine systematically the world-view which was recorded in the *Mythus* and expanded in further writings by Rosenberg[44] is not so useless as Bollmus assumed.[45] Its basic characteristics were repeatedly analyzed during the Third Reich and in the period immediately following.[46] They will be clarified here in a brief overview and by emphasizing the relevant aspects for folklore and cultural scholarship.[47]

Rosenberg's image of the world is based in the assumption of a racially determined, Nordic-Aryan or Germanic-German folk-nation with a racially pure world-view and a high culture. From the very beginning of its history, through the Middle Ages, and into the present it finds itself in an unceasing struggle with foreign racial powers who were conceived to be enemies and who had a different world-view and culture. The last historical documentation of this battle for life of the Germanic-German folk-nation is seen as the loss of the First World War, which also represented the renewed victory by those powers opposing Germandom.

The First World War means for Rosenberg, in more than one way, a decisive historic caesura. During this time the later "chief ideologist" of National Socialism apparently begins with the conceptualization of his world-view; he expands it further during the Weimar Republic and finally publishes it in 1930 in the *Mythus* as a still unfinished version of the "theme developed by fate."[48]

As fateful as the lost world war was on racially determined Germandom, it was for Rosenberg not in vain but was, on the contrary, the beginning of a "world revolution" of the Germanic-German folk-nation and of his world-view "in all areas." For the dead of the world war were indeed the sacrifices of an epoch which brought on the catastrophe of defeat because racially pure values had been forsaken. They were "martyrs of a new day, a new belief";[49] they were the guarantors of a new epoch which was beginning and in which a racially pure world-view would be victorious.

With this new epoch the dead of the world war are united in a racially mysterious way: the "blood of those who died begins to come to life. Under this mystical sign a new cellular construction develops in the German folk soul."[50] That comes by way of the "blood" trait, out of which a race is constituted, to a "folk renewal" of ostensibly Germanic-German but in reality of National Socialist provenence, and which Rosenberg as the visionary of the new age declares as the "fateful assignment." This is the primary statement of the *Mythus* and represents at the same time the legitimization of the "role" of its "genial" creator.

A primary constituent of Rosenberg's world-view is the assumption of a blood-bound "racial soul" with specific "values" or "soul values." Rosenberg defines this racial soul with an irrational circular reasoning. It was a concept which enjoyed validity in the racial studies of that period, i.e., that "soul values" could be read from the physiognomy of a man. "Soul, however, means race seen from within. And vice versa, race is the outer side of a soul." The racial soul which has remained unchanged through all times is a "highest value," under whose primacy all other values are given their "organic position" in the state, arts, and religion.[51]

The fundamental reordering of German culture "in all areas," according to values set by the racial soul and through the overcoming of an "inner breakdown" of an "epoch which has become valueless," had been taking place since the First World War. It can only happen, according to this fascist ideologist, in a battle against counterpowers of other races and world-views, through the "confrontation between blood and blood, race and race, folk and folk. And that means a battle of soul values against soul values."[52] The principle of an incessant warlike confrontation[53] with an opponent, which comes from this "new world image" of a racial view of history,[54] is of significance as a general method of procedure and for the behavior of the individuals who are participating in it.

In the realization of the "task of our century"[55] the *Mythus* world-view is supposed to be carried out in public realms as well as in private life, and wherever necessary with the "survival of the fittest." With its pseudo-ethical values in a special ideological context, it is supposed to be binding for all Germans. For Rosenberg intends to create from "the new life mythos a new human type": the new man of the fascistic Third Reich or, as Rosenberg himself expressed it more precisely, of the "first *German* Reich,"[56] that is, the "German master race" which stands above all other peoples.

Rosenberg's world-view meant an attitude toward the world, toward external fate, and toward the drives within the soul, i.e., toward the values of his racial soul. This attitude was determined through bravery, pride, and freedom. Since the world-view was to be reestablished as a "Germanic unity" and included religion, science, and art, and since from these "primordial activities of mankind" all other branches of activity grew, the world-view attitude must be the same everywhere, and it must determine all expressive forms of religion, science, and art. Only then could the harmony of folk and life be created,[57] i.e., only then, according to Rosenberg's intention, are German culture and the German folk totally coordinated and ready to be led by a totalitarian fascistic regime which is in agreement with the "setting of racial-soul values."

Just like the Germanic-German folk-nation, the world-view state of the future which arises out of the *Mythus* is constantly being threatened by foreign-racial enemies who must be fought and destroyed. Their internationally guided sets of values stand in absolute contrast to the national values of the racial soul of German-Nordic man. Enemy powers are first of all Judaism—for the leading anti-Semite of the National Socialist regime it was quite simply the Jewish "counterrace"[58]—and there are others under their dominating influence who stand in close intellectual contact with them.

Marxism, or as Rosenberg formulated it, Bolshevism, subverts with its "teachings of internationalism" the folklike foundations of all thinking and feeling. It destroys with its "class struggle" the "living organism" of the nation and completes this act of destruction through "pacifism," which cripples or emasculates foreign policy, and through the removal of the "concept of possession" which is most closely related to the Germanic ideal of personality.[59] Liberalism and free Masonic "humanity" represent the "teaching of a democratic raceless 'human rights,'" which is not rooted in a nationally based concept of honor,"[60] i.e., in the fundamental rights and unity of all humans before the law. The "equality of all humans before

God" which is counter to this racial postulate, the "compulsory belief of limitless love," of pity, is taught by Christian churches. " 'Love' plus 'humanity' " had become a "teaching which destroyed all life commandments and life forms of a folk and a state," and European society had " 'developed' precisely as a protector of the inferior, the sick, the crippled, and the criminal and those who were rotten."[61]

The Christian churches, especially the Roman Catholic Church, are sharply attacked by Rosenberg. The Roman Church is indeed the existing counterforce in the "world-view battle of the Third Reich."[62] Catholics are accused of making "Jewish-Asiatic confessions" of false religion, of overpowering scholarship with Biblical dogmas and compulsory statements of faith, and of reducing art to merely praising the Bible and the Roman Church.[63] The churches had made human values dependent on their compulsory statements of faith, which bound mankind through their souls to the particular church organization.[64]

Rosenberg contrasts these ecclesiastical "compulsory statements of faith" with the "character values" of the human type he wanted to create, Christian *love* in the sense of humility, mercy or pity, subjugation, and asceticism with Germanic-German *honor* in bravery, duty, pride, freedom, and willingness to do battle. These two values of love and honor are above all the ones through which the entire contrast between church and race, theology and belief, compulsory statements of faith and pride of character had been revealed through nearly two thousand years.[65]

The idea of "love" contained "no [human] type forming strength," "for even the organization of the 'religion of love' was built without love," i.e., the Roman Catholic Church.[66] The idea of "honor" however, had been the center of existence, particularly in the Nordic world, the Germanic occident.[67] There had been thousands of years of battle around this concept of honor, "when Nordic Europe saw itself in conflict with the armed Roman south and finally was subjugated in the name of religion and Christian love."[68]

Christians and especially the Roman Catholic Church fought for thousands of years against Nordic-Germanic high culture, suppressed it, covered it over, and estranged it by means of racially contrasting cultural values of Asiatic-Jewish and African origin. The church Christianized the Germanic gods and put in their place its own saints; it changed the former "pagan" festivals into Christian ones but still could not completely destroy the "ancient force of old Nordic tradition."[69]

In connection with this accommodation procedure it introduced much to Germandom, things which were originally foreign, such as magic, low-level ecstasy, sacrifices, and superstitions,[70] which came from the "magical world of Africa-Asia." In the same way "Christian legends are made known to Europeans in all seriousness still today: 'the virgin birth,' the material 'resurrection' of Christ, 'the ascent into heaven and the descent into hell' as well as the various 'visions' of Catholic saints to whom the Virgin Mary appeared just as really as did Jesus Christ."[71] In contrast to this the greatest accomplishment in the history of Nordic man was the "Germanic recognition . . . that nature could not be overcome through magic . . . also not through rational schemes . . . but only through the innermost observation of nature."[72]

The renewal movement which came from the *Mythus* in Germany has the "historical task" of consciously securing "the previous *foundations* of our culture insofar as they have been changed through Roman-Jewish ecclesiastical teachings and a Syrian-African world-view, and to help these values win out." "Germanic religion," "Germanic science," and "Nordic art" are to play an important role.[73] The goal is the reestablishment of a "Germanic unity" world-view.[74]

The ideological and fictitious "rebirth of Germandom," the creation of a single German folk and of a real German folk culture out of the *Mythus*, are legitimized through the axiom of "organic truth" which can no longer be questioned.[75] This is a concept which Bollmus has described as the " 'Archimedean point' of Rosenbergian thought"[76] and which raises Rosenberg's ideology from a racial *mythus* to a form of belief.

This "total truth" propounded by Rosenberg consists of a "logical part," which is presented by means of critical recognition with understanding and reason; an "observable part," which is revealed in art, in *Märchen*, and in the religious *mythus*; and a "willful part," symbolized through ethical teachings and religious forms. "If they are real they all stand in the service of organic truth; that means: in the service of a racially bound folk-nation. . . . And in this they all find their most decisive criterion, whether they advance the form and the inner values of this racial folk-nation, whether they educate it more purposefully, whether they structure it in a more lively manner or not."[77]

The "organic truth" is thus presented through race or through the racially pure Germanic-German folk-nation. This is then hypostatically made the center and the object of veneration of the "new belief." The "organic truth" embodied in the folk-nation is not to be viewed as the concern and the result of constant and searching inquiry, "i.e., as something which is technically impossible but something almost reachable." For that "nearly impossible final 'knowledge' of a race is embedded in its first religious *mythus*."[78] For Rosenberg it is faith in the unique, absolute, eternal truth of his world-view, with its blood *mythus* of the Germanic-German folk-nation, which cannot be verified through a critical evaluation of understanding but can be experienced only emotionally, through a voice in the blood. He writes: "The individually experienced, wise observation of the world and the organic self-fulfillment mean experiencing the bloodstream which unites the old Germanic poets, the great thinkers and artists, the German statesmen and military generals. It is a mythical reminiscence. . . . "[79]

Scholarly criticism, artistic creation, ethical norm, and religious attitude are evaluated solely according to their usefulness for that imaginary axiom of "organic truth," or of the racially pure folk-nation and its world-view to which they are absolutely subordinated. Scholarship, art, ethics, and religion have the exclusive task of helping secure the "renewal" of the folk-nation and world-view or to work with the construction of the totalitarian world-view state with the Rosenbergian stamp and to help it continue to exist henceforth.

One must agree with Bollmus that the author of the _Mythus_ proclaimed "a naïve utilitarian ideology . . . from which all requirements could be derived, in favor of the 'Germanic race' and in the name of an ostensibly higher law,"[80] i.e., in the name of the "organic truth" of the Germanophilic blood _mythus_.

"What unpolitical educated citizens of the Weimar Republic had proclaimed, without thinking about the consequences," writes Wolfgang Emmerich,[81] namely the connection between blood and soil on one hand and the postulate of Germanic-German continuity on the other, "now becomes the central piece of fascistic ideology and, as a consequence, the exercise of power. . . . The _Mythus_ as a means of interpreting, one which provides for a hidden ideology in real history and real society, is certainly not unique to fascism alone. However, fascism employed social and historical myths for the first time in a very specific way, and this distinguishes it radically from previous tendencies toward the mythic."[82]

Instructions for political implementation of the teachings of Rosenberg are found everywhere in his _Mythus_ and subsequent writings. They are concerned with the battle against ideological opponents and the construction of the new world-view state, and together they present a rather clear picture of the political intentions of the "chief ideologist" of the NSDAP. In the 1939 "Theses from the _Mythus_" (see appendix I.3) Rosenberg summarizes the tendencies of his cultural politics to affirm the fascistic world-view state and to negate Christianity. As usual, he does this with martial-art-like words:

The birth of the folk-nation and of racial ideas are today destroying the international body of Christ with an inner necessity and are replacing it with a pure German community as a supreme community of clans guarded by an alliance of warriors which is today called the National Socialist Reich.[83]

A distinguishing trait of Rosenbergian tactical rhetoric, the disguising of the political intent, is quite obvious in this quotation. "The inner necessity" of destroying the Christian churches, which is what is intended here, comes from Rosenberg's and the National Socialists' will to exclude that which was defined ideologically as racially foreign. In the _Mythus_ of 1930 Rosenberg treats with absolute clarity the justification of this measure as well as those who are actually affected.

There it is stated, in contrast to both the Christian-ecclesiastical ethic of mercy and love and the free masonic ethic of humanity, that "honor" is placed as the highest value for all action; closely associated with this is the protection of the Nordic-occidental race. A nation whose central core is represented through honor and duty would not include that which is rotten and criminal—the inferior, sick, crippled, criminal, and spoiled—but would exclude them, would of necessity separate out "those who did not measure up racially and in their souls for a Nordic life form."[84]

"Rotten and criminal," in the sense of that which has become "spoiled," "sick," and "crippled," are for Rosenberg not only those who are mentally sick, different, homosexual, or repeat criminals, many of whom were seized during the Third Reich in euthanasia actions,[85] put into concentration camps,[86] and murdered. Generally the "inferior" are those who do not correspond to the Germanic-German folk-nation "racially and in their souls." For their "separation" and "exclusion," i.e., their liquidation, Rosenberg proclaims a *Recht als Rasseschutz* (right for racial protection). It is based on the ominous ideological concept of honor and is "associated eternally with specific blood [lines]."[87] This is supposed to assure it primacy, and it was widely propagated by law during the Third Reich, e.g., through the Nürnberg racial laws.

This so-called right, which was "in the service of our highest racial values," requires "as its most important element the most complete implementation of folk and racial protection."[88] This is expanded even more, so as to forbid all "unrestrained breeding by idiots, children of syphilitics, alcoholics, and the mentally deranged," to make hereditarily sick people sterile, to deny non-Jews sexual intercourse with Jewish-Germans and to take away their citizenship, and in regard to immigration to Germany "to carry it out in the future according to Nordic-racial and hygienic standards."[89] With a new German law Rosenberg wants "to reestablish a gradient of values, between that which is honorable and that which is dishonorable, to increase the punishment for dishonorable crimes," because only in this way can "once again a German human type arise."[90]

The concept of honor or of "that which is honorable" is attributed to this German human type which is being striven for but which is already predestined through the concept of Germanic-racial continuity. In Rosenbergian thinking, punishment for what is perceived to be dishonorable is directed toward the opponents of the racially bound German folk-nation or simply toward "all of those who are incapable racially and in their souls for Nordic life forms."[91] Their "dishonorable crimes," which consist of hesitation or inability to view "the folk-nation and folk honor" as the highest value and "rejection of the Germanic ideal in Germany," are ultimately looked upon as folk and state treason. The punishment planned for these "crimes" runs the gamut, from "separation of foreign types and racially alien beings" all the way to imprisonment and death.[92] They are intended to apply to and destroy all of those who are mentally ill, who are Jews, who belong to Christian churches, and who are both alleged and real opponents of the teachings of the *Mythus*.

Rosenberg's "right for racial protection" is a political instrument for securing the "Germanic ideal" of a racially determined German folk-nation as an "organic truth . . . which can allow no compromise but promotes its own *predominancy*," even in regard to Christian beliefs. It is not supposed to be a "purpose in itself, but rather a changeable means in the service of National Socialist life feeling and Germanic character values," from which "ethics" grows. For "ethics" was not brought to the Germans by Christianity, since "it owes its own lasting values to its Germanic character." A "real ethic" or a racially pure life-style begins only when "the pure German existence has forced its laws of life on the churches," when the eternal German character values have prevailed through a German re-birth.[93]

"A man, however, or a movement which intends to aid these values toward a complete victory, has the ethical right of not sparing that which is in opposition," Rosenberg writes. He and the National Socialists are thus obligated "to overcome spiritually" the opponents and thus the Christian churches, "to let them waste away organizationally and to maintain their political weakness."[94] The destruction of the Christian churches as independent institutions and the changing of their teach-ings into National Socialist ones are prerequisites "for a coming German folk church, whose essential basis seems to be clearly outlined."[95]

A German folk and national church, still to be founded, raises Rosenberg's racial teaching to "a religion of blood" and of the racial soul,[96] to a religion of a "racially bound folk-nation, of organic truth." The later National Socialist adherents to this religion or this religious world-view, who called themselves "believers in God," were basically honoring themselves with this racial soul and this blood-bound folk-nation. Rosenberg proclaimed expressly: "The god whom we honor would not be, if our souls and our blood did not exist. . . ."[97] The "divine" portion of this "new belief" thus lives in the blood; it is identical with the racial soul and the folk-nation, and the Germanic-German "master race" is made equal to God.

"Trust in God becomes a trust in oneself," Künneth stated; "belief in God becomes a belief in oneself."[98] This total reversal of the Christian teaching cor-responds to the political-ideological tasks which Rosenberg is assigning to what Künneth called his "pseudo church."[99] Rosenberg states that the "high breeding of *all* honor values, of pride, of inner freedom, the 'noble soul' and of belief in their indestructibility,"[100] the "*creation of a high feeling of value*" in the sense of a deep inner trust in one's own type, and a heroic concept of life[101] all serve to educate the new fascistic human type who is remote from "individualism" and "universalism" and is supposed to become a folk and racial man who is on one side totally politically coordinated[102] and on the other side a ruler and a conqueror.

"To give a German church to the 'Nordic racial soul,' in the sense of a folk *mythus*," is for Rosenberg "among the greatest tasks of our century."[103] With this sacred institution, which will encompass the entire German folk, his world-view teaching would also be politically established for a long time, and he himself, as the "chief ideologist" of German fascism, would be the "founder of a religion." Thus a German folk church is to be understood even more as a central part of his political concept for the Third Reich, but on whose specific structure and cultural form the *Mythus* offers only a little information, mostly just brief presentations.

Nordic religious history, Rosenberg says, is supposed to "form the sourdough which is to penetrate the former Catholic and Lutheran portions of the German Church." "Nordic legends and fairy tales" are in the beginning only told briefly but later they are to be understood as symbols. Lacking precise insights into Germanic culture and religion, however, it is to be left to a "genial hand" to gather "from the spiritual sediment through the millennia these rather disparately treated jewels of the German spirit and unite them organically."[104]

Even if Rosenberg has to restrain himself here, he copies the apparent accommodation procedure used by the Christian church for the conversion of pagan Germanic tribesmen and turns it against the Christian cult. Instead of the bothersome crosses in churches and on village streets which present the crucifixion, he wants in his German church to "present the hero in the highest sense"[105] as one who "is always beautiful," and that means he is "of a certain racial type."[106] The churches and the congregations of his German church are supposed to have German artists replace "at the old holy pilgrimage places," little by little, those "bastardized art pieces of the Baroque age with a Jesuit stamp, with paintings and statues of the one who brings life," so that "finally God appears with a spear. . . . "[107]

People are not supposed to gather on Sundays around columns to the Virgin Mary but around memorial stones put up in German cities and villages and around heroic statues of those German soldiers from the front of the Franco-Prussian War of 1870–1871 and the First World War of 1914–1918. It is the duty of the coming German race "to name with honor the names of those who . . . fought for the greatness and the honor of the German folk and to honor them for what they are: martyrs of pure German belief."[108] The fallen German soldiers replaced the saints of the Catholic Church as witnesses of pure German blood and belief. Their "heroic monuments and memorial groves are being created by a new generation, at pilgrimage sights for a new religion."[109]

Among the "heroes" of the proposed German church, the world war dead play a significant role. As "martyrs of a new day, a new belief," they are united by their blood and in a mystical way with the "world revolution" of the Germanic folk-nation propounded by Rosenberg and with his own racially pure world-view.[110] Rosenberg dedicates the *Mythus* to them, and they especially are to be assured immortality through religious worship by the "new generation." Likewise, however, in this "coming German generation . . . everyone is 'in his own way immortal.' Everyone bears the stamp of his ancestors on this world, and is at the same time the forefather of the deeds of his followers."[111]

The "high breeding" of the new type of man predestined by his forefathers is specifically associated with the epoch of National Socialism. The elite of the world-view state, which arises out of the Germanic-German folk-nation, and in which the Rosenbergian folk and national church acquires an outstanding meaning, are the pioneers of German fascism. The task of the state founder—which meant "Hitler, the one who awakens the racial soul"—is supposed to be a "union of men, let's say a German order, to be founded, which is made up of personalities who have taken part in a leading way in the renewal of the German folk."[112] Through those "men, however, who have stood in the foremost positions in the battle for the coming Reich—intellectually, politically, militarily," there is also "the basis for the development of a *new nobility*." Blood and efficiency are requirements for membership in this "German noble order," which will have to be in the first place a peasant nobility and a nobility of the sword.[113]

Rosenberg, visionary and expert on a "German folk religion of the future," "of an authentic German Church," and "of a unified German folk culture,"[114] viewed himself apparently as the creator of a world-view and of a religion, even though he carefully tried to hide this pretension. He presented his book of 1930 not as a "fulfillment of the great theme placed on us today by fate" but more as a clarification and a summarizing answer to questions about the basis for the future.[115] The assertion, to have been assigned "by fate" with a concept for the future new order of German culture, sounds like the statement of a monomaniac who consciously needed to verify his own mission. It is a messianic self-evaluation by Rosenberg, who saw himself as one of the "great dreamers" honored by the people and at the same time "a great man of deeds,"[116] as a "religious genius,"[117] as "a coming *German* statesman and thinker." He was *"a man"* whom we can thank for the creation of the "Fifth Gospel"[118] and who, as the "greatest of our time . . . through a powerful new mythical structure has laid the foundation stone for that which until now *never* existed, but which has always heightened the yearning of our searchers: a German folk and an authentic German folk culture."[119]

Rosenberg did not associate, in any place in the *Mythus*, these *epitheta ornantia* with himself. He did not dare do so because he held a subordinate position in the hierarchy of the National Socialist party and because it would have endangered his own political influence. His need for validity, to propound his teaching not only in his own name but also officially for the fascist party, was however already limited at the time of the first publication of his *Mythus* in 1930. Because of domestic political considerations he had to say that his "thoughts and conclusions" were "completely *personal* confessions and not programmatic points of the political movement to which I belong."[120] This documents the tactic of disguise used everywhere by Rosenberg. This statement, which conflicts with his own self-consciousness, is basically rejected throughout the *Mythus* and should be looked upon as a simple tactical maneuver. There he writes openly: "The symbol of organic Germanic truth is today without a doubt the black swastika."[121]

Rosenberg saw himself as the chief ideologist of National Socialism, as the propounder of the biological, of the *"mythus* of blood" which was associated with natural laws.[122] He intended during the Third Reich to build this into a German national and folk church, into a political instrument which controlled all realms of public as well as private life. It was reserved for his "genial hand," with the support of those scholars who belonged to his cultural institutions and who worked for them, to gather "from the spiritual sediment through the millennia these rather disparately treated jewels of the German spirit and unite them organically" and to clarify and determine the "isolated points to be carried out" in his undertaking.[123] The success of this enterprise would have created for him a unique position in the party and the state.

Scholarship and research had to be free, according to Rosenberg.[124] To be sure, however, this requirement meant simply the freedom of scholarship to follow the *Mythus* with no stipulations. "Belief," which made demands, and "knowledge" were "not to be in opposition with each other." The researching and the presentation of the laws of the universe and thus of nature made up the "essence of Germanic scholarship." "European scholarship" arose "because great researchers *sought* laws, which they prescribed."[125] Likewise there was for Rosenberg "no scholarship which had no prerequisites, but only scholarship with prerequisites. . . . "[126] Just as art was the creation of a certain bloodline and the form-bound essence of art was to be understood as in reality creations by the same bloodline, "science" was also the result of blood. "Everything that we today call abstract science is the result of Germanic powers of creation."[127] Scholars who do not belong to the Nordic-Germanic race were thus excluded in principle from the research and the "renewal" of German culture. With the help of this scholarship of "faith" applied in his cultural-political institutions, the "chief ideologist" planned the reestablishment of "Germanic unity" through science, art, and religion, and its expansion into a National Socialist world-view of the German folk.

INSTITUTIONS OF THE PRACTICAL CULTURAL POLITICS OF ROSENBERG

Years before the establishment of the Rosenberg Bureau, Rosenberg's cultural-political Service Branch in the Reich leadership of the NSDAP, Rosenberg had brought institutions into existence with a Reichwide claim to validity. Here cultural and folk-national cultivation and to a certain degree scholarly *Volkskunde* were carried out along the lines of the world-view in the *Mythus des 20. Jahrhunderts*. Rosenberg's Kampfbund für deutsche Kultur (KfdK, Battle Union for German Culture),[128] which was founded in 1929 but had its beginnings in 1927, had as its goal "to defend the values of the German essence in the midst of cultural degeneration at the present time and to promote all racially pure expressions of German cultural life," as well as "to create the prerequisites for an education in school and university which recognized the folk-nation as a first value."[129] Its pure German proclamations correspond to the guidelines of the "preservation of that which is indigenous before acquiring that which is foreign"[130] and read in places like John Meier's Reich institute plan of 1917[131] or like the introduction of the "classic" *Germanische Wiedererstehung* (Germanic Rebirth) published in 1926:[132]

Endangered and partially damaged is that which the past has left behind in living goods; subverted and choked off are the creations of values during the present; the future, however, the holy right of our youth, is being forsaken.[133] . . . The Battle Union for German Culture is supposed to "save that which can still be salvaged, . . . to lay out the entire *problem of German culture so threatened in its substance.* Here the very first thing is a recognition that through faithless surrendering of one's own essence and through a tolerance of that which is foreign, even of that which is inimical, that we have taken great guilt onto our shoulders; for exactly from this insight a second thing arises for us: that it is also in *our* hearts and hands to complete the revival, the internal and external rebirth through our own powers."[134]

From the leadership group of the Battle Union came the directors and functionaries of the later Rosenberg Bureau, such as Gotthard Urban, Walter Stang, and Hans Hagemeyer,[135] as well as Hans Reinerth, who in 1932 founded the Battle Union Special Group for Prehistory and who published his plan for a total restructuring of German prehistory.[136]

In the area of folklore and as far as we now know, the following people were working. There was the charter member Robert Mielke;[137] there was Richard Beitl, who had belonged to the Battle Union for German Culture "as long as it had existed";[138] and there was Anneliese Bretschneider, who occupied the "referee position for the disciplines of linguistics and *Volkskunde.*"[139] At the 1933 "Nordic Meeting," the first large public state meeting of the Battle Union in the Rhine-Saar District which took place in Bonn, the Viennese mythologist Karl von Spieß spoke about "Schicksalsgestalten in der arischen Überlieferung" (Fate Figures in Aryan Tradition), Hans Naumann about "Führertum und Gefolgschaft als deutsches Schicksal" (Leadership and Followership as German Fate), and Richard Eichenauer about "Musik und Rasse" (Music and Race). There was a puppet theater and local youth groups offered "well-chosen folk songs and folk dances."[140]

The main field of activity of the Battle Union was certainly "high culture," whose representatives it subjected after the National Socialist power seizure, e.g., in Thuringia, to a "politics of cultural destruction," people and works such as those by Otto Dix, Lyonel Feininger, Vassily Kandinsky, Paul Klee, Ernst Barlach, Oskar Kokoschka, Franz Marc, and Emil Nolde. This was "without example in recent German history," and it tried to coordinate these institutions politically.[141]

In April 1933, under Rosenberg's protective umbrella and Franz Lüdke's directorship, there arose the Bund deutscher Osten (BDO, Union for the German East), which was to politically coordinate the various regional boundary associations.[142] It was divided into sixteen regional groups with a large number of subgroups and local groups and served "for the cultivation of boundary-land Germandom."[143] The teamwork of the BDO and the Battle Union for German Culture in the boundary areas was promoted though adult education, kindergartens, music, laity work, folk dance, folk costume, museums, writing, and art as well as through the libraries.[144] Leading an active role in the BDO was the man who later became a collaborator of Adolf Spamer's in the Department of Folklore of the Reich Community for German Folk Research and a co-worker of Matthes Ziegler's in the Rosenberg Bureau, Ernst Otto Thiele.[145] Anneliese Bretschneider took on the historical investigation of a boundary-land council by considering the nationality problem which used folklore criteria.[146]

In the summer and the fall of 1933 various National Socialist cultural organizations appeared which competed for folk-national cultivation projects with those of Rosenberg.[147] The Reich Union Folk-Nation and Homeland was directed by Werner Haverbeck, a student who later was supposed to be a doctoral candidate with Spamer but who finally completed his doctorate under Eugen Fehrle in Heidelberg.[148] In the middle of December 1933 the Reich Union acknowledged the authority of the National Socialist Labor Union Deutsche Arbeitsfront (DAF, German Workers' Front) of Reich Leader Dr. Robert Ley, who created for Haverbeck the Office of Folk-Nation and Homeland in the DAF.[149]

In November 1933 Ley founded the leisure-time association National Socialist Community "Strength through Joy,"[150] and with Ley's help Rosenberg was named on January 24, 1934, by Hitler himself as the Führer's commissioner for the supervision of all intellectual and world-view schooling and education of the NSDAP.[151] Rosenberg then created his cultural-political Service Branch in the Reich leadership of the NSDAP, the Rosenberg Bureau. He created on June 6, 1934, the National Socialist Cultural Community by uniting the Battle Union for German Culture with the German Stage (a theater organization). Based on an agreement between Rosenberg and Ley on the same day, the Cultural Community of the Community "Strength through Joy" was added to this.[152]

This was the complicated procedure which led to the development of Rosenberg's Department of Folk-Nation and Homeland of the Cultural Community. After the dissolution of the Reich Union Folk-Nation and Homeland and the removal of Haverbeck, it published a journal for a brief period beginning in 1936[153] called *Volkstum und Heimat*.[154]

Volkskunde and folk-national work were obligated to the Department of Folk-Nation and Homeland of the Cultural Community which had created a totalitarian need for the National Socialist world and cultural view, as Alfred Rosenberg had developed it in his *Mythus des 20. Jahrhunderts*. According to the *Völkischer Beobachter* "practical cultural work" affected all areas of "folk cultural life in the work of constructing" or rather in the "battle for the spiritual and soul renewal of the German folk." The goal was "the development of a comprehensive folk culture . . . music, theater, architecture, painting were being based on the foundation of the folk-nation: from simple customs all the way to the work of a genius there is a great and unified line which comes from the blood and from the race."[155]

This comprehensive concept of Rosenbergian folk-national work goes far beyond the traditional concept of *Volkskunde*, as Hermann Bausinger has pointed out.[156] In its entirety it did not correspond in any way to the understanding of the discipline of *Volkskunde* by Ziegler, who was supposed to become, in the early phase of the development of a world-view *Volkskunde* within the Rosenberg Bureau, one of the outstanding theoreticians and organizers of the discipline.

THE WORLD-VIEW *VOLKSKUNDE* OF MATTHES ZIEGLER

Reich Leader Rosenberg was primarily dependent on Ziegler's competence in the discipline for establishing a Reichwide *Volkskunde* institution after the Reich Community for German Folk Research of the German Research Council (DFG) in 1936–1937 had been destroyed by combatants from the ranks of Reichsführer-SS Heinrich Himmler. During the first half of 1937, as a result of the rivalry between Robert Ley and Rosenberg, the Cultural Community was also dissolved at Hitler's command and its institutional holdings taken over by Ley.[157] Ziegler, who had been Rosenberg's specialist for *Volkskunde* and religious studies[158] since the end of 1936, was active as the organizer for folklore scholarship in order to balance out this loss of power by the Rosenberg Bureau. The unique experiences which he had gained as the intermediary to the Presidium of the German Research Council aided him in building the new Rosenbergian Reich Working Community for German Folklore, whose scholarly theoretician was none other than Ziegler himself.

Johann Matthäus—called Matthes—Ziegler was born on June 11, 1911, the son of a foreman in the former Reich city Nürnberg. Upon completion of schooling he studied Protestant theology and Germanistics for three semesters at the nearby University of Erlangen. For the winter semester 1931–1932, the twenty-year-old Franconian transferred to the University of Greifswald in Pommerania. There his course of study was "decisively determined by my distinguished teacher, Herr Prof. L. Mackensen."[159] From the fall semester 1932 until the spring semester 1933[160] Ziegler followed this Germanist and folklorist Lutz Mackensen[161]—who later also became an honorary collaborator of the Rosenberg Bureau—to the Herder Institute, i.e., Herder University in Riga, Lithuania.

Certainly also under the influence of Mackensen, Ziegler changed from his study of Protestant theology to the study of *Volkskunde*, Nordic philology, Germanistics, and religious history, giving up the "plan to become a theologian, after serious considerations."[162] It was also Mackensen who promoted this obviously gifted and industrious student. "Based on my high grade for my semester paper 'Family Relationships in the *Märchen*,' I chose for my doctoral dissertation the theme 'Woman in the *Märchen*.' Professor L. Mackensen gave me then the words *family, woman*, and *siblings* to work up for the *Handwörterbuch des deutschen Märchens* (Handbook of the German Fairy Tale)."[163] Even though they were published somewhat later, these works probably represent Ziegler's earliest scholarly works in *Volkskunde*.[164]

Ziegler spent the summer of 1933 in Copenhagen with the master archivist

Hans Ellekilde and in Lund with docent Dr. Carl Wilhelm von Sydow "in order to work through the archives there for my doctoral work and in order to broaden my knowledge of the living Nordic languages."[165] During this time and after having been a folklore assistant with Mackensen in Riga,[166] he was offered a position as German assistant for the Swedish docent for *Volkskunde* in Stockholm, Dr. Waldemar Liungman, but he refused.[167]

There were thus several well-known folklorists who advised and promoted Ziegler or were ready to promote him, particularly his highly honored teacher Mackensen, all of whom could thus have had a decisive influence on his understanding of the discipline. Evidence of these influences on the part of university scholars and their schools of thought can be clearly seen in the later scholarly work of the young man, who was being promoted from all sides. They do not have much to do, however, with his special object of study in folklore and his methodological procedures. These must be sought in other political, ideological, and scholarly realms.

Ziegler made preparation for his doctoral dissertation in Denmark and Sweden, but he did not return to study with Mackensen at the Herder Institute in Riga. Instead he spent his last semester at the University of Berlin in the winter of 1933–1934[168] and completed his doctorate in the winter of 1936 at the University of Greifswald. Ziegler submitted his dissertation, "Die Frau im Märchen. Eine Untersuchung deutscher und nordischer Märchen" (Woman in Fairy Tales: An Investigation of German and Nordic Fairy Tales),[169] to the Department of Germanic Philology. His nominal *Doktorvater*[170] was the docent for Germanistics and *Volkskunde*, Karl Kaiser,[171] who was also a collaborator in the Rosenberg Bureau. The three years he spent between 1933 and 1936 promoting his career and developing his scholarly works in the Reich leadership of the NSDAP were of decisive importance, specifically for the development of Ziegler's understanding of the discipline of *Volkskunde*.

The first portion of his political career was not in any way untypical for a gifted and industrious student of the Weimar Republic, one with a pure German inclination[172] who had devoted himself to fascism. As a pupil of the Nürnberg Reform High School in 1929, Ziegler had joined the National Socialist Youth Union Adler und Falken (Eagle and Falcon). On November 1, 1930, during his student years at the University of Erlangen, he joined the National Socialist German Student Union, and on March 1, 1931, he joined the NSDAP with membership number 786 463. He belonged to the SA until September 30, 1933.[173]

In the Eagle and Falcon union, which had worked since 1930–1931 with Rosenberg's Battle Union for German Culture[174] and had, according to Ziegler's own words, "been since 1929 clearly National Socialistic," the Erlangen student occupied "the leadership of the Racial Office and of the *Gau* Franconia." During this same period he was "active in the completely National Socialistically oriented fraternity Germania." In Greifswald, in addition to his "SA service and the work in the

Eagle and Falcon union (racial and world-view essays and lectures) . . . he participated in the educational service of the student body and the Reich Military Kasern, and during Easter of 1932 visited one of the first student military camps, in Wünsdorf in Mark Brandenburg." In Riga it seemed to him that the "acquaintance with Baltic life and the monumental times for practical boundary struggles" were "very valuable for [my] development. . . . During my Riga period I was in close contact with the Racial and Settlement Office of the SS and worked in other ways and through small contributions for the *NS-Monatshefte*."[175]

A few months after the seizure of power by the National Socialists a second but most unusual phase in his political development followed. Just as Ziegler promoted himself with his academic teachers through sentiment, intelligence, and talent, he also did with influential party leaders. He did not accept the university assistantship with the Swedish folklorist Waldemar Liungman in Stockholm because he preferred "to answer a call within the Reich, to the Racial and Settlement Main Office of the Reichsführer-SS."[176] Still in hopes of being able to complete his university studies as soon as possible, he returned in August 1933 to Germany and was

> accepted by Herr Dr. Rechenbach, the deputy chief of the Racial and Settlement Office SS, into the staff of the Reichsführer-SS, and was recommended by Herr Reichsminister Darré. Herr Reichsminister Darré called me to Berlin and assigned to me the task of building a Department of Nordic-Scandinavian Peasant Studies for the Past and the Present in his staff office.[177]

Since Ziegler joined the SS on October 1, 1933,[178] this could also be the time when he was accepted into the staff office of the Reichsminister and Reich Farm Leader R. Walther Darré.[179] As a collaborator of this office he directed the construction of a special exhibition on peasant culture during the "Green Week 1934" in Berlin and put together a *Deutsches Namenbuch* (German Book of Names).[180]

His lightning career continued to develop: "As of May 1, 1934, Reich Leader Alfred Rosenberg named me the editor-in-chief of the *NS-Monatshefte*, the central scholarly and cultural-political monthly journal of the NSDAP,"[181] which had been published until 1933 by Hitler and had been under the editorial supervision of Rosenberg. At this same time, i.e., with the acceptance of Ziegler, the *NS-Monatshefte* and the party newspaper *Völkischer Beobachter* also became the responsibility of the Reich leader. Ziegler said that Rosenberg

> appointed me shortly thereafter to the position of Central post leader in the Reich leadership of the NSDAP and as a department leader in his Office for Overseeing the Entire Schooling and Educational Work of the NSDAP. Based on this new activity, the Reichsführer-SS arranged for my transfer into the Main Office for Security of the Reichsführer-SS with a direct special assignment.[182]

The twenty-three-year-old Ziegler had climbed by April 1, 1934, to the position of Reich Central Post leader of the Central Post "World-View," i.e., the Rosenberg

Bureau founded by the Führer's order on January 24, 1934.[183] The Central Post
was elevated two years later, on April 1, 1936, to the Amt für Weltanschauliche
Information (Office for World-View Information),[184] and Ziegler was promoted on
November 1, 1937, to the position of Reich Office leader.[185] The "direct special
assignment" is found in the assignment by Rosenberg to Ziegler at the beginning
of December 1934

> to take over an intermediary post, yet to be created, between the Secret State
> Police Office and the Reich Overseeing Office of the NSDAP concerning ec-
> clesiastical-political questions. I had the opportunity to personally present this
> plan to the Reichsführer-SS; the Reichsführer gave his blessing to the plan and
> ordered my transfer into the Security Service in order to work on these ques-
> tions.[186]

Ziegler functioned thus as the intermediary between the Reich leader and the
Security Service (SD) Main Office,[187] that is, as an intermediary in the ecclesias-
tical-political area between Rosenberg and his Reich Overseeing Office, or the
Rosenberg Bureau, and the Secret State Police (Gestapo) as well as the Security
Service of Himmler.

The astonishingly high positions reached so rapidly by the young Ziegler, as
collaborator and discussion partner of several influential vassals of Hitler, leaves
questions concerning the actual basis for such promotions. That the young man
had joined the party early on, was a gifted and ambitious student, and had studied
the appropriate scholarly disciplines for NS cultural politics were not sufficient
reasons for this unthinkably rapid career rise in the academic world.

Personal contacts were created by Ziegler in the Eagle and Falcon Youth Union,
in the NSDAP and its subdivisions, but particularly in the Racial and Settlement
Main Office of the SS, where in the summer of 1932 he was made "an honorary
collaborator."[188] As someone who aspired to high party service he could refuse
the offer for a scholarly position with Waldemar Liungman during his study period
in Sweden, in the summer of 1933. When he was permitted to make the personal
acquaintance of Reich Leader Rosenberg in 1934 "during a guided tour of the
exhibition 'Green Week'" and was later appointed by him to a position in his
office, this change took place "in full agreement" with his previous party superiors.[189] Ziegler occupied an intermediary position during the entire period when
he belonged to the Rosenberg Bureau. As an SS member he was committed on
one side to Himmler. On the other side he was obliged as a "political leader" to
the latter's political competitor Rosenberg, but this did not make his career development in any way difficult if we can judge by the unbroken optimism of his
many autobiographical statements.

The real reason for Ziegler's rapid climb in the Reich leadership of the NSDAP
is to be attributed to his convincing acceptance of the party and his unique usefulness for the National Socialist ideology, particularly for the special activities of

Reich Leader Rosenberg. This can be seen in the cultural-political and scholarly writings which he published from this point on in rapid succession, his official correspondence, his promoting of the needs of the Branch Office, and his carrying out of the world-view presented in his Reich leader's main work, *Der Mythus des 20. Jahrhunderts*,[190] which members of the Rosenberg Bureau were obligated to carry out.

Rosenberg was made aware of Ziegler's cultural-political writing activity through the latter's Hölderlin article in the *NS-Monatshefte*[191] and even more so through a pamphlet[192] which bore the title *"Kirche und Reich im Ringen der jungen Generation"* (Church and Reich in the Struggle for the Young Generation), most likely published in 1933.[193] A note by Ziegler to Rosenberg, which is unfortunately undated, could have been sent along with this world-view call to battle:

> Most Distinguished Herr Rosenberg! In memory of your Baltic homeland, which became my second home, I am pleased to send you a copy of this booklet which I put together in the fall of 1933 in Riga under the auspices of the Central Institute for Education. In faithful obedience, Your Matthes Ziegler.[194]

The pamphlet, directed primarily against the Christian churches, contains the central theses of the future Rosenberg collaborator: Marxism, liberalism, and Christianity, especially "Catholic Action," which ostensibly was attempting to gain a primary position in the cultural area, are degraded as racially alien attitudes, while Ziegler looks favorably on a singular and acceptable Nordic world-view. He opposes materialism (Marxism, Bolshevism), rationalism (liberalism), and oriental-Jewish-Christian "dogmatism" (churches). All conflict with the Nordic-German state and the Reich concept, as well as with "Germanic feelings for ethics." The Nordic world-view offers a racially fitting experience, for at its center "stands the relationship to God, indeed an unbroken and pure connection with God through life."[195] Life, however, is subject to the eternal law of dying and becoming, and that means the battle which National Socialism is conducting. The young generation is proudly and relentlessly carrying out its fateful task. Its assignment is "the Reich," and indeed the "Nordic Reich of the German Nation," which has been expanded to include other "Germanic" states.[196]

Ziegler shows here that he knows and adheres to the *Mythus des 20. Jahrhunderts*; he follows its ideology and borrows significant concepts from it. Reich Leader Rosenberg was thus well advised to trust this follower who was so well informed ideologically, who was such a gifted writer, and who had been recommended as a developing scholar. He gave him the leadership and allowed him to develop the central world-view post which later became the Office for World-View Information and which was being planned to do battle with the churches. He also entrusted him with the editorship of the *NS-Monatshefte*, which stood in the service of the *Mythus*. In addition, Ziegler had put himself and his abilities in the service of the staff office of the Reich farm leader.

Overseeing and opposing the international and national world-view counter-movements[197] was the negative side of the Rosenberg Bureau and its many departments. Its activities were conducted as of 1934 both within and beyond the Reich boundaries. The other side, with a positive tendency, had to do with the special National Socialist world-view of Rosenberg, to defend the "new belief" of the "mythos of blood, belief, and through blood[lines] also the godly essence of man. The belief embodied the most distinct knowledge that Nordic blood represented that mysterium which replaced and overcame the old sacraments."[198]

Ziegler associates himself with this Rosenbergian ideology or world-view in his pamphlet, particularly with the thesis of the Germanic tribesman's union with God through life,[199] i.e., through blood. In this way he equates God and Nordic man, as Rosenberg did. In order to completely expand and implement this uniquely fascist replacement religion—or racist religion of the "master race"—the Rosenberg Bureau needed the help of a series of scholarly disciplines including philosophy, racial studies, prehistory, and religious history, but *Volkskunde* occupied a primary position.[200]

It speaks for Ziegler's perspicacity that he takes note of this desideratum in his brochure, that he had studied those disciplines, including *Volkskunde*, and thus indirectly recommends himself to Rosenberg. In the next-to-last chapter, "Unsere Aufgabe: Das Reich" (Our Task: The Reich), he postulates "Nordically determined culture as a task." He sees "Nordic peasantry" as a "blood and soil conscious relationship to God" and as a prerequisite for the "Reich" which was conceived of as countering the church[201] and which was in fact the National Socialist state of the future. In the last chapter, "Wege und Notwendigkeiten" (Ways and Necessities), he lists "the guidelines for the total needs of the total state, especially in those areas, . . . which the church designated as its unique cultural task, as its undeniable service to folk and state."[202] There are three large areas ("Festivals of Kinship in a Life Span," "Festivals of the Folk during the Calendar Year," and "Festivals of the Nation") for which *Volkskunde* was supposed to produce new and organically developed festival forms. They were born "out of the necessity of our immediate present" and in order "to establish connections between the racially pure spirit of the past and the life of today."[203] For this, German artists "of the past and the present" are supposed to work together. "With words and songs which tell of Nordic life laws, with a visible creation and a dramatic structure, which gives powerful expression to a nation's willingness to do battle," they can "become the most formal leaders for the total folk."[204]

Ziegler's euphemistic speech does not express clearly that the "total state" is being identified with a totalitarian world-view and with the new Germanic religion of Alfred Rosenberg. It is supposed to lead through education and school work to a uniform, or in Ziegler's words, a "total folk."[205] This is the task which the Rosenberg Bureau assigned itself. *Volkskunde* was also assigned a central task, to create functional festivals and celebrations.[206]

With his pamphlet and even before he began his service, Ziegler had submitted to Reich Leader Rosenberg a kind of framework and an ideological basis for his cultural-political and scholarly activities in the world-view post as well as in the Working Community for German Folklore[207] founded at the beginning of 1937. The battle against the Christian churches and the promotion of a National Socialist *Volkskunde* faithful to the *Mythus* were the two primary working areas of Ziegler. They were related to one another in their world-view, and they enhanced each other. This can be documented for the early years only by means of the sparse archive materials which have been preserved. The publications by Ziegler, by his colleagues and subordinates in the Rosenberg Bureau, and by collaborating scholars, however, give us sufficient insight.

As a forum for publication there was in the beginning the *NS-Monatshefte*, which Ziegler edited. A reading of this journal, completely apart from other existing information possibilities, had to open the eyes of every scholar at the time concerning the objectives of the cultural and scholarly politics being conducted. Ziegler carried out the church struggle, which is not of primary interest for our study, with ruthless and decisive openness.[208] The incessant attacks from the Rosenberg Bureau caused church leaders to take political steps with high governmental offices in order to counter the *Mythus*, whose biased historical constructions and dangerous ideological potential were known. The real effect of the Rosenbergian opus during the Third Reich has been seriously questioned,[209] even though it had a publication run of over a million copies. Its teachings were spread far and wide by means of direct and mass-media communication through the many subdivisions of the NSDAP, and it carried out the schooling and education of the party and of the folk.[210] The *Mythus* had to be defended against the criticism of the church by its author and his co-combatants, among them Ziegler, in several publications.[211] In this way the Reich leader's specialist for folklore and religious studies[212] acquired a very dubious reputation.[213]

In ecclesiastical-political and folklore treatments, reports, and reviews, Ziegler, with his colleagues and subordinates, used a more-or-less veiled language when it concerned the final objectives of the ersatz religious function of the *Mythus*. They did not fail, however, to make their statements absolutely clear concerning what they wanted in a National Socialist *Volkskunde* apparatus. The negative acts of cultural politics by Rosenberg were repeated in his folklore writings. He turned against the assumed or real opponents of a racist German *Volkskunde* based on the *Mythus*, particularly against the religious and most especially the Catholic confessional *Volkskunde*, against "liberal" and "Marxist-Bolshevist" *Volkskunde*. Numerous lines of connection were constructed among these three main opposing camps, or presumed enemies, and they were aligned with the "liberal" or National Socialist researchers of other directions. The palette of the battle program was thus very broad. Those who were attacked had to fear for their professional positions and their material existence, and thus they sometimes joined other National Socialist cultural organizations such as the Office of Ancestral Inheritance of Himmler, founded in 1935,[214] thereby becoming enemies of the folklorists in the Rosenberg Bureau.

There was practically no Marxist subdivision in German *Volkskunde* before or after the seizure of power by the National Socialists in 1933. The attacks on them are thus correspondingly rare, mostly a brief mention of the presumed enemies during the first years when Rosenbergian *Volkskunde* was being established. They are little more than stereotypical exercises, so to speak, since the Reich leader himself had already passed judgment on the Marxist-Leninists in various writings.[215] Only with the beginning of the Russian campaign does the Bolshevist *Volkskunde*[216] of the Soviet Union receive much attention. To legitimize the German conquest of Soviet territory and the subjugation of the Slavic "subhuman beings," there is a pursuit of the ostensibly original Aryan folk tradition and the Germanic cultural influence in Russia.

Ecclesiastical-confessional *Volkskunde* receives Ziegler's verdict as early as 1934. It reflects the "compulsory dogma of the *ex oriente lux*," and scholarly contributions by its representatives are written *sub specie orientis*.[217] Its alleged oriental-Jewish-Christian direction stands, for Ziegler, in absolute opposition to a Germano-centric, Nordic *Volkskunde*. In his "Kirchliche oder religiöse Volkskunde?" (Ecclesiastical or Religious Folklore?) of 1935, which had not yet been recognized as a guide, he explains that German *Volkskunde* is an area "that scarcely, like no other today, presents the basis of operation by our world-view opponents," and *Volkskunde* scholarship is "only then National Socialist when it is based on racial thinking."[218] It has "the task of exposing the fountain of racially pure folk tradition in legendry and material goods which has often been covered over and has deviated [particularly by the ecclesiastical-confessional group in the discipline], and to secure its undisturbed flowing through all times. The necessity of implementing this challenge as soon as possible is quite clear, especially in light of the need for totality which is raised by the confessional side in the area of religious *Volkskunde*."[219] At the pinnacle of the alleged totalitarian, ecclesiastical folklorists stands "the Prelate Professor Dr. Georg Schreiber of Münster, who was well known among the National Socialists."[220] Following him are the university docent, Dr. Karl Meisen, Bonn,[221] and the Austrian folklorist Hanns Koren.[222]

Hans Naumann of Bonn is looked upon as the leading figure of "liberalist" *Volkskunde*, a man who sees "in the separation of upper and lower strata, of a culture-bearing and educated stratum and an uneducated, primitive stratum the great methodological ordering principle of *Volkskunde*."[223] With his innovative reception theory or his teaching of *gesunkenes Kulturgut*[224] Naumann becomes one of the most dangerous of those "world-view opponents" who covered over and deviated from the "fountain of racially pure folk tradition."[225] Ziegler attacks him as early as 1934 in "Folklore on a Racial Basis"[226] (see text in appendix I.9) and contrasts Naumann's theory with the *Volkskunde* of the Rosenberg Bureau. The latter "does not think in upper and lower strata, but proceeds by contrasting racially pure essence with racially alien influence, the historical conflict between the Nordic cultural realm in general and of the German soul in particular . . . with the estrangement brought on by foreign racial ethics."[227]

This "estrangement" is brought about through the liberal, internationally oriented, educated members of the bourgeoisie, especially Naumann, whose *Volkskunde* stands in a close relationship to that of the Jewish scholar Lucien Lévy-Brühl, particularly in regard to the intellectual type and the thought processes of primitives.[228] "National Socialist *Volkskunde* can never again equate the folk with a 'lower stratum.' For it the folk is the entirety of the nation."[229] It only places the peasantry in the foreground "because the blood and soil bound peasant is closest to a racially pure essence" and because the task of an applied *Volkskunde* is understood to be "the new creation of the German peasantry from its blood and soil . . . the guarantor of the German future."[230] "Racially pure essence" could simply not be in agreement with "a cultureless primitive stratum."

In his "Ecclesiastical or Religious Folklore?" of 1935 Ziegler supposes a close world-view connection and singles out an oppositional front in "liberalism" and "Catholic Action." He equates Naumann's concepts of upper-lower strata with ideas of Georg Schreiber and with confessional folklorists' conceptions of high-religion and primitive religion, "whereby both concepts are totally conceived of as claiming validity for all peoples, all races, and all times."[231] The personified images of the enemy by the Rosenberg Bureau are thus firmed up. In the expanded version of "Folklore on a Racial Basis" of 1936 and 1939, Naumann and Schreiber function even more as representatives of the two *per definitionem* separate groups of scholars in the discipline who collaborate against National Socialist *Volkskunde*, groups that thus have "totalitarian" claims.

Associating the primitive lower stratum and primitive religion among the broad strata of "Germanic" peoples and the German folk in particular was an inconsistency in itself for Rosenberg's folklorists. Nor did they recognize the bourgeois upper stratum as the bearer of tradition in the real sense, or Christianity as a high religion. Ziegler's *Volkskunde*, which was associated "in the area of religious folklore essentially with the questioning and the conclusions of Germanic studies," was supposed to be a positive tendency "of discovering in custom and legendary materials the sources of religious life and ethical behavior which had until now had been covered over intentionally or through a lack of care."[232] It was supposed to help establish as *"religiöse Volkskunde"* the new Germanic high religion of Reich Leader Rosenberg, or rather the National Socialist world-view of the present.

Rosenberg's *Mythus* presented the party's political-ideological framework for Ziegler's scholarly and applied *Volkskunde*. Since Rosenberg was the architect, writer, politician, and, in his view, chief ideologist of the NSDAP but was not a trained scholar, it does not come out clearly in his basic work just which methodical path his scholarly objectives for folklore were to take or which specific disciplinary traditions were supposed to be primary and thus continued. Ziegler probably had to make this decision. His "Folklore on a Racial Basis," just like his earlier programmatic "Church and Reich" of 1933,[233] concentrates on festivals and celebrations and on the realm of customs.

To uncover the "sources of religious life and ethical behavior" in custom and legendary material,[234] we have to reach back methodologically to the scholars and theoreticians of the discipline who appear in Ziegler's publications. They are for the most part not the academic teachers and conversational partners of his student years. Nor are they the scholars of the discipline of the early 1930s who were the recognized authorities, who were well known to him from his studies and from his cultural-political activity in the Rosenberg Bureau and with whom he had worked a little in the Reich Community for German Folk Research. The German Research Council (DFG), whose honorary president was Rosenberg, appointed Ziegler as its DFG referee for folk research from November 1, 1935, until December 1, 1936, and he "could gain in this way a complete overview of the material, personnel, and organizational questions in the area of *Volkskunde*, prehistory, and racial studies."[235]

Most influential for the savvy folklorist Ziegler were the representatives of the Viennese Mythological School, Leopold von Schroeder, Georg Hüsing, Wolfgang Schultz, and especially Karl von Spieß and Edmund Mudrak.[236] Schultz directed the paperwork empire of the Department for Aryan World-View and Folklore of the Rosenberg Bureau,[237] in which Spieß and Mudrak later were to take on important positions for the discipline. Ziegler added their scholarly opinions to the world-view teachings of Rosenberg. Only on this theoretical-ideological basis is the *Volkskunde* of Ziegler and of the Rosenberg Bureau understandable.

In the fall of 1934 Karl von Spieß published his *Deutsche Volkskunde als Erschließerin deutscher Kultur* (German Folklore as the Key to German Culture), in which he summarized his own theory, methods, and research conclusions as well as those of the Viennese Mythological School.[238] By December of the same year Ziegler had praised the book of Spieß, which had been critically labeled by other scholars of the discipline as the promising beginning of a "new method of viewing folklore." As obvious as Spieß's action appeared to every National Socialist, it had a revolutionary effect on contemporary folklore scholarship.[239] In the two subsequent reprintings of Ziegler's "Folklore on a Racial Basis," Spieß's introduction to *Volkskunde* is preferred to that of Adolf Spamer, Wilhelm Peßler, and Arthur Haberlandt,[240] because it had made "the first and until now only attempt at an organically complete picture of the essence and the breadth of German *Volkskunde*."[241]

Spieß is concerned with the meaning of German *Volkskunde*, whose bases are for him represented in three closely related areas of race, language, and the traditional world, and to which he dedicates separate sections in his book. The main impetus is the traditional world, "because it is at the moment the most unknown area since it includes a world-view, and because it is from here that the buildup must begin."[242] The scholarly objectives of German *Volkskunde* are becoming clear. The practical task is the reestablishing of the complete unity of the Nordic traditional world which had been separate at an earlier time—and which includes not only German traditional material "but also the Germanic and in the final analysis the Aryan (Indo-Germanic)"[243] as well as the racially pure world-view contained therein. "All of this obligates us to the cultivation of the area of tradition, a cultivation whose guidelines are the same as those for racial questions. The preservation of the healthy tribal inheritances and the slow removal of that which is inherently sick is contrasted here with the preservation of that which is racially pure and the removal of that which is racially alien."[244]

Spieß subdivides those "inherited goods" of the Nordic or Aryan traditional world into three areas: legendary material (*Saggut*), the calendar, and custom. Calendar[245] and customs are in a close relationship to legendary material. Particularly the old, indigenous Aryan Folk Festival,[246] with its common mealtime and its dramatic presentation with song and dance which forms the central core of customs, is found again in legendary material. This legendary material preserves mostly for us the fate of the figures acting in the old festival.[247] The narrative or legendry, which has been transmitted from generation to generation, documents therefore the old festival and helps to reveal and reenliven it today.[248]

The entire work of this young cultural politician in the Reich leadership of the NSDAP is clearly imprinted with the thought processes of the Viennese Mythological School, and by Rosenberg. Primary impetus for accepting the mythological premises was transmitted to the school pupil and university student Ziegler by the nationalistic youth union Eagle and Falcon.

For the development of "a folk-national [*tümlich*] German education," Georg Hüsing, founder of the Viennese Mythological School "in the narrower sense,"[249] had created the *Laich*, a dramatic presentation with song and dance. It was a dance song "from the primeval Aryan past and from which all of the rhetorical arts had developed,"[250] and was the expression of a perception "which we would today most likely call a 'religious one.' It presumes a certain devotional atmosphere and creates one. It represents, so to speak, a church procession and a cult activity which probably indeed was later added by the Aryan peoples to the *Laich*."[251]

From this "complete art work of the Aryan past" there developed "the individual expressions of folk dance, folk song, mythical fairy tales and children's songs." Hüsing reconstructed "with the help of comparative scholarship of all related elements . . . eleven stylistically pure *Laiche*,"[252] which were published after his death by his wife, Emma, in 1932. Pure German youth unions had helped during the preceding years "to bring the *Laiche* to life again which we [the Hüsings] worked up by means of happy, dancing activity."[253] These unions include the Eagle and Falcon.

The Ninth Union Meeting of the Eagle and Falcon took place from July 28 to August 4, 1930, in Koblenz and nine hundred young people participated. On the program there was an exhibition called "Folk-Nation, Tribal and Racial Studies."[254] There also were lectures on a racially appropriate Nordic world-view in contrast to the oriental and the degenerate by speakers such as Schultz and Darré, and there was a war game by boys and girls with a memorial celebration for heroes at the cemetery. According to Konopath, an especially deep impression was made by the Union Acting Troupe, "which caused a cultic expressive form to arise before our eyes, through a reenactment of an ancient song-game-dance in the form of a 'Laich.' "[255] Two years later, after the appearance of the textbook by Georg and Emma Hüsing, the Eagle and Falcon did not celebrate a single festival without presenting one of these curious initiation plays.[256] According to the teachings of the Viennese mythologists, the *Laich* written by Hüsing and the "legendary material" arrived at by him documented the ancient Aryan festival and served to reveal it in the present. Ziegler wrote his dissertation, certainly not by chance, on the important areas of legendry and oral narrative transmission.[257] In his pamphlet of 1933 he placed festivals center stage of his *Volkskunde* and continued to maintain their priority.

In accordance with the Viennese school, the inherited goods of the Nordic traditional world played an important role. They represented an internally consistent documentation for an a priori objective, a racially pure world-view. In the final two printings of "Folklore on a Racial Basis" in 1936 and 1939, versions which differed little from one another, Ziegler made an important but brief comment concerning the canonical categories and the practical tasks of German *Volkskunde*: "It is most certainly not our task to create a system of religion by interpreting these survivals of a once complete world-view [too quickly[258]]. That would be an inorganic path and the beginning of a new dogmatism."[259] The limitation based on the Rosenbergian concept of dogmatism, or an ecclesiastical compulsory dogma of faith, changes quite obviously in Ziegler's theory of *Volkskunde* and with no difficulty into its opposite. It only needs to be correctly interpreted, and then the organic path to the rebuilding of the once complete world-view will have been taken. The language of the Rosenbergians, which concealed the real needs and work objectives for political reasons, can also be found elsewhere.[260]

Ziegler's *Volkskunde* begins "with the earliest appearance of the Nordic race," its division into various ages, and "the developmental stages of the Nordic race and the development of the German folk from the peoples of the Nordic race."[261] It has the task of extracting this world-view from its "remains," or survivals, which existed in a pre-Christian historical stage, and from folk-national traditions, and to implement it in the National Socialist present.

The substance of Ziegler's *Volkskunde* is made up of five large groups of traditional materials or canonical areas[262]: (1) settlement and material culture, (2) narrative and legendary material (*Saggut*), (3) custom and symbol research, (4) cultivation of folk speech, and (5) research of the history and form of communities, which were and are the bearers and creators of these traditional goods.[263]

Special canonical tasks for *Volkskunde* are given. In the first group the task is the "cultivation of noble and useful forms of tools, . . . the observation of genuinely harmonious colors in costumes, . . . or the care used in accomplishing unity in building shapes, settlements and landscapes."[264] In the second group the task "most especially" is the uncovering and making useful of "mythical elements which were used in dramas and plays . . . useful in shaping calendrical ceremonies."[265] In the third group there is the documentation of "the reality of German popular belief and an indigenous, true piety."[266] In the fourth group there is an emphasis on the meaning of the "education and power of form in a language that is pure to its roots," and its cultivation. In the fifth group the task is the documentation of continuity "from the Germanic clan and the German tribal confederacies to the professional and work communities" and to the family of the present.[267]

Ziegler's racially based folklore called for research on the Germanic-German traditional world, for treating it in a scholarly manner, and for transposing it into a National Socialist folk-national cultivation or folk renewal. In place of the "division into upper and lower strata, educated and primitive culture," there was to appear "a division into racially pure and racially alien essences," whereby as a "measure" there was "the value sensibility of the races" in practice but in fact there never was an exact methodological means of help which could be verified.[268] It is this racial postulate which reveals in the clearest way the arbitrary procedure and the ideological-utopian character of Ziegler's *Volkskunde* scholarship and his folk-national cultivation.

The political tasks[269] of this *Volkskunde* are already contained in or at least can be heard in these special canonical tasks. All five canonical areas are directed toward fascist festival and celebratory structures. Everything culminates here, and Ziegler describes it by paraphrasing the metaphor of the Brothers Grimm, that of the fragments of a belief dating back to the most ancient times, a mythical element which resembles small pieces of a shattered jewel which "are lying strewn on the ground all overgrown"[270] and which, according to Ziegler, can be reconstructed in their original form:

National Socialist organization of festivities represents a condensed description of our national powers of belief. Germanic piety and Nordic faith in God (*Gottglaube*) are like those brightly colored jewels, strewn in among the traditions in the legends, *Märchen*, and songs, in the world of popular customs, and they are discernible in the holy signs and symbols which we can find everywhere on our farmhouses and on the creations of our handicrafts.[271]

Ziegler thought of Jacob and Wilhelm Grimm as the ancestral fathers of his theory of the discipline. The brothers, who were sure of their instincts, had expressed "the realization of a united world-view of our entire intellectual and material traditional world and its Nordic-Aryan origin."[272] This world was "for the Grimms the world of the *Mythus* and of belief." Ziegler adds:

> From this understanding of the mythical, which was lost more and more through time and philological narrowness, there is a straight path to the *Mythus* concept of Alfred Rosenberg.[273]

With this statement the circle from the past to the present is closed for the National Socialist mythologist Ziegler. His *Volkskunde*, whose ideology of the *Mythus germanischer Kontinuität* (mythus of Germanic continuity), analyzed by Wolfgang Emmerich,[274] is being legitimized in the discipline by circular reasoning.

Toward the end of 1936, after two years of activity in the Rosenberg Bureau and after completing his doctorate at the University of Greifswald in Pommerania, Ziegler, at age twenty-five, had by and large completed his prethinking about the theoretical foundations of his fascist *Volkskunde*. Its Reichwide institutionalization, in which he would play a decisive role as the scholarly organizer, could now be undertaken. Everything transpired under the pressure of the cultural-political happenings which were so disadvantageous for the Rosenberg Bureau: dissolution of the DFG Working Community for Folk Research and the Rosenbergian National Socialist Cultural Community. Ziegler's fascist *Volkskunde* had become absolutely necessary.

THE PREDECESSOR OF THE ROSENBERG REICH INSTITUTE

The Reich Working Community for German Folklore (see pertinent material in appendices I.1–8) was founded on January 5, 1937, at Ziegler's instigation, was supported by the Reich leaders of the NSDAP R. Walther Darré (Office of Agrarian Politics, Reich farm leader), Heinrich Himmler (Reichsführer-SS), Konstantin Hierl (Reich work Führer), and Baldur von Schirach (Reich youth Führer), and was directed by Alfred Rosenberg.[275] It was supposed to become quite simply the *Volkskunde* institution of the party in the German Reich. Thus, in addition to the leaders just mentioned, other Reich leaders interested in *Volkskunde*, folk-national cultivation, and celebration development were courted[276] in order to create for the new institution and within the Reich leadership a broad agreement as soon as possible. By 1939 ten others from the circle of "heads of the remaining subdivisions and associated leagues" had joined the Working Community for German Folklore, among them Robert Ley.[277] They all bore the title of Reich leader, even though they did not represent this high committee at all and functioned simply as nominal overlords. Reich Organization Leader Ley and Reichsführer-SS Himmler, Rosenberg's active competitors in the area of cultural politics, were obvious proofs that one could be both a supporter and an opponent of the Working Community.

The tasks and the objectives of this Working Community, formulated in various ways by its real initiators from the Rosenberg Bureau, were partially disguised for political reasons. It was "from the very beginning not supposed to become an autonomous service branch, but rather a *Beratungs- und Mittelstelle* (advisory and intermediary post)." The results of its work were to be made available to the entire party, its divisions, and its allied leagues, "without limiting in any way its independence and personal responsibility." It was thus years later directly subordinated to Reich Leader Rosenberg in his Service Branch.[278] There was, however, in Ziegler's Office of World-View Information a Main Office for Folklore with "political leaders" Ernst Otto Thiele, Hans Strobel, Erich Kulke, and Karl-Heinz Henschke. They served the Working Community through their personal alliance and as scholarly referees.[279] Ziegler's office indeed directed the Working Community, which was destined to become the primary organization for the Reichsinstitut für deutsche Volkskunde within the future Advanced School of the NSDAP of Rosenberg. The planning was begun in the same year, 1937.

In the chartering document of the Working Community, signed by Rosenberg on January 5, 1937 (see text, appendix I.1), the objectives were spelled out. In addition to "advising all party offices (*Parteidienststellen*) interested in questions on folklore" there was, as expected, "the defense against the world-view opponents of National Socialism in the realm of folklore research and practical folklore work."[280] There was an absolute claim for sole representation, since all folklorists who did not adhere to Rosenberg's *Mythus* ideology were considered to be "opponents" or at least deviates from "pure teaching" and thus sectarians. Related to this, Ziegler declared the Working Community as "official for the party." Through its founding, the NSDAP (i.e., the Rosenberg Service Branch), has "brought its high need for the realm of German folklore to full expression" and will "never relinquish" it.[281] In his later autobiography Ziegler formulates the working principle for the *Volkskunde* organization of the Rosenberg Bureau in this way: "It had to make the results of scholarly research useful for the practical tasks of the party, and at the same time assign important party research tasks to scholarship."[282]

The "practical tasks" consisted, as the first sentence of the chartering document indicates, in "schooling and educating the party," for which *Volkskunde* was given an ever-increasing role. Hitler, as Führer, had assigned to Rosenberg the task of "supervision of all intellectual and world-view schooling and education of the NSDAP"—and thus of the German folk. Rosenberg was not satisfied with the role of controller and censor of National Socialist ideology but aspired to a dominant power position in the Third Reich. He himself handed out "important party research assignments" to co-workers and collaborators of the Working Community which he directed, in order to make the results of this scholarly research useful for his service branch in the sense of the *Mythus*, i.e., for the construction of the planned fascist world-view state.

Rosenberg's and Ziegler's Working Community for German Folklore—and later the Institute for German Folklore in the Advanced School of the NSDAP—was supposed to subjugate and make useful all bourgeois-national and National Socialist scholarship in the discipline, including folk education. Without exception this was to serve the fascist or—better said—the special ideology and the strong-armed ambitions of the Reich leader who had been singled out by Hitler as the "party dogmatician."[283]

It was obviously not sufficiently understood by the Rosenbergians that what Bollmus has called a "mission compulsion" in the "leadership chaos of the Führer state"[284] had to be limited by other Reich leaders who were defending their *Volkskunde* fiefdoms and were deceptively invited to work together. The need for success which they took on with missionary zeal made them compensate everywhere for their real and imagined hindrances and setbacks. Everything was carried out through a random choice of procedures and tended to intensify their fascistically determined behavior.

With the founding of the Working Community for German Folklore, the participating Reich leaders named high functionaries of their service branches as their deputies. Darré and Himmler named SS Brigadeführer Reischle, Hierl named General Work Führer Decker, von Schirach named Oberbannführer Brennecke, and Rosenberg named SS-Obersturmführer Ziegler, the egghead of Rosenbergian folklore. The *spiritus rector* of this new institution was also its business leader and director of its scholarly "objects of study."[285]

Among the scholarly referees was the former Greifswald student, now Dr. Karl-Heinz Henschke.[286] This man, the only one who had formerly belonged to the Rosenberg Bureau, now assumed the position of "referee for scholarship." Rosenberg's comrade-in-arms in the Union for the German East, the Spamer collaborator Dr. Ernst Otto Thiele,[287] received the position of referee for press and publication. He brought with him the Kurmark Regional Post for Folk Research as the only large piece of "booty" from the Department of Folklore of the Reich Community for German Folk Research. There was also SS-Hauptsturmführer Dr. Hans Strobel,[288] the most important *Volkskunde* functionary after Ziegler and like the latter a member of Eagle and Falcon and a former student at the University of Erlangen, where he completed his doctorate with the Germanist and folklorist Friedrich Maurer.[289] He came from the staff office of Darré and directed the post of referee for schooling. Dr. Karl Haiding-Paganini,[290] an ethnic German from Austria and thus an adherent of the Viennese Mythological School, came from the Cultural Office of the Reich Youth Leadership and administered the post of referee for folk-national work. The leader of the post of referee for celebration structuring, General Work Führer Dr. Will Decker, left the Working Community in 1938. His successor was Work Führer Thilo Scheller from the Reich Work Service, a worthy co-organizer of celebrations for the Nürnberg Reich Party Days of the NSDAP.[291]

These scholarly referees, except for Decker, were later regularly employed functionaries of Rosenberg's Service Branch and formed with Ziegler the hard core of the *Mythus* folklorists. They had served partially as referees in the small working group formed one year before the development of the Working Community. They were "scholarly and capable world-view folklorists" in the Main Lectureship for Folklore, which had been founded and directed by Ziegler as part of the Rosenbergian Reichsstelle zur Förderung des deutschen Schrifttums (Reich Office for Promotion of German Writing).[292]

The founding of the Working Community for German Folklore was announced in German newspapers and journals, including those of the Rosenberg Bureau.[293] German *Volkskunde* was thus presented as the core area for all educational and schooling work, by means of which all folk-national work of the NSDAP was supposed to be distinctly marked.[294] Franz Alfred Six, commissioner for the Reich Professional Competition of German Students,[295] called folklore work the most urgent area of student activity at the pedagogical institutes, which in the best sense contributed to the work area of the Working Community for German Folklore.[296] The National Socialist Teachers Union instituted a subdivision of folk-national pedagogy in order to research folk-cultural goods along with the Working Community.[297]

The Working Community had already arranged during 1937 agreements with the National Socialist Student Union, Teachers Union, Docent Union, Women's Community, and Legal Aid Union; the Supreme SA Leadership; the German Workers' Front; the Main Office for Communal Politics; the Testing Commission for the Protection of National Socialist Publications; and the Office of Racial Politics of the NSDAP.[298] In this lively activity of concluding agreements for collaboration, it is of course not proved that advice in folkloric questions on schooling and educational work came every time from the Working Community of the Rosenberg Bureau. In the beginning only the necessary contractual prerequisites were created in order to be able to exercise a decisive influence on those subdivisions of the NSDAP already named or to be developed later.

The first meeting of members of the Working Community took place on May 5, 1937,[299] in Berlin. It was held in conjunction with a meeting of the Reich Office for Promotion of German Writing, and there was a paper by Ziegler entitled "Aufgaben und Planungen für die nächste Zeit" (Tasks and Planning for the New Era) and one by Decker on conducting National Socialist celebrations.

At the second meeting, on October 22, 1937 (see the report of this meeting, appendix I.2), the results of the common organizational work could be presented.[300] Henschke reported on the post of referee for scholarship, stating that with the presumption of "scholarly thoroughness and world-view industriousness," German *Volkskunde* could become "the outstanding national scholarship." The employment of the Working Community in the scholarly area was divided into three tasks: to gain by means of one's own systematic, impeccable research work "the basis and the materials for schooling, educating and reshaping of German social life by means of the party and its units"; to defeat and push aside "those who oppose the National

Socialist world-view in the realm of scholarship"; and to expand folklore scholarship "into a fortress for the National Socialist world-view." One had to establish a scholarly circle of collaborators and acquire the necessary financial means for all of this work already underway. Certain research had already been undertaken: farm house research (under the direction of Dr. Kulke); investigations of German folk customs, especially in light of the new celebration planning (under the direction of Dr. Decker and Dr. Strobel); work on the German folk song, folk and children's games, and folk dance (under the direction of Dr. Haiding). According to Henschke,

> These scholarly works are organized in such a way that the appropriate group leaders, aided by stipends, travel funds, and specialists' help (for archives) treat the individual research theme independently within the framework of the whole. Evaluation is carried out by the group leaders. In this way the Working Community exercises a decisive influence on all folklore research work.

These scholarly works served mainly for practical folklore work but were also destined for indirect and direct confrontation with the confessional opponents.

The Working Community, Henschke states, intends to be actively employed so that German *Volkskunde* acquires validity as a scholarship and can fulfill the tasks assigned to it, i.e., to find secure research and teaching positions at German universities. This will be done so that a scholarly tradition can be developed (at that time there were only five chairs of *Volkskunde*), and it will be so elevated that it will be able to administer its own examinations. Work with German *Volkskunde* is to become a goal for professionals, and regular positions at research institutes, museums, libraries, etc. are to be arranged.

Erich Kulke,[301] who brought the Intermediate Post for German Peasant House Research from the staff office of Reich Farm Leader Darré into the Working Community; Karl Haiding, who created the Intermediate Post for Game Research; and Hans Strobel and Will Decker all clarify their research plans and their accomplishments. Kulke and Strobel at least have access to financial subventions from the German Research Council, which in the future will also promote the Working Community for German Folklore.

Kulke says his tasks are:

> 1. Developmental history of the Germanic farmstead from the Nordic, not from the Roman-Celtic standpoint. 2. Expansion of the farm*stead* concept in contrast to the previous one-sided work on *house* research. Viewing the farmstead as a portion of the village community and of village delimitation (farm order, community order, field order, settlement order). 3. Expansion of previous knowledge of Germanic-German land acquisition and the associated German settlement history. 4. Purification and renewal of peasant construction methods. Exhibition of a new construction tradition. Battle against the urbanization of village construction. 5. Cultivation of valuable old farmsteads in the sense of state monument preservation, since the farmstead represents at least as meaningful national common property as monasteries, castles, churches, and fortresses.[302]

Investigations had been undertaken on log construction, settlement history, round villages (*Rundlinge*), and the arbored houses (*Vorlaubenhäuser*) of the Kurmark. There was also the preliminary work for a dictionary on German farmhouse research, collaboration on new plans to publish a large work on farmhouses, investigations on the living conditions in the country, and suggestions for structuring a village house (*Dorfhaus*). In addition there was preparation for an exhibition on the house and farmstead of the German peasant and gathering of a picture collection.

Strobel designates the objective of his research task as an attempt at "a systematic gathering of material for the relationship of churches to folk custom. From this presentation and evaluation in schooling especially, as well as from a scholarly and political viewpoint, valuable results can be expected." Strobel is in the process of establishing a picture archive on living customs.

Haiding is concerned with collecting, investigating, and publishing on games, dance, song, and custom, and he works in the division of fairy tales, song, game, and dance for the bibliography of the Working Community. Especially notable are his "investigation on the religious political coordination of German folk songs" and the "preparation of a publication of later Christianized songs in their original form," as well as the "collection of material for the racial investigation of dance melodies."

Decker gives an overview of the structuring of large political celebrations "which are more than just marching and which present a celebration of faith to the National Socialist world-view," such as the Celebration Day for German Work (May 1), the Reich Party Day of the NSDAP in Nürnberg, the ninth of November in Munich (a festival in memory of the November 1923 putsch by Hitler). In the realm of family festivals and clan celebrations the Working Community was to carry out preliminary work in the form of investigations "where clan celebrations (baptism, wedding, funeral) are already being conducted in the sense of a National Socialist world-view" in order to gain "suggestions for clan celebrations of a German type." This had begun with the establishment of an appropriate library and picture archive.

Thiele, as leader of the post of referee for press and publication, announces a "list of folklore publications," the guidelines published in 1938.[303] He summarizes the informational lectures of the Working Community that were held during the year for Berlin and the German press representatives in Berlin. They were given by collaborators of the Rosenbergian Working Community, by the staff office of Reich Farm Leader Darré, and by Himmler's Ancestral Inheritance.

To "correct the numerous but false meanings about expressive forms of the folk-nation" which commonly appear in the press, Strobel, Thiele, Haiding, and von Spieß spoke to about twenty-five or thirty representatives of the daily press. Friedrich Rehm from the staff office of Reich Farm Leader Heinrich Appel, Karl Theodor Weigel, and Otto Huth from Ancestral Inheritance spoke about calendar customs, symbols, dance, peasant art, costumes and their renewal, and folk-national cultivation.

The Versuchsstelle für Volkstumskunde (Experimental Post for Folk-National Studies), which was associated with Ziegler's Office for World-View Information, came out of Thiele's work in the Kurmark Regional Post for German Folk Research. Its task is "to carry out investigations whose conclusions are of value for practical folk-national work, or to make possible new knowledge for judging the development of our folk-nation and the relationships to closely related folk groups." The "investigation of rural dwelling conditions," which was under way at the time, was supposed to help clarify the reciprocal relationship between man and his house. It was especially important for future settlement work. Studies on Christmas and New Year's customs are being carried out throughout the entire Reich through collaboration with the Teachers Union and are based on reports of experiences by school pupils. Thiele and Strobel also are working on the establishment of folkloric film and slide series for educational purposes.

Strobel, leader of the post of referee for schooling, has put together a "card file of collaborators" of over five hundred persons who worked officially and unofficially within the NSDAP and the associated leagues on folklore questions. Their appropriateness and abilities for the most part still had to be proved.[304] There was a preliminary speakers' list of the Working Community for the "most varied presentations, some of which were public in nature, others within the framework of various divisions of the movement." With its thirty-three names it offers a first overview of the supporters and helpers of Rosenbergian *Volkskunde* who had mostly been educated for scholarship.[305] In addition to the Rosenbergians themselves, such as Haiding, Henschke, Kulke, Karl Ruprecht, Scheller, Strobel, Thiele, and Ziegler, they were party functionaries and scholars in the discipline who worked together with the Rosenberg Bureau in the folklore and folk cultivation area.

For the service branches of Darré and Himmler, for example, there is SS-Untersturmführer Dr. Heinrich Appel (Racial and Settlement Main Office SS), SS-Standartenführer Dr. Wilhelm Kinkelin, Dr. Hans Lorenzen, Friedrich Rehm (all from the staff office of the Reich Farm Leader), SS-Brigadeführer Dr. Hermann Reischle (staff office, Reich Farmer Rank), Dr. Siegfried Lehmann and SS-Sturmbannführer Karl Theodor Weigel (both from Ancestral Inheritance), Wolfgang Hirschfeld and Otto Schmidt from Ley's branch office (Community "Strength through Joy"), and General Work Leader Dr. Will Decker, acting referee of the Working Community, from Hierl's branch office.

Folklore specialists are Gustav Bebermeyer (University of Tübingen),[306] Heinz Diewerge (Teacher Education Academy, Lauenburg/Pommerania),[307] Eugen Fehrle (University of Heidelberg),[308] Georg Fischer (Teacher Education Academy, Frankfurt/Oder),[309] Herbert Freudenthal (Teacher Education Academy, Hirschberg/Silesia),[310] Gerhard Heilfurth (University of Leipzig),[311] Karl Kaiser (University of Greifswald),[312] Gustav Friedrich Meyer (Kiel),[313] Bruno Schier (University of Leipzig),[314] and Martin Wähler (Erfurt).[315] The bourgeois-national folklorists who joined the NSDAP and who are on the list of speakers will also be available to the Rosenberg Bureau in the future and partially take on its fascist *Volkskunde*.

Several of the folklore scholars who sympathized with the Rosenberg Bureau had already appeared together with the Rosenbergians at the Second Nordic Scholarly Congress "Costume and Decoration,"[316] which took place in Lübeck from August 30 to September 4, 1937. This congress was arranged by the Nordic Society,[317] which was under the influence of Rosenberg; by the Rosenbergian Reich Union for German Prehistory under Reinerth; and by the Reich Working Community for German Folklore under Ziegler.

In the section on costume and decoration of the Germanic tribesmen past and present, papers were presented by Hans Strobel on costume and fashion,[318] Ernst Otto Thiele on Nordic spinning wheels,[319] and Bruno Schier on prehistoric elements in European folk costumes.[320] Josef Hanika (German Karls University, Prague) spoke about structural types of European headdress.[321] Eugen Fehrle lectured on the bridal crown,[322] Arthur Haberlandt (Austrian Folklore Museum in Vienna) on textile art of the Germanic and Indo-Germanic tribesmen,[323] Rudolf Helm (Germanic National Museum in Nürnberg) on Germanic decoration forms in German peasant costumes,[324] and Misch Orend (Hermannstadt/Siebenbürgen, Transylvania, Romania) on jewelry of the Siebenbürg Saxons.[325]

In addition to a few lecturers from the Netherlands, Scandinavia, and the Baltic states, once again representatives of the SS Office of Ancestral Inheritance are found among the folklorists in 1937 in Lübeck. Siegfried Lehmann presents a paper on symbol in costume and decoration[326] and Joseph Otto Plassmann talks about decoration in Nordic folk belief.[327] They are the last ones of a rather significant list of speakers at this Rosenbergian congress. They were mostly well known or were at least "Nordic." Representatives of various scholarly disciplines from almost all the "Nordic-Germanic" states of Europe participated,[328] and the success was emphasized at the October 1937 meeting of the Working Community for German Folklore.[329]

The international congress on costume and decoration national meetings followed, including the one by the Intermediate Post for German Farmsteads in the Reich Working Community, under Kulke. The first Reich Working Session of the Intermediate Post took place in Berlin from March 17–19, 1938, to point out "new paths for farmstead and house construction research in Great Germany" and to pass on the "farmstead of past centuries" as the "pioneer for recognizing our Germanic-German essence . . . in its best expressive forms, and for coming generations."[330] The second Reich Working Session, in cooperation with the Reich Food Ministry and the Party Branch Office of Reich Farm Leader Darré, was convened in Eger in the Sudetenland (Cheb/Czechoslovakia) from May 31 to June 3, 1939.

At the first Reich Working Session of house researchers the annexation of Austria (now called the Ostmark) to the German Reich a few days earlier was celebrated. At the second one the defeat of Czechoslovakia was celebrated, i.e., the creation of the Reich protectorates of Bohemia and Moravia and the alignment of these two Czech states in March 1939 into Hitler's Great Germany.

At the second Reich Working Session in Eger it was primarily a matter of solving, as Kulke says, "perhaps today's most intense problem in German agriculture," fleeing the land, through folk-national cultivation and in the form of "building conservation." Thus the question was to be addressed "just how far professional construction is to be called on to help take care of an emergency situation which is gnawing at the roots of our folk strength." That means nothing less than "how much can healthy and true peasant construction help the German landworker and peasant—indeed German people in general—acquire a homeland in the countryside which will bind him for all eternity through inner values to the soil?"[331]

John Meier had already proposed stopping this flight from the land in his Reich institute plan of 1926, as a task of *Volkskunde* and of folk-national cultivation.[332] It is now about to be successfully enacted, at the wish of the totalitarian fascist regime, by representatives of high party and state service branches who were invited to the Reich Working Session in Eger. It will be with the help of the "construction experts of Great Germany, who are connected in any way at all to the rural construction of the present," says Kulke.[333]

This social-reactionary project for stopping rural mobility, which was being promoted by those in authority in the Reich Working Community for German Folklore, took on a new dimension in comparison to the bourgeois-national proposal of 1926. In fact, Kulke, much as Meier had already done, also stresses the very essential and necessary economic viewpoint. In addition, however, there is the disguised ideological aspect of the "inner values" that were ostensibly guaranteed by the continuous settlements of the rural populace. This meant, according to Kulke, the *"working and economic requirements* in reshaping our farmsteads in order to be able to have increased efficiency through an intensification of German agriculture."[334] Shortly before the outbreak of the Second World War and as a result of the realization of Hitler's geopolitics and Rosenberg's world-view in his *Mythus*, national or, better said, strong-armed objectives now dominate. For Kulke it is "necessarily the *'recreation of the German peasantry'* which is in the foreground" of the great rural building tasks. It is a "verification of how the new farmsteads to be built can offer, through their structure, through their economic efficiency, through the details of their handicrafts, etc., a reflection of our times to other peasantry."[335]

This means the politically planned new settlement of German peasants on "new farmsteads"—first in prewar Germany,[336] later in the vanquished lands abroad, in the "reclaimed east German living space"[337]—and finally the "high breeding" of the new German type of man with a Rosenbergian stamp who was bound to blood and soil. This is then made into one of the tasks of fascist house research and as part of an applied folk revival. It means that with Kulke's concepts published in 1938, "Wunschbild eines nationalsozialistischen Siedlerdorfes" (Desired Image of a National Socialist Settlement Village)[338] and the "village house" (*Dorfhaus*) with its "future role in village community life,"[339] a far-reaching contribution by the discipline had been made to a settlement and construction politics now logically subjected to the objectives of the Rosenbergian world-view and Hitler's plans for conquest.

Kulke's "Desired Image" presents a sketch for the expansion of a small farming village in a central German region which is increasingly influenced by industrialization and urbanization: old and new buildings surround the village center in a highly structured system. The overall layout, or the "new unity," that gives in a bird's-eye view an impression that it is militarily arranged, almost like a fortress.[340] Peasants and farm workers are supposed "to be bound to the homeland, but so are industrial workers, employees, craftsmen, and tradesmen," which means stopping the flight from the land "of German people." A "new kind of village center" forms the central point of the layout and "of village life in general," with a village green as a "festival place for village community." It is to be surrounded by a community house with service rooms for the party, by the "Strength through Joy" house, as well as a neighboring "celebration hall"[341] with a clock tower with monuments and flags.

The celebration hall "is conceived of as an intellectual and cultural gathering place for the entire village, not put up from one day to the next, but rather growing slowly out of a well-thought-out plan and from offerings made by the community, as once the old places of worship did." School, fire brigade houses, and National Socialist Folk Welfare children's home are near the village center, while cemetery and chapel, Hitler Youth Home and sport field as well as the inn with a post office and a bus stop are situated on the outer boundary of the village."[342] There is no church for Christian worship services. It is quite obvious that the celebration hall has replaced it and has become the "intellectual and cultural centerpiece." The church tower is now replaced by a "clock tower with monuments and flags" as a monument to those who died in war, and for the NSDAP.

Villages which are far from the city and industry and which are made up primarily of old buildings or are limited by the financial burdens of new construction cannot count on a series of new central structures, as was the case with the National Socialist settlement village, but have to be satisfied with a single building. Kulke takes this into account in his proposal for the "village house" as its "future role in village communal life."[343] Recommendations for structuring this village house had already been made in 1937 at the October meeting of the Reich Working Community.[344] Now they appear in *Odal*, Reich Farm Leader Darré's *Monatsschrift für Blut und Boden*.

In the multifunctional "village house" there was to be the "village hall" (*Dorfhalle*) for celebrations, the Hitler Youth Domicile, the service offices for the mayor, the village library, kindergarten, the village "showplace" museum, the village baths for hygiene, and the National Socialist communal nursing station for health maintenance. A large games, marching, amusement, and festival area was planned for the village house. Including the Hitler Youth Domicile and the kindergarten would also promote later connections by the young people growing up there with the village house. The village showplace, with its folk educational emphasis, presented the history of the village as well as the working and living world of the peasants and passed this along to coming generations. Official marriages could take place there, "for nothing can offer a more beautiful framework for carrying out such a celebration than those bits of ancestral wisdom in the form of documents preserved on the walls and in the rooms."[345]

The most important arrangement of the village house is without a doubt the village hall. It was a room sufficient in size to hold the entire village community. In its dignified confines were to be held the parents' evenings of the Hitler Youth, the radio broadcasts of Hitler's speeches, and "all of the village calendrical festivals."[346] Among these there was May 1 as the "Celebration Day for German Work" and the harvest festival in the fall,[347] but as one can see from the additional proposal for special celebrations, there was also November 9 as the day of the Hitler putsch in Munich in 1923. Into every pillar of the celebration hall the name of one of the sixteen who died at the Munich Feldherrenhalle[348] was to be hewn, and at the foot of the clock tower planned to stand beside the celebration hall, "a fitting monument for those who died in the world war and for the movement was ordered."[349]

These offer striking indices for Kulke's real intention. His proposal was to prepare the celebration hall for the National Socialist settlement village, or more precisely the "village hall" was to be the sacred rural structure of the "German Folk-National Church" of Rosenberg's *Mythus* ideology. Kulke wisely avoids, for domestic political reasons, clarifying his real intention in a journal which was available to everyone.

Other passages in his village house proposal of 1938 spell this out. It is "an incontrovertible fact that numerous houses of worship are no longer fulfilling their unifying tasks. . . . " It can be verified *"that almost nowhere can the churches of today be called on to be the gathering place for village life. . . . Strong and binding,"* however, is the *"political life force of the German homeland and thus also of the German peasant folk which grows out of the folk-nation. The faith of German man is fighting here for new and authentic values for us."*[350]

"Because, however, our age is the expression of a new faith and of the high communal awareness of a nation unified under National Socialism, the new domestic union which is growing on the soil of pure German life values needs a new image within the city and the countryside, in the lecture halls and factories, in the dwellings and in the celebration halls." Thus also the call for "ennobling the village image" goes out, for communal voluntary work by the entire populace of the village. The "village house" arises as the "centerpiece," as the "crowning glory of this will, as a new expression of a faithful communal affirmation of our village folk."[351] Its most important structure is the "village hall," which serves primarily for party propaganda and calendrical festivals, i.e., the Rosenbergian neopagan religion and the breeding of the Germanic-German master race.

The "village house," which grew up like the old village worship places through many years of construction, must *"never be in its appearance a poor imitation of urban building styles."* It "must fit the peculiarities of the village and landscape buildings. *It will not look much different than a large and cleanly kept peasant's house."*[352]

The rejection of the modern urban construction style, e.g., that of the internationally famous Bauhaus, and the turning toward a traditional peasant building style which is bound to the landscape are only superficial. Still there are in a large number of publications by Kulke harsh words about aesthetically inappropriate applications of urban building styles in the countryside. There are also traditional peasant house types which are researched scientifically by the Intermediate Post for the German Farmstead and other cooperating institutes throughout Germany and they are presented as exemplary prototypes.[353] But the postulate of adherence to racially pure continuity in the new fascist rural building style is just as shallow ideologically and as far from reality as that of the unalterable union of German man to his blood and soil.

This ideological imaginary world is a facade for clear political objectives. The ostensibly traditional peasant building style, much like the unification of Nordic man with the inner values of his racial soul, serves to build the totalitarian world-view state envisioned by the "chief ideologist" of the NSDAP and his bureau, Rosenberg, for whom a totally politically coordinated populace is necessary, according to the *Mythus*.

Rosenberg's co-conspirator, Kulke, admits this himself indirectly. In spite of the industrial and urban influences, he maintains that "by far the majority of our villages . . . will maintain their clear peasant essence," even if the nonpeasant professions increase there. Then all of these changes "should and will become clearly and carefully united and shaped in a National Socialist way. Thus the German village of the future will gain a new face, as a structure of the new age, but it will always bear witness that it has grown meaningfully through the millennia from ancestral estates."[354]

This means that the strategists of the NS world-view are planning to oversee social and cultural changes in the rural area and to channel it in a direction that is ostensibly traditional but in reality is new and is being determined by political powers. Quite logically the monumental fascist building style for public structures being propagated by the Intermediate Post for the German Farmstead utilizes traditional peasant building elements only as movable scenery.[355] The sketches and models presented by Kulke as a pattern for his "village house," "village halls," and "village celebration halls" look more like presentations of those monumental urban structures of the Third Reich, just reduced in size and remodeled for the rural setting.[356] This is then the "new face" of the National Socialist village, which allegedly grew out of Germanic-German building continuity.

Much like Kulke's house research and building cultivation, the other papers described in the minutes of the October 1937 meeting of the Working Community for German Folklore, or the later Intermediate Posts, were laid out and their directors and collaborators conducted a lively scholarship and a cultivation of the folk-nation. The results were published in part in the quarterly journal of the Working Community founded in 1939, *Deutsche Volkskunde*.[357] The chief editors were first of all Matthes Ziegler and Georg Fischer, who was named in the same year director of the referee's post "scholarship" of the Reich Working Community.[358]

The ideological prerequisites as well as the specific scholarly-political assignments came from Reich Leader Rosenberg himself. Reich Office Leader Ziegler had to see to their implementation as a working practice in folklore, or he had to do them himself. Ziegler, the skilled scholarly theoretician and organizer, was thus the real head who carried out this undertaking. With justification he can be called the *Volkskundeprimus* of the Rosenberg Bureau, since he played a leading role in the activities of the Reich Working Community.

In his Jena autobiography of 1940 Ziegler attributes much to himself. Not only did he suggest the founding of the Reich Working Community but it was also he who founded its journal *Deutsche Volkskunde* and directed a series of book exhibits and special meetings of the scholarly Intermediate Posts. He expressly includes the two working sessions of the Intermediate Post for the German Farmsteads in Berlin in 1938 and Eger in 1939. Furthermore, his special attention was directed toward the cultivation of close connections to the Scandinavian lands based on the Nordic Society in Lübeck. One result of this work was the German-Nordic Scholarly Congress for Prehistory and Folklore in Lübeck in 1937.[359]

It may be that Ziegler, by sensing the previous accomplishments of the Reich Working Community, is putting his own service in too favorable a light. But the Führer principle so self-evident for fascism placed on him a strict power to command and the responsibility for all the activities of the Reich Working Community. Often, however, he had to stand to the rear of his collaborators or even Rosenberg himself, as was the case at the second session in 1937, where he merely greeted those present and then let the individual specialists speak.

The early scholarly, organizational, and folk cultivation successes of the Reich Working Community for German Folklore were, however, without question. Now it was a matter of expanding them, spreading the folklore institution systematically to all of Germany, and carrying out its claim of sole representation, ostensibly sanctioned by party politics, but in reality not written down anywhere, and to carry this out even among those with whom he was competing. After the liquidation of the Reich Community for German Folk Research, with its Department of Folklore under Spamer, there still existed Meier's League of German Societies for Folklore, which represented several camps of world-view opponents, and Himmler's SS Ancestral Inheritance, with its folklore departments. The latter was still in its developmental stage and was thus only now becoming an opponent.

Ziegler and his followers began to take over the expansion of their *Volkskunde* institutions, with the active help of Rosenberg, by establishing Reichwide *Gau* working communities for German folklore. They were supposed to be built up on the pattern of the Reich Working Community and its professional referee posts, or intermediate posts. They were to carry out the work and they were to be careful and "special attention [was to be] paid to those who participated." Only those who were responsible collaborators and who were unobjectionable were considered. Ever since July 1937 the Rosenberg Bureau had been used by the *Gau* schooling leaders of the thirty-two NSDAP *Gau* leaderships of the German Reich for setting these up. Since Reich Leader Rosenberg's competency for leadership of the *Gau* schooling leaders, whom he viewed as his representatives or deputies in the various *Gaus*, was not clearly delineated, it is probable that these enterprises were not carried out without difficulty. Strobel, leader of the schooling referee post in the Reich Working Community, was nevertheless able to report at the October 22, 1937, meeting seven such *Gau* working communities, in Danzig, Düsseldorf, Halle-Merseburg, Hamburg, Hessen-Nassau, Mecklenburg-Lübeck, and Württemberg-Hohenzollern.[360] Others were added later. By placing the *Gau* Working Community for German Folklore with the *Gau* schooling leaders, which was to be directed from the main office in Berlin, the establishment of a Reichwide instrument for folk-national work or renewal by the Rosenberg Bureau was planned. This would secure the political, scholarly, and disciplinary primacy of the Reich community, from which the folkloric Reich institute was supposed to grow.

ROSENBERG'S "BROWN" VS. HIMMLER'S "BLACK" *VOLKSKUNDE*

For Reichsführer-SS Heinrich Himmler, "struggle . . . [means] a primary principle of nature," a "general life principle, even a 'law of god,' "[361] which assured individual and collective survival and thus human existence overall. In this way the Nordic-Germanic race had distinguished itself, through a process of selection spread over thousands of years which was unmerciful, sober, and horrible, but still natural. In the "struggle for existence" everything weak and inferior will be annihilated, and only that which is strong and vigorous will multiply.[362]

Hitler shared this vulgarized social Darwinistic concept[363] of the survival of the fittest in the struggle for life, and it was raised by Himmler to a guiding principle of his actions. It also corresponded to the world-view teaching recorded by Rosenberg in the *Mythus* and was made a binding principle in his branch office, the Rosenberg Bureau.[364]

The principle of continuing "warlike" confrontations in virtually all realms of life and using all conceivable means was valued for its usefulness and became a central piece of fascist behavior during the Third Reich. It was shared by the members of Himmler's Schutzstaffel (SS) as well as by Rosenbergian functionaries,[365] and it was promoted by both camps into the schooling and the education of the entire party.

It is certainly not an exaggeration to view the millions of people who were murdered by the fascist regime for racial and strong-armed political and ideological reasons as inferior "weak people" and the sacrificial offering of this thought and behavior pattern which was making a mockery of all ethical standards. It was based, like fascism itself, on a hatred of humankind.

The ideological "law" of fascist behavior patterns was valid for the scholars of the Ancestral Inheritance and of the Rosenberg Bureau, and this quite obviously included folklorists. They carried out their duties in the black uniforms of the SS or the brown ones of the party leadership, and were thus called by their second names "Black" or "Brown" folklorists. This extended quite logically to the innermost core of German scholarship and the university community as we can see from the rivalry battles for the presidency of the German Research Council (DFG) and the Reich Community for German Folk Research and its Department of Folklore. Traces of this are still evident at German universities today.

Those "world-view opponents" who were branded as scholarly competitors were affected existentially and their professions were damaged, e.g., the bourgeois-national folklorists and popular piety researchers Adolf Spamer and Georg Schreiber. The fascist principle of mindless struggle being propagated as a "law of nature and god" was also part of the regular dealings between the rivals Himmler and Rosenberg. Both Reich leaders were also driven by an ambitious personal sense of calling and each wanted to create for himself a new National Socialist religion.[366] In this way he would secure absolute predominance during the Third Reich for his ideological strong-armed political intentions and institutions with their own scholarly departments, including folklore departments. As a result the collaborators of the SS Ancestral Inheritance and of the Rosenberg Bureau were divided into two adversarial camps. It would be incorrect to maintain that representatives of the one camp stirred up a battle on their own, through their actions, or that those of the other camp placed people being persecuted under their protection for unselfish reasons.[367] The confrontation and the way it was carried out were in principle determined ideologically.

The founding of Rosenberg's and Ziegler's Reich Working Community for German Folklore at the beginning of 1937 was still under the favorable star of partial cooperation with Himmler's Ancestral Inheritance, which had been brought into existence only one and a half years earlier, on July 1, 1935. In addition to Himmler, two other founding members of the Ancestral Inheritance, Richard Walther Darré and Hermann Reischle, had joined the folklore Reich Working Community, and worked for it with yet another of its charter members, Erwin Metzner, and with a member of the Ancestral Inheritance Presidium, Wilhelm Kinkelin.[368] Reischle, Metzner, and Kinkelin represented the Darré faction. The latter functioned not only as the Reich farm leader of the NSDAP and the nutrition minister of the Reich government but had also been installed as leader of the Racial and Settlement Main Office by Himmler. In the beginning Himmler adhered to Darré's "blood and soil" ideology, profited from it, and exposed the SS and the Ancestral Inheritance to its influence. Reischle also occupied the position of deputy curator and was thus the deputy of Himmler in the Ancestral Inheritance Presidium. Further, he occupied the position of leader in Darré's Staff Office of the Reich farm leader, where Metzner was one of the collaborators with authority,[369] and from whose cultural-political scholarly departments several leading functionaries of the folklore Reich Working Community had come, like Ziegler, Strobel, and Kulke.

The Darré faction, especially the Staff Office of the Reich farm leader, established a barely tolerated bridgehead for initial cooperation between the Reich Working Community and the Ancestral Inheritance. Ziegler and Strobel, both SS officers like Wolfram Sievers, the Reich business leader of the Ancestral Inheritance,[370] apparently arranged for this cooperation. Ziegler, for example, reported to Sievers that he was basically willing to let his collaborators support a lecture program by the Ancestral Inheritance.[371] Strobel, who was on a first-name basis with his SS comrade Sievers,[372] asked to receive photographs in order to "build a scholarly picture archive on living customs."[373] Representatives of "Black" *Volkskunde* worked thus alongside "Brown" folklorists at meetings and to employ speakers.[374]

The Reichsführer-SS had already inquired and decided in February 1937 that collaboration between the Ancestral Inheritance and the Working Community for German Folklore should take place "as much as possible."[375] The period of cooperation, limited from the very beginning by the tactician Himmler, thus ceased at the very latest when Darré and his faction no longer influenced the SS and the Ancestral Inheritance. Based on ideological differences with Darré, Himmler had continued to chop away at the realm of activity of the Reich farm leader and his people in the SS.[376] The personal tensions which grew out of this led to Darré's resignation in February 1938 from Himmler's Schutzstaffel and to surrendering his function as chief of the Racial and Settlement Main Office of the SS.[377] Reischle, Metzner, and Kinkelin also departed in the same year from the Ancestral Inheritance. One year before, in March 1937, Walther Wüst had ascended to the presidency and replaced the original charter member Herman Wirth.[378] Supported particularly by his faithful combatants Wüst and Sievers, Himmler could now set out on a most controversial political path in regard to Reich Leader Rosenberg's bureau. Here too very important preliminary work had been accomplished.

In a letter dated January 5, 1937, Rosenberg had written to Reich Educational Minister Bernhard Rust, in the name of the Working Community for German Folklore founded on that same day, and suggested that the leadership of the *Atlas der deutschen Volkskunde* be assigned to the private docent at the University of Greifs-wald, Dr. Karl Kaiser.[379] The date on the letter was not chosen by chance but leads rather to the conclusion that Rosenberg's Working Community was being conceived of as the successor institution of the Department of Folklore of the Reich Community for German Folk Research. The minister was made cognizant of the founding of this community by an enclosed circular (see text, appendix I.1).

Rosenberg, in his request to assign the *Atlas*, the showpiece of German *Volks-kunde*, to Kaiser, who had been a volunteer collaborator in his Service Branch and the doctoral mentor of Ziegler,[380] makes reference to the "new structuring of the relationships of the German Research Council" (DFG). With forethought Ro-senberg sends his letter to the Reich educational minister as the work supervisor of Rudolf Mentzel, who had been named commissioner in November 1936 and president at the end of January 1937.[381] Reich Educational Minister Rust, as a weak personality, however, is being controlled by his own collaborators, and his ministerial officer Mentzel, as an SS officer, is close to Himmler. The latter's Ancestral Inheritance receives one piece at a time of the disintegrating Department of Folklore of the DFG Reich Community.[382]

Here the complaint by the ideology expert Rosenberg is of no use, that the various periods of influence in regard to world-view which the *Atlas* had to undergo, had decisively determined the type and the contents of the individual questionnaires and had thus restricted the results which were now waiting to be published. Nor was the Reich leader's offer of any use to allow "objective sifting and sophisticated evaluation of the varied materials for their world-view." This had been of great importance for "the great folk political meaning of the *Atlas* work and its increasing respect abroad" and was being carried out by Kaiser, and thus by the folklore Working Community of the Rosenberg Bureau which was behind it.

Kaiser, with scholarly merits especially in the area of the folklore *Atlas* work,[383] is singled out for his world-view reliability and seems most likely to measure up to Rosenberg's requirements for "directing large scholarly undertakings."[384] With this recommendation, however, he is poorly served, as the immediate results show. He was born in 1906 and received his doctorate at the University of Greifswald in 1928 and his *Habilitation* in 1933. As a young Germanist and folklorist he worked from February 1931 to December 1932 in the Central Office of the *Atlas* in Berlin. He then took over the direction of the Pommeranian Folklore Archive from Lutz Mackensen[385] and of the Pommeranian Regional Post of the *Atlas* in Greifswald.[386] He taught successfully as a private docent at the University of Greifs-wald, i.e., without a continuing appointment and a sufficient salary. His numerous publications for the folklore *Atlas*[387] were crowned in 1936 with the publication of the *Atlas der Pommerschen Volkskunde* (Atlas of Pommeranian Folklore).[388] In spite of his young age of thirty years, Kaiser was singled out as a specialist for the edition planned for him by Rosenberg. He was, however, considered to be "*menschlich schwierig*" (difficult as a human type), as one says in German scholarly circles about unconventional, i.e., unaccommodating or obstinate colleagues. Because of the Reich leader's protection he became a dangerous competitor and a desired object of attack for the folklorist Heinrich Harmjanz and later also for the SS Ancestral Inheritance, a "dog that one slays in front of a lion."[389]

Harmjanz took over the *Atlas der deutschen Volkskunde*, the Photo Archive, and the Central Archive of German Folk Narrative (ZA) on May 5, 1937,[390] from the holdings of the DFG Department of Folklore, exactly one day after Spamer resigned[391] but many months before the final takeover by the Ancestral Inheritance. After Harmjanz had had the first *Atlas* map publications[392] brought in—those of Spamer, who was also being persecuted by him[393]—he published them with his willing helper Erich Röhr as their own intellectual property.[394] He also promoted Röhr's professional career all the way up to the position of *Ordinarius* for German *Volkskunde* at the University of Bonn.[395] He and the former Spamer collaborator Röhr thus were the usurpers at the end of a long series of scholars who had built up the *Atlas* and who now were being denied the fruits of their labors.

Siegfried Elimar Heinrich Harmjanz played an important role for the discipline of *Volkskunde* during the Third Reich, indeed for intellectual endeavors in general. Born in 1904, he was by 1930 a member of the NSDAP and the leader of the National Socialist German Student Union at the University of Königsberg in East Prussia. Here he also joined the SS in 1931, which he then left again in 1933 for unknown reasons.[396] As a student of the Germanist Walther Ziesemer he completed his *Habilitation* in 1935 at the age of thirty-one[397] with a scholarly folklore investigation.[398] He quickly became full professor for *Volkskunde*, first in 1937 at the University of Königsberg and then in 1938 at the University of Frankfurt am Main.[399] His own publications for *Atlas* folklore do not compare in quantity and importance in any way to those of the Greifswald private docent Kaiser.[400]

Harmjanz was furloughed from the obligations of his professorial career in order to become a referee for the humanities in the University Department of the Reich Educational Ministry in Berlin. He assumed this position on March 22, 1937, and was soon to rise to the position of chief of the Ministerial Bureau and became a personal referee to Rust.[401] He became directly responsible for appointing most of the humanities professors at German universities, including folklore,[402] and through his office he could participate in the overseeing of all these scholars. The important scholarly-political influence of this folklorist was unique, and was never reached by any other member of the profession in the entire history of the discipline.

Harmjanz's dealings with other people have been variously interpreted by scholars. He is supposed to have been captivating, jovial, unbureaucratic, and comradely toward his followers and friends. His need for success is also pointed out,[403] which meant those people whom he viewed as his opponents had to suffer, and he persecuted them pitilessly.

In 1937 he had assumed the position of an opponent of the Ancestral Inher-

itance and its founding father, Herman Wirth, who was not well respected in scholarly circles.[404] One year later, however, Walther Wüst could report a substantial
improvement in dealings with Himmler,[405] and in the fall of 1938 Harmjanz joined
the Ancestral Inheritance after he had previously applied for reacceptance in the
SS.[406] There he directed the Teaching and Research Post for Folk Narrative, Fairy
Tales, and Legendry at the Central Archive and the Teaching and Research Post
for Folk Research and Folklore with the *Atlas* in Frankfurt am Main.[407] He had
brought his "booty" from Spamer's DFG Department of Folklore along to the
Ancestral Inheritance.

Rosenberg and his co-combatants were justified in seeing in this Himmler
paladin, Harmjanz, one of their most dangerous opponents. Together with his ministry colleague Mentzel, a natural scientist, he had robbed them of the *Atlas* and
further "booty pieces" from Spamer's inheritance. He hindered their Service
Branch, specifically "Brown" *Volkskunde*, because of his antipathy and his scholarly-political sense of power, and he caused difficulties for the collaborators in the
Working Community for German Folklore, difficulties in getting professional appointments.[408] The Rosenberg Bureau did not overlook any opportunity to attack
the usurper Harmjanz and to exclude him if at all possible from his political and
his scholarly position so that it would be possible for Rosenberg scholars to have
an unobstructed path to the professional positions at German universities.

As a countermove, Harmjanz joined the hated Rosenbergians, particularly his
Atlas rival Kaiser. It is not insignificant that the latter was two years younger but
had completed his *Habilitation* two years earlier, and he outdid Harmjanz in regard
to his work on *Atlas* folklore studies. From the application of the Reich leader
dated January 5, 1937, for reassignment of the *Atlas*, a bitter exchange of letters
took place between the Rosenberg Bureau and the Reich Educational Ministry.
Rosenberg and Rust signed them, but they were prepared by their referees.

A new inquiry by Rosenberg on October 19, 1937, was answered in a letter
by Rust on March 10, 1938.[409] It serves as an example for the fascist method of
damaging the career of a scholar, even one from the ranks of the NSDAP. It was
not possible, according to this shrewd document of information, to name Kaiser
to the leadership of the *Atlas*, since the position had already been occupied by
Spamer. Furthermore, subsequent questioning by the ministry had revealed that
Kaiser did not view himself as adequate for this job, neither as a scholar nor as
a person. He had participated in a National Socialist docent camp (*Dozentenlager*)
but only after much hesitancy; his National Socialist understanding was inadequate,
his general ethical talents limited; his character pedantic. His general pleasure in
serving was contrary, and he had been criticized formally as an aesthetic loner
without ardor and character strength.

Since Kaiser was described at that time, including by those from his Greifswald
posts, to the Reich Educational Ministry as a secluded, completely unpolitical, and
difficult human type, he was officially apprised in May 1936 "that he had no

opportunity of becoming a tenured university docent." His financial support through the ministry was cut off after the Reich Docent Union leader, in October 1937 in Munich, called any further promotion of Kaiser unjustified.

This was still not enough. Kaiser had recently "shown considerable lack of ability in working folk-politically in a National Socialist sense in the area of German *Volkskunde*." Immediately before the appearance of the *Atlas der deutschen Volkskunde*[410] he had warned foreigners about it and had even looked upon Pommerania as originally being Slavic. He did this in an article[411] in the international journal *Folk* published by the Dutch freemason and alleged freemasonic grand master Jan de Vries.[412]

The Official Party Testing Commission[413] and the Secret Prussian State Archive would have objected to this procedure and would have called for a reprimand of Kaiser. Reich Minister Rust expressed extreme disapproval and threatened removal of his teaching license if the situation was repeated. He did not do this "out of consideration for Kaiser's otherwise satisfactory accomplishments in Pommeranian *Volkskunde*, and with the hope that he would let this case serve as a lesson."[414]

The "extreme disapproval" of Kaiser was expressed in a decree with similar wording by the ministry on the same day and sent to the curator of the University of Greifswald. The decree expressly denies that the person being reprimanded "could be given any special support other than his college fees" by the German Research Council, unless the DFG wanted to give special support.[415] The private docent, who had material needs, is then employed as of May 1938 by the Rosenberg Bureau on an honorarium basis.[416]

Behind this plot against Kaiser was no doubt the professional worker responsible to the Reich Educational Ministry, Harmjanz, who had already participated in the persecution of Spamer. At the beginning of 1939 he refused the financial security for Kaiser which the University of Greifswald had requested.[417] In the same year he harshly criticized Kaiser's *Lesebuch zur Geschichte der deutschen Volkskunde* (Reader on the History of German Folklore),[418] which was loaded with a National Socialist spirit.

Harmjanz turns against Reich Leader Rosenberg himself and ridicules him indirectly in an audaciously arrogant way in a ministry letter signed by Rust on March 10, 1938. He denounces the journal *Folk* promoted by Rosenberg's office as well as the subsequently liquidated Reich Community for German Folk Research, calling it the product of freemasonry, which had been declared the ideological opponent of the *Mythus* world-view. In addition he insinuates that the "chief ideologist" of the NSDAP and the author of the *Mythus* had promoted with Kaiser his own real world-view opponent. Harmjanz's unscrupulous tactic, however, was successful only insofar as it briefly interrupted the university career of the Rosenberg protégé, thereby destroying the financial relationships of Kaiser and his family, and kept his rival under further psychic terror.

It is not the scholarly accomplishment of Kaiser which is being judged through this condemnation. The ministry letter to Rosenberg, which addresses Pommeranian *Volkskunde* and thus indirectly the *Pommerscher Volkskunde Atlas*, judges the scholarly accomplishment as "adequate."[419] Rather, his necessary political reliability is brought into doubt through massive accusations which are reduced to "state endangerment." These factually unprincipled denunciations, which were extremely brusque even for the Third Reich, were countered by the Rosenbergian Karl-Heinz Henschke in a letter of safe conduct for Kaiser sent to the docent leader of the University of Greifswald.[420] Rosenberg himself also wrote a letter on April 11, 1938, to Reich Minister Rust,[421] in which all accusations were convincingly rejected point by point, but without allowing improvement in the unfortunate situation of the scholar being affected.[422]

Kaiser was a National Socialist: on November 1, 1933, he became a member of the SA, on July 1, 1934, a member of the university teaching group of the NS Teachers Union, and on May 1, 1937, a member of the NSDAP.[423] He did not approach the Rosenberg Bureau as a result of the dangerous intrigues by Harmjanz.[424] With the Rosenberg Branch Office he had worked "in close collaboration" since the beginning of 1936.[425] Its chief and the "grail protector" of the National Socialist world-view wrote him a glowing recommendation with deep conviction, concerning his political reliability in the matter of all those harsh accusations made by the Reich Educational Ministry.[426] It must be remembered that Kaiser was persecuted only because he was a representative of "Brown" *Volkskunde* and thus represented serious competition for Harmjanz and the Ancestral Inheritance, and, true to the fascist behavioral norm, had to be fought against and shut out if at all possible.

Much of this Kaiser affair will seem strange to us today, but not the realization that the Reich leader's *Primus* for *Volkskunde*, Ziegler, was deeply involved in it. Ziegler and Harmjanz, as capable professional workers, were certainly assigned by their superiors to write the many letters that are filled with so much folklore detail, or they oversaw their composition. They worked with all their might to carry out the battle in the areas reserved for them personally. Thus Rust took precautions against Rosenberg. A dossier on Kaiser presented to him by Ziegler, which the Reich leader most likely knew about, "contained, among other things, suspicions about the unprejudiced attention to detail by my professional worker [Harmjanz]." Rust had the latter's actions investigated by two lawyers in his ministry. Both verified "that not even the smallest accusation could be made in any way against this professional worker, that on the contrary he had acted absolutely correctly and humanely, and with the greatest understanding in regard to Kaiser."[427] Even this cool and holier-than-thou attitude was part of the confrontational style of Harmjanz which, most likely, cut his opponents to the quick.

Ziegler emphasized that it was not personal but rather substantial motives which separated him from Harmjanz.[428] The contested problems of dominance by one or the other folklore direction led again and again and of necessity to personal sensitivities and antipathies. After Harmjanz assumed office in the Reich Educational Ministry, Ziegler made a visit to offer his advice as representative "of the party office responsible for the general structuring of the sector of *Volkskunde*," but this new referee did not respond. The latter, on the contrary, pretended not to understand Ziegler's and the Rosenberg Bureau's desire, and when he was reminded of it later he covered up his aversion with the insulting words: "I had no time to concern myself with this, whether it was Herr Müller here or Herr Meier there who was full of flatulence." Since Harmjanz, according to Ziegler's statement, affected the work of the Working Community for German Folklore very little after this,[429] the Rosenbergians, who were now looked upon as "Tom, Dick, and Harry," declared war. Ziegler persecuted him "step by step," particularly after the takeover of the desired "showpiece" of German *Volkskunde*, the *Atlas*.[430] Still the Kaiser affair shows that Harmjanz knew how to behave congenially.

Already one year before the founding of the folklore Working Community "a small working circle of folklorists who were sound in their scholarship and in their world-view" had developed in the Rosenberg Bureau under Ziegler. In 1937, supported by further collaborators, it was "employed for the new scholarly tasks of the Working Community."[431] In addition to the Main Lectureship for Religious Studies it created the Main Lectureship for Folklore,[432] founded and directed by Ziegler within the Rosenberg Bureau, i.e., in the Reich Office for the Promotion of German Writing, also known as the Office for Literary Promotion, which was the censorship office under Reich Office Leader Hans Hagemeyer.[433] As lecturers, or better as censors, Ziegler and his comrades criticized German folklore publications from this vantage point according to the guidelines established in the *Mythus* conception of the discipline, and published their conclusions in the form of reviews in various party journals. In the beginning this working circle of folklorists was small, and Ziegler was proud of it. Harmjanz had reason to be suspicious that it was "hatching plans against him."[434] The membership consisted of scholars from the Reich Working Community, such as Ziegler himself, Strobel, and Thiele, and included the Greifswald private docent Kaiser[435] and the Leipzig *Volkskunde* professor Bruno Schier,[436] who was an energetic volunteer collaborator and a frequent speaker at meetings for Rosenbergian *Volkskunde*.[437]

In October 1936 Heinz Diewerge[438] subjected the *Habilitation* study of Harmjanz to a detailed review[439] in the *Nationalsozialistische Monatshefte*. The review addressed the importance of this very perceptive investigation of concept formulation in *Volkskunde*.[440] In spite of harsh criticisms of individual points, the theoretical accomplishments of this "innovator" of folklore is praised. Harmjanz is criticized, for example, for not treating the assumption of the confessional influence on the shaping of *Volkskunde* and for not taking into account the works of various folklore theoreticians, including von Spieß and Ziegler, or doing so in too limited a way. In conclusion the author is reminded and condescendingly advised "that he is not a pioneer and does not stand alone with his convictions and discussions, but is rather *one* in a series of similarly inclined forces"[441]—quite obviously a challenge that he join the folklore phalanx of Rosenberg. But Harmjanz did not do so.

In April 1938 the *Deutsche Volkskunde im Schrifttum* (Index of German Folklore Publications), announced by Thiele in October of the preceding year,[442] was published under the auspices of the Office for Literary Promotion and the party's Official Working Community for German Folklore.[443] This work draws together for the most part reworked and shortened reviews previously published by the lecturers of the Main Lectureship for Folklore, i.e., reviews by virtually all well-known German-speaking folklore authors of that and earlier times. As stated in the subtitle, "Guidelines for the Schooling and Educational Work of the NSDAP," German *Volkskunde* is reduced to Ziegler's "Archimedean" point, i.e., divided according to the *Volkskunde* of the *Mythus* into the various world-view camps. The guidelines are, however, stated to be available not only to party members but to anyone interested, for 1.80 Reichsmarks from the Central Publishing House of the NSDAP, Frz. Eher Nachf. GmbH.

The *spiritus rector* of this catalogue, Ziegler, remained faithful to the common practice of the Rosenberg Bureau of concealing reality. The goal, according to the subtitle and as clearly stated in the introduction, was not to establish a scholarly but rather a world-view qualification for practical schooling, "so simple and clear, but written so directly . . . , that even the simplest man out there on the school front can use it." The author was committed to this kind of simplicity in those judgments, even if there was the danger of making himself unpopular.[444]

The authors of the individual reviews were carefully left unnamed. The only person who could make himself unpopular was Ziegler, who signed the introduction, and the leader of his referee for publishing, Thiele, who was singled out by name, unlike the professional workers of the Working Community, who were only cursorily mentioned.[445] The aggressive style of the reviews as well as the introduction defamed the scholarship and the person of professional colleagues who were not acceptable to the Rosenberg Bureau and who were thus to be persecuted, particularly "the authoritative German folklorists," as Harmjanz warned.[446] The example of Spamer more than adequately documents this.[447]

In addition to several other "authoritative folklorists," judgment was also passed on Harmjanz himself. Just as in the case of Spamer, i.e., by means of the SS camarilla of the Reich Educational Ministry, now the National Socialist "innovator" of the discipline was to be brought down by the Rosenberg Bureau and his scholarly-political influence and folklore "booty piece" taken away. His *Habilitation* publication, previously praised by Diewerge,[448] is only briefly recognized in the guidelines as a "destructive confrontation with liberal folklore research, particularly with an ethnological bent." Because it lacked a presentation of the religious influence on *Volkskunde* and a racially oriented viewpoint, it had to be convincingly put down.[449] It is even worse with a second publication, his *Volkskunde und Sied-*

lungsgeschichte Altpreußens (Folklore and Settlement History of Ancient Prussia).[450] The settlement history part offered useful material, but the folklore portion broke down considerably; it seemed to be disjointed, and the necessary evaluation was completely missing. The primary thesis of the author was to be completely rejected: "Every fact of a folklore nature is based first in the soil of the folk, then in folk history, and only then in folk man." In this way the common overestimation in the past of the environment is promoted and the decisive importance of human structuring on the establishment and the growth of culture is unjustly pushed into the background.[451]

Through the fortunate discovery of the "primary thesis," Rosenbergian *Volkskunde* was put in the position of branding the folklorist Harmjanz, who rejected the blood and racial theory, as eternally outmoded. In the introduction to the guidelines, even though he is not called by name, he is singled out as the defender of a "space ideology" which runs counter to the *Mythus* world-view.[452] In the National Socialist *Monatshefte*, this time by name, he is made the representative of an "environmental thesis" and is thus associated with Naumann's liberalistic *Volkskunde*.[453] This was a damaging volley, and it had its effect on the person being reprimanded.

Harmjanz, obviously under fire from the Rosenberg Bureau, apparently gave up his antipathy to the Ancestral Inheritance and fled with his folklore "possessions," the *Atlas*, the Central Archive, and the Photo Archive, to the scholarly umbrella organization of Himmler. According to Harmjanz, Rosenberg's staff leader, Gotthard Urban, in the name of Ziegler's Working Community, had finally called for new personnel in the office of the Reich Educational Ministry run by Harmjanz and recommended the *Mythus* folklorist Henschke. Ostensibly an attempt had been made by Ziegler's Working Community to block Harmjanz's reacceptance into the SS by means of telephone calls.[454] That was not successful, and in his letter of gratitude to Himmler on June 16, 1938, Harmjanz writes: "As a member of the SS I ask you, Reichsführer to grant me the protection of the SS. For months now I have been subjected to the worst kind of hostility, both verbally and in writing by Dr. M. Ziegler."[455]

From this process of converting Harmjanz into an Ancestral Inheritance scholar, it becomes evident how professionally and existentially dangerous it was to actively oppose the Rosenberg Bureau and its "official party" *Volkskunde*, even for someone who was a high ministry officer and an NS folklorist. Harmjanz did not see the threats incorrectly, for it was only a few years thereafter that the Rosenbergians succeeded in bringing him down forever. In the meantime, however, Himmler took him in, and with his more careful and clever tactics he had gained the victory in the struggle for Harmjanz.

Ziegler, Strobel, and Karl Ruprecht were giving courses in Gmunden am Traunsee on German *Volkskunde* for schooling leaders from Austria soon after that country had been returned at the beginning of the year *"heim ins Reich"* (home to the

Reich). On July 26, 1938, the Reichsführer-SS unexpectedly visited their camp. In an interview of nearly an hour with Ziegler and Strobel, Himmler received a report on folklore questions, including the *Deutsche Volkskunde im Schrifttum*. Ziegler explained that the galley proofs had been sent to the deputy of the Reichsführer in the folklore Working Community, Hermann Reischle. Himmler thus absolved Ziegler from trying to circumvent him, but he asked for changes in a second edition of those sections concerning Harmjanz. He wanted to see them before they appeared. Furthermore, he called on Ziegler to seek an exchange of views with Harmjanz in preparation for cooperative work.[456]

During this interview Himmler knew how to awaken the impression that he was satisfied with the existence of the Reich Working Community: he wished for cooperation between it and his Ancestral Inheritance[457] and was "thinking about good terms" with Reich Leader Rosenberg himself and with his Branch Office. Ziegler appears to have taken this at face value, since it corresponded to his own desires. In any case, he reported the good news quite euphorically to his Reich leader and offered himself as the intermediary between "Scylla and Charybdis."[458]

Ziegler could have known just how inevitably the confrontations between Rosenbergians and those in the Ancestral Inheritance were determined by the "fundamental strife between Rosenberg and Himmler,"[459] and just how hopeless the situation already was in spite of the tactical ploys of Himmler.[460] He also could have surmised this from the troubled interview with Harmjanz which took place in Copenhagen on August 1, 1938, outside the International Congress for Anthropology and Ethnology, which both combatants were attending.[461] The unbridled need by Harmjanz to take revenge on Ziegler and the Rosenberg Bureau for the injustices he suffered causes one to assume that Himmler had quite consciously chosen his new vassal as a useful "spearhead" against the competition.

After the report by an angry Ziegler, the meeting continued without any positive results. They talked about a series of related matters of dispute, with reciprocal attestations of guilt, tactically hiding their own methods and intentions, in short with self-justifying one-sidedness. Ziegler complained among other things about the difficulties over the past months of getting the money applied for from the German Research Council for carrying out the scholarly tasks of his Working Community. In the past and the present fiscal years it was a matter of sums from 80,000 to 100,000 Reichsmarks. Harmjanz pretended to know nothing about these scholarly works—and thus about the applications—even though according to Ziegler all applications of over three hundred Reichsmarks to the DFG had to be presented to him. Harmjanz maintained he had nothing to do with the Kaiser case. Attempts by Ziegler and his "accomplices" to put up loquacious professors such as Adolf Helbok,[462] Bruno Schier, and Otto Maußer[463] as witnesses against him, to discredit him and his publications in the *Index*, the 1938 list of publications, represented "sowlike methods."[464]

If we can believe Ziegler's attempt to write his own self-justification, Harmjanz finally lost his patience. As a prerequisite for cooperation with him he demanded from Ziegler and his Working Community an official and public explanation. It was supposed to include an admission that "sowlike methods" were used against him, as well as a recognition that his view was the only correct one in all matters of strife. Ziegler was, of course, not ready for such an unconditional capitulation. He complained in these same words to Reichsführer-SS Himmler, to the Gruppenführer and head of the Main Office for Security of SS Heydrich, as well as to Reich Leader Rosenberg.[465]

Ziegler had, for ideological reasons, repeatedly and irrevocably opposed a folklore core team in the Ancestral Inheritance, those representatives of the Viennese "male societies" school of Germanic folk and antiquities studies so respected by Himmler.[466] Their traditional opponents were those representatives of the Viennese Mythological School who were committed to a *Mythus*-type *Volkskunde*, like von Spieß, Mudrak, and Haiding.[467] In developing his own *Volkskunde* theory, Ziegler had drawn on the Viennese mythologists.[468] In 1936, in a study with the revealing title of "Germanische Religionsforschung im Weltanschauungskampf" (Germanic Religious Research in the Struggle for World-View),[469] he condemned Otto Höfler,[470] one of the leading exponents of the male societies school and a volunteer collaborator in Himmler's Ancestral Inheritance.

Höfler's *Habilitation* study, *Kultische Geheimbünde der Germanen* (Secret Cult Unions of the Germanic Tribesmen),[471] did not correspond in the decisive axioms to the teachings of the Viennese mythologists nor of the Rosenbergians. According to Ziegler, Höfler saw in the dramatic treatment of cult customs the source of all myth and legend traditions. As correct as this thesis was, there was reason to doubt its claim for exclusive validity. This is even more the case when it is associated with the secret societies which, as can be shown, did not exist exclusively in Germanic antiquity. The members of these societies, according to Höfler, were possessed with demons and were not just representing cult demons, but had been filled in an ecstatic and frenzied experience with the certainty of their equality with these demons. They had not only felt like them, they had acted like them, and like these wild ones they attacked the peaceful world with robbery and murder. In the legends of the Wild Hoard and of the werewolf, according to Höfler, one could still see a reflection of such a Germanic secret cult.[472]

Ziegler accuses Höfler of depending on a confessional viewpoint, according to which the pagan Germanic tribesmen were overcome by a primitive fear of demons, and also of borrowing the society principle from ethnology. Höfler and his followers are thus categorized as enemies, as liberals. Ziegler is concerned with the world-view effect of "misunderstood conceptual language" in Höfler's investigation. The Germanic image of the world was, for the Rosenbergians, faithful to the *Mythus*, to "an image of order," Germanic spirit was "at all times a spirit of creative clarity," and the Germanic tribesman himself was "neither priest nor nomad nor robber, but rather an artist, a peasant, and a warrior."[473] Höfler had sinned against this indisputable gospel truth, and his failures unfortunately continued to work through his book and his school.

The conclusions or the presuppositions of Höfler's investigation are in any case doubtful because of their unproved theses and their Germanophilic prejudices. They have continued to be doubted until today by bourgeois-national and by non-National Socialist scholars,[474] not so much because of their requirements for faith as for more rational reasons. Through Ziegler's damning judgment it becomes clear how forcefully the ideology of Rosenberg—and of the Viennese mythologists— determined the perception and the behavior pattern of those who had intensified it as a replacement for belief. A tolerable cooperation between "Brown" *Volkskunde* and "world-view opponents," even with the "Black" folklorists organized within the Ancestral Inheritance, was thus impossible from the very beginning, that is, unless the primary point of the *Mythus* world-view was recognized and with all the conclusions which could be derived from it for *Mythus Volkskunde*. Himmler, who was interested in folklore, behaved more diplomatically, even though the special ideological-political attitudes and needs for power finally assumed absolute primacy.

Ziegler and his comrades in faith produced the official party publication *Index* in 1938. It documented positively a group of people without fault, who were faithful to the world-view line. It was made up of authors who represented no real difficulties in regard to their National Socialist or traditional pure German attitudes, and it included the publishers of collections of pure material. All others were left dangling, partially or completely, filtered out through *Mythus* criteria, and were filed away conveniently into such categories as liberalism and confessionalism and were found only in trendy publications that were remote from their world-view. Overlaps of several of these categories in the case of a single author were not unusual, but Bolshevists or Marxists were totally missing. Instead there were intermediate categories of "political actualists," who called "in so many words for the political actualization of *Volkskunde*" and in contrast to this "for simultaneously getting rid of the romantic world-view questioning in *Volkskunde*, i.e., together with the representatives of the liberal research epoch."[475] The *"Volkskunde"* here means Ziegler's.

Harmjanz and most probably the Viennese male society group in the SS Ancestral Inheritance are identified as "political actualists," not as "Black" folklorists in general. Lily Weiser's little book *Jul, Weihnachtsgeschenke und Weihnachtsbaum* (Yule, Christmas Gifts, and Christmas Tree) does "not proceed logically . . . in its interpretation from a Germanic-peasant world-view."[476] Her 1927 *Habilitation* study *Altgermanische Jünglingsweihe und Männerbünde* (Ancient Germanic Youth Initiation and Male Societies) presents "a collection of very varied references taken mindlessly from ethnology," builds "on false scholarly and world-view presuppositions," and must be treated "as a failed construction."[477] Richard Wolfram's *Habilitation* publication *Schwerttanz und Männerbund* (Sword Dance and Male Societies) includes "now in the realm of the sword dance the viewpoints of Otto

Höfler,"[478] and Höfler's *Dämonisierung der Glaubenswelt unserer Vorfahren* (Demonizations of the Faith World of our Forefathers) leads "to misguided and dangerous conclusions,"[479] which Ziegler had pointed out a year and a half earlier.[480]

Höfler was the "trusted man" of the Ancestral Inheritance in the Ostmark, i.e., recently annexed Austria. Wolfram[481] was supposed to begin in July 1938 directing the Salzburg Department for Germanic-German Folklore within the Regional Branch Southeast of the Ancestral Inheritance. The competition, "Brown" *Volkskunde*, took root in Salzburg in 1938.[482] According to Himmler's plan it was for the work of the Ancestral Inheritance and for his own position of power "of inestimable importance" to drop his anchor in the newly acquired Ostmark of the Reich.[483] Rosenberg thought so too. It was Ziegler himself who expanded the "Brown" folklore institution into Austria and, supported by his footmen from the Viennese Mythological School, as a power instrument of his Reich leader.

Concerning this power struggle for supremacy by Himmler's and Rosenberg's *Volkskunden*, which was now being conducted throughout the entire Great German Reich, there is not a single word in the "Secret Situation Reports" of the Security Service (SD) of the SS for the year 1938 and the first quarter of 1939.[484] There it is stated for 1938 that the official party Reich Community for German Folklore had increasingly tried to work counter to liberal and confessional forces. The League of German Societies for Folklore, under the leadership of John Meier, represented then as now a *Volkskunde* of the liberal type and was based on an ethnological and thus international foundation. By means of his League meeting held in September 1938 in Basel, he had once again proved "that he represented the reservoir of the old, liberal and confessional folklore thrust, and was neither willing nor capable of promoting National Socialist thought processes through his work."[485]

Reich Leader Rosenberg could have written this sentence. He was extremely angry about the "folklore meetings" in the Swiss city of Basel and in Freiburg im Breisgau, which he had been unable to stop.[486] Rosenberg's "Brown" *Volkskunde* answered this last demonstration of independence by the bourgeois-national umbrella organization with the quickly arranged First National Socialist German Folklore Meeting in Braunschweig.[487] Here "the unified guidelines for National Socialist racially determined folklore work were distributed for the first time to all *Gau* schooling leaders and other party branches of the Reich."[488] The meeting seems to have been successful, as reported by the Secret Situation Reports. Based on the results of the meeting, various communities, societies, and institutes had resigned from the League of German Societies for Folklore, and they had then joined the Reich Working Community for German Folklore.[489]

It remains unclear whether the leadership requirement presented by the folklore Reich Working Community could "up until now not be enacted in a single *Gau*,"[490] as it was stated for the first quarter of 1939. *Mythus Volkskunde* had no doubt not accomplished its main objective of absolute dominance in Germany, even though there was significant initial success.

The same was the case for the folklore and folklore-related departments in Himmler's Ancestral Inheritance. In 1938 or 1939 these were, insofar as we can determine,[491] the Teaching and Research Posts for Germanic Studies (under the direction of Joseph Otto Plassmann and Bruno Schweizer), Inscription and Symbol Studies (Herman Wirth and Karl Theodor Weigel), Germanic-German Folklore (Richard Wolfram), Folk Narrative, Fairy Tales, and Legendry (with the Central Archive of German Folk Narrative), and *Volkskunde* and Folk Research (with the *Atlas der deutschen Volkskunde*, (both teaching and research under the direction of Harmjanz);[492] the Research Posts for the History of Indo-Germanic Belief (Otto Huth), Germanic Architecture (Martin Rudolf),[493] and House Signs and Kinship Symbols (Karl Konrad Ruppel); and the Department of Nordic Music (with the honorary collaborator Fritz Bose).

The yearly budget of the Ancestral Inheritance from April 1, 1937, until March 31, 1938, ran around 250,000 Reichsmarks. About one-third of the total was spent on folklore and departmental and research plans which were relevant to folklore.[494]

The scholars of "Black" *Volkskunde* competed in 1939 with those of "Brown" *Volkskunde* at two public meetings of the Ancestral Inheritance, in Kiel[495] and Salzburg. During the Salzburg Scholarly Weeks,[496] which Rosenberg tried in vain to stop, as he had done one year earlier with the folklore meetings of Meier in Basel and Freiburg im Breisgau, the Second World War began, on September 1, 1939, with the attack of Nazi Germany on Poland. It was to bring, with the unconditional surrender of Great Germany in 1945, the end of National Socialist *Volkskunde* organizations. During the war the braintrust of Himmler and Rosenberg included ethnic Germans and militarily subjugated peoples of Europe; both strengthened their scholarly and "folk cultivation" endeavors and continued to expand their scholarship, including *Volkskunde*, into Reich institutions.

In comparison, the bourgeois-national League of German Societies for Folklore withered away during the course of the Second World War into a meaningless condition. With a different ending to the war and a continuation of the totalitarian rule it would most likely not have been reactivated, but rather would have been taken over before the death of its aged chairman Meier, along with the German Folk Song Archive in Freiburg im Breisgau, by the SS Ancestral Inheritance.[497] The Reichsinstitut für deutsche Volkskunde apparently planned by the Ancestral Inheritance in Freiburg im Breisgau, including the German Folk Song Archive,[498] was never realized. Therefore it must have appeared inopportune to the SS scholarly organizers to appoint the bourgeois-national scholar Spamer to the folklore chair at the University of Freiburg. Probably for this reason it was stopped by Harmjanz, the hatchetman of the Ancestral Inheritance politics in the Reich Educational Ministry.[499] It was no longer possible to think about the state promoting a non-National Socialist *Volkskunde*, its leading representatives, or its disciplinary goals, such as the bourgeois-national Reich Institute plans.

4

The Rise and Fall of the Reichsinstitut für deutsche Volkskunde

THE TWO National Socialist *Volkskunde* umbrella organizations, those of Alfred Rosenberg and Heinrich Himmler, were declared during the Second World War and after a short initial phase of uncertainty about their usefulness as being "important for the war."[1] They were supported with large sums of money given by the German Research Council to the Ancestral Inheritance and the Reich treasurer of the NSDAP to the Rosenberg Bureau, as well as by other public sources. Under the auspices of the "War Implementation by the Humanities"[2] they furthered their interest.[3] They were used by Reich Leader Rosenberg and Reichsführer-SS Himmler in the same way, for the construction of the Germanic or National Socialist world-view state as well as for defense against domestic and foreign world-view opponents, and they were to be guided in each case by a central Reich Institute for German Folklore. The rivalry struggles between the two NS camps, which were ideological and power political in nature, did not in any way cease after the initial military successes by Hitler. On the contrary, even after the war was expanded into large areas of Europe, they received more and more opportunities for implementing the primary fascist behavioral principle of the survival of the fittest in the struggle for life.

During the world war the abundance of offices of the two Reich leaders and paladins of the Führer increased, but not equally, which had an effect in the final analysis on those scholarly disciplines, such as *Volkskunde*, that were a part of their braintrust. Himmler, who was head of the regular SS, the military elite unit of the Waffen-SS, and the German police force, became at the beginning of the war the Reich commissioner for solidifying the German folk-nation.[4] In this function he employed two special service branches of the Ancestral Inheritance in the north Italian province Bozen (Bolzano) and in the north Yugoslavian area around Laibach (Ljubljana). The Cultural Commission South Tyrol, under the leadership of the Reich business leader of the Ancestral Inheritance, Wolfram Sievers, and the Cultural Commission Gottschee under the geography professor Hans Schwalm, as of 1940–1941 had to register, secure, and transfer into the new homeland, according to respective agreements with the Italian officials, the private "cultural possessions" of the South Tyroleans and the Gottschee ethnic Germans who were to be resettled in the European regions conquered by Germany.[5]

Under "cultural possessions" was understood the materials of traditional folk culture, such as narrative, song, custom, dance, symbol, etc., which were collected in South Tyrol and Gottschee by several working groups that were oriented toward different themes and who used folklore fieldwork methods.[6] In the new homeland these "traditional" expressive forms, collected by utilizing selective scholarly world-view criteria, were to be used after they had been essentially reworked by ideological experts for building and practicing of a National Socialist world-view and religion. They were supposed to help create, by overcoming the Christian tenets of faith, a fascist "master race." This concept of Himmler's SS scholars for a "Germanic folk renewal" reflects *Mythus Volkskunde* in custom, festival, and celebration planning, all the way to the celebration house in the village center which included a place of worship for the ancestors and the deceased.[7] This obvious agreement is an indication that Himmler and the Ancestral Inheritance scholars were epigones of the "chief ideologist" Rosenberg and his cohorts in the area of NS *Volkskunde* and NS folk renewal, and it makes even clearer the political power rivalry of the two camps. Their continuing battle was carried out even in South Tyrol. The initial work of a small group of *Mythus* folklorists under Ernst Otto Thiele that was allowed by Himmler at Rosenberg's request came to a quick end because of an intrigue among the Ancestral Inheritance colleagues.[8]

Another Himmler project that was an example of ideology and power politics was the Germanic Scholarly Activity Plan of the Ancestral Inheritance, set up for the militarily occupied "Germanic" states of Belgium, the Netherlands, Norway, and Denmark. It was to help realize in fact the vision of a Great German Reich under German leadership. Participating in the broadly based activity of the Germanic Scholarly Activity Plan there were German cultural scholars and folklorists as well as scholarly collaborators from several of the affected countries, all under the leadership of Hans E. Schneider.[9] Through cooperation by the two groups the problematic objective was to reveal the common roots of European Germandom, its historical continuity down to the present, and the real spatial unity, including race and family, law, speech, the folk-nation, folk belief and folk custom, myth, legend and song, house and farmstead and the creative, artistic documents of the folk spirit, and "to employ them with the willpower that resulted from this insight, in the struggle for the renewal of the German community."[10] According to the linguistic principle used by Ancestral Inheritance scholars, "renewal" was understood to mean the world-view reeducation and totalitarian political coordination of the Belgian, Dutch, Norwegian, and Danish folk.

As of 1939 Himmler's Ancestral Inheritance took part in the "salvaging action in favor of German cultural goods" in the Baltic states of Latvia and Estonia, even though according to the nonaggression treaty between Hitler and Stalin they had been declared in the sphere of interest of the Soviets.[11] They continued from 1939 to 1941 through the appropriation of public and private cultural goods in Poland. The leader of this Polish action by the Reich commissioner for solidifying the German folk-nation, this "clever robbery of foreign possessions,"[12] was the general trustee Heinrich Harmjanz and his business representative, Wolfram Sievers. Among the collaborators of this and later marauding expeditions in the Soviet Union, which had been attacked by German troops on June 22, 1941, there were other folklore scholars.

Rosenberg, just like Himmler, participated in the systematic plundering of the peoples subjugated by Hitler's Germany. The "Implementation Staff of Reich Leader Rosenberg,"[13] founded for this purpose in 1940, carried out its tasks first of all in France and then was expanded on July 17, 1941, into Eastern Europe, after Rosenberg's appointment as Reich minister for the Occupied Eastern Regions. It was ideologically self-evident to the Rosenbergians that it was a matter of "acquiring the material for a planned spiritual struggle with the world-view opponents of National Socialism."[14] A Führer decree on March 1, 1942, named these world-view opponents, Jews, freemasons, and their cohorts, declared them to be those who caused the Second World War, and set their "spiritual defeat" as a task necessary for the war. It granted Rosenberg unrestricted rights to search through and expropriate "libraries, archives, lodges, and other world-view and cultural establishments of all kinds for appropriate material."[15]

With this decree the Implementation Staff was put in a position to confiscate art and cultural objects of all kinds, especially scholarly libraries, and to bring them to Germany in order to expand Rosenberg's scholarly institutes. In the summer of 1943 there were outposts for acquiring the foreign cultural possessions in the Netherlands (Amsterdam), in Belgium (Brussels), in France (Paris), Yugoslavia (Belgrade), Latvia (Riga), Estonia (Dorpat, Reval), Poland (Vilna), in the Soviet Union (Minsk, Gorky, Smolensk, Kiev, Charkov, Dnjepropetrovsk, Simferopol), as well as in Germany itself (Füssen-Hohenschwangau). Additional outposts were planned in Africa, Greece, southern France, and Sweden. The central office was in Berlin.[16] The collaborators of this Implementation Staff were divided into "special staffs" for art, music, prehistory, etc., which for the most part corresponded to the offices of the Service Branch of Rosenberg. It comes as no surprise that on their service trips they came into conflict with the competing Ancestral Inheritance, even on the Russian peninsula of Crimea.[17]

In the Implementation Staff of Reich Leader Rosenberg there existed also a "Special Staff for Folklore," which was reported on at one of the service discussions in December 1941.[18] During the Second World War the Special Staff gave *Mythus Volkskunde* an opportunity to expand its criminal activity into the occupied regions and to enumerate "in detailed scholarly investigations the influence of German culture on the eastern regions."[19] Several of these investigations have been published, and virtually all of them slander Marxist-Leninist folklore research as well as the peoples of the Soviet Union.[20]

Even more revealing is Karl Haiding's July 4, 1941,[21] sketch in a memorandum to Reich Leader Rosenberg, "Die Aufgaben der Volkskunde bei der politischen Neuordnung Europas" (The Tasks of Folklore in the Political New Order of Europe). It is concerned with the military subjugation of the Soviet Union and the politically helpful role of *Volkskunde* in regard to the real intentions. In place of Bolshevism there must be in Eastern Europe "in part, the introduction of a rigid foreign rule, partially, however, there must also be a *cultural new order*."[22] There are three special reasons for the planned acquisition of the rich folkloric holdings of Petersburg (Leningrad) and the numerous research and collecting activities of the last decades: "1. The *cultural-political direction* and control of the peoples of Eastern Europe. 2. The *working up of the original Aryan folk tradition* which in certain areas of Russia seems to be especially well preserved. . . . 3. *The Germanic cultural influence on Russia*," which was to be pursued also among the Baltic peoples and the Finns. Haiding thus suggests creating a Special Staff for *Volkskunde* to be in close cooperation with the Outpost (Institut) Volkskunde in the Advanced School and to include all well-known folklorists, e.g., von Spieß, Mudrak, and Kulke. Like the "Outpost (Institut) Volkskunde" it was to be under the "General Direction of Dr. Hans Strobel."[23]

The Special Staff for *Volkskunde* suggested by Haiding to Reich Leader Rosenberg was apparently put in place in the second half of 1941 and was led by Strobel;[24] collaborators were Haiding,[25] Hans Lorenzen, Karl Ruprecht, Kurth Speth,[26] Thiele, Arthur Haberlandt, von Spieß,[27] and others. The Institute for German Folklore of Rosenberg's Advanced School mentioned by Haiding was founded in 1942. The Special Staff and the institute suggest a second phase in the institutional development of *Mythus Volkskunde* with which especially the names of the political leaders and scholars of the discipline, Strobel and Haiding, are associated.

Ziegler is no longer mentioned in these plans. He had asked the Reich leader one month earlier, in an interview on June 4, 1941, for his understanding that he was leaving the Rosenberg Bureau. He gave as a reason his criticism of other political leaders of the Service Branch with whom he obviously was in internal conflict; it was not a criticism of the Reich leader himself. It was only too clear to him "what I have learned under you and from you; the inner association which I have gained toward you and your work is undeniable."[28] To be sure, this upright spiritual association and further the unique usefulness of Ziegler were probably the reasons why Rosenberg waited six days, until June 10, 1941, to call for his official discharge. He did it in a curt and rejecting tone which revealed how personally he was hurt.[29]

A little later the Reich leader was to react in an even more troubled way when he learned by chance that Ziegler had made contact with the Party Chancery of the NSDAP and with Reich leader Martin Bormann. The latter highly valued Ziegler's NS soldier's breviary which had been written as a special assignment by

Bormann,[30] who now had received a memorandum from Ziegler that included a plan for establishing a central office for European religion and ecclesiastical questions.[31] Since Rosenberg protected the world-view and confessional battlefield as his own personal domain, he immediately protested to the Party Chancery.[32] Bormann, who was more than equal in sophistication to the Rosenbergians, tried to fend off the protest in a response full of deviation and deception.[33] Whether he actually was able to calm Rosenberg down is not known. In any case Ziegler moved over to the Party Chancery of the NSDAP and from this point on conducted anti-confessional works for Bormann and Himmler.[34]

With the departure of Ziegler, his superior of several years, Hans Strobel had now become the most important folklorist of the Rosenberg Bureau, since he had long ago made a name for himself as a *Mythus* scholar and political functionary. His developmental path resembles to a great extent that of Ziegler. Born on November 28, 1911, as the son of a gendarmerie officer in the Franconian village Heinersreuth, Strobel[35] completed his *Abitur* (university preparatory school diploma) in the nearby city of Bayreuth and studied Germanistics, *Volkskunde*, history, art history, geography, and geopolitics from 1931 to 1933 at the universities of Munich and Erlangen. In Erlangen he completed his doctor of philosophy degree on December 18, 1933, under Professor Friedrich Maurer with a dissertation on the place-names of his home village of Heinersreuth[36] and imbued it with a Germanistic-folkloric and National Socialist spirit.

Strobel was, like his Franconian compatriot Ziegler, a member and functionary of the pure German Youth Union the Eagle and Falcon, in which he rose during 1931–1932 to Führer (*Gauwart*) of the *Gau* of Franconia. He joined the NSDAP on December 1, 1930, one month later than Ziegler, and on November 1, 1931, he joined the SS in Munich. Within the realm of his educational work in the Eagle and Falcon union, as well as in the seminars of his studies, he found in his own words continuous opportunity to deal with racial questions and to speak and write about themes like race and art, race and culture, the politics of the population, etc. During political campaigns he occasionally appeared as a speaker and a group leader of the NSDAP.[37]

The associations gained by his political activity led Strobel to the Reich capital Berlin. Immediately after completing his studies he was appointed by the Reich commissioner for peasant customs, Erwin Metzner, on January 1, 1934, as his co-worker in the Staff Office of the Reich farm leader Darré. Strobel rose there to the position of departmental chair in Ziegler's Department for Nordic-Scandinavian Peasantry, left the Protestant Church at the beginning of 1935, and declared himself, like his superior, as "believing in god." Returning from a brief official assignment in the Racial and Settlement Main Office of the SS[38] to the Staff Office of Darré, he worked intensively in the Rosenberg Bureau from about 1936 on under the leadership of Ziegler.

He became a lector in the "Main Lectorship *Volkskunde*" of the Rosenbergian

Reich Office for Promotion of German Writing, or the Office for Literary Promotion,[39] and co-author of the guidebook *Deutsche Volkskunde im Schrifttum* (Index of German Folklore Publications).[40] He was leader of the referee for schooling of the Reich Working Community for German Folklore.[41] He was also personally associated as the leader of the referee for schooling to the Central Post for Folklore in Ziegler's Office for World-View Information.[42] On June 24, 1939, Reich Leader Rosenberg endorsed him as leader of this main post,[43] which earlier was under the commissarial direction of Thiele. In the course of its changing history it had control over the referee positions for schooling (Strobel), Germanic tribal studies (Eberhart Achterberg), folk-nation and church (Karl Ruprecht); the intermediate posts for the cultivation of scholarly associations (Henschke), game research (Kulke, later Haiding), the German farmstead (Kulke), folk custom (Strobel), the post for festival and celebration planning (Thilo Scheller); and the experimental post for folk-national studies (Thiele).[44]

After Ziegler's departure from the Rosenberg Service Branch, his Office for World-View Information was upgraded to the Hauptamt Überstaatliche Mächte (Main Office for Supra-National Powers) under Hans Hagemeyer,[45] and in 1941 the Central Post for Folklore became the Amt für Volkskunde und Feiergestaltung (Office for Folklore and Celebration Planning) under Strobel.[46] Strobel also took over the main lectorship for *Volkskunde* in the Main Office for Literary Promotion[47] and the directorship of the Special Staff for Folklore in the Implementation Staff of Reich Leader Rosenberg,[48] thereby receiving the title of Reich office leader,[49] which Ziegler had also had.

The emphasis on world-view and scholarly work by the political multifunctionary and folklorist Strobel lay in the areas of Germanic racial and peasant custom research and its application for National Socialist festival and celebration planning. He followed the ideological and methodological prescriptions of the Rosenbergian *Mythus*, the Viennese Mythological School, and the folklore theory of Ziegler. Ziegler had already called in his 1933 publication "Church and Reich in the Struggle for the Young Generation" for the development of new and organically increased festival forms for the present, from the racially pure spirit of the past by means of *Volkskunde*, in order to carry out the requirement for completeness of the total state in regard to the church.[50] Then, in his lead article of 1936–1939, he related all five canonical areas of his *Mythus Volkskunde* to National Socialist festival and celebration planning.[51]

Strobel took up the work without any difficulties and devoted himself completely to this central area of endeavor in Rosenbergian world-view scholarship and folk renewal practice. In several independent books,[52] a large number of articles which appeared in party publications and scholarly journals almost to the end of the war and were even reprinted in collections,[53] and many lectures, he presented the results of his world-view research concerning the schooling of the party, its formations, scholars, and the German folk.

Strobel's usefulness came about because of his political and ideological faithfulness of mind, his university education in the discipline, and his organizational, didactic, and publishing capabilities.[54] He was continually promoted by Ziegler and the Rosenberg Bureau. Thus he was also assigned, for example, the keynote lecture on customs at the first National Socialist German Folklore Meeting in 1938 in Braunschweig[55] and the direction-setting primary lecture of the first Working Week for Celebration Planning of the Working Community for German Folklore in 1939 in Berlin.[56] Together with the practician for celebration planning in the folklore Working Community, Thilo (Theodor) Scheller, he offered a programmatic piece on the Festival and Celebration Concept in the first volume of the Rosenbergian journal *Deutsche Volkskunde*[57] as well as an article about custom questions in Rosenberg's *Handbuch der Romfrage* (Handbook on the Roman Question), which was edited by Ziegler.[58] Strobel was able to extend his world-view schooling to the students at the University of Berlin, where he frequently accepted teaching assignments for German *Volkskunde*[59] and even taught Spamer's students.

For Strobel, racially pure custom was anchored in belief and world-view and was bound to the natural communities of the family and clan which included the entire village, the complete folk, as well as the calender arrangements of life or of the year. Custom as a part of life structuring meant more than games, passing the time, or amusements, it bore "within it the deepest imaginable moral seriousness: the task of always serving life."[60] It documented the eternal order of the universe which was part of the Germanic world image, "reflecting the forces which promoted and were hostile to life, in the eternal battle between summer and winter, day and night, seed and harvest, life and death." These counterpoles together determine "the real, the *complete* godly life." The meaning of this eternal combative reflection was, however, always the victory of life and the continual renewal of life.[61]

As a result Strobel transferred the ideologically determined fascist behavioral principle of incessant combative confrontation onto customs and celebrations. He based this "on natural laws" in the sense of "death and rebirth," i.e., "*Stirb und Werde* [die and become]." Racially it was "godly revelation," a "moral life assignment" prescribed by blood, to align oneself with this "fateful order."[62] He accomplished with the theoretical principle of customary action an outstanding contribution to the manipulation of "National Socialist" man.

The National Socialist celebrations were not primarily different, according to Strobel's theory, in their essential traits from racially pure customs. Like those they were all the expression of a world-view, based on this through belief, shaped by inner necessity, bound to their bearers, the natural communities, and part of National Socialist life structuring.[63] Their general and compulsory establishment in Germany was still lacking, except in political or national celebrations during the course of the year. They were supposed to be brought into being by means of the world-view and the scholarly leadership of the Rosenberg Bureau, and especially through *Volkskunde* in the spirit of the *Mythus*.

This *Mythus Volkskunde* preferred to reach back to the preliminary work done by the Viennese Mythological School for its celebration theory. Karl von Spieß, in *Das arische Fest* (The Aryan Festival), convincingly presented in historical and contemporary customs the following "as constitutory parts of our celebrations since time immemorial": fire, water, tree, symbolic actions (dramatic presentations), song, dance, sayings, meals (food and drink), ancestor worship.[64]

These "old traditional symbols of our world-view,"[65] which had already been combined by means of the prejudicial associations of Karl von Spieß into an ideological image, run like a red flag throughout the publications of Strobel. In 1939 they are applied by the Working Community for German Folklore, through their programmatic conception of the festival concept, to the festivals of the peasant's year (calendrical festivals) and clan festivals (personal festivals).[66]

In the theoretical studies by Strobel there are seldom concrete instructions given for the organization of racially pure celebrations, since these all arise out of living traditions in the specific community. They are to be put on "only from inner necessity,"[67] and then also only by the Führer or a member of the community, not by external schooling directors or professional middlemen.[68] Strobel on occasion passes judgment on celebrations which have failed in his eyes.[69] As a rule this is to be attributed to the opponents and competitors of the *Mythus* ideology, and through this criticism suggestions for racially pure planning are indirectly passed on.

At the pinnacle of world-view opponents of the Rosenberg Bureau and its celebration planning are, obviously for Strobel, the Christian churches and confessional *Volkskunde*. He attributes to them in his 1938 polemic a *"Bekämpfung und Gleichschaltung des Volksbrauches"* (Resistance to and Political Coordination of Folk Custom), i.e., historical and contemporary annihilation, disdain, suppression, or "ecclesiastical political coordination" of racially pure custom.[70] Applying this to the Roman Catholic church he explains on another occasion that world-view, read National Socialist celebration planning, was not so much in need of its "own new medium." Rather, "the solution to the German question of faith" could be "the occasion for creating an organization specifically for this purpose ('ersatz church' with 'consecration warders')."[71]

In this way—hidden as usual—the real political objective of the German Folk and National Church of the National Socialist world-view state is being addressed in terms of the *Mythus des 20. Jahrhunderts*. The entire celebration and life structuring of the Rosenberg Bureau is directed toward this. Strobel indirectly affirms this intentional connection himself. In one of his later and most important studies, the breviary *Zur deutschen Lebensgestaltung* (On German Life Structuring) of 1943, he summarizes once again the basic postulates of his schooling program, develops them further, and discusses portions of the planned *Mythus* cult, such as the worship forms for the soldiers or heroes who died during the Second World War and the construction style of the celebration halls with clock towers in German communities.[72] Here Strobel is concerned with *"overcoming the racially alien mythos once again with racial and organic purity."* He then adds: "And in this undertaking celebration planning can accomplish for us the best imaginable services."[73]

The leading representative of this most important working area for *Mythus Volkskunde* had first to ascertain the centuries-old "ecclesiastical political coordination"[74] of Germanic custom. Now, under the power structure of the Third Reich and faithful to the guidelines given in Rosenberg's *Mythus*, the reversal of behavior that had been accommodated by the church appeared to be politically possible. Strobel thus demands the National Socialist political coordination of church festivals and celebrations in his instructions to the schooling leaders of the party. The customs of remembering the dead, which had been taken over by the church's All Souls Festival, were transferred to November 9, the "old" May customs which the church had associated with Pentecost were to move back,[75] the "old" parade rides and meadow walks which were estranged and had been attached to pilgrimages and processions were to be *heimgeholt* (brought home) in a correspondingly purified form for National Socialist life structuring.[76]

The examples of this kind of "bringing home" could easily be multiplied, which Strobel readily admits. For "political folk-national work" lends itself here to a wide-ranging field of activity, "namely the reappropriation, the de-confessionalization and the *reacquisition of the folk's own customs.*"[77] The impression arises that the celebrations of a "National Socialist religion"[78] planned by the folkloric service branches of the Rosenberg Bureau were to be established for the most part by the appropriation and revision of the traditional festivals and celebrations of the Christian Church, with little of the ideology concealed, particularly since they did not have any other innovative ideas.

In May 1940 *Mythus Volkskunde* used a very favorable opportunity to try out its theoretical requirements in practice and to work together on the fascist political coordination of a church custom. Thiele was invited to participate as adviser in a preliminary discussion for restructuring the Corpus Christi Festival in Kirchberg in the region of Kitzbühel. Here the Catholic Church was to be completely shut out. The Brixentaler meadow ride, which allegedly reached back to a pre-Christian origin, was the largest and most beautiful rider festival of Tyrol and was to be accompanied by political leaders of the NSDAP instead of the usual clergy. Thiele reported to the Rosenberg Bureau on the successful course of the preliminary discussion in Kirchberg and asked for permission to travel there in order to be able to record on film this National Socialist "premiere."[79]

The meadow ride, which took place on May 26, 1940, a Sunday, in "purified form," was written up by Thiele and published with pictures in a house journal.[80] Around one hundred and fifty farmers from the area rode in a star shape toward Kirchberg, on festively decorated horses and accompanied by NS functionaries. At the head of the parade they were led not by church banners but rather by a storm banner from the Tirolean freedom wars at the beginning of the nineteenth century and the swastika, the "banner of the Reich." On the open field it was not a clergyman who said a weather blessing but a local peasant leader who gave a benediction. In the village of Kirchberg all of the riders rode past the *Gau* leader and the Reich governor of Tirol and circled the Maypole, not the church as in the past. Political speeches by the *Gau* leader and the local leader replaced the mass and the sermon. After a *Sieg Heil* to Hitler and his German soldiers there was a judging of the best horses on the festival grounds.

Thiele does not fail at the end of his study to list in a scholarly and critical fashion the local pre-Christian roots of the ride and the bygone misleading "church political coordination."[81] The attempt to exclude the Brixentaler clergy from the Corpus Christi ride, to simply take over the formal elements and to give the festival a totally different meaning, was carried out apparently with success. It can be assumed that it was continued in this or in a similar form at other locations.

There can be no doubt that the Christian churches would have been completely wiped out following a successful conclusion of the Second World War for the National Socialists. Hitler himself made this decision known in the war years 1941–1942, and Rosenberg knew about the Führer's will to annihilate them.[82] He had already planned this out programmatically in the *Mythus* so that he could put his own church in the place of the Christian one. There seems to have existed a principal understanding concerning the destruction of the institution of Christian churches and a National Socialist replacement among the leading ideologists and power practioners of the Third Reich, like Rosenberg and Bormann.[83] The confessional churches and their members began to suffer soon after the NS seizure of power from this existential "world-view struggle,"[84] from the suppression of their religious confessions and their meaning in private and public life.[85]

Rosenberg was certainly bound by domestic political considerations, especially during the war, to avoid what seemed to the NS regime to be the inopportune unrest of those in the populace who were faithful to the church. He was more concerned with the power claims and existing power relationships being competed for among the fascist leadership groups. These were cutting deeply into his intentions at realizing his political world-view.

Consideration of the confessions was avoided by Rosenberg wherever possible by means of his own characteristic double-tongued tactic of disguise. Thus he forbade in his "command" of January 27, 1942, in "agreement with the leader of the Party Chancery," Bormann, "until further notice," the treatment of confessional questions in general schooling work so as not to fire up some undesired confessional battle. In the same command he added, however, that the world-view schooling must be continued in a most decisive way, and allowed once again the treatment of historical and political-confessional educational questions with non-committal limitations.[86] The example of Strobel, his speeches and studies, gives ample proof of the unbroken polemic of the Rosenbergians against the church until the end of the war.

It was more difficult for Reich Leader Rosenberg to prevail over the power claims of influential party leaders such as Himmler, Reich Organization Leader Dr. Robert Ley, and Reich Propaganda Leader Dr. Joseph Goebbels, who competed with him in the area of schooling the party and the folk. Even here, however, he understood how to unscrupulously get around contractually binding competition, wherever it seemed necessary and possible, and to dupe his opponents within the party.

Nevertheless Rosenberg looked upon himself as chief ideologist of the party, the "one who proclaims a singular" world-view and the former creator of the "National Socialist religion." His ideological competence, which was widely recognized during the Third Reich, created for him and the institution in the Reich leadership of the NSDAP that carried out his political will, the Rosenberg Bureau or the Reich Overseeing Office, and gave him at least high prestige among the high functionaries of the regime. It brought out among the middle and lower functionary levels what Raimund Baumgärtner has called a "strong resonance"[87] that Rosenberg could by other means, however, not attain because he lacked the competency to administer and direct the service branches of the party and the state.[88]

In the area of celebration planning, Goebbels, Rosenberg, and Ley made a pact on May 23, 1942,[89] which was mediated by the leader of the NSDAP Party Chancery, Bormann. It gave Goebbels the responsibility for the "celebrations of the Reich and of the calendar,"[90] as well as public proclamations. Rosenberg got the internal party morning celebrations,[91] as well as the so-called nonpublic "world-view celebration hours"[92] and the "life celebrations." Ley gave organizational help at several of Goebbels's celebrations after his wide-ranging claims were wiped out by a "statement by the Führer."[93]

Rosenberg did not do badly in the pact of May 1942. He laid primary claim to the calendar celebrations which had long since been worked up, "for the most part" by his collaborators, but he seemed to be in overall agreement with the delimitation suggested by Bormann between Goebbels and himself. He rejected, however, the intrusion of Ley, whose service branch had never delivered a direct contribution to the treatment of life celebrations. These were for Rosenberg "of decisive world-view importance" and "had to be dealt with directly"[94] by him. This reflected namely "a wish by the Führer to establish clarity here," since there had been increasing inquiries by party comrades to the Party Chancery asking for the publication of "guidelines." Bormann had reported Hitler's wish to Rosenberg on April 6, 1939, and had added his own suggestions for implementation, but he had left open just which party service branch outside the Party Chancery was supposed to be entrusted with the task.[95] The Rosenberg Bureau had already looked into this. After years of correspondence and the constant support of Bormann, this was officially assigned to him by the party and the state in the pact of May 1942.

For Rosenberg's "life celebrations," Strobel was responsible through his Main

Post for Folklore, which had been upgraded to the Office for Folklore and Celebration Planning, both institutions being so to speak identical with the Working Community for German Folklore. In 1938 the Working Community had sent out a confidential questionnaire to all *Gau* schooling leaders and to the subdivisions of the NSDAP which were attached to the Working Community in order to evaluate "festival and celebration planning outside the church." One year later about 1,600 answers had been sent back.[96] In June 1939 a *Handbuch zur Feiergestaltung im Lebenskreis* (Handbook for Celebration Planning in the Life Circle) was being prepared by the Working Community.[97] And by the middle of 1942 the *Richtlinien für die Gestaltung der Lebensfeiern* (Guidelines for Planning Life Celebrations)[98] was sent from the Office for Folklore and Celebration Planning to the "service branches of the party, including the local groups of individual service branches and subdivisions."[99]

The guidelines were thus distributed over the entire Reich, into every German community. The instructions "only for service use" of the NSDAP—they were not to be used by the public—were invalidated, since they regulated birthday celebrations, weddings, and funerals through minute directions and included local officials of the party and state offices for the families of "believers in god."[100] The guidelines were too inclusive, too complicated, and thus for the simple party functionary too difficult to deal with. These instructions were followed, as had been announced, by generally understandable examples[101] for planning of the various life celebrations, some of which had already been tried out in *Gaus* of the Reich.

The local group leaders of the NSDAP or their schooling leaders were responsible for the organization and planning of these celebrations according to the guidelines. They had to take care of the celebration halls, the music, chorus, poetry, and decoration, to advise the party and folk comrades on how to carry out these celebrations. They conducted the "honoring" of children, or their mothers and parents, of bridal couples, and of the dead with a speech and a "statement by the Führer." They displayed documents and memorials, cultivated indigenous and essential folk customs, watched over racially just and appropriate world-view forms of life celebrations, and fought against kitsch, abuses, and distortions.[102]

The structuring principle was laid down so as to conform to the world-view by Strobel and his Service Branch of the Rosenberg Bureau. It was for the "life celebrations of the movement"[103] that the NSDAP conducted, like action,[104] word and honor, music and song, hall, decoration, uniform and festival dress, documents and memorials, gifts and offerings.[105] It used a series of borrowings and transformations of church customs for births, weddings, and funerals.[106]

According to statements by Rosenberg and his folklore co-combatants, it was in no way intended "to dogmatically establish the life celebrations and to turn them from the outset into petrified forms."[107] "A healthy balance of living pure German tradition and new National Socialist will to plan" was to be created. "Once and for all every new intermediary or National Socialist ersatz priesthood" should be excluded, "the family" was once again to be made the "bearer of life celebrations" and the NSDAP should "give advice or work actively where folk comrades ask for it of their own free will or desire."[108]

These programmatic statements of intent let us see the thought processes of Rosenberg's *Mythus* and the festival and celebration theory of Strobel, which together with those of Thilo Scheller in his conceptional study *Gedanken zur Feiergestaltung* (Thoughts on Celebration Planning) represent the cornerstone of the guidelines[109] and which Strobel later worked out in writing. According to Strobel's axiomatic assumption, life celebrations were shaped during the "early age of our folk" by the Nordic clans. The Führer of the clan, just like the Führer of the tribe or the folk at the celebrations of the larger communities, "was the born keeper of clan customs." As a result of the takeover of these celebrations by the Christian Church the clan community had become unfit in the course of the centuries to plan the life celebrations by itself,[110] a condition which now in the Third Reich and with the help of a National Socialist *Volkskunde* was to be set right.

National Socialist *Volkskunde*, by separating customs into racially pure and racially alien, "has to display the useful values of tradition for folk-national work and celebration planning," so that racially pure customs which are alive and capable of being transmitted can be made "once again the unfalsified goods of the folk"[111] and the clan or the family can be made the "bearers of life celebrations." In the meantime the NSDAP has the assignment of taking over the further structuring of these life celebrations and developing National Socialist forms "which later can become the customs of the German folk."[112]

Strobel's innovative statements of intent present an exemplary case for the ideological bias of the Rosenbergians. This had, however, already been thought out in principle by bourgeois-national folklorists, e.g., by Spamer in his memorandum on a Reich institute in 1936.[113] The guidelines and examples for planning of celebrations grew of course less out of "living," i.e., "pure German tradition," that were suited for transmission and came exclusively from a "National Socialist will to plan." Far from any celebration plan which derives from the "inner necessity" of the private family "community,"[114] it documents the public intermediacy of an "ersatz priesthood," the totalitarian need by National Socialism, read Rosenberg and his world-view, to rule the German folk elements with a "belief in god."

It is still necessary to ask about the resonance of the guidelines that were so boldly planned and distributed throughout the Reich, or even of the examples of planning for life's celebrations, i.e., their reception in Germany during the last years of the fascist regime. There is no exact information concerning the practice of all local party service branches and offices. This still needs to be extracted wherever possible in order to be able to determine reliably the part played by Rosenbergian festival forms at births, weddings, and funerals. Their acceptance may have been blocked by the struggle with Reich Organization Leader Ley, who had been disadvantaged through the pact of May 1942 and was thus in disfavor.

When Rosenberg complained in July 1942 to Bormann, Ley tried to thwart the collaboration of the deputy for celebrations of the *Gau* schooling leaders who were necessary for organizing life celebrations in the individual *Gaus*.[115] Measured against the "strong resonance" which Rosenberg in general was able to record at the middle and—in the case of the life celebrations especially meaningful—lower functionary levels in the communities, it is completely imaginable that there was a considerable reception of the folkloric celebration forms of the Rosenberg Bureau. In the final analysis this was what the Führer wanted, and it was supported by the Party Chancery under the influential Bormann.[116]

Viewed statistically the introduction of the "life celebrations of the movement," which were "to be separated strictly from all confessional and cultic celebrations,"[117] depended on that portion of the populace which "believed in god," and which was to increase after the final victory and the annihilation of the Christian churches. *Mythus Volkskunde* couched this future task indirectly in these words: "During the war this development will naturally proceed slowly, but after the war the problem of the life celebration must be solved for those who believe in god, also in regard to the celebration halls. These guidelines represent preliminary work in this matter."[118]

The establishment of institutes with Reichwide functional spheres for scholarly disciplines that were important for the Rosenberg Bureau reflected the power political intentions and the need for implementing ideologically conforming private and public celebrations as instruments for creating a "National Socialist religion," or the world-view cult of Rosenberg, throughout Germany. These disciplines were to be directed from the Reich institutes and were to be made useful for the *Mythus*.

For the discipline of *Volkskunde*, the Working Community for German Folklore was founded at the beginning of 1937 as a forerunner of the Reich institute. To conceal the actual and power political objectives toward the other high service branches of the NSDAP that were part of it, the Working Community answered not to the bureau but to Rosenberg himself. It was flanked already at that time by the Main Post for Folklore in Ziegler's Office for World-View Information and controlled by Rosenbergian *Mythus* directives. The Main Post for Folklore and the Office of Folklore and Celebration Planning which grew out of it in 1941 could scarcely be distinguished. Their political leaders and scholars of the discipline were frequently the same and their ideological-political objective was identical to that of the Reich Working Community. Their structural makeup, with referees or intermediate posts that were later to be taken into the Reich Institute for German Folklore, was primarily more concentrated in the political and scholarly canonical areas of the discipline. But even so, these areas are also found in the Main Post for Folklore and in the Office for Folklore and Celebration Planning, where they are listed as posts or main posts. We can thus with some justification assume a certain identity among all these "official party" *Volkskunde* institutions, as they were called.[119]

Just as the Reich Working Community had begun to establish *Mythus Volks-kunde* in the *Gau* working communities and among the *Gau* schooling leaders during the prewar period, there followed now, during the second phase of the institutional development in wartime, an attempt to achieve a "breakthrough into the realm of the universities"[120] of the Great German Reich by founding the Reich Institute for German Folklore. One can easily ascertain in the Rosenberg Bureau, in its cultural-political studies and reviews as well as in the guidelines *Deutsche Volkskunde im Schrifttum* of 1938, that the university professors had, with few exceptions, not yet gone over to a *Mythus*-type scholarship, and that they had been hindered in their traditional scholarly understanding from adhering absolutely to its ideological premises. It was now time to totally imbue the German universities with these scholarly premises that were looked upon as "believable." The universities were to be subjugated for the future to the *Mythus* and made useful.

Reich Leader Rosenberg created for himself two very different but equally important instruments which were extremely effective in their combined application. On one hand it was the official permission granted to him in 1941 by the Party Chancery under Bormann to participate in the appointment of professors to German universities, which he carried out through the Office of Scholarship of his service branch.[121] This did not result in complete success, however. Other service branches of the party and the state, like the NS Docent Union, the Party Chancery, and the Reich Educational Ministry—here particularly the SS camarilla and Heinrich Harmjanz, who belonged to the Ancestral Inheritance—took some part in the competition to select professors who were acceptable to the regime. The Rosenbergians were underrepresented in their attempts to gain university positions, and many of their nominees were without *Habilitation*, e.g., Edmund Mudrak, who came into his *Volkskunde* professorship in 1943–1944 from the Reich University in Posen.[122]

In the later years of the Third Reich a situation arose which may have made the appointment of *Mythus* scholars like Mudrak to professorial positions much easier. The Rosenberg Bureau succeeded in bringing down its archrival in the Reich Educational Ministry, Heinrich Harmjanz. He was the editorial officer for most of the humanities disciplines in the University Department of the Ministry, and was the personal referee and head of the ministerial bureau of Bernhard Rust. The effect of this intrigue must not be underestimated. It was initiated in the Main Office for Scholarship of Rosenberg's service branch against the cultural politics of the ministry and worked to the advantage of the Rosenberg Bureau.

In two letters of July 16, 1942, Reich Leader Rosenberg accused SS-Sturmbannführer Professor Harmjanz of plagiarism. One letter was sent to Bormann, the other to Himmler. Even more serious was the accusation that Harmjanz relied in several of his scholarly studies on the work of Jewish authors, an accusation Rosenberg tried to document by including a few references. He then called categorically for harsh punishment of the accused, removal from his position in the

Reich Educational Ministry, and the "initiation of a reappointment for this post through agreement with the suggestions made by my service branch."[123]

Harmjanz was furloughed from SS service on July 27, 1944, by a secret order of the Main Office of the SS Court and in the name of the Reichsführer-SS, and he was temporarily denied all his honorary SS offices, including his leadership position in the SS Ancestral Inheritance. He had already gotten around the SS disciplinary investigation in April 1943 by being furloughed from his functions in the Reich Educational Ministry and by joining the Wehrmacht. The Rosenbergians thus came out victorious in this old and bitter struggle with their familiar enemy and placed their hopes on his successor in the ministry. The none-too-strong association between the SS, or the Ancestral Inheritance of Himmler, and the Reich Educational Ministry just got worse through this Harmjanz affair and in National Socialist eyes it was eminently scandalous. After Harmjanz's departure, Rudolf Mentzel, who was the "reserve force" of the Ancestral Inheritance in the Ministry, seems to have been put under pressure by the Rosenbergians to make him submissive to their power political intentions.[124]

The other instrument of Reich Leader Rosenberg for conquering the German universities seemed to be more promising. He had been planning since 1936 or 1937[125] an alternative university, what he was calling the Advanced School. According to Bollmus, this was supposed to create a "pinnacle of the entire educational work of the NSDAP, all its subdivisions and all of the associated leagues. Practically speaking it was supposed to become an intellectual educational and guiding center for the entire German folk."[126] In addition, the results of the Advanced School were supposed to "become obligatory for the party *and* the state wherever the National Socialist idea was in question. . . . " Rosenberg had in mind "establishing certain institutes independent of universities even though most were in the closest association with universities." He assumed "in this way to help *both* parts: the Advanced School by drawing in academic recruits, and by leading the universities toward new scholarly life in the spirit of our world-view through specifically assigned tasks. Later results of National Socialist research would further yield the prerequisites for a reform of all universities. . . . "[127]

There can be no doubt that this "university reform" meant the total implementation of *Mythus* scholarship. Bollmus thus speaks correctly about the "attempt to politically coordinate the universities," which we know failed "in the inclusive way it was planned here."[128] "In the event of a National Socialist victory it would probably only have been a question of time until the alternative university would have penetrated into the corpus of the traditional university in numerous places, from whence it would have carried out the 'university reform' announced by Rosenberg . . . at least as an experiment."[129]

For one thing Rosenberg's Advanced School was supposed to get a central office in a monumental construction on the Bavarian Chiemsee. On the other hand it was supposed to be housed in the form of outposts or external institutes for certain disciplinary areas, specifically in German university cities, and be supported there at the universities.[130] This direct intrusion into state universities was aided by the attempted and partially successful personal union of the outpost leaders, as Advanced School directors and as professors at the various universities, appointed by the Reich Educational Ministry, i.e., with the assistance of the Rosenberg Bureau. Here they and their collaborators were primarily "members of the Advanced School and thus a party service branch." They had to appear at all posts of the party and of the state "as followers of Reich Leader Rosenberg," and thus they had only, as it was said so nicely, the task of a "peacemaking function" in regard to the universities and their faculties. Their real task was, in accordance with the objectives of the Advanced School, to "set that scholarship in motion which was not advancing the world-view at the universities with their ancient traditions." They were to "develop existing tendencies under the intellectual leadership of the Reich leader and organize a scholarly communal work which is clearly equipped in its world-view."[131]

The architectural plan for a monumental construction on the Chiemsee[132] never was carried out. According to a memo of 1937 from Rosenberg to Hitler, it was to have a large central lecture hall which was to be equipped with all kinds of technological media, such as an organ, film equipment, television, etc.; its own radio station; seminar, lecture, and working rooms for the four large supradisciplinary areas, or working centers for the "research on the history of the German folk and the party, the world-view opponents of our age, also philosophical-racial-pedagogical individual research, and general cultivation of culture";[133] working, sleeping, and living rooms—approximately two hundred individual rooms—for every Advanced School inmate except for the teachers, who lived in the houses separated from the main building; a large library wing for hundreds of thousands of books; working and living quarters for Hitler, Rosenberg, and the commandants of the Advanced School; buildings for schooling of the party, its service branches, and associated leagues and for an Adolf Hitler School; further, there were to be sport fields, motorboat docks, etc. The very first thing to be mentioned, however, is a large festival hall equipped with all kinds of technical media. The organ music is to be accompanied by bells in a tower and "it was perhaps later to be turned into a memorial place of intellectual and world-view warriors of German history."[134] Clearly this would have turned into the holy place for Rosenberg's world-view cult.

According to another programmatic announcement from the Rosenberg Bureau,[135] the Advanced School was divided into a department of research and teaching and a department of schooling and teaching, or schooling and education. In the research department there was a division between basic and special disciplines. Basic disciplines, which were also supposed to form main research offices, were philosophy; education, science, and sociology; *Volkskunde*; science of religion; anthropology and racial studies; biology; prehistory; the old Germanic world; German history; contemporary Germany (NSDAP); the new European world—Italy, the southeast, the east, the north, the west; and the non-European world. By far the so-called humanities disciplines dominate. Special disciplines were various branches of orientalistics, such as "Indology, Iranistics, oriental languages, but also natural science and technology," which were to be represented partially in the outposts of the Advanced School. "In every case care is taken that in all world-view disciplines a complete scholarly study can be conducted within the realm of the Advanced School and its outposts."[136]

This plan, like many of those which were not realized, sets out a division of those studying into two main groups, both of which must go through the research department to get a scholarly degree, for example the doctorate. The students of the first group will "belong to the scholarly recruits of the Advanced School (and the universities of the Reich)," whereas those of the second group "are at the disposal of the research work of the Advanced School in the educational activity of the NSDAP."[137] After they complete their study of a basic discipline in the research department and after "sufficient practical education at the schooling front" they transfer into the department of schooling and education of the Advanced School. Here they receive the scholarly-political degree of Reich schooling teacher, which entitles them in collaboration with the *Gau* schooling leaders to teach any-where they might be employed,[138] which means for the education of the NSDAP and of the German folk in the *Mythus* teachings of Rosenberg.

After years of dealings and also controversial ideas between Rosenberg and other high party leaders about carrying out this Advanced School project, it finally came to pioneering arrangements. In a written agreement among Reich Leaders Rosenberg, Ley, and Schwarz dated January 18, 1939, Rosenberg is granted re-sponsibility for the planning and structuring of the Advanced School "insofar as the Führer does not make any decisions himself." Ley is given the right to vote on the employment of the commandant, on the development, and on the educational work. Reich Treasurer Schwarz is entrusted with the construction and the admin-istering of all matters which have to do with the Advanced School at the Chiem-see.[139]

One year later, on January 29, 1940, Hitler signed the command which Ro-senberg presented to him concerning the preparatory work on the Advanced School. It was, so to speak, the chartering document. This decree by the Führer maintained that the Advanced School was to be built right after the war was over as the "central place of National Socialist research, teaching, and education." However, in order to promote the preliminary work already under way, Reich Leader Rosenberg was to continue "especially in the area of research and in the establishment of the library" and thus should receive all necessary support on the part of the service branches of the party and the state.[140] The state was not responsible for the financing of this undertaking, but rather the party, and here it was understood Reich Treasurer Schwarz.[141]

During the following years the construction of the center on the Chiemsee was postponed and emphasis was placed for the time being on the establishment of the outposts. On June 26, 1940, Rosenberg created his own service branch for the preparatory work with the departments of organization (Leader Hans-Wilhelm Scheidt), research (Leader Alfred Baeumler), administration (Leader Kerksiek), and library (Leader Walter Grothe), which was later the Central Library of the Advanced School.[142] Adding to the command of June 26 he ordered on November 1, 1940, that "all necessary measures in preparation for research at the Advanced School" were to be carried out according to his, the Reich leader's, instructions, by Alfred Baeumler and "all planning, personnel, and research proposals" were to be sent to the latter, who was then to collect them and pass them on to Rosenberg.[143]

After Scheidt's transfer into the Reich Ministry for the Occupied Eastern Regions, the Planning Office of the Advanced School in Preparation[144] was developed in 1942 by Baeumler and was under the deputy direction of Dr. Kurt Wagner. It was responsible for all portions of the "preparation." Baeumler, who was a professor of philosophy and the former head of the Office of Scholarship in Rosenberg's Service Branch,[145] was to a certain degree the chartering rector of the Advanced School in Preparation, if one does not attribute this function to Rosenberg himself. But it was Baeumler and his deputy Wagner[146] who decisively rejected *Mythus Volkskunde* that was based on the theories of the Viennese Mythological School. This was to have an effect on the folklore outposts of the Advanced School. In addition to personal confrontations which were passed on from the Ziegler era[147] to the era of Strobel,[148] the negative criticism of Baeumler and Wagner of the Viennese mythologists Spieß, Mudrak, and Haiding, was to turn into a basic frontal assault. One can thus assume that the office establishing the Advanced School in Preparation followed partially differing concepts from those of Strobel and Haiding in the building of an Institute for German Folklore.

Using the Führer's decree of January 29, Rosenberg ordered on October 30, 1940, the establishment of outposts of the Advanced School. They were research institutes and received their research assignments from Rosenberg personally. He also appointed and removed the leaders and the collaborators. The administration, i.e., all financial matters, was under the control of Reich Treasurer Schwarz.[149]

By the end of the war several outposts or institutes had been developed: the Institute for Research on the Jewish Question in Frankfurt am Main (under the leadership of Wilhelm Grau and Klaus Schickert), for Religious Studies in Halle/Saale (under Wilhelm Brachmann), for Overseas Research and for World-View Colonial Research in Hamburg (under Adolf Rein), for National Socialist Folk Cultivation in Marburg an der Lahn (under Richard Benzing), for Indo-Germanic Intellectual History in Munich (under Richard Harder), for Biology and Racial Studies in Stuttgart or Schelklingen/Württemberg (under Walter Gross, represented by Werner Hüttig), and for German *Volkskunde* in Berlin and Monastery Rein near Graz (for the duration of the war under the commissarial leadership of Haiding). There were in addition the Research Post for Educational Science in Nürnberg (under

Karl Seiler), the Central Library of the Advanced School in St. Andrä near Villach/Carinthia (under Walter Grothe),[150] and the Institute for Research on Bolshevism (under the deputy leader of the Office for Scholarship in Rosenberg's Service Branch, Heinrich Härtle).[151] At least five of the outpost leaders—Brachmann, Rein, Benzing, Harder, and Seiler—were also professors at the local universities.[152]

Planned were institutes for research on freemasonry in Frankfurt am Main, for eastern research in Prague, for research on Germanism and Gallicism in Straßburg, for Germanic research or German-Scandinavian relationships in Kiel, for folk welfare cultivation in Tübingen, and for art education in Leipzig, Munich, or Dresden.[153] Negotiations took place for taking over the Institute for Eastern Work in Cracow[154] and for the construction of outposts in Vienna, Agram (Zagreb, Yugoslavia), and Amsterdam.[155] The preparatory planning included the Hoheneichen publishing company[156] as the "publisher of the Advanced School, Hoheneichen-Verlag";[157] two working communities of the Rosenberg Bureau, one for continental European research and another for research of the relationships between world-view and practical life structuring;[158] and six areas of the Advanced School, for music, art, theater, prehistory and early history, philosophy, and educational science. This latter one was to be coordinated with the already mentioned Nürnberg Research Post for Educational Science[159] and the Working Post for Celtic Research[160] as obvious preliminary stages of the outposts.

Complete files on the plans no longer exist, since the main building of the Rosenberg Bureau in Berlin was destroyed on November 22, 1943, during an air raid and thus a large portion of the files on the construction of the Advanced School were wiped out.[161] The attempts by the Rosenbergians to establish their *Volkskunde* at several universities nevertheless allow us to reconstruct at least in part the origins of the Institute for German Folklore by using those portions of the files which we have.

Already during the prewar phase of the Advanced School planning, Matthes Ziegler wrote—glossed over for outsiders—about a "healthy and necessary development and reconstruction of the humanities and especially the folk-historical scholarly disciplines which perhaps could not be seen in their entirety."[162] In February 1939 a Berlin ministerial councilor, J. Roth, had "told him very *confidentially*" about the removal for ecclesiastical-political reasons of the Catholic theology faculty at the University of Munich that would open up about ten ordinary teaching positions. He had recommended that several of them be requested for the humanities, especially for the coming Advanced School on the Chiemsee, for which Munich would be the nearest university. Roth made the proposal that "this be presented to the Herr Reich Leader so as to be able to lay out a plan of action at that moment when the removal of the Catholic faculty is finished and is made public." Ziegler responded to the man who delivered this information with gratitude and a request for two chairs, one for religious studies/*Volkskunde* and one for religious history.[163]

Rosenberg, who from the very beginning of this action had been kept completely informed by the man pulling the strings, Bormann,[164] succeeded in having the teaching chairs vacated by the closing of the Munich Catholic faculty at the end of February 1939. They were to be assigned by Reich Educational Minister Rust to scholars who were close to his service branch. Of these, however, no one was appointed with the exception of the Kiel classicist Richard Harder, who thereafter directed the Advanced School Outpost for Indo-Germanic Intellectual History. The attempts by Rosenberg for the rest of the teaching positions came to naught. The resistance of the Rosenberg opponents, among them Rudolf Mentzel from the Reich Educational Ministry and the rector of the University of Munich and head of scholarship for the SS Ancestral Inheritance Walther Wüst, was clearly more successful. The Reich Finance Ministry consistently hesitated in the continuing negotiations until well into 1943 to release further professorial positions during the war and to refill them.[165]

Wilhelm Brachmann, a collaborator of Ziegler's in the office of World-View Information and later leader of the Outpost for Religious Studies at the University of Halle/Saale,[166] suggested in 1940 an Advanced School institute "for researching of Aryan intellectual history (within the philosophical faculty) of the University of Munich." A chair for *Volkskunde* was also planned,[167] or as it was sketched out by Brachmann in the Advanced School project, "a new faculty in Munich" with the "objective of a revolutionarily restructured university" including a chair for "*Volkskunde* (German contemporary *Volkskunde*)."[168] The appointment of a scholar from the discipline recommended by Rosenberg for this folklore professorship had already been set forth by the Reich educational minister at the beginning of 1942.[169] It was Kurt Ranke, at that time a docent at the University of Kiel,[170] who had possibly been recruited by Richard Harder along with candidates from other disciplines.[171]

Ranke was supposed to receive the *Ordinariat* for German *Volkskunde* and antiquity studies. He was among the final six professors for classical antiquity studies (Professor Harder, University of Kiel), pre-Indo-Germanic cultures of the Mediterranean Basin (Docent Heidenreich, University of Leipzig), Assyriology (Professor Falkenstein, University of Göttingen), Indo-Iranian antiquity studies (Dr. habil. Anatol Waag, German lector in Agram/Zagreb), and the representative for the secondary discipline Slavic folklore and antiquity studies (Dr. Alois Schmauß, leader of the German Scholarly Institute in Belgrade).[172] Together with the other new appointees to the positions of the former theological faculty the goal was to "be able to make positive contributions to solving of foreign world-view traditions by means of an Indo-Germanic one."[173] Based no doubt on his qualifications for this assignment, Ranke had also presented a paper in 1939 at the Kiel meeting of the SS Ancestral Inheritance, which was also interested in him.[174] The professorship which he wanted was not supposed to be flanked by a central "Reich" Institute for German Folklore. Instead, the folklorist and antiquities scholar Ranke was supposed to be integrated into the Rosenbergian Institute for Indo-Germanic Intellectual History.

The attempt to moor *Mythus Volkskunde* as an independent institute of the Advanced School at a university was undertaken in Münster in Westphalia. Here the institutes for *Volkskunde* and foreign studies of Professor Georg Schreiber were closed by the Secret State Police and the extensive book collections, including the Görres Collection from Freiburg im Breisgau, as well as cash sums of 300,000 to 350,000 Reichsmarks were confiscated.[175] This action was conceived by Ziegler and reached back to an announcement by Rosenberg on October 22, 1938, to the Party Chancery.[176] Rudolf Heß, deputy of the Führer, had decided then "that there were no objections to stopping the political and questionable world-view activities of Prelate Dr. Schreiber in his German Institute for Folklore, but also in his German Institute for Foreign Studies." Heß wished, however, that the "extensive material" collected by Schreiber in his institutes and "especially the extensive relationships of these institutes domestically and abroad" should remain intact insofar as possible. Rosenberg should make his suggestions as soon as possible "in what form the valuable acquisitions of these institutes [could] be maintained most purposely under National Socialist leadership." Thus wrote Bormann on February 4, 1939, in a letter, a copy of which was sent immediately from the Rosenberg Chancery to Ziegler.[177]

Rosenberg first wanted to establish the Advanced School Outpost for German Folklore, with the help of the institute holdings of the persecuted and dispossessed prelate and in connection with Himmler's Ancestral Inheritance in Detmold,[178] but then later in the university city itself (Münster). This was so that, as the Rosenbergian Hans-Wilhelm Scheidt expressed it, "in the chain of development of the *Volkskunde* question, Münster would quite demonstrably be the last link of the chain closed, where National Socialist scholarship would occupy the building of the Catholic *Volkskunde* pope."[179]

In conjunction with this goal the second National Socialist German Folklore Meeting of the Rosenberg Bureau was planned for Münster from October 1 to 8, 1939. It was to include an exchange of experiences by the *Gau* schooling leaders concerning festival and celebration planning during the course of the preceding year and with a special exhibition, "Folk Art Implements for Festival and Celebration Planning," for which contributions were requested from the *Gaus*.[180] The outbreak of the Second World War on September 1, 1939, caused the meeting to be called off.

The original plan to place the institute in Detmold was changed in favor of Münster because Himmler did not follow through with his agreement for possible collaboration between the Ancestral Inheritance and the Advanced School Institute for Folklore,[181] even though he had stated this in an interview with Rosenberg. On the contrary he, as chief of the German police, did not release Schreiber's library, which had been requisitioned for the work of the Advanced School.[182] Himmler's resistance possibly caused the plan for an Outpost for German Folklore to collapse, even though there were continuing negotiations with the local *Gau* schooling leader, the university curator, and the senior mayor as well as planned petitions to the Prussian finance minister and the Reich educational minister.[183]

At the end of April 1941 the negotiator and leader of the Advanced School Organization Department, Hans-Wilhelm Scheidt, had suggested to Reich Leader Rosenberg that the head of the Office of Scholarship, Alfred Baeumler, had to "take up negotiations immediately with Herr Reich Minister for Folk Education concerning the transfer of the chair for *Volkskunde* at the University of Münster to Pg. Dr. Strobl [sic]. (Here one must proceed exactly as in the case of Brachmann)."[184] The sketch written by Reich Leader Rosenberg, "Description of Assignments for the Outpost of the Advanced School, Münster. Institute for German Folklore," seems to have been directed in substance toward the scholarly-political work of Strobel.[185]

The institute clearly planned for Strobel received the "central task of researching the various elements of German symbolism in German customs, separating them from various confessional overlays and presenting the continuity of the oldest traditions down to the present." From this research it will then be possible to "make a selection of those elements which are useful for modern National Socialist custom planning." But even the newest NS custom must be researched, since it too will also be part of German customs in the future.[186]

Further assignments for the Münster institute are the collecting of the entire corpus of writings concerning German *Volkskunde*, the integration of all large individual research undertakings (the folklore atlas, etc.) into the planned tasks, the preparation of extensive picture and map materials, and the establishment of connections in a number of German *Gaus* "in order to carry out research directly and to avoid any purely literary work." Beyond the borders of the German Reich it will be necessary "to test the customs of ethnic Germandom in other countries and to publish this as part of the common richness of German folklife." Here it is necessary to establish a connection with the German Academy, which has the task of researching German cultural accomplishments abroad.[187]

This is Rosenberg's Reich institute plan for the discipline of German *Volkskunde*. It follows on one hand in many ways the previous outlines of bourgeois-national folklorists such as John Meier and Adolf Spamer.[188] On the other hand, it clearly exemplifies the specific ideological thought processes of the autodidactician Rosenberg and his *Volkskunde*. Since the plan could not be carried out at that time at the Westphalian University of Münster, another way was found. Under the limited conditions of the war years a provisional Institute for German Folklore was founded at the seat of the Rosenbergian Service Branch in the Reich capital Berlin. It could later be moved as an Advanced School outpost to a traditional university—as Rosenberg and his collaborators planned, e.g., into the Ostmark university city of Graz.[189] Indeed it was housed in the vicinity for the first years of its existence, which were to be its last.[190]

Before the founding of the Institute for German Folklore in the Center for the Advanced School in Preparation on June 5, 1942,[191] its research posts were developed out of the intermediate posts of the Reich Working Community for German Folklore and were financed by internal funds approved by the Reich treasurer of the NSDAP. These research posts were in folk belief and folk custom, or folk custom studies, under the direction of Strobel in Berlin with 935 Reichsmarks monthly; folk games (game research), or games and sayings, under Haiding in Berlin with 1,425 RM monthly; folk speech under Prof. Dr. Bernhard Martin in Marburg an der Lahn with 3,260 RM monthly; costume and decoration under Dr. Gertrud Pesendorfer in Innsbruck with 1,270 RM monthly; German farmstead, or farmstead and settlement, under Dr. Erich Kulke in Berlin or Schöneiche near Berlin with 700 RM monthly; folk belief, or peasant life forms, under Dr. Karl Ruprecht in Salzburg with 1,215 RM monthly; folk art and handwork, formerly the Experimental Post for Folk-National Studies, under Dr. Ernst Otto Thiele in Berlin; and, as a new enterprise, myth studies under Prof. Dr. Karl von Spieß with the collaboration of Dr. Edmund Mudrak in Vienna. The last two research posts applied for monthly support of 2,100 or 1,680 RM respectively.[192]

Out of the Intermediate Post for Festival and Celebration Planning in the Working Community for German Folklore[193] there developed the "teaching post for celebration planning" with a monthly stipend of 33,300 RM for "steering the *life* celebrations within the movement," according to the mandate given to Rosenberg by the Führer. It was to be located within the walls and the accommodations of the celebration place Stedingsehre in the *Gau* of Weser-Ems[194] of Rosenberg's personal friend, *Gau* Leader and Reich Governor Röver. According to a command by Rosenberg on July 2, 1942, however, it was taken over by the Rosenberg Bureau and was placed temporarily in Berlin, under the direction of Thilo (Theodor) Scheller. Once again it was excluded from the Advanced School in Preparation and thereby from the Institute for German Folklore. In Berlin it was "essentially responsible to the Office of Folklore and Celebration Planning," i.e., its leader Strobel. The task of the teaching post was "to work up the foundations and the plan for National Socialist celebrations, to test them and supply them to the responsible leadership of the entire movement. It is urgent that the prerequisites for planning of life celebrations be created. In order to carry out these tasks, teaching programs are to be instituted."[195]

Strobel was an authority in the planning and later participated in the working organization of the Institute for German Folklore. At the end of 1941 he presented the monthly budget for the research posts, which—excluding the teaching post for celebration planning—received 8,805 RM, i.e., 105,660 RM yearly. There was also the yearly budget for the institute still to be founded in the sum of 156,840

RM (including the teaching post for celebration planning, it was 399,600 RM).[196] The leadership of the new institute was not taken over, however, by Strobel. The reasons for this decision by Rosenberg and probably also by Strobel are clear.

The plans did not materialize for moving Strobel's research post "folk custom," or "folk belief and folk custom,"[197] to Münster in Westphalia.[198] In the later war years it does not show up much and was almost inactive, and the Rosenbergian plan to appoint him to a *Volkskunde* professorship at the university there did not come about. The *Primus* of *Mythus Volkskunde* was hindered by other important tasks, including his administrative duties, from taking over the leadership of the provisional Reich institute, as Haiding had suggested.[199] Strobel was simply not available for this less topical assignment.

Haiding was named instead as the director of the Institute for German Folklore on its charter day, June 5, 1942, but only "for the duration of the war."[200] This limitation may reach back to the machinations of Baeumler and Wagner. It was on the other hand based on the personality and the scholarly qualifications of Haiding, who was clearly controversial in the planning office of the Advanced School in Preparation. Before the end of 1943 Kurt Wagner recommended that because a "successor for Dr. Haiding is not available at this time," the latter "be left alone for the time being, but (a) his functions on the technical side in the preparation of the Folklore Institute be limited, and (b) he remain as director for only one year, which means from now until December 31, 1944. We would accomplish by this continuation having a director for the institute, but the scholarly plans by Spieß and his circle, which do not match the central plans of the Advanced School, would not be incorporated."[201]

This was not the only negative judgment passed on the commissarial institute director. Of significance for his appointment was the lack in Rosenberg's Service Branch of better-suited scholars of the discipline, his miserable health condition which made him, in contrast to most of the other political leaders, unfit for military or war service,[202] his frequently attested and unwavering faithfulness to the political idea of the *Mythus*,[203] and his undeniable eagerness to do his duty. Until his appointment as the caretaker of the Reich institute, which was continually under preparation, he was always in the second row but was granted important political assignments. Even his family name was a second choice.

Karl Paganini was born on July 3, 1906, in Vienna and completed his first degree at the Federal Technological Trade School for Construction. As a construction worker he financed the second or complementary degree, which he began in 1929 at the University of Vienna and completed in 1936 with a dissertation for his Ph.D. on children's games[204] under Arthur Haberlandt. In 1923 in Vienna he became a member of the NSDAP and temporarily led the NS local youth group Gersthof. In 1924 he joined the Free Corps Oberland, and in 1929, just when he began his studies, he joined the Austrian Federal Army. He was discharged in 1933 for political reasons, i.e., as a sympathizer with the National Socialists. In

1933 he renewed his NSDAP membership, which he had given up during this four-year stint as a professional soldier. In the spring of 1935 he successfully appealed to the Viennese magistrate to change his Italian family name Paganini into Haiding, because the church "formerly called the rural populace who did not want to accept Christianity 'Paganini,' i.e., heathens."[205]

After this controversial Nordicizing of his name[206] and the origins of his family, which excellently fit in with Reich Leader Rosenberg's *Mythus* ideology, this convinced supporter of the Viennese Mythological School[207] emigrated to Nazi Germany. It offered him a secure professional existence in the cultural office of Baldur von Schirach's Reich Youth Leadership, something he did not have in his Austrian homeland. Haiding belonged to this office without interruption until well into the first half of 1943. In 1938 he acquired the rank of Obergefolgschaftsführer and became a main referee.[208] Only then was he placed formally in Rosenberg's Advanced School and paid from there—incidentally for the first time in his professional career, and with a considerable sum.[209] The Reich Youth Leadership had made him available to the Reich Community for German Folklore as of January 5, 1937, its founding day, and to its leader Rosenberg, as a scholarly collaborator and a political functionary. It was thus Reich Leader Rosenberg who offered the great chance of a lifetime, as Haiding said, and for which he frequently expressed his gratitude. Haiding-Paganini, who had up until then been neglected and disadvantaged, was now named the commissarial Reich institute leader on June 5, 1942.

According to a decision made by Rosenberg in 1942, the Institute for German Folklore was "not, like the other institutes of the Advanced School in Preparation, to build up its own extensive research apparatus, but rather . . . have the scholarly works carried out essentially by the already existing research posts. Only that which must be accomplished for the unified direction of works by the research posts and for the political evaluation of that work (creation of scholarly bases for political folklore work, including celebration planning), should be taken up by the institute itself." A relatively small personnel staff would be sufficient for this limited activity. In addition to the director there would be a scholarly specialist, a scholarly assistant, a librarian, a photographer, a secretary, and one typist.[210]

Even in the year of founding Rosenberg did not intend to make the institute into an outpost during the war years. Only after the war was over was a decision to be made about the final location. The institute was to belong for the present to the Center for the Advanced School. The commissarial director, in addition to the institute and his own Research Post for Games and Sayings, was also the director of folklore research in the *Gau* of Styria. Because *Gau* Leader Uiberreither placed emphasis on his presence, Rosenberg agreed to transferring the service office of Haiding and his few collaborators there. Reich Treasurer Schwarz agreed to rent the necessary space,[211] which was found in the Monastery Rein near Graz.[212] The Research Post for Games and Sayings moved with Haiding from Berlin to Styria.

Individual works accomplished before the end of the war by the scattered research posts of the Institute for German Folklore still need to be researched.[213]
They were in and near Berlin and in Marburg an der Lahn, Vienna, Salzburg,
Innsbruck, and the Monastery Rein. Institute Leader Haiding's activity was marked
by an abundance of political contracts and a corresponding disunity. From the
beginning of 1942 he was wartime editor[214] for Rosenberg's journal *Deutsche Volkskunde*.[215] He had also been employed ever since its founding by the Special Staff
for Folklore in the Implementation Staff of Reich Leader Rosenberg.[216] In March
1943 he reported that he soon wanted to "begin with the practical implementation
in the ethnic German forest villages in the Carpathians,"[217] whatever he might
have meant by that. In April 1943 he reported, "based on his trip, concerning the
relationship between Lithuania and the Reich."[218] He was moved by the question
whether, in one of the "cemetery primers" planned by Rosenberg's *Volkskunde*,
"monuments in the shape of a cross" should be considered.[219]

In November 1943 the establishment of the institute in the Monastery Rein
"was so far advanced that a plan of work for all research posts can begin more
energetically."[220] This work plan still consisted of confrontations between Haiding
and Thiele, for each one despised the other. During Thiele's work in the Ministry
for the Occupied Eastern Regions, Haiding had taken all of Thiele's collaborators
in the Research Post for Folk Art and Handwork without asking him.[221] Or there
were confrontations between Haiding and the touchy Professor Bernhard Martin,
who wanted to publish a book concerning the name given to potatoes as a valued
institute publication, and whom Haiding tried to convince otherwise.[222] Only with
the entrance of Reich Leader Rosenberg or of Strobel, who traveled to Marburg
an der Lahn, were they able to calm the angry seas.

On the other hand, Haiding himself, who wanted to start "by carrying out our
work in the scholarly confrontation . . . immediately with works for the public,"[223]
was stopped by the Planning Office of the Advanced School and was thus saved
from blind activity. A list found in the archives[224] reveals that the publications
planned by Haiding were for the most part republications of well-known narrative
anthologies. Kurt Wagner kept the ideas of the Reich leader before Haiding's eyes,
noting that the publication of "*Märchen* collections and such was not the task of
the Advanced School."[225]

Haiding's duty-conscious working reports from the Monastery Rein to the Planning Office of the Advanced School or to his personal friend Strobel speak for
themselves against scholarly or politically meaningful activity by the Central Office
of the Institute for German Folklore. Here the talk is about conferences with party
functionaries and scholars, about folklore lectures and practicums of the Herr director in smaller circles of students, teachers, Styrian schooling leaders, ethnic German girl kindergartners, members of the leadership school of the Union of German
Girls near Rein, of folklore collecting in camps of resettlers from the east, of

Haiding's collaboration with the Styrian newspaper *Sonntagsblatt*, of a celebration on the Führer's birthday, and after completing folklore practicums, a children's festival in Rein.[226]

All of this is covered over by Haiding's concerns for the future of Rosenbergianism. He had not been able to speak to the personal referee of the Reich leader, Dr. Koeppen, on his last visit to Berlin. Haiding thus decided to write a personal letter to Koeppen, literally—"the relationships in the daily life of the local group and of the community [Rein], reveals however a considerable weakness in regard to world-view opponents [the Catholic church], which cannot be overcome by propaganda." Here it is a matter of the core question: "Will it still in the next few years be possible to reap the successes of the *Mythus* by having several men, who see clearly and who are pure and capable, create the foundations for individual areas and implement them politically? For the entire life work of Rosenberg is one of the most indispensable prerequisites for making National Socialism a reality in our folk, through which we can then crown peace with a victory."[227]

Haiding's worries were more than justified. The Second World War and with it the totalitarian National Socialist regime were nearing their end. Rosenberg bore to a large degree the intellectual guilt for the inhumanity and the expansion of an orientation toward a racial-religious world-view state for the future. In the interest of total war and the mobilization of all available forces for the "final victory," Rosenberg, under pressure by Bormann,[228] had released all men and women collaborators of his service branches in the Reich leadership of the NSDAP, including those of the Advanced School in Preparation, for immediate deployment to the war front.

From the detailed personnel lists or post plans of 1944,[229] only a little information can be extracted. In the working areas of the Advanced School during the last three years, twenty-two establishments were carried out, for which the "Reich treasurer, in agreement with the Party Chancery—in consideration of the war conditions—[had approved] 272 planned posts." Of these, in August 1944 only 123 (and twenty-eight honorary posts) were still occupied, since previous war-determined measures of February 1943 had led to a limitation "of the very small personnel apparatus to less than 50 percent, considering the emergency conditions of war." According to this tabulation on August 12, 1944, by Dr. Kurt Wagner from the Planning Office of the Advanced School, the Institute for German Folklore had "employed all together only twenty-two workers in its seven research posts."[230] According to a second tabulation dated November 1, 1944, i.e., after the closing down of the establishments of the Advanced School, 111 workers were released from the Institute for German Folklore and its seven research posts. Names were laid out in precise lists, including the few people who remained and were recorded according to their activity and the institution to which they belonged.[231] This noticeable difference could be explained by the fact that the majority of the personnel were paid from budgets other than those of the Advanced School, a common practice in the Rosenberg Bureau.

Haiding, who was not fit for deployment in the war, received the responsibility in November 1944 of carrying on in Rein near Graz. At the request of Strobel it was "for the duration of my absence" and "as my representative for folklore matters" of the Rosenberg Bureau, "including the Special Staff for Folklore in the Implementation Staff of Reich Leader Rosenberg." In support of Haiding, party comrades Dr. Rosemarein Rossbach and Dr. Kurth Speth were being considered.[232]

The last months still left for the Third Reich were spent by Rosenberg in his office in Berlin and by Haiding in the Styrian monastery. Both men were increasingly isolated in surroundings which were becoming more and more inimical. Nevertheless, Haiding sent his Reich leader at Christmas 1944 and New Year's 1945 "also in the name of all collaborators of the institute, best wishes" and his final faithful confession: "More than ever before the past months have shown what a decisive meaning the world-view has which we are fighting for as your followers. Thus the new year shall also find us without fail at work."[233]

Haiding's wishes and hopes were clearly illusionist. The dream of a Reichsinstitut für deutsche Volkskunde was now finally vanishing because of the rapidly advancing National Socialist *Götterdämmerung*[234] and the downfall of the Third Reich.

Guide to the Appendixes

I. Documents of the Rosenberg Bureau

1. Circular to Found the Working Community for German Folklore, January 1937 (complete)

2. Report of the 2nd Meeting of the Working Community for German Folklore, October 1937 (slightly abbreviated)

3. Theses from the *Mythus* of Alfred Rosenberg 1939 (excerpts)

4. Memorandum: Alfred Rosenberg's "The Advanced School of the NSDAP and Its Tasks" from June 1937 for Presentation to Adolf Hitler (excerpt)

5. Führer's Order of 1940 to Establish the Advanced School in Preparation (complete)

6. Command by Rosenberg to Establish Outposts of the Advanced School 1940 (complete)

7. Command by Rosenberg to Found the Institute for German Folklore 1942 (complete)

8. Central Offices and Offices of the Service Branch [Rosenberg Office], Institutes of the Advanced School, Research Posts of the Institute for German Folklore 1944 (excerpt)

9. Matthes Ziegler, "Folklore on a Racial Basis: Prerequisites and Tasks" 1939 (complete)

II. Documents of the SS Office of Ancestral Inheritance

1. Departmental Directors' Meeting in Munich 1941 (excerpt)

2. Memorandum on the Office of Ancestral Inheritance 1944 (complete)

III. Documents by German Folklorists

1. Call by the Union for German Folklore, Inc. 1933 (complete)

2. Adolf Spamer, Unpublished *Reichsinstitut* Plan 1936 (excerpts)

3. John Meier, "Ultimate Goals of Research" (Conclusion of a Larger Work) 1940

Appendix I.1
Circular No. 1/1937
The Working Community for German Folklore

German National Socialist Workers Party. Reich Administration. The Führer's Commissioner for all Intellectual and World-View Education of the NSDAP. Berlin W 35, January 5, 1937. Margaretenstr. 17.

In view of the steadily growing importance of folklore for the work of schooling and educating the party, Reich Leaders Darré, Hierl, Himmler, Rosenberg, and von Schirach, who participate directly in questions about folklore through their fields of competence, have concluded the following agreement:

1. To guarantee a permanent collaboration in the area of folklore, Reich Leaders Darré, Hierl, Himmler, Rosenberg, and von Schirach have founded an Arbeitsgemeinschaft für deutsche Volkskunde [Working Community for German Folklore].

2. The Working Community sees as its assignment the warding off of ideological opponents of National Socialism in the area of folklore research and in practical folklore work as well as in advising all party offices [*Parteidienststellen*] interested in questions on folklore. This assignment does not affect the particular plans, tasks, and works of the individual party offices and organizations, nor the absolute responsibility of their leaders.

3. Belonging to the Working Community are: Central Office Director SS-Brigadeführer Dr. Reischle as commissioner of Reich Farm Leader R. Walther Darré and of Reichsführer-SS Heinrich Himmler, General Work Führer Dr. Will Decker as commissioner of Reich Work Führer Konstantin Hierl, Senior Battalion Leader Brennecke as commissioner of Reich Youth Führer Baldur von Schirach, and Chief Post Leader Dr. Matthes Ziegler as commissioner of Reich Leader Alfred Rosenberg. The Working Community will be directed by the Führer's commissioner for the supervision of all intellectual and world-view schooling and education of the NSDAP, Reich Leader Alfred Rosenberg. The aforementioned Reich leaders welcome into this Working Community the dispatching of commissioners at other party offices interested in questions on folklore.

4. The Working Community will establish topical offices for the execution of their assignments. Guidance for these offices lies in the hands of SS-Obersturm-

führer Dr. Matthes Ziegler, leader of the Central Post for World-View Information, for the Führer's commissioner for the supervision of all intellectual and world-view schooling and education of the NSDAP, Berlin W 35, Margaretenstrasse 17 (telephone: B.2. [Lützow] 9541).

In agreement with Reich Leaders Darré, Hierl, Himmler, and von Schirach, I have appointed as topical referees to the Working Community for German Folklore, which is under my direction:

For the *Office on Schooling*: SS-Hauptsturmführer Dr. Hans Strobel, Staff Office of the Reich farm leader.

For the *Office on Festival Development*: General Work Führer Dr. Will Decker.

For the *Office on Folk-National Work*: Dr. Karl Haiding, Cultural Office of Reich Youth Leadership.

For the *Office on Scholarship*: Dr. Karl-Heinz Henschke, referee for the Führer's commissioner for the supervision of all intellectual and world-view schooling and education of the NSDAP.

For the *Office on Press and Literature*: Dr. Ernst Otto Thiele, leader of the Regional Institute Kurmark for Folk Research.

Berlin, January 5, 1937   Signed: Alfred Rosenberg

Checked for accuracy:
Signed: Urban
Staff leader

cc: G.

Source: Bundesarchiv Koblenz, FRG, File NS 8/128, Fol. 45–47.

Appendix I.2
Report of the Second Meeting of the Working Community for German Folklore (Arbeitsgemeinschaft für deutsche Volkskunde) on October 22, 1937 (slightly abbreviated).

The business leader of the Working Community for German Folklore Dr. Matthes Ziegler greeted those in attendance and then allowed the individual specialists to speak.

Dr. Karl Henschke, director of the Division of Scholarship:

Scholarly thoroughness and *world-view industriousness* are the two primary presuppositions for German folklore. If they are accomplished—and that is our purpose today—then German folklore is what it should be: the outstanding national scholarship.

The application of the Working Community in the realm of scholarship is divided into three tasks:

1. The basis and the materials for training, educating, and reshaping of German social life by means of the party and its units must be carried out by means of systematic, impeccable research.

2. Those who oppose the NS world-view are to be defeated in the realm of scholarship and pushed aside.

3. It is necessary to develop German *Volkskunde* scholarship into a fortress for the NS world-view.

For these tasks which have been taken on by the Working Community it was necessary (1) to create a scholarly staff of workers; (2) to receive the required funding.

At the founding of the Working Community in January of this year there had existed for a year already a small working circle of scholarly and, in their world-view, reliable folklorists in the Hauptlektorat Volkskunde der Reichsstelle zur Förderung des deutschen Schrifttums [Main Lectorial Office for Folklore of the Reich Office for Promotion of German Writing, the overseeing organization of the Rosenberg Bureau]. This circle was employed for the new scholarly tasks of the Working Community and expanded through further workers who were named in the *Gaus* after special inquiries were made. Individual gatherings of the scholarly workers have taken place thus far at the Second Nordic Scholarly Congress "Costume and Decoration" in Lübeck (from August 29 to September 5, 1937), which was partially developed by the Working Community, and in Berlin discussions on May 5 and November 20, 1937, on the occasion of the Reich Office Meeting.

In view of its meaning for the practical work in the party and its sub-organizations, the following research areas were taken up first:

Farm house research (under the direction of party comrade Dr. Kulke)—investigations of German *folk customs*, especially in light of the new *celebration planning* (under the direction of party comrade Dr. Decker and party comrade Dr. Strobel)—work on the German *folk song, folk and children's games*, as well as *folk dance* (under the direction of party comrade Dr. Haiding).

These scholarly works are organized in such a way that the appropriate group leaders, aided by exhibitioners, travel funds, and other financial help (for archives) treat the individual research theme independently within the framework of the whole. Evaluation is carried out by the group leaders. In this way the Working Community exercises a decisive influence on all folklore research work.

If the scholarly work mentioned here serves mainly as practical folklore work, they are simultaneously both directly and indirectly intended for *confronting the confessional opponents*. It would lead us astray to go into these confrontations on an individual basis. . . . * The 30 (!) volumes of Prelate Schreiber published in the series *Forschungen zur Volkskunde* [Research on Folklore] are sufficient to show just how necessary a *systematic* application of scholarly works on our part is.

With this I come to the third task which has been placed on the Working Community and which—generally speaking—consists of *making German folklore valid as scholarship*, and to see that the jobs assigned to it can be fulfilled. Here the Working Community does not play an organizational role in the area of scholarship but rather an activating role. It sees that (1) German folklore finds secure *research and teaching posts* at German universities, so that a scholarly tradition can be established (as of now there are five chairs for German folklore!), (2) German folklore correspondingly is raised to an independent *discipline for testing*, and (3) working with German folklore must be a possible professional goal, i.e., that *regular positions at research institutes, museums, libraries, etc.*, must be opened up; here the majority of the work is to be accomplished.

In summary it can be asserted: the application of the Working Community for German Folklore in the area of scholarship is for: (1) the founding and deepening of the entire schooling and educational work in the Party and its suborganizations, (2) the systematic scholarly confrontation with world-view opponents, and (3) the furthering in general of German Folklore as scholarship.

Dr. Ernst Otto Thiele, director of the Division of Press and Publication:
From the previous activity of the Office of Publication and Press three specialized areas are to be emphasized:

1. The Working Community for German Folklore is now preparing a *Verzeichnis des volkskundlichen Schrifttums* [published as *Deutsche Volkskunde im Schrifttum*, Index of German Folklore Publications] which will for the first time offer a critical overview of folklore literature of the past and the present. This publication will offer an in-depth evaluation of all the pertinent publications, arranged according to subject. It will work out especially in the numerous new works the widespread liberalistic thoughts and the concerns with political Catholicism which are appearing more and more frequently in the area of folklore. The list will be available in the spring and in the interest of wide coverage the price will be kept down.

In addition to this inclusive work, several reviews will be presented monthly as special issues of the *Mitteilungen zur weltanschaulichen Lage* [Reports on the World-View Situation], which will treat the most recent publications. These monthly overviews have been appearing since June 1937.

2. The Working Community will present monthly an *information lecture* for Berliners and the German *press* represented in Berlin. These gatherings have been well received and are regularly attended by twenty-five to thirty representatives of the daily press. The purpose is for mutual discussions through which it is possible to correct the numerous but false meanings about the expressive forms of the folknation which commonly appear in the press. The following have spoken:

February: Dr. Strobel, Staff Office of the Reich farm leader, on "Carnival Customs."
March: Dr. Appel, German Ancestral Inheritance, on "Easter Customs."
April: Rehm, Staff Office of the Reich farm leader, on "Spring Customs."
May: Dr. Strobel, Staff Office of the Reich farm leader, on "Cultivation and Renewal of Costumes."
June: Karl Theodor Weigel, German Ancestral Inheritance, on "The Condition of Symbol Research."
July: Dr. Thiele, Rosenberg Bureau, on "Folklore at the Second Nordic Scholarly Congress in Lübeck."
August: Dropped because of the Congress.
September: Dropped because of the Reich Party Day.

October: Dr. Haiding, Reich Youth Leadership, on "Dance in Culture Work."
November: Prof. Dr. Karl von Spieß, Vienna, on "Peasant Art—Its Type and Meaning."
December: Dr. Huth, German Ancestral Inheritance, on "Christmas Tree and Christmas Custom."

3. Working together with the Reichsstelle für den Unterrichtsfilm [Reich Office for Instructional Film] the Working Community has developed a test of film material which is possibly suitable for folkloric school work, and has thus given its approval to the *films on "customs"* produced by the party or by state offices. The result is so insufficient that the Working Community sees that it is necessary to produce new films, in association with the Reich Office for Instructional Film, which are intended to be impeccable in their world-view, with technical completeness and professional structure.

The Versuchsstelle für Volkstumskunde [Experimental Post for Folk-National Studies] has grown out of the Landesstelle Kurmark für deutsche Volksforschung [Regional Institute Kurmark for German Folk Research]. It is the job of this office, which is attached to the Amt für weltanschauliche Information [Office for World-View Information, the office for countering the Christian churches under the direction of Matthes Ziegler], to carry out investigations whose conclusions are of value for practical folk-national work, or to make possible new knowledge for judging the development of our folk-nation and the relationships to closely related folk groups.

In process at this time is an *investigation on rural living conditions* which is especially important for future settlement work and which is supposed to help clarify the reciprocal relationship between mankind and his housing. The work will most likely be completed in the spring.

Simultaneously preparations are being made for an *investigation of Christmas and New Year customs*. This investigation will be carried out in collaboration with the National Socialist Teachers Union in the entire Reich and is based on the reports of school children's experiences of the custom which they have witnessed this year in their parents' houses and in public. The evaluation of this material will take place during the summer of 1938.

Dr. Hans Strobel, Director of the Division of Schooling:
Design of a Workers Catalog. Based on reports of the various service posts, organizations, etc., more than five hundred people have been assembled who are working full time or part time within the movement and its associated leagues on folklore questions. The catalog will become useful only with time since . . . for the majority of the people their aptitude and abilities can be known only in the course of their work.

Gau-Working Communities for German Folklore. In July the *Gau* schooling directors received instructions to create in their own areas *Gau* Arbeitsgemeinschaften für deutsche Volkskunde [*Gau* Working Communities for German Folklore] which corresponded to the structure of the Reich Working Community for German Folklore. Since it was clearly pointed out that it wasn't a matter of representative corporations but rather communities capable of work and for which only impeccable and responsible workers came into question, it was of course required that the founding of the *Gau* Working Communities for German Folklore can only come from an especially careful choosing of the participants. The following *Gaus* have to date reported *Gau* Working Communities for German Folklore: Danzig, Düsseldorf, Halle-Merseburg, Hamburg, Hessen-Nassau, Mecklenburg-Lübeck, Württemberg-Hohenzollern. In various other *Gaus* the preparations are under way, e.g., in Kurhessen, Silesia, Schleswig-Holstein, etc.

School Material. This appears irregularly in the *Mitteilungen zur weltanschaulichen Lage* and in the press. The schooling activity of the participatory service posts will not be replaced by the Working Community for German Folklore, only unified in its setup. Together with the National Socialist Community "Strength through Joy" the booklet *Deutsches Erntedankfest* [German Thanksgiving Festival] could be published. . . . *Film strips* or rather glass-framed slides which can also be recommended for schooling have been started by workers from the Working Community for German Folklore. Thus far the following have appeared: K. Th. Weigel: "Runes and Symbols" (46 pictures); H. Strobel: "Peasant Customs during the Year" (61 pictures) (Verlag Lipropa, Berlin W 50, Bambergerstr.). Preparations are under way for producing a carnival film.

Use of Speakers. A preliminary list of speakers could be announced in the *Mitteilungen zur weltanschaulichen Lage.* Agreements exist with the Deutsches Volksbildungswerk [German Folk Education Works, which belonged to the office of Dr. Robert Ley], the Nordic Society [closely associated with the Rosenberg Bureau, it put on the Nordic scholarly congresses], and the Ancestral Inheritance. Individual referees and speakers of the Working Community for German Folklore have spoken on several dozen occasions at the most varied presentations, some of which were public in nature, others within the framework of various suborganizations of the movement.

Research Tasks. Mittelstelle für deutsche Bauernhausforschung [Intermediate Branch for German Farm House Research] in the Working Community for German Folklore. Director Dr. Ing. E. Kulke (Staff Office of the Reich farm leader). Tasks:

1. Developmental history of the Germanic farmstead from the Nordic, not from the Roman-Celtic standpoint.

2. Expansion of the farm*stead*-concept in contrast to the previous one-sided work on *house* research. Viewing the farmstead as a portion of the village community and of village delimitation (farm order, community order, field order, settlement order).

3. Expansion of previous knowledge of Germanic-German land acquisition and the associated German settlement history.

4. Purification and renewal of peasant construction methods. Exhibition of a new construction tradition. Battle against the urbanization of village construction.

5. Cultivation of valuable old farmsteads in the sense of state monument protection, since the farmstead represents at least as meaningful national common property as monasteries, castles, churches, and fortresses.

In collaboration with various scholars and researchers the following works were taken on and made possible through the research help of the German Research Council: investigations on log building methods, investigations on settlement history, investigations on *Rundling* [ring-shaped village around a central square], investigations on the *Vorlaubenhaus* [porch house] in Kurmark, preliminary work for a dictionary on German farmhouse studies, collaboration on new farmhouse work to be published, investigations on rural living conditions and suggestions for the structure of a village house [according to Dr. Kulke a community house for festivals, celebrations, kindergarten, and offices for the mayor], preparation of an exhibition "House and Farmstead of the German Peasant." The *Mittelstelle für deutsche Bauernhausforschung* has also begun putting together a picture collection and a publication collection.

Research Assignment. "Folk Custom and Churches," Director Dr. H. Strobel (Staff Office of the Reich Farm Leader):

The goal of the work planned for the next years is to undertake a systematic gathering of material for the relationship of churches to folk custom. From this presentation and evaluation in schooling especially, as well as from a scholarly and political viewpoint, valuable results can be expected. From the funds made available by the German Research Council several workers with monthly research subventions can be considered. Various regions and periods of history and of the present are being worked up. Working connections exist with appropriate service posts and important researchers.

Exhibition of a Picture Archive "Living Customs." From the most varied regions of the German settlement area pictures about folk customs are being purchased. The archive will have about two thousand pictures in the coming fiscal year.

Dr. Karl Haiding, director of the Division of Folk-National Work:

1. *Mittelstelle für Spielforschung* [Intermediate Post for Game Research]. Practical evaluation of the work of the Nationalsozialistische Volkswohlfahrt [National Socialist Folk Welfare] and the Bund deutscher Mädchen [Union of German Girls]. Planned are regional booklets on children's games, picture collections on games and dances. Thus far there are seven thousand handwritten recordings from Austria which are now being transcribed. A questionnaire is in press and will be sent out after Christmas. Before the publication the questionnaire was tested in German speech islands and in the Allgäu.

2. Dance as a general foundation. Publication of the booklet *Tänze unserer Gemeinschaft* [Dances of our Community]. A picture book on dance is being prepared.

3. Folk song. Investigation on the religious political coordination of German folk songs. Preparation of a publication of later Christianized songs in their original form.

4. Custom. Publication of a picture book, "Christmas."

5. Collection of material for the racial investigation of dance melodies.

6. Work on the bibliography of the Working Community for German Folklore sections *Märchen*, song, game, dance.

General Work Leader *Dr. Will Decker*, director of the Division of Celebration Planning:

General Work Leader Dr. Decker gives an overview on the planning of great National Socialist celebrations. The great political celebration took shape particularly at the last Reich Party Day, even though several new attempts were unsatisfactory. It is of significance to note the participation for the first time of the Young Women's Work Service during the parade by the Working Service. This has shown that it is possible, while taking into consideration the living rules of women, to let them participate in celebrations which are more than just marching and which present a celebration of commitment to the National Socialist world-view. For the celebration day of German work, the Reich Party Day, November 9 [Hitler putsch in Munich in 1923] celebratory forms have been created which will remain clear and meaningful for the future.

Far more difficult is the realm of family festivals and clan celebrations. Here important preliminary work is to be accomplished through the Working Community for German Folklore by investigating where clan celebrations (baptism, wedding, funeral) are already being conducted in the sense of the National Socialist world-view. From these investigations then suggestions for clan celebrations of a German type are to be located.

The implementing of a library for festival and celebration planning as well as a picture archive for collecting pictures of National Socialist festivals and celebrations has been undertaken.

Following this Prof. Dr. Nelis spoke about "Catholic Action in German Folk-National Scholarship and in Folk-National Work."

Source: Bundesarchiv Koblenz, FRG, File NS 21/281.

*See Karl Ruprecht, "Deutsches Volkstum und konfessionelle Volkskunde." *Nationalsozialistische Monatshefte* 8:92 (1937) 962–969.

Appendix I.3
Alfred Rosenberg
Theses from the *Mythus* (Excerpts)

PREFACE

Many times I have been asked to publish the *Mythus* in an abbreviated version. I have refused because the *results* of an investigation would have stood alone, without the thought development which had led to these results. Furthermore, a *work* has a unity, which cannot simply be cut apart at will.

I have had to defend the *Mythus* from attacks on several sides through two articles.

I have also been asked again and again to formulate the theses of our world-view "programmatically," thereby to produce a "catechism" or at least to stimulate its creation. I have also refused to do that: *the new world-view is not a dogma, but rather an attitude*. A dogma can be "declared," an attitude can only be presented, explained, or at the most kindred spirits can be *called forth*. Standard answers to a thousand questions make the questioner lazy and portly. We want to maintain German inquisitiveness and intensity. That is what distinguishes priests from comrades. It is not omniscience, but keeping oneself firm, that is the goal of teaching and education.

Nevertheless, our work of the last twenty years has required of us that we take a position on almost all life's questions. The renewed activity of the priesthood throughout the world is trying once again to win back lost ground through a new "Counter Reformation," by roundabout "cultural" ways. Thus it is often necessary to work out a *positive attitude* along with a firm *defense*.

Even though I have considered those clear wishes, I have not chosen for this third writing of the *Mythus* the form of a continuous presentation (everything else to be said must wait for a larger work), but I have rather simply listed short statements without writing those otherwise necessary stylistic transitions. I hope, by doing it this way, to have escaped the danger of a "catechism," and still to do justice to an impressive version. The formulations should *never* be conceived of dogmatically, but I have very much tried to offer a lasting and clearly presented *guide* for an awakened will to a heightened sense of complete consciousness. I would like to stress here again that I am not advancing any official requirements for general agreements with the "confessions." Insofar as the German and National Socialist is willing to follow with a free will, that is how strong the effect of the submissive will can and will be. A world-view revolution requires centuries to be fulfilled, and we shouldn't attempt to *demolish* old perceptions, but *overcome* them.

Some formulations can be found in other contexts in various of my speeches over the last few years. I have taken them up again because they, scattered as they were but united here, express most clearly what I want to say. Furthermore, one should reuse a fortuitously expressed form instead of using a new one which is not quite as fitting. It was once the wisdom of Greek builders to reuse the forms of the Doric temple, which all recognized as having been perfect.

In this text, there will be no attempt to outline the complete scope of the battle, and only those areas will be described and sketched out which directly touch on the world-view. National rights, technology, social problems have not been treated, from this basic attitude a judgment will be forthcoming and knowledgeable compilers will be found.

Thus I hope to contribute something through this text to the firming up of attitudes and to a will for greater distance.

The political victory will be followed by our battle for world-view. We must also accomplish that in order to guarantee permanence to the great revolution of our age.

Alfred Rosenberg
Bad Elster, July 1939

I

World-view means looking at the world in a certain way. World-view is thus attitude, not dogma.

+

Attitude toward the world: that means toward external fate and to the soul's driving forces.

+

An attitude is brave or cowardly, proud or submissive, free or subservient.

+

He who is brave does what his conscience type bids, the coward is looking for possible dangers, the proud faces fate, the subservient asks about the requirements of its commandments, the free man recognizes unity with his own kind, the servant waits for the command of others.

+

To call for bravery, pride, and freedom means to educate in a Germanic-German way; to teach humility and to instill fear is the basic educational principle of the Christian churches.

+

A world-view includes religion, science, and art. From these ancient activities of mankind grow all of the other branches of work. The harmony of folk and life will only then be accomplished when the attitude found in religion, science, and art are the same and when it is apparent that all expressive forms are dependent on this attitude.

+

We had those Jewish-Asian confessions which were falsely called religion. We had a science which was overpowered by Biblical dogma. We saw art which was only allowed in praise of the Bible and the Roman [Catholic] Church. Germanic man exploded these forms. He created an ideal beauty which suited him; today it has become a conscious idea for all Germans. Europe has fought for and won the freedom [to conduct] natural research, contrary to all Biblical dogma. Today's Europe, particularly the German folk, is getting rid of the Syrian-Jewish church dogma and oriental ceremonies.

+

To create that Germanic unity of religion, science, and art in attitude and expression is the essence of the world-view revolution of the twentieth century.

II

Religion and confession have become different concepts.

+

Religion means: soul unity of a man or a folk with that which is godly and stands over this life. Religion is just *one* part of the complete world-view attitude. There is confession as well as providence included in belief in god or in a godhead as well as in fate. *This* confession is an essential part of religion.

+

Confession means the sum total of those required belief tenets (dogmas) of a certain church.

+

One confession requires a belief in the Bible, in the tradition of the Church, in the infallibility of the Pope, in the so-called sacraments, in a raceless and unified humanity, in priestly control of heaven. Another requires belief in the Bible, in a so-called unique revelation recorded in the New Testament, in the teachings of Luther or Calvin.

Because there are *two* large confessions—and hundreds of sects—in Germany, they no longer offer a general religious basis for the entire German folk. Christianity was once an absolute power, but through the development of many confessions it has become a particular phenomenon.

That one-time absolute power broke down because its effect was anti-Germanic and became more and more anti-German. A new—Germanic-German—attitude could not be brought about by a new Protestant attachment to the Bible.

Thus: whoever strives for a unique religious attitude for all Germans must first overcome the previous confessions.

[. . .]

Education through fear has been overcome. No one who has been awakened can make his salvation depend on a belief in an old assertion of some confession. The fight over confessions is over, the great struggle over values has entered its decisive stage.

+

Belief in the spiritual worth of honor and freedom as the *highest* value of life and death means the greatest religious revolution since the appearance of Christianity in world history.

+

Everybody is "in his own way immortal." Everyone bears the legacy of his ancestors in this world and is at the same time the forefather of his successors' deeds. Just as nature has given each being the abilities which are necessary for achieving his own possible goal, so we also believe that the belief in some kind of acquired immortality represents the human ability for only reaching a mere surmised goal.

Everybody is thus essentially "the architect of his own happiness"—but also the deciding cause of his own unhappiness. Everybody determines through his own *type* in this world the form in another inconceivable next one.

The "hereafter" is not determined through a belief in the teaching and actions of the church, not through its blessing or threats of excommunication, but instead through value-guided will and the will-guided deed of man himself.

We believe therefore:

Whoever sacrifices for his *Volk* cannot be in opposition to a true religion. When this seems to come about, then this "religion" has no right to exist.

Whoever strives to follow the most noble values fulfills a metaphysical, religious mandate. He joins his life's task to the highest manifestation of existence and not to the human-church organizations, dogma, and ideology. Restless service to the highest values is the stamp of the true *Germanic* religious genius. Religion is not the renunciation of will but rather the development of will in the service of the noble spiritual type. With this recognition, the influence of all previous religions from the orient ceases. From the chaos of the confessional disintegration, the opportunity for a German religion has been born.

[. . .]

Freedom today—after 1,500 years of disciplined-education [*Zucht-Erziehung*] through fear—is not good for everyone. Whoever *needs* shackles in order to walk, should not remove them but die in them.

+

From confessional disciplining to the disciplining through Germanic values, the steps of many generations are required. *We* are the link between the one kind of disciplining and the other. We are the conquerors of an age and the founders of a new—also religious—era. We bear a heavy and therefore important fate. In the midst of the struggle for the future, we must respectfully preserve the greatness of the past, yes, even protect discarded lifeforms, out of respect for the honest beliefs of living people.

+

To destroy images, every revolution has had that capacity. But to leave one's own matters to chance and still not to burn all one's bridges behind, that is the nobility of character of the National Socialist new epoch.

+

To perceive something as noble, that is a judgment. Nature is neither good nor bad; it *is*. Man stands *in* it and is *sub*servient to it. But that he can make judgments about it, that is a sign of his freedom, i.e., a strength which does not derive from this nature as we comprehend it.

+

When the man of the *orient* perceives himself as sinful—then let him do so. Nothing obligates the Germanic people to take on the same attitude in regard to nature and man. When the church teaches sin and original sin, then it is showing her oriental, Jewish-Syrian Near Eastern soul. To divorce this Biblical teaching is the first step to religious recovery.

The German folk is not originally sinful but rather noble by birth.

[. . .]

So that the German folk, after a thousand years' search, may find a religion which it has outgrown, then it must understand Christianity as part of the past and lift up those values in one's own being which have come forth through all ages, and make them the guiding stars of its own deeds of the soul.

+

The signs of the times declare: whoever will not recognize the honor of the awakened soul will break down under the pressure of this "fortress" of new life.

+

We grew up without church bells and in opposition to all priests; we will in the future continue to grow without the sounds of bells from the church.

Bells, however, were and are symbols of a *community* that is to be called together; therefore the bells of the fortresses of the National Socialist order will one day admonish a new community and will call out across the German fields and forests and hills to the members of this new community.

+

Religion is a bond to something godly—but it is also a bond to the people for whom soul values must be expressed and proved. The new folk community

(National Socialism) has been prefigured and there have been presentiments, but it has not yet been formed. To acquire form, great all-encompassing form, many generations will have to take each other by the hand.

[. . .]

Communities will only become reality through a willing belief as a true representation of the soul. One can only believe when the human representatives of this hard-won community prove themselves to be worthy of their founders. Values, which are not represented by the leaders [*Führer*] will not be defended by the community. That is the harsh law of selection, even in moral-religious life.

+

To create an international organization Christianity had to strive to destroy the pure German communal conscience. When a Germanic count . . . was to be baptized, he first asked if he would encounter the fallen members of his clan in heaven. When this was answered in the negative, he withdrew his consent to baptism, with the remark that he did not want to be separated from his dead ancestors for all eternity. Out of the scattered millions of individuals, the church formed the spiritual "body of Christ." The birth of the folk nation and of racial ideas are today destroying the international body of Christ with an inner urgency and are replacing it with a pure German community as a supreme community of clans guarded by an alliance of warriors which is today called the National Socialist Reich.

[. . .]

In place of Christian love, the idea of National Socialist, Germanic comradeship has come in.

+

Liberal charity was secularized Christian love. A hundred millionaires provided money for hundreds of thousands who were to sacrifice to the deeds and the actions of the same millionaires. Church and capitalism "donated" as the upper class to the "lower strata." Today we do not sacrifice out of presumptuous charity, but out of justness. We do not wish to make the recipient humble but to elevate him. Do not practice mildness but duty.

+

The oriental damnation of labor has been replaced by the honor of labor. The new work ethic is an exaltation against the monastic ideal of the Roman Church. The spade of the German Workers' Service [*Arbeitsdienst*] has overcome the "rosary."

+

The biggest danger for a new world-view is often not the old and still existing ideologies but the sectarians of the new movement. A sectarian sees only *one* point which hypnotizes him; he makes it the center of attention and loses through unbounded imagination his balance of judgment. He overextends himself, storms when rejected, conducts himself like an abused genius—and when a new movement has no steadfast and firm people, then the growth of a great idea can be thwarted, often for centuries, through unbridled sectarianism. Political sectarianism was tamed, keeping it apart from the world-view; that is the task of all leaders. Furthering of iridescent sectarians out of fear that a genius will be hindered in his works is evidence of the same subordinate attitude, just like the subjective worshiping of old idols simply because they are old.

+

Death is not the price that we must pay for sin. It is not at all the opposite of life but is subservient to life. Being born and dying, that the *individual* does, not life. Birth and death are therefore absolute *signs* of life.

[. . .]

The fighting camaraderie of a great revolution is always a dynamic combination. Only self-willed dispositions will independently conduct a war against an old world. Thus there still are explosions of temperament despite unifying service. What is left *after* death, is the *work*. Just as the *Führer* represents the symbolic unity and core of the will, so do the old comrades in arms, insofar as they are of a pronounced personality, represent a suprapersonal notion. That which they create remains behind as a continuing deed, and the unity of these related deeds is the discipline notion for coming centuries. Therefore the *community* of later times can possibly seem more closed than even the battle camaraderie of the present. The subjective rests in the grave or is suppressed by life, the [newly] formed eternity lives as personality with utmost strength for the further shaping of the suprapersonal folk nation. What was whitewash, affectation, and appearance will dissolve, just like those who glowed with pretense, without associating their person with a higher notion than an iridescent glowing self-vanity.

To leave behind a *work* and to fulfill the idea of completeness with *one's* personality, that is highest goal of a National Socialist life.

A work can be important for the community of a village, a town, the countryside, all the people, a racially related folk family, for all of Europe. Each work is only then *real when* it is at the center of a tangible community. Therefore *every* creation is ensured respect and love by *all*: the extent of these possibilities is a *gift* of fate—and industry of those who have been touched by destiny.

+

Monumental structures are not houses but stone notions of a community. The imperial palace, the hall of the king, was the image of knighthood. It was made into the knave, just as German knights were made into crusaders. The *Gau* houses of National Socialism, the castles of order [*Ordensburgen*], the meeting halls, the Advanced School of the NSDAP are new concepts of a new community—a folk knighthood. They as well as those monuments still to come are supposed to show that we have thought highly about ourselves and that we have respected our ideas expressed, just as the Christians in their times did for their ideal.

[. . .]

Research must be free for all aspiring minds. The old confessions were and are bound by their "revelations" to an out-of-date world image. The discovery of the heliocentric system was the end for the legends of the New Testament.

+

Belief and knowledge generally cannot to be made into opposites; that was only possible through the Judeo-Christian dogmatism which places a "belief" over all knowledge, but which then did want to prove it on an historical and legendary basis.

+

True religion, however, is neither proved through discoveries in nature nor overthrown by it. Religion is the result of an *inner experience*, not the consequence of some scientific proof of God or a resurrection legend; it has generally nothing to do with miracles and magic.

The more a person believes in miracles the less religion he has. Therefore the Jew is a religionless person and the Jewified [*verjudet*] Christian deludes himself about his religious poverty through an abundance of stories from the Old Testament and magical legends from the New Testament.

+

The greatest miracle is the laws of the universe. The existence of matter is just as incomprehensible as the existence of life. To research and describe laws constitutes the nature of Germanic science, to follow the noble commands of the soul is the nature of Germanic religion.

+

Through the magical deeds and spells of the priest, that means through *someone else*, in order to change the hereafter or to want to influence nature, that constitutes the nature of African–Near Eastern demonism. The mass-celebrating priest stands religiously at the same level as the African medicineman. Therefore he teaches us—in spite of all efforts at Germanizing—a racially alien religion. He has tried with all his might to hinder the development of scientific research, using poison, prison, and burning at the stake.

+

European science did not originate because man discovered "certain laws" after a thousand years of observation, but because great researchers *searched* for laws, presupposed them. Counter to the dogmas of the Church.

+

Universal originality appears as a mechanistic causality: cause and effect, biologically as stimulus and response, humanly as motive and deed. These branches are being treated: physics and chemistry, physiology, racial studies, and psychology. Complete originality must be—even if it is never reached—the goal of true European science.

+

The researcher must not be frightened away from any question and any possible answer. His truthfulness is that attitude which matches the courage of the soldier, the confession of the religious leader. This true scholarship arises out of a proud attitude. *This* is what it is which unites him with another fighter in our life.

[. . .]

Race, soul, and spirit are all the same, just seen once from the outside then from the inside. "Race is the outside of the soul, soul is the inside of race." In a racial soul lie those abilities limited in structure, which appear in life. Serving them, forming them, transfiguring them and defending them, is to embody religion in life itself, after the example of the great figures of this earth.

That is not "materialism," but in the language of the church, real "divine service" and true "respect for creation." Materialism: that is that ostentatiously jewel-bedecked priesthood of a church which claims "not to be of this world."

All great creations are a structured parable of a racial soul. The Parthenon and Faust show the range of Nordic humanity. Confucius is China's soul. Tenno is the warrior mythos of the Japanese.

+

Soul and nature come together in art, to create a new form. The beauty of man and the world is a parable of the inner will. Homer was therefore as great an artist as a religious founder because he created through soul and structure a cosmic force of fate for his people.

+

Gods are the creation of the religious, world images are the creation of the researcher, temples and dramas are creations of the artistic will. They are all parables (symbols) of the inner world-view which has been transferred to the outside. Every real parable is a final answer in and of itself to questions of an age or of a folk nation. Parables are pictures, never dogmas. Great *races* live in their images, *ideologies* through schematic compulsory tenets of belief.

+

Parables, born out of a real inner self, racially pure projections to the outside, always stand as *friends* to those who shape them. Dogmas always come from the outside: as masters or as enemies. Zeus was the friend of the Hellenics, the Yahweh church is an enemy of the Germanic people.

+

Every great parable: religious idea, scientific theory, image of beauty, all are perceived as a spiritual-godly inspiration. Godly revelation is repeated a thousand times in creative hearts; it is *not* at home in the Sinai manifestation.

+

Every *Volk* especially likes its *own* thoughts and ideas. They are assured our respect, but there is no obligation. For us Beethoven's Fifth Symphony is a higher godly revelation than all the sayings of the Old Testament put together.

+

At the first awakening of a racial soul, religious hymns are both world images and songs of art. They prove clearly the *unified* motivation of will of every real world-view. When religion, world image, and art are separated, no longer understand each other, or even deny each other and do battle, that is proof of the alienation of one or all areas through a hostile racial soul.

+

Christianity has made an effort through its hard-fought religious position to destroy research. *That* is the final proof of its estranged attitude of the soul. It has made an effort to place art only in its service. All of this did not succeed and for this we are indebted to the unbroken character of the Europeans.

There where our culture shows unity is the *Germanic* attitude. To ensure this everywhere—and that means to overcome those valued teachings of Christianity—is the future goal which has been placed on Europe.

Only when this has succeeded will the new harmony of the creative racial soul be possible.

[. . .]

The longing of Walther von der Vogelweide: "German discipline [*Zucht*] has priority over all else" is now becoming a reality. The intellectual-spiritual forced discipline of Christianity is past. Soul, spirit, body are beginning to move unhindered and are becoming more self-confident. *Our* times have made them free, the future will bring harmony. It will be able to bring it, if it has grasped the meaning of a great age and is committed to defending it.

Translated from Alfred Rosenberg, *Thesen aus dem Mythus* (Excerpts). Source: Bundesarchiv Koblenz, FRG, File NS 8/22. Published by Seraphim 1956: 197–212.

Appendix I.4
The Advanced School of the NSDAP and Its Tasks
Memorandum from Alfred Rosenberg on June 1937 for presentation to Adolf Hitler (Excerpt)

The branching of the complete schooling and education of the NSDAP, its sub-organizations, and the attached associations has made it necessary for the purpose of securing the unity of the National Socialist world-view through a centralized production and compilation of teaching methods and teaching materials as well as through the education of responsible teachers and instructors to establish the Hohe Schule der NSDAP [Advanced School of the NSDAP]. This understanding has resulted in the development of essentials for the tasks and methods of this central education office of the National Socialist movement. Any thoughts about this should be submitted to the Führer later for a decision. . . .

The National Socialist movement has incorporated all of life and comes from the understanding that even if secure foundations had not been forged for all areas of this life by the men who have gained victory by fighting, for the future the danger remains that the old ideologies could reappear, in order to form new political groups after this reappearance and through that to change the victory of the National Socialist movement into a mere *episode*, even if an important episode, of German history. It therefore appears necessary . . . to secure the foundations for a complete intellectual-cultural and world-view education effort so that a unified attitude can be passed on to future generations.

Source: Bundesarchiv Koblenz, FRG, File NS 8/175, Fol. 45–46.

Appendix I.5
Führer's Order of 1940 to Establish
The Advanced School in Preparation

Information Concerning Offices of the Party and State

The "Hohe Schule" [Advanced School] shall henceforth be the center of National Socialist research, teaching and education. Its establishment will take place after the war. In order, however, to promote the preliminary work already begun, I order that Reich Leader Alfred *Rosenberg* carry on these preparatory works, particularly in the area of research and the establishment of the library. The offices of the party and state are obligated to lend their support to him in this undertaking.

Berlin, January 29, 1940   Signed: Adolf Hitler

Source: Archive of the International Military Court in Nürnberg, FRG, File no. PS-136.

Appendix I.6
Command by Rosenberg to Establish Outposts of the Advanced School 1940

Command
Concerning the Establishment of the Outposts of the Advanced School

Based on the proclamation of the Führer of January 29, 1940, I order the establishment of the Outposts of the Hohe Schule [Advanced School].

The Outposts of the Advanced School are Research Institutes. They will receive their research directives from me.

The Directors of these Outposts and their coworkers on research assignments will be appointed and recalled by me.

The Administration of the Outposts of the Advanced School will be under the Reich Treasurer of the NSDAP.

Berlin, October 30, 1940   Signed: A. Rosenberg

More detailed procedural guidelines will be forthcoming in the near future

Source: Bundesarchiv Koblenz, FRG, File NS 8/265, Fol. 125.

Appendix I.7
Command by Rosenberg to Found the Institute for German Folklore 1942

The Commissioner of the Führer for the Supervision of all Intellectual and World-View Teaching and Education of the NSDAP. Berlin-Charlottenburg 2, May 6, 1942. Bismarkstraße 1. Telephone: 34 00 18. R./K. 942.

Within the Central Office of the Hohe Schule in Vorbereitung [Advanced School under Preparation] an Institute for German Folklore is herewith founded. The Institute for German Folklore still must establish research posts outside the Central Office of the Advanced School under preparation. As Director of the Institute for German Folklore, I am naming, for the duration of the war, Dr. Karl Haiding.

Signed: A. Rosenberg

R[osenberg]/K. [unknown secretary]

Source: Bundesarchiv Koblenz, FRG, File NS 8/137, Fol. 103.

Appendix I.8
Central Offices and Offices of the Service Branch [Rosenberg Office], Institutes of the Advanced School, Research Posts of the Institute for German Folklore 1944 (Excerpt)

Institutes of the Advanced School

Institute for Research on the Jewish Question
Director: Dr. Klaus Schickert

Frankfurt/Main
Bockenheimer Landstr.
Nr. 68
Tel.: 79 354

Institute for Religious Studies
Director: Dr. Wilhelm Brachmann

Halle/Saale
Am Neuwerk 7
Tel.: 252 95

Institute for Overseas Research
Director: Prof. Dr. Adolf Rein

Hamburg-Gr. Flottbek
Elbchaussee 160

Institute for National Socialist Folk Cultivation
Director: Dr. Richard Benzing

Marburg/Lahn
Universitätsstr. 48
Tel.: 27 52

Institute for Indo-Germanic Intellectual History
Director: Prof. Dr. Richard Harder

München 22
Ludwig-Str. 14
i. Aufgang

Institute for German Folklore
Director for the duration of the war:
Dr. Karl Haiding

Stift Rein bei Graz
Tel.: Rein 6

Institute for Biology and Racial Studies
Director: Prof. Dr. Walter Gross
Deputy Director: Dr. Werner Hüttig

Schelklingen/Württ.
Schlösschen
Tel.: 84

Central Library for the Advanced School
Director: Library Director
Dr. Walter Grothe

St. Andrä Post St.
Ruprecht bei Villach
(Kärnten)
Tel.: Villach 6047

Research Post for Pedagogical Studies
Director: Prof. Dr. Karl Seiler

Nürnberg
Egidienplatz 25

Research Posts of the Institute for German Folklore

Research Post for Peasant Life Structures
Director: Dr. Karl Ruprecht

Salzburg
Hofstallgasse 5a

Research Post for Peasant Handicrafts
Director: Dr. Ernst Otto Thiele (in the
East Ministry at this time) (The business
is being carried out by the Director of
the Research Post for German Farmsteads,
Dr. Erich Kulke).

Schöneiche bei Berlin
Blücher-Str. 41
Tel.: 64 62 47

Research Post for German Farmsteads
Director: Dr. Erich Kulke

Schöneiche bei Berlin
Blücher-Str. 41
Tel.: 64 62 47

Research Post for German Folk Speech
Director: Dr. [Bernhard] Martin

Marburg/Lahn
Ketzerbach 1

Research Post for Mythology
Director: Prof. Dr. [Karl] von Spieß

Wien
Joseph-Bürckel-Ring 3a
Gauhaus

Research Post for Games and Sayings
Director: Dr. Karl Haiding

Stift Rein bei Graz

Source: Bundesarchiv Koblenz, FRG, File NS 15/102.

Appendix I.9
Folklore on a Racial Basis:
Prerequisites and Tasks
by Matthes Ziegler

"The study of the *Volk* and not of political systems should be the beginning point for all politics. The statesmen of earlier centuries certainly come nowhere close to our own thorough schooling, but they saw the actual life of the *Volk* every day with fresher eyes and therefore at least carried out their regimen with a practical surety that has become very scarce today."

These sentences by Wilhelm Heinrich Riehl, the grand old man of German *Volk* research, were written in the middle of the last century and yet they could serve as precepts for a National Socialist, German science of *Volkskunde*, connected to the *Volk* and beholden to it. With an uncanny clarity they show the task and the content of German *Volkskunde*, which, by virtue of being a "science of the *Volk*," can claim to be the most proper means of educating the German *Volk*.

The first prerequisite of a German *Volkskunde* seen in this manner is, of necessity, a consideration of the object which it treats, the essence and development of the German *Volk*. By the term *Volk*, *Volkskunde* does not mean *Volk* per se, but rather deals in each instance with a very specific *Volk*. The whole problem of our modern science of *Volkskunde* comes about because of its inability to recognize these basic facts and to draw the necessary conclusions. Not until our time, which has learned consciously to see and think racially, are we ripe for an organic recognition of the essence of *Volk*.

A proud series of great Germans in the eighteenth and nineteenth centuries have helped to prepare this understanding.

The historical philosophy of the Enlightenment was based on the educational community which, by means of its preoccupation with foreign countries and foreign peoples, discovered an interest in the perceptual world of the so-called common people. The common folk was in the eyes of the Enlightenment the scorned mass of the uneducated which is present in every civilized nation and forms the lowest stratum. Whereas rationalistic Protestantism exhausted itself with the pastoral teachings on the lack of purpose, nonsense, and idiocy of superstitious customs and habits, cosmopolitanism, or the brotherhood of mankind concept that was then dominating European thinking, worked to include common people into its educational system for mankind.

The first person who turned his attention away from the rantings and the fanaticism of well-meaning apostles of humanity, the first to recognize specifically the despised and poverty-stricken lower strata as the protectors and preservers of indigenous stability and *Volk* consciousness, was the Low German, Justus Möser. He placed peasants at the center of his social and historical conception and produced in his 1768 *Osnabrückische Geschichte* the following sentences, which were revolutionary for the sensitivities of the aesthetically active man of the Enlightenment: "In my opinion, Germany has hope of a great turning point in its history, if we take the common land owners (i.e., the peasants) as the true components of the nation and follow them through all their changes, form our substance from them, and look upon the greater and lesser servants of this nation as the good or bad fortunes of this body. We could then develop the origins, progress, and the differing relationships of the national character with much greater order and precision than if we only describe the life and efforts of doctors and don't consider the sick body." Möser recognized quite properly that which has become law in the National Socialist state, that the farmstead can remain a germ for indigenous stability only when it represents an inalienable and indivisible inheritance. From Justus Möser comes the famous study of the Low Saxon farmhouse, a song of praise to peasant ranks. In his *Osnabrückische Geschichte*, in that exemplary history of the *Volk* bound to its blood and earth [*Blut und Boden*], he writes: "The peasant dwelling is so perfect in its design that it cannot conceivably be improved on and can serve as a ideal pattern. The hearth is just about in the middle of the house and constructed in such a manner that the wife who sits next to it can oversee everything at once. No other type of building has such a large and comfortable field of vision. Without getting up from her chair she can simultaneously view three doors. She thanks those who come in, asks them to take a seat near her, keeps an eye on her children and the domestics, the horses and cows, watches over cellar and larder, constantly does her spinning and cooks. Her sleeping area is behind this hearth, and from there she has the same good view, sees her domestics get up for work and go to bed, sees the fire die down and start up, sees all the doors open and close, hears her livestock eating, and watches over cellar and larder. Any incidental task is part of the chain of everything."

In addition to this sociopolitical insight by Möser, which was described in greater detail in his *Patriotische Phantasien*, we find a history of ideas which, though slowly at first, was to produce the conditions for an actual science of German *Volkskunde*.

Johann Gottfried Herder was the first to speak of a creative *Volksgeist* [folk spirit] which exists in every *Volk* and imprints itself again and again on each *Volk's* essence and shape. From him comes the statement: "Each nation has the center of its happiness within itself, just as every globe has its center of gravity." Thus the essence of the *Volk* is lifted from the level of pure metalanguage and is seen again in the essential context of life. *Volk* is no longer an abstract supportive conceptualization which could be applied to any sort of community whatsoever, but is rather a very specific reality.

The path that Herder set was spoken of with an instinctive surety by the brothers Jakob and Wilhelm Grimm, i.e., the realization of a united world-view of our entire intellectual and material traditional world and its Nordic-Aryan origin. Even if contemporary *Volkskunde* science sees the relationship between myth and *Märchen* differently, the following statements by Wilhelm Grimm about the *Märchen* are nonetheless characteristic of the Grimms' general viewpoint. Wilhelm Grimm states: "Common to all *Märchen* are the survivals of a belief . . . dating back to the most ancient times, a belief in which spiritual things are expressed in a figurative manner. This mythical element resembles small pieces of a shattered jewel which are lying strewn on the ground all overgrown with grass and flowers, and can only be discovered by the most far seeing eye. Their significance has been long lost, but it is still felt and imparts value to the *Märchen*, while satisfying the natural pleasure in the wonderful. They are never the iridescence of an empty fancy. The farther back we go, the more the mythical element expands: indeed it seems to have formed the only subject of the old fictions."

Even if the Romantics of German *Volkskunde* were concerned primarily with *Volksgut* [folk goods] and the pure German traditions, it was Ernst Moritz Arndt and Friedrich Ludwig Jahn who out of direct, practical, and political necessity came to the demand for a *Volkstumskunde* [folk-national study] and coined the term *Deutsches Volkstum* [the German folk-nation].

Continuing the train of thought of Justus Möser, Friedrich Ludwig Jahn says this about the essence of the folk-nation: "Nowhere on earth does humanity appear isolated and pure; it is always manifested and represented through folk-nationalities. In these folk-nationalities lies the special value of each *Volk* and its true contribution to the evolution of humanity. What the noble character of accomplished men is to the confusion of daily life, the folk-nation is to national spirits. The folk-nation is the consecrational gift of a guardian spirit, an unshakable bulwark, the only natural boundary. Nature herself created this division of peoples from natural conditions; it has continued to shape it through time, blessed it with language, assured it through writing, and made it eternal in hearts and spirits."

For Arndt and Jahn folk-national study was the task and the means for both theoretical and practical popular education and training. In this sense Arndt's pupil, Wilhelm Heinrich Riehl, named his main work of 1853 *Die Naturgeschichte des deutschen Volkes* [The Natural History of the German People]. His main concern was presenting the relationship between traditional *Volk* material and the bearers of the folk-nation. In contrast to the beginning philological specialization of certain branches of *Volkskunde*, he correctly emphasized, "*Volkskunde* is unthinkable as

a science until it has found a center for its diverse studies in the idea of nationality."
Riehl's thoughts about the people as a living organism and *Volkskunde* as a "foyer
to the political sciences" were suppressed or twisted more and more by progressive
Marxism. German conservatism in the nineteenth century, which found its programist in the Jew Julius Stahl, was incapable of stopping this development because
it lacked any comprehension of the essence of *Volk*.

Thus the liberal age in the area of German folk research began, as elsewhere,
to have a more and more noticeable disintegrative effect. The intellectual and cultural history of the Aryan-Indogermanic family of nations, termed with bold far-
sightedness *Germanistik* by the Grimms, was dismembered, divided into a series
of special disciplines under the guidance of so-called objective and unprejudiced
science. These specialized areas were no longer viewed from the perspective of a
unified whole of folk history, but rather were set up according to supranational
[*übervölkisch*] "generally applicable laws," claimed to be binding for the whole
world. The pure German consciousness that arose in the period of the wars of
liberation had to make way for a cosmopolitan, i.e., supranational, way of thinking,
which saw the *Volkskunde* of Grimm and Riehl as a mere footnote to general
studies of primitive culture and ethnology overseas. Using the liberal Marxist slogan
of equality of anything that bore the face of man, it was believed that from the
primitiveness of the so-called natural peoples in the Australian outback and in
Central Africa one could extrapolate a prehistoric primitiveness of the European
cultured nations, which remained preserved up to the present in the so-called lowest
strata, i.e., among the peasants and workers.

The science of *Volkskunde* attempted to prove its lack of prejudice at first
through collecting for its own sake. The ethic of this epoch of *Volkskunde* is the
l'art pour l'art viewpoint, which also dominated the world of art at that time. The
peasant was essentially of interest only as a scientific object; among the peasantry
"the folklorist will find the richest and most easily graspable material for observation."

With a considerable Jewish participation, the idea of a primitive communal
culture was developed by ethnologists on the supposed developmental ladder of
"one" humanity, from a half-animal dweller in the primitive forest to "the lord of
creation." In the attempt to pay lip service to fashionable realism, the primitive
element overseas and in inner Africa was equated with the German and Scandinavian peasants.

This school of thought found its programmatic representative in the Bonn university teacher, Hans Naumann,[1] who attempted to clarify the interplay between
the purported primitive lower stratum and the educated upper stratum through the
terms "primitive communal property" [*primitives Gemeinschaftsgut*] and "sunken
cultural property" [*gesunkenes Kulturgut*], and for whom the task of a German
science of *Volkskunde* is exhausted in the following question: "in which of the

two realms, in the realm of ethnology or in the realm of intellectual and cultural history, lies the origin of all those things whose representation and description is necessary for presenting the life of the *Volk*?"

"The folk doesn't produce, it reproduces"—this guiding sentence of "modern" *Volkskunde* is used by Hans Naumann in the following manner: "Folk costume, folk custom, folk song, folk drama, rustic furniture, etc., are sunken cultural property, down to the smallest detail and they become this only slowly and in an almost calculable time span." According to Hans Naumann, folk costume is merely sunken cultural property, "fashionable clothing of the upper stratum in the minds of the uneducated lower stratum." He professes thus not to know that from the archaeological finds of the clothes of the Germanic peoples of the Bronze Age to the fundamental forms of German costumes of our era there runs a line which cannot be destroyed, even by constant alien influences infiltrating by way of the "upper stratum." He doesn't know and doesn't want to know that folk song and folk drama have preserved a very ancient heritage and that the decorative forms of rustic furniture don't represent primitive attempts at imitation of the curlicues of "high art," but are rather symbols and very ancient emblems of fortune and life. No, for him these are all manifestations of a bottomless primitivity. He takes great pleasure in the following characterization of our German peasants:

"Primitive man dislikes continued and systematically organized, physical and mental effort, except perhaps the dance. Our primitives still dislike work and only do what is absolutely necessary. They prefer to live from hand to mouth, work for the most part to subsist, not to earn a profit. In any case, they still like to believe that work is dirty. They don't know the maxim of the modern cultured stratum, 'work or despair,' and they are most certainly at ease and happy when they don't have to work."[2]

Characteristically, the representatives of confessional *Volkskunde* greet the methodological statements of the so-called modern science of *Volkskunde* most warmly.[3] The Bonn university teacher Karl Meisen felt it appropriate in a programmatic study in honor of Prelate Schreiber to speak of the "monstrous damage" which the Brothers Grimm had imposed on the science of German *Volkskunde* by directing "their gaze almost without exception to the oldest time of our people, to the Germanic, heathen epoch." And why was the perception of the Brothers Grimm, of the unity of our whole set of traditions in its Nordic-Aryan origin, in the words of Karl Meisen, "a fatefully wrong path"? Because they neglected to use as their starting point the "real" source of the folk-nation, namely the Roman Church, and because they blocked the understanding of the only true perspective, i.e., the "supranational, Western perspective," by their combination of *Volkskunde* with the national philologies and especially with Germanic studies. On the basis of his supranational attitude Karl Meisen arrives at the following goals for the study of German *Volkskunde*: "We cannot solve from the point of view of one *Volk*, one nation, or even one region the multitudinous problems that the folk-nation in general, and each nation in particular, assigns to its research. This view contradicts completely the folk-nation shape and development of the Western nations, where since the early Middle Ages it has not been so much those characteristics of national and racial constituency [*volklich*] that have been determinative for the essential points of the folk-nation but much more that gradually completed integration into the Western cultural circle."

It is only consistent with his supranational way of thinking that Karl Meisen speaks out enthusiastically in favor of introducing into *Volkskunde* the ethnographic concept of primitive culture that is not bound to *Volk* or race, nor time or space. Therewith dies the idea of a national *Volkskunde* of itself.

If the Catholic action of today is trying to present saints of the Roman Church to today's German youth as heroic figures and leader [*Führer*] personalities, then it is doing this apparently out of necessity. If, however, Karl Meisen places German *Volkskunde* in the service of this temporally limited functional objective, then we will be on guard against this for the sake of honor in German science. Every scholar of history knows that saint worship in the Roman Church was not able to displace Germanic god and hero worship. Indeed, around any single Roman saint who was set up by the Christian missionaries in the place of a unified deity, there was a concentration of customs that could not be suppressed and which had nothing to do with the saint, but revealed instead the connection to a confounded Germanic deity. The Roman Church did the wisest thing it could do, it tolerated these customs and also allowed the saint to take on the characteristics and functions of the Germanic deity. It made a virtue out of necessity and eventually brought about a celebration of itself by its "scientific representatives," claiming to be the preserver of Germanic heritage and *Volk* property, proudly pointing out its places of pilgrimage as great manufacturers and concentrations of popular customs (Prelate Schreiber). You almost need the disposition of a magician to twist it and say that because this or that saint was probably born in this or that year as a non-Germanic, and further, because his cult can be proved to be Christian, then those ostensible Germanic customs and those ostensible remains of a racially pure set of beliefs which "Romantic mythologies" associated with him were not Germanic at all, rather that they had been brought in with the saint from the old cultural area of the Mediterranean. The whole thing is apparently a contribution to the role of the Roman Church as a provider of culture to us barbarians in the north. The method does not get better when it is carried out on a large scale and when one's business is camouflaged with the harmless title of an "Institut für Volkskunde," such as is located in Münster.

In contrast to all these attempts from both liberal and confessional sides to subject German *Volkskunde* to some supranational dogma or other, our National Socialist criticism must start by firmly establishing that the object of German *Volkskunde* can never be the expressions of the community per se. It is a half-truth to claim that *Volkskunde* is concerned with the expressions of a community, "up to that point where the individual steps in as a determining and directing factor," without stating which community one has in mind. It is a half-truth when historic verification is claimed as a characteristic of true *Volk* property but the question of racial nativeness or racial alienness is neglected. And finally, it is a half-truth to call on Wilhelm Heinrich Riehl to support a traditional social teaching which plays the bearers of *Volk* property off against traditional *Volk* goods instead of directing its attention to the biological function which every popular tradition has in folk life.

The key to a National Socialist understanding of *Volkskunde* is given neither by sociology, nor ethnology, nor any confessional system, but rather only by biological and racial thinking. By continuing the thought process of a Herder, a Jakob Grimm, and a Wilhelm Heinrich Riehl, we can today, by way of contrast, say the following about the object of *Volkskunde: German* Volkskunde *is the study of the essence and the conditions essential for life of that racial and traditional world of the German* Volk *which is purest and most alive in those communities having shown most eternal contacts with the blood and soil* [Blut und Boden].

Therefore, the basis of German *Volkskunde* must be the concern with the biological and the ideo-historical being and becoming of the German *Volk*. What follows is a presentation of the breadth of range of German *Volkskunde* and a clarification of its tasks.

*

Racial studies teach us to look for the home of the Nordic race in the late Neolithic period, i.e., some 5,000 years ago, in the Saxon-Thuringian district and in the area of the northwest German giant stone graves, and to recognize the North Sea–Baltic as the actual center of Indo-Germanic migrations.

Western tribes from Asia Minor in southwest and western Europe and Lapp-Mongolian tribes in northeast and eastern Europe came in the course of centuries into the realm of power of Indo-Germanic peoples and were subjugated by a Nordic conquering stratum. This stratum forced the defeated to take on their language, which in the mouths of the new, racially alien speakers experienced a slow but sure transformation. The completion of a racial transformation came about much quicker within the ever-expanding Indo-Germanic language area. Naturally, on those most daring and exposed frontiers where there was huge loss of blood from never ending battles, the change was most effective. Thus, until today the Indo-Germanic language has been preserved in the Far East and in the Mediterranean countries to a greater or lesser extent. However, the tradition-bearing power of the blood of those erstwhile speakers from the north dissipated, but not until it had carried out major cultural achievements.

In the North Sea and Baltic area, the very kernel of the Nordic–Indo-Germanic region, the Nordic blood must have been conserved best, and in those nearby border regions its formative power must have been the strongest. In the course of historic development the Germanic tribes of central Europe guarded this decisive region for the Nordic race and welded together the German *Volk*. In the Middle Ages, it protected the Nordic race from the masses of people from Africa and from the hordes of Mongolian horsemen out of Asia in a series of decisive battles. National Socialism also considers the actions of the Knights of the Teutonic Order and the Prussian kings and the blood sacrifice of the Great War from this large perspective of a racial consideration of history.

The German *Volk* was once able to ward off the mass invasions from Africa and Asia. But it couldn't hinder the penetration by the dying Classical world. It was all the less able to do so because the technologically more advanced potpourri of peoples of the Mediterranean had appropriated the cultural values of the former Nordic ruling stratum and presented themselves to the Germanic tribes as their tradition bearers and heirs. The glory of an undermined but empty life covered up the racially alien contents which were hidden behind racially related forms. When the true danger was recognized, at first unconsciously, later more and more consciously, all pure German life had been forced into technologically unopposable but rigid forms of foreign thought systems. To shake these off intentionally and successfully, we were lacking the intellectual schooling that could work to organize and create an exemplary model. As long as this type of intellectually superior leadership was missing the new lords could choke off the continual and elemental flare-ups of healthy blood by playing off "rebel" against "rebel." They succeeded all the more easily because they continually set new values in invalidating the previous leader [*Führer*] principle as well as previous customs and ideas of common law, and further, by supporting foreign races within the Germanic-German realm that had till then been under the influence and rule of the Nordic race. Equating of freemen and slaves, of members of the Nordic race and of mixed breeds, must have had an increasingly devastating effect for the Nordic race. The new value system chose a leadership which effectively created models before the opposition could take shape. Gradually a stratum was formed, small at first but constantly spreading, which was clearly distinguished from the rest of the *Volk*. There arose the so-called educated stratum, in contrast to the "uneducated." Just these two terms illuminate graphically the nature of the matter. The educated stratum, through its new values of experience and training, was self-contained. Their unity was a foreign thought system and a body of knowledge based on claims of absolute validity. In contrast, the unity of the "uneducated" existed solely in a negation of this system of values and its representatives. The rebellious movement of the "uneducated" who had been degraded to a lower stratum (which was characterized, to name only the most prominent stages, by a line from the Peasant Wars to the Reformation with its consequences for the German workers' movement of the Second Empire) were doomed to failure as long as they did not adhere to those values through which a counterblow could be struck. Only National Socialism has succeeded, by the means of its goal-oriented leadership, in creating the organizational conditions for coming to power and thus being able to destroy the foreign value system. However, a complete break with that intellectual world was only possible by means of an uncompromising affirmation of the eternal values of the Nordic race, which had to be and were most alive precisely in that lower stratum of the so-called uneducated. Peasantry and workers protected these model-building powers out of which the German folk community grows.

This knowledge of the cartography of German history is the decisive precondition for a truly German *Volkskunde*.

*

What is then the object of German *Volkskunde*? In light of the numerous published collections of material from recent years a limitation to the basics will be permitted here.[4]

For the most part there are five large areas with which German *Volkskunde* ought to concern itself: settlement and material culture, narrative and legend material [*Saggut*], custom and symbol, folk speech, and communal forms.

Settlement studies and research into material culture are mainly concerned with the material forms of living, and of ceremonies and everyday life, starting with settlement form and structure of house and yard, with economic life and labor, including folk costumes and all kinds of handcrafted expressions relating to usage and to decorations. The cultivation of noble and useful forms of tools is here just as essential as the observation of genuinely harmonious colors in costumes, or the care used in accomplishing unity in building shapes, settlements, and landscapes. In this manner *Volkskunde*, by dealing with the relationship between settlement and space in its diversity and by including in its field of observations both field and forest and roads and paths, can become regional study in the true sense of the word.

Narrative research and legend research [Saggut] include all forms of oral reporting, especially *Märchen*, legend, song, game, jest, and saints' legends, as well as fable, riddle, and proverb, including the simple joking question. It attempts most especially to discover the structure of mythical materials in its dramatic structure, i.e., the mythical elements which were used in dramas and plays, and strives to make it useful in shaping calendrical ceremonies. Its duty is, above all, to secure the foundations of a healthy and genuine sociability in the realm of our folk-national work.

Research on customs and study of symbolism is concerned most especially with customs and practices, holy signs and symbols in the course of life and of the year, on holidays and workdays. It testifies thus to the reality of German popular belief and an indigenous, true piety.

But certainly not least is the *cultivation of folk speech* an honorable duty, precisely for a way of looking at things, which can recognize the significance of perception, of graphic strength, and color, but also of education and power of form in a language that is pure to its roots. In addition there is the preservation of the rich treasure of German given names as well as research devoted to geographic and place names.

Closely associated with the numerous manifestations of folk-national traditions is our research into the *history and structure of communities, which were and are the bearers and shapers of this traditional material.* Thus *Volkskunde* closes the circle, from the Germanic clan and the German tribal confederacies to the professional and work communities of the present, and deals at the same time with the role of women and the relationship between the mother and child.

Naturally, with such a completely new picture of the canonical areas for German *Volkskunde* there must be new research goals which go to the heart of the matter. Thus it is a racial, cultural, and sociopolitical necessity for this newly designed folkloric research to dispense completely with the division into the upper and lower strata, educated and primitive culture. In their place must come the division into racially pure and racially alien essences. The standard of measurement is the value sensibility of the Nordic race. This summons does not represent a call to arms for a racial battle. It comes about rather by professionally establishing that the Nordic race represents, through its proven values and through its historic goals, the best means for securely cementing the folk-national existence of a racially mixed German *Volk* which is still united by the Nordic blood in all its people.

It is also the task of German *Volkskunde* to lay bare the sources of Nordic tradition that have been buried by a foreign overburden and to secure their undisturbed course into the future. This splendid political task requires a tremendous ability to empathize with the cartography of German development, in order to hear and feel the pulse of Nordic blood even where it has taken on foreign forms.

From this, however, comes for German *Volkskunde* the obvious duty of closely and constantly rubbing of shoulders with German research into prehistory in the spirit of a Gustav Kossinna, and with racial studies in the sense of the programist of Nordic thought, Hans F. K. Günther. Today we see *Volkskunde*, prehistory, and racial studies as a firmly cemented block, as the science of German *Volk* research.

Although *Volkskunde* may have stood for too long in a fateful dependency relationship on ethnology, it has now turned the tables and can offer ethnology a new and infinitely useful working principle: the thesis of the independence of the folk-nation which is represented by National Socialist *Volkskunde* and which is also able, especially in the realm of ethnology, to guarantee the multitude and the diversity of phenomena and traditional values and to extrapolate their real nature. National Socialist ethnology does not subject foreign folk-nationality to a universal construction, but rather allows it its own dignity and respects its own essence.

If we also believe that a modern study of *Volkskunde* must start with the peasantry, this is not because of a false romantic notion about peasants, but rather because the peasant is still more closely associated with the primal powers of our being than a town and city dweller who is much more likely to be subjected to continuing change. Using this as a basis it becomes most nearly possible to strengthen and deepen the consciousness of tradition of a worker to whom, like the peasant, National Socialism has given a consciousness of the honor of his name and rank.

Thus the practical tasks of German *Volkskunde* become visible as well. They consist above all in shaping ceremonial and everyday life. The celebrations of life's stages, the seasonal festivities, and especially the great celebrations of the nation present a large area of research that is conscious of its responsibility to National Socialism. The shaping of leisure time in all of the organizations of the movement [NSDAP] and the new state poses question after question for *Volkskunde*. A youth that has grown up for the most part in the city is placed through the *Reichsarbeitsdienst*[5] and the *Landjahr*[6] for longer or shorter periods directly into a rural setting. This youth observes and experiences, makes comparisons between city and country. Without fail he is forced quite instinctively to the psychological and practical attempts to reshape his living conditions. It is here that German *Volkskunde* takes on the decisive task of advising and overseeing the lot of German *Volkskunde* regarding questions about *house construction, clothing, and creativity in handicrafts*.

For the questions about the organization of festivities which has rightly taken a front-row seat in folkloristic observations, Wilhelm Grimm's image of a shattered jewel whose pieces are widely strewn, all overgrown, can serve as a good road sign.

National Socialist organization of festivities represents a condensed description of our national powers of belief. Germanic piety and Nordic faith in God [*Gottglaube*] are like those brightly colored jewels, strewn in among the traditions in the legends, *Märchen*, and songs, in the world of popular customs, and they are discernible in the holy signs and symbols which we can find everywhere on our farmhouses and on the creations of our handicrafts.

It is most certainly not our task to create a system of religion by interpreting these survivals of a once-complete world-view too quickly. That would be an inorganic path and the beginning of a new dogmatism. But a knowledge of the continually changing historical development of the intellectual and material traditions of our ancestors can first open our eyes and then sharpen our ears for racially pure and racially alien essence. Then we will also be able to sense the warp and the weave of the eternal powers of belief of our people, powers that have been alive from prehistoric times to this very moment, and which exist today, precisely in the festivities of the battle-ready organizations of the movement [NSDAP] and in the great national festivals. Here we find the expressive forms of our time, which document the new-found unity of our *Volk*. Concerning the desire to shape, however, there is that great statement by Ernst Moritz Arndt, "To be a *Volk*, to have a feeling for something, . . . that is the religion of our age. Because of this belief you must be harmonious and strong, for it you must overcome the devil and hell. Leave all petty religions and do your great duty to the single highest religion, and unite yourself to one belief, far beyond the Pope and Luther."[7]

Translated from Matthes Ziegler, *Volkskunde auf rassischer Grundlage. Voraussetzungen und Aufgaben*. Deutsches Volkstum. Eine Schriftenreihe über deutsche Volkskunde für die Schulungs- und Erziehungsarbeit der NSDAP. Hrsg. vom Beauftragten des Führers für die Überwachung der gesamten geistigen und weltanschaulichen Schulung und Erziehung der NSDAP in Verbindung mit der "Arbeitsgemeinschaft für deutsche Volkskunde." München 1939. Hoheneichen-Verlag München.

Appendix II.1
Departmental Directors' Meeting of the Research and Teaching Community "Ancestral Inheritance" [Forschungs- und Lehrgemeinschaft "Das Ahnenerbe"] in Munich, April 23–24, 1941. Report (Excerpt)

List of participants at the Departmental Directors' Meeting:

SS-Standartenführer Professor Dr. Wüst
SS-Obersturmbannführer Sievers
SS-Obersturmbannführer Weigel
SS-Sturmbannführer Professor Dr. Harmjanz
SS-Sturmbannführer Professor Dr. Jankuhn
SS-Sturmbannführer Professor Dr. Tratz
SS-Hauptsturmführer Dr. Komanns
SS-Hauptsturmführer Dr. von Lützelburg
SS-Hauptsturmführer Dr. Plaßmann
SS-Hauptsturmführer Dr. Scultetus
SS-Hauptsturmführer Dr. Schäfer
SS-Hauptsturmführer Professor Dr. Brand
SS-Obersturmführer Professor Dr. Christian
SS-Obersturmführer Dr. Willvonseder
SS-Obersturmführer Dr. von Rauch
SS-Obersturmführer Dr. Fitzner
SS-Obersturmführer Rampf
SS-Untersturmführer Professor Dr. Till
SS-Untersturmführer Boehm
SS-Untersturmführer Dr. Rudolph
SS-Untersturmführer Dr. Huth
Professor Dr. Dirlmeier
Professor Dr. Wolfram

Professor Wimmer
Dr. Bohmers
Dr. Schweizer
Dr. Haarnagel
Dr. Hielscher
Secretary: Fräulein Dafner
Excused were:
SS-Sturmbannführer Dr. Greite
SS-Hauptsturmführer Professor Dr. Schleif

Wednesday, April 23, 1941
In the meeting room of the Philosophical Faculty of the University of Munich, the curator, SS-Standartenführer Professor Dr. Wüst, began the Departmental Directors' meeting at 10 A.M. He greeted those who came and explained the purpose and business of the two days: here the wish of the Reichsführers-SS would be fulfilled, to maintain their personal connections during the war. This opportunity today will be utilized to prepare the work of the "Ancestral Inheritance" for peacetime, in contrast to other culture-political organizations. Peace will bring about special problems for Germany, which can't be solved with the sword alone. It is a matter of Germany, German scholarship, and German culture going to work now to pacify the Western world, and employing the influence of the German science decisively. No organization, like the "Ancestral Inheritance," has such an opportunity to assist with this problem. The duty has arisen primarily with us, to show the peoples [of the world] the great communal accomplishments in all areas; whether we are dealing with excavations, symbols, language, or folk customs, we possess the necessary tools. Put simply: our work is first and foremost the establishment of Indo-Germanic community. In open conversation and in a sense of comradeship, these two days should serve to accomplish preparatory work on these thoughts.
Three large problem areas are to be distinguished:
1. A discussion about the community works of the "Ancestral Inheritance," about the existing ones as well as the ones planned for the near future.
2. The publications of the "Ancestral Inheritance," a task which now during the war has met with unexpected difficulties.
3. The question of scholarly succession.
Primary here is the basic order of the Reichsführers-SS of November 27, 1938, to incorporate the scholarly goals and scholars of the "Ancestral Inheritance" into the universities in order to become secure there. The Reich business leader can report now on community works.

SS-Obersturmbannführer Sievers made lengthy statements about the war activity of the "Ancestral Inheritance." The work was in the beginning mostly cur-
tailed but that will soon be changed. In the eastern regions it came first of all to
special activities. Caring for the culture goods made the creation of individual
service branches necessary within the framework of the "Ancestral Inheritance."
In addition there were the tasks of solidifying the German folk-nation, for German
history a new and unique area. The acquisition and treatment of the entire spiritual
inheritance of those ethnic Germans being resettled, and tending to their cultural
life was a difficult and demanding job. These people were either separated from
their old homeland or they had to overcome more or less great difficulties and
hindrances in the new homelands. In the Baltic this work was completed relatively
fast. The University of Posen, which will open this coming Sunday, represents one
more accomplishment in the new eastern regions. Reflecting the wishes of the
Reichsführer an Institut für Volkstumsforschung [Institute for Folk-National Re-
search] has been created, and that is the first teaching post for folk-national studies
in cooperation with a university.

The cultural action in South Tyrol which was assigned to the "Ancestral Inheritance" and which is under its direction (i.e., of the Reich business leader) has
been carried out for a year now with thirteen working groups and fifty-six men
and women workers. The work is laid out with a breadth and detail such as has
never been accomplished before. Things have been verified which the people themselves had said did not exist and which scholarship had assumed without being
able to offer proof. Establishing this proof was now possible for many things. He
named for example house types which up until now were only known to exist in
Gotland or South Sweden.

It is not only the resettlement areas but the newly occupied regions which
have come into question for the action of the "Ancestral Inheritance." Here all of
our previous accomplishments in all of these areas would benefit us especially.
The Department of "Prehistory" has worked here in an exemplary way. Experience
in the importance of aerial photography for prehistory, photographs of the military
roads, of prehistoric lands, exhibitions, etc., have become primary concepts of the
working technology which we have mastered. In this way many monuments could
be secured.

The Reich business leader mentioned further the various actions in Scandinavia,
France, and Holland and commented on the work of Jankuhn, Plaßmann, and Schnei-
der. The limited number of scholarly workers both here and there is a problem.
He touched upon the future activity in Lorraine and in the western regions.

A further important question is the science of colonization. Within the
Reichsforschungsrat [Reich Research Advisory Board] a working society for colonization scholarship with twenty-seven sections has been founded. The question
arises just how far the individual departments and departmental directors in this

working society can be brought together for action in the colonies and can work together in a practical way. New areas of work are emerging now in the south and the southeastern areas. It has happened that wherever military action is successful and completed, that the "Ancestral Inheritance" is then called in. All scholars of the "Ancestral Inheritance" must be employed for these necessary work problems.

The Reich business leader emphasized emphatically the strictly confidential nature of this discussion. Beyond this circle no questions are to be discussed, no matter what kind.

Following the presentation of the Reich business leader, Prof. Dr. Richard Wolfram was allowed to speak. He reported extensively on his folklore work in South Tyrol, which was for him, as he described it, a treasure chest and fountain of happiness. In the relict area an abundance of material was collected: customs, folk beliefs, folk dances. With one example he explained the unique fact that songs of a special quint-form previously known only in Iceland had been found in South Tyrol. In the lively activity of everyday life, symbols could be recognized everywhere. He has in his possession forty-two still-unpublished folk dramas. That led, among other things, to the question just how the steadily growing material could be worked up and applied.

SS-Obersturmbannführer Sievers answered this question in detail and pointed out the prohibition on publications of such results. Only in light of the eastern work has this prohibition been lifted somewhat. The decision on individual cases of publication by specialists is made exclusively by the Reich commissioner for solidifying the German folk-nation [Reichsführer-SS Heinrich Himmler]. The film material, however, can now be worked up and spliced together. At the next meeting of the departmental leaders the pictures from South Tyrol can be shown. . . .

Source: Bundesarchiv Koblenz, FRG, File NS 21/229.

Appendix II.2
The Research and Teaching Community
"The Office of Ancestral Inheritance"
[*Das Ahnenerbe*]. Tasks and Structure

The Research and Teaching Community of the "Office of Ancestral Inheritance" was founded in 1935. It grew out of the situation at the time in the liberal arts which had not followed the radical change accomplished in the political realm; instead they remained in part stuck in an old world-view, and in part, in a painful effort not to miss out on annexation with National Socialism, they forcefully violated scholarship. Certainly there were individualists who honestly strove to find new paths. It was worthwhile to gather them in, to bring them closer together.

The Reichsführer-SS had recognized that there could be only one way to give a firm foundation back to this rootless scholarship that is so lacking in its pure German relationship, and thereby to this new "world-view" as well, this means "becoming who you are"—contemplation of our own being and essence, e.g., of one's ancestors, their essence and deeds.

"A *Volk* lives happily in the present and the future as long as it is aware of its past and the greatness of its ancestors"—that is the guiding thought coined by Heinrich Himmler, which covers the work of the "Office of Ancestral Inheritance."

In the beginning the work of the "Ancestral Inheritance" was above all intended to uncover the Germanic elements of our culture. It was an effort to trace the Germanic essence and deliver it from the numerous foreign elements, brought about by the confessions and other influences. The first research posts established therefore were those for "Germanic studies," for "*Märchen* and legends," for "script and symbol studies," for "excavations," for "house signs and clan symbols." The magazine *Germanien*, as a "magazine for all friends of German prehistory," helped make scholarly material accessible to larger circles. At the same time the Schriftenreihe Deutsches Ahnenerbe [German Ancestral Inheritance Series] was founded with its three branches: primary work, investigations by special branches of science, folk-national writings.

A knowledge grew out of this work, that in our search for the "whither" and "whence" of our existence, we cannot stop at the Germanic sources but must reach back to the original connections among all *Volk* of Nordic blood within the Indo-Germanic realm. The Reichsführer-SS has called as head of the "Office of Ancestral Inheritance," as his scientific director (curator), the ordinary professor for Indo-Germanic–Aryan culture and linguistics at the University of Munich, Dr. Walther *Wüst*. The "German Ancestral Inheritance" received in the "Ancestral Inheritance" its absolute goal, which included a number of new tasks and thus new research posts.

Hand in hand with that was the establishment of natural scientific research institutes, since the separation into arts and sciences, a result of the liberal thought process, had to be overcome and the unity of the soul and body, spirit and blood, god and world had to be made a prerequisite of a new Indo-Germanic–Germanic world-view.

The activity of the "Ancestral Inheritance" should not just be limited to research but should see as its most distinguished goal the education of a new scientific generation, who can spread the information and knowledge acquired in the working society "Ancestral Inheritance" to the universities and schools.

On January 1, 1939, the "Research and Teaching Community of the Office of Ancestral Inheritance" received its final, legitimate form in the statute given to it by its president, Reichsführer-SS Heinrich Himmler, from which only the introduction, defining the assigned tasks, is quoted:

"The Research and Teaching Community of the 'Office of Ancestral Inheritance' has the task of researching the space, spirit, deed, and inheritance of the Nordic races of the Indo-Germanic realm, to structure the results of research in a lively way, and to convey them to the *Volk*. The execution of this task must follow exactly applied scientific research procedures."

Its realization occurs through:

1. the organization of research and teaching posts,
2. the granting of research assignments and the accomplishment of exploring expeditions,
3. the publication of scientific papers,
4. the promotion of scientific works,
5. the arranging of scientific meetings.

The Research and Teaching Community "Ancestral Inheritance" shall promote and support all similar and like endeavors, including in the area of international [*zwischenvölkischer*] cooperation. The Research and Teaching Community "Ancestral Inheritance" is of value to the community through lawful acts.

The "Ancestral Inheritance" today includes thirty-four research, respectively research and teaching posts which are listed below.

The directorship of the "Ancestral Inheritance" consists of the following:

President, Reichsführer-SS Heinrich Himmler
Curator, Ordinary University Professor SS-Oberführer Dr. Walther Wüst
Reich Business Leader, SS-Standartenführer Wolfram Sievers.

The Scholarly Departments:

1. Teaching and Research Post for Indo-Germanic–Aryan Linguistics and Cultural Studies. Director: SS-Oberführer Dr. Walther Wüst, Ordinary Professor and Rector of the University of Munich.
2. Teaching and Research Post for Germanic Cultural and Landscape Studies. Director: SS-Obersturmbannführer Dr. phil. habil. Otto Plassmann, Extraordinary Professor at the University of Bonn.
3. Research Post for Germanic Linguistics and Landscape Studies. Director: Dr. Bruno Schweizer, Munich.
4. Teaching and Research Post for Indo-Germanic–Germanic Language and Cultural Studies. Director: Dr. Richard Kienle, Ordinary Professor at the University of Hamburg, on the battlefield at this time.
5. Teaching and Research Post for Orientation and Landscape Symbols. Director: Dr. phil. habil. Werner Müller, University Docent at the University of Straßburg, on the battlefield at this time.
6. Teaching and Research Post for Indo-Germanic Religious History. Director: SS-Obersturmführer Dr. phil. habil. Otto Huth, Adjunct Professor at the University of Straßburg, in the Waffen-SS at this time.
7. Teaching and Research Post for Indo-Germanic–Germanic Legal History. Director: SS-Untersturmführer Dr. Wolfgang Ebel, Ordinary Professor at the University of Göttingen, in the Waffen-SS at this time.
8. Teaching and Research Post for Runic and Symbol Studies. Director: Dr. Wolfgang Krause, Ordinary Professor at the University of Göttingen and SS-Obersturmbannführer Karl Theodor Weigel.
9. Research Post for House Signs and Kinship Symbols. Director: Not occupied at this time.
10. Teaching and Research Post for Folk Research and *Volkskunde*. Director: SS-Obersturmbannführer Dr. Heinrich Harmjanz, Ordinary Professor at the University of Frankfurt/M, on the battlefield at this time.
10a. *Atlas der Deutschen Volkskunde*.
11. Teaching and Research Post for Narrative, *Märchen*, and Legends. Director: Killed in action, not occupied at this time.
12. Teaching and Research Post for Germanic-German *Volkskunde*. Director: Dr. Richard Wolfram, Ordinary Professor at the University of Vienna, in the Waffen-SS at this time.
13. Teaching and Research Post for Excavations. Director: SS-Obersturmbannführer (Division Leader [Sonderführer] in the Waffen-SS) Dr. Herbert Jankuhn, Ordinary Professor at the University of Rostock, on the battlefield at this time (Waffen-SS).

14. Teaching and Research Post for Germanic Architecture. Director: SS-Obersturmführer Dr. Martin Rudolph, University Docent at the Technical High School [University] in Braunschweig, in the Waffen-SS at this time.
15. Research Post for Wurten [*Wurten* (or Low German *Warften*) are earth mounds or little hills used as dwellings, i.e., prehistorical or ancient Germanic house research]. Director: SS-Untersturmführer Dr. Wilhelm Haarnagel, Wilhelmshaven, on the battlefield at this time.
16. Teaching and Research Post for Prehistory. Director: Dr. Assien Bohmers, University Docent at the University of Groningen.
17. Teaching and Research Post for Classical Antiquities. Director: Dr. Franz Dirlmeier, Ordinary Professor and Dean of the Faculty of Philosophy at the University of Munich, and SS-Obersturmführer Dr. Rudolph Till, Ordinary Professor at the University of Munich.
18. Teaching and Research Post for Middle Latin. Director: Dr. Paul Lehmann, Ordinary Professor at the University of Munich.
19. Teaching and Research Post for Celtic Folk Research. Director: SS-Untersturmführer (Division Leader [Sonderführer] in the Waffen-SS) Dr. Ludwig Mühlhausen, Ordinary Professor at the University of Berlin.
20. Teaching and Research Post for the Near East. Director: SS-Sturmbannführer Dr. Viktor Christian, Ordinary Professor and Dean of the Faculty of Philosophy at the University of Vienna.
21. Teaching and Research Post for North African Cultural Studies. Director: Dr. phil. habil. Otto Rössler, University Docent at the University of Tübingen, in the Waffen-SS at this time.
22. Research Post for Indo-Germanic-German Music. Director: SS-Untersturmführer (Division Leader [Sonderführer] in the Waffen-SS) Dr. Alfred Quellmalz, Berlin.
23. Research Post for Astronomy. Director: Not occupied at this time.
24. Research Post for Geophysics. Director: SS-Sturmbannführer Dr. Hans Robert Scultetus, on the battlefield at this time.
25. Teaching and Research Post for Biology. Director: Not occupied at this time.
25a. Reich Union for Biology. Union Leader: Dr. Hermann Weber, Ordinary Professor at the University of Straßburg.
26. Research Post for Botany. Director: SS-Obersturmbannführer (Division Leader [Sonderführer] in the Waffen-SS) Dr. Philipp von Lützelburg, Dachau/Upper Bavaria.
26a. Pfohl Institute for Plant Preparation. Director: Professor. Dr. Pfohl.
27. Teaching and Research Post for Central Asia and Expeditions. Director: SS-Sturmbannführer Dr. habil. Ernst Schäfer, University Docent at the University of Munich.
28. Teaching and Research Post for Plant Genetics. Director: SS-Untersturmführer Dr. habil. Heinz Brücher, University Docent at the University of Jena.
29. Research Post for Chalk Formations and Cave Studies. Director: SS-

Standartenführer Prof. Dr. Hans Brand, on the battlefield at this time (Waffen-SS).

29a. Reich Union for Chalk Formations and Cave Studies. Union Director: SS-Obersturmbannführer Prof. Dr. Eduard Paul Tratz, Salzburg.

30. Teaching and Research Post for Folk Medicine. Commission Director: SS-Hauptsturmführer Dr. habil. Alexander Berg, University Docent at the University of Berlin (in the Waffen-SS at this time).

31. Research Post for Natural Scientific Prehistory. Commission Director: SS-Obersturmführer Dr. Rudolf Schütrumpf, Dachau/Upper Bavaria. (Waffen-SS).

32. Teaching and Research Post for Representative and Applied Natural History, "*Haus der Natur.*" Director: SS-Obersturmbannführer Prof. Dr. Eduard Paul Tratz, Salzburg.

33. Research Post for Applied Geology. Director: Prof. Dr. Josef Wimmer, Munich.

34. Institute for Research of Applied Military Scientific Goals. Dept. P: Commission Director SS-Hauptsturmführer Dr. habil. Plötner, University Docent at the University of Leipzig. Dept. H: Director SS-Sturmbannführer Dr. August Hirt, Ordinary Professor at the University of Straßburg. Institute for Entomology: Director Dr. phil. habil. Eduard May, University Docent at the University of Munich.

Naturally their establishment is dependent on peaceful conditions. In the course of the war a large number of research posts had to be closed; other institutes, which have an immediate relationship to the necessities of war, have been newly organized. In addition special activities have been implemented.

In the area of cultural science, the first special activity [*Einsatz*, the military term for attack against an enemy] implemented was the assignment of the Reichsführer-SS as Reich commissioner for solidifying the German folk-nation for seizing and securing the spiritual and material cultural property of all resettled German nationals.

Scholarly activity in Germanic lands followed, whose tasks, because of their topicality, are detailed as follows:

The new community of the European-German nation will grow out of the great common battle experience. The rediscovery of the self, a newly unifying achievement derived from the mandate for historical leadership, must be restored through exhibiting and making us conscious of the common roots out of which the European-German nation lives. It is of value to point out unbroken German continuity in the historical sense as well as living and true German completeness in the spatial realm, e.g., race and family, spirit and state, law, speech, nationhood, belief and custom, in myth, legend, and song. This unbroken German continuity and living true German completeness have also been consolidated in home and hearth and in the creative artistic manifestations of the folk spirit, and it continually materializes as a living tradition of the individual branches of the Germanic folk family. It is also of value to implement the strength of will which has grown from insight in the battle for regeneration of the Germanic community.

This summons encompasses first of all an important concept for German scholarship and that of other Germanic lands, which can only be fulfilled through cooperation. For its realization and implementation, the *Germanische Wissenschaftseinsatz* [Germanic Scholarly Activity Plan] was called to life. Its task in Germanic lands will be carried out, for the time being, through Regional Branches in the Hague, Brussels and Oslo which are part of the Germanic Directive Posts [*Germanische Leitstellen*].

The Germanic Scholarly Activity Plan, therefore, has the task of gathering together the German scholarly work force in the fields of prehistory, Germanic studies, and Germanic folk research, and in regard to these Regional Branches, to bring together in the Germanic lands those who are being considered for collaboration and those who are already prepared to work together. It will then propose for all of them, in the context of the above outlined goals, both joint and individual assignments. It will be concerned with the publication of goal oriented research results in scholarly or popular books, in scholarly journals and even in such big illustrated monthly journals as the *Hamer*, which has appeared for years in Dutch and Flemish editions and now appears in German (*Hammer*) as well. Here the special concern is above all to bring to life the results of scholarly Germanic studies in those Germanic lands where research still lags behind or where, in their questioning, they have not found ubiquitous and common Germanic foundations.

In the Netherlands and in Flanders, the work of the "Ancestral Inheritance" in the Germaansche Werkgemeenschap Nederland [Germanic Workers' Community Netherlands], or the Germaansche Werkgemeenschap Vlaandern [Germanic Workers' Community Flanders], which is corporately attached, has already established a firm footing and discovered its organizational form.

Military goals in the framework of the Waffen-SS serve the medical and scientific research posts which are combined in the Institut für wehrwissenschaftliche Zweckforschung [Institute for Research of Applied Military Scientific Goals]. Belonging to this same series of institutes for war related tasks is also the Forschungsstätte für Pflanzengenetik [Research Post for Plant Genetics], whose primary task is to breed frost- and drought-resistant grain types for the settlement of the east. Almost all of the research posts still working today have individual assignments important to the war effort.

Mandates for securing monument preservation in the occupied territories, as in the war zone on the eastern front, led to specialized activities for implementation in Denmark, Serbia, following the SS-Panzer Grenadier Division Wiking.

From the Teaching and Research Post for Chalk Formations and Cave Studies came the Karstwehrtruppe [Chalk Formation Group] of the Waffen-SS, whose commander, as director of the Research Post, made use of the theoretical knowledge in military practice gained there.

In conclusion, one should point out that a great number of individual research mandates unites scholars in all branches of scholarship to the "Office of Ancestral Inheritance," which thus has the opportunity to present the SS spirit to the German universities.

The "Ancestral Inheritance Foundation Press" which should not go unmentioned, publishes, in addition to an abundant number of scientific books, a series of leading scientific magazines.

The abundance of tasks, which because of the farsighted goal setting of the Reichsführer-SS cannot be outlined here, gives to everyone who feels himself called, the opportunity for a fulfilling activity in life.

The Reichsführer-SS has forged for himself in the Research and Teaching Community of the "Office of Ancestral Inheritance" an effective instrument of power. Detached from all cumbersome administration and from various prejudices that are burdened down by armchair scholarship, it will push open the gates which lead out onto the fields where the fruits for creating a new Germanic Reich to guide Europe will come forth.

The way of thinking and attitude, through which all the work of the Research and Teaching Community of the "Office of Ancestral Inheritance" is determined, and will be determined, bear on their shields, for their defense and their esteem:

> Noble as it is fitting for the German-Germanic man, never narrow-mindedly imprisoned in dogmas and doctrines, truthful and rigorous in research and scholarship, National Socialist in courage to his creed.

Ahnenerbe-Memorandum (1944). Source: Bundesarchiv Koblenz, FRG, File Number NS 19/1850.

SCHRIFTEN DER
BREMER WISSENSCHAFTLICHEN GESELLSCHAFT
Reihe E

Niederdeutsche Zeitschrift für Volkskunde

Herausgegeben von

ERNST GROHNE und HERMANN TARDEL

Jahrgang 11

BREMEN 1933

G. WINTERS BUCHHANDLUNG
FR. QUELLE NACHF.

Appendix III.1
Call by the Union for German Folklore, Inc.
[Bund für deutsche Volkskunde, e.V.] 1933

German *Volkskunde* awakens and preserves the knowledge of the most authentic cultural goods that the German folk possesses. The digging is deeper and deeper, more and more relationships are being established, more and more knowledge is being gained. Precisely the world-view foundations for National Socialism and the national movement have been prepared in the past through folklore research, as the names Jahn, Riehl, etc. prove.

Lacking however was unity, large-scale cooperation, penetration into the broad folk strata, a consciousness that everyone must work together.

Great things have already been accomplished: the associations and institutes that have promoted German *Volkskunde* through collections and research have joined together in a League; the German Folk Song Archive has collected German folk songs throughout the entire German cultural area since 1914; the great German folklore *Atlas* is in process; folk art is promoted throughout the widest area; handbooks that bring together synoptically the materials of superstition, fairy tales, etc., and numerous other works have had a far-reaching effect.

Still, it is of value to preserve what has been done, and it is of value to expand it, to find champions for *Volkskunde* in every city and every village—not hundreds, no, but thousands.

In order to reach this goal, and at that moment when the great pure German and National Socialist renewal has made *Volkskunde* into a public affair of the German nation as research and instruction of the folk-national thought and life forms in the past and the present, we have founded the

Bund für deutsche Volkskunde

Yearly dues RM 1,—; for associations and corporate public sector bodies RM 3,—.

Those who are members of an association for folklore which is allied with the League of German Societies for Folklore, need pay only RM 0.60, but may voluntarily increase this to RM 1,—.

Every Mark contributes to giving *Volkskunde* new assignments, to deepening its scholarly base, preserving threatened folk material from extinction.

What do we want to do with this small fee, which becomes powerful when it is given by many hands?

1. Publish annually a folklore work that all members will receive without further payment;
2. have lectures held on a regularly scheduled plan about folklore, whose scholarly value is guaranteed;
3. publish a folklore newsletter that supplies newspapers and magazines with impeccable contributions;
4. support the editing of scholarly works in the realm of folklore;
5. supply school libraries and scholarly institutions that are not able to buy folklore works with valuable pieces;
6. further the work of individual folklore associations and dispense new scholarly assignments.

Is that not a lot?

It can only take place, however, if in fact thousands contribute, if it is all of Germany, indeed all Deutschtum [Germandom], wherever our language is spoken, wherever it has validity.

Verify your participation in this great task by sending in the attached membership declaration, and solicit other members.

Every German of Aryan heritage and every politically coordinated association can become a member of the Bund.

The Bund für deutsche Volkskunde will be recorded in the list of associations and will be directed by an executive committee which is made up of a business chair and eight to sixty advisers.

We ask that payment be made through a postal money order to the Treasurer, Berlin No. 1337 57: Dr. Gerhard Lüdtke, Berlin W 10, Genthinerstr. 38.

Patron
Herr Prussian Minister for Science, Art and Folk Education
Bernhard Rust

Executive Committee for Business

Chairs
Prof.Dr. John Meier   Prof.Dr. Otto Lauffer   Prof.Dr. Hans Naumann
Freiburg i./Br.   Hamburg   Bonn a./Rh.

Secretaries

Prof.Dr. Adolf Spamer   Prof.Dr. Herbert Freudenthal   Prof.Dr. Ernst Bargheer
      Dresden   Halle a./S.   Berlin

Treasurer

Dr. Gerhard Lüdtke, Berlin

Advisors

Senior Head Master Dr. A. *Becker*, Zweibrücken; Dr. Fr. *Boehm*, Berlin-Pankow;
Book dealer H. *Cram*, Berlin; Senior Head Master Dr. G. *Faber*, Friedberg i./H;
Ministerial Officer Prof. Dr. E. *Fehrle*, Karlsruhe; Senior Reverend Dr. h.c. Ch.
Frank, Kaufbeuren; Museum Director Prof. Dr. K. *Hahm*, Berlin; Prof. Dr. H.
Hepding, Gießen; Prof. Dr. A. *Hübner*, Berlin; Prof. Dr. Fr. *Karg*, Leipzig; Head
Master's Assistant Prof. Dr. J. *Klapper*, Breslau; Head Master's Assistant Dr. *Klin-
kott*, Schneidemühl; Prof. Dr. *Künzig*, Lahr; Conservator A. *Lämmle,* Stuttgart;
Prof. Dr. O. *Lehmann*, Altona; Prof. Dr. Fr. *v.d. Leyen*, Köln a./Rh.; Prof. Dr.
L. *Mackensen*, Riga; Author G. Fr. *Meyer*, Kiel; Docent at the Technical University
Prof. R. *Mielke*, Berlin; Prof. Dr. W. *Mitzka*, Marburg; Prof. Dr. J. *Müller*, Bonn
a./Rh.; Prof. Dr. E. *Nägele*, Tübingen; Privy Councillor Prof. Dr. Fr. *Panzer*, Hei-
delberg; Museum Director Dr. W. *Peßler*, Hannover; University Director Prof. Dr.
K. *Plenzat*, Elbing; Prof. Dr. Fr. *Ranke*, Breslau; Conservator Dr. J. M. *Ritz*, Mu-
nich; Assistant Master Dr. H. *Schewe*, Freiburg i./Br.; Prelate Prof. Dr. *Schreiber*,
Münster i./W.; Prof. Dr. J. *Schwietering*, Frankfurt a./M.; Privy Councillor Prof.
Dr. Th. *Siebs*, Breslau; Ministerial Officer Dr. *Stier*, Weimar; Prof. Dr. H. *Tardel*,
Bremen; Prof. Dr. H. *Teuchert*, Rostock; Prof. Dr. J. *Trier*, Münster i./W.; Dr.
h.c. *Wagenfeld*, Münster i./W.; Prof. Dr. M. *Waehler*, Frankfurt a./M.; Head Master
Prof. Dr. *Wirth*, Dessau; Prof. Dr. R. *Wossidlo*, Waren; Prof. Dr. W. *Ziesemer*,
Königsberg i./Pr.

Translated from "Aufruf des Bundes für deutsche Volkskunde, e.V." *Niederdeutsche
Zeitschrift für Volkskunde* 11 (1933): 255–256.

Appendix III.2
First Thoughts on the Tasks and the Possibility of Establishing a Reichsinstitut für deutsche Volkskunde (Excerpts) by Adolf Spamer

I. Goal and Meaning of *Volkskunde* as a Science

The task of *Volkskunde* as a science is a recognition of the intellectual and spiritual forces within a pure German community, in their substance and in the interplay of their respective expressive forms. To this end *Volkskunde* attempts to include all educational factors of an historical, suprahistorical, temporal, and atemporal (biological, psychological) type which give the intellectual-spiritual life of a folk its external and internal shape. The beginning points of its research are those expressive forms of the inner folk life, in word and deed, which can be grasped with the senses, i.e., folk speech, folk song and folk music, folk dance, games, dramas, folk belief and folk custom, folk narrative and folk reading materials, folk wit, folk law, as well as the works of folk art. In this, the observation of speech, song, custom, narrative, art, etc., can never be an end in itself, but simply the means for penetrating into the depths of the soul of its bearer. The working goal is thus not the item but rather the person, i.e., the "*Volksmensch*" [folk man] bound up with the pure German community, or expressed somewhat differently, the recognition by the folk-nation of its folk roots. Reflecting this the view of *Volkskunde* is directed toward the mother soil of the nation, toward the deep roots of the intellectual-spiritual forces while the individual accomplishments of the intellectual hero who has come from the folk is of interest only insofar as his creations are not estranged from the mother soil or have had a fruitful effect back on it.

II. The Importance of *Volkskunde* Research for the Entire Folk

The importance of folklore knowledge for the folk cultivator and the folk educator of every type, from the least village schoolteacher to the leading statesman, was recognized by the founder of "Folklore as a Science" around the middle of the last century. Nevertheless his call to expand the state-economic faculties at the universities into state-scientific ones whose foundations were supposed to be economics *and* folklore found no resonance in the intellectual life of the time. The social restructuring as a result of the overly rapid technologizing of numerous branches of the economy and the closely associated great capitalistic buildup left little time for understanding that behind and above all economic life processes there are other stronger and more timeless powers of the spirit and of the soul in which the possibilities and the limitations of life are prescribed for every folk-nation. With the *dogma* that the intellectual-spiritual life of a folk is simply a more or less inconsequential reflex of economic-historical happenings, the incorporation of folklore into university teaching, which Riehl had striven for, fell by the wayside for decades. While economics and sociology stepped into the center of university life, as a political economic philosophy, folklore withered as a scarcely noticed appendage to the philosophical-historical subject investigations of German studies (song, legend, fairy tale, etc.) or of the research of individual motifs of a literary type. Not until the twentieth century did a change come about which has solidified once again during our age the conviction concerning the meaning of folkloric work for the cultivation and the preservation of the folk-nation. It is concentrated in the requirement: no folk-national cultivation without folklore, no folklore without folk-national cultivation! Thus it is clear on the part of folklorists as well as folk-national cultivators that there exists an agreement concerning the service role of folklore as a science, which has the task of delivering the knowledge and the theoretical base for folk-national cultivation. Fulfilling this requirement, however, places two great assignments on the folklore research of our age. First is the exposing of the almost completely unrealized sources which shed light on the historical development of individual expressions. Second is the continual search for the intellectual-spiritual life processes within our folk from which alone can be gained a clear distinction of the static and dynamic parts of our pure German course of life.

III. Previous Organizations of Folklore Research

It must also be clear to the person who believes that, as a rule, from the work of the individual will comes a decisive penetration into new realms of understanding, that a number of basic answers to folkloric questions can be accomplished only in a well-organized gathering together of similarly inclined work forces. On one hand this is through proceeding hand in hand with other arts disciplines (prehistory and history, racial studies, etc.), on the other hand through a joining of one's own disciplinary work endeavors into a firm marching plan. In this way the creation of a well-directed collector and observer network on a potentially broad (pan-German) base is often indispensable, that is, with the help of a broad circle of those interested in questions of folklore and homeland studies. From such thought processes have come since 1890 a series of regionally associated folklore associations which have mostly published their own journals and which joined together in 1904 into the Verband deutscher Vereine für Volkskunde [League of German Societies for Folklore]. With the relatively limited means which were available to the League as well as the impossibility at that time of acquiring a firmly based and voluntary helping organization for an extended period anywhere in the entire German Reich or even in the territory of ethnic Germans, the League tried (with the exception of broad attempts at affecting this) to prepare collections for a series of important research work areas as a basis for individual research. Thus arose the great *Handwörterbücher der deutschen Volkskunde* [Handbooks of German Folklore], from which the *Handwörterbuch des deutschen Aberglaubens* [Handbook of German Superstition] has been appearing since 1927 and the *Handwörterbuch des deutschen Märchens* [Handbook of the German Fairy Tale] since 1931. The *Volkskundliche Bibliographie*, begun by the Hessische Vereinigung für Volkskunde [Hessian Folklore Society], was also placed in the hands of the League and further expanded. The greatest undertaking by the League, however, was created by John Meier in his *Deutsches Volksliedarchiv* [German Folk Song Archive], founded in 1914 in Freiburg im Breisgau and still directed by him, and which now includes almost 250,000 individual documents of old and new German folk songs. He also has a Musikarchiv des deutschen Volksliedes [Music Archive of the German Folk Song] in Berlin which has recently grown far beyond the scope originally planned by him. The far-reaching meaning of both archives remains undiminished even though it was not possible for them to pursue this in addition to primary material collecting of individual texts and individual melody research, i.e., to question the life of songs within German folk singing of the present. Thus the philological-historical appears to be stronger than the folkloric objective. Only with the founding in 1927 of the *Atlas der deutschen Volkskunde*, which was cared for by the Notgemeinschaft der deutschen Wissenschaft [Cooperative Council for Aid to German Research] (the German Research Council today) was the decisive step taken toward folklore as contemporary research. With its 23,000 volunteer workers and thirty-six regional offices throughout the entire German-speaking realm, the *Atlas* and its first fascicles, which are now available, represent the most inclusive communal undertaking in the area of scholarship in the arts which has ever been attempted. The *Atlas* would scarcely be able to justify the large financial sums (about one million Reichsmarks) as a one-time undertaking on contemporary folk life (as important as such a synoptic overview is). However, its ultimate meaning consists in the fact that it is a scarcely dispensable research instrument not only for folklore research work but for all investigations in the pan-German realm. For its maps reveal both the interdependence of racially pure education (racially pure knowledge) as well as the interdependence of intellectual education which is historical, and they represent the starting points for individual research projects in more or less problematic areas. With the founding of the Landesstelle für Volksforschung und Volkstumspflege im NSLB (Gauverband Sachsen) [Regional Institute for Folk Research and Folk-National Cultivation in the NSLB (*Gau* League Saxony)] there followed in 1933 a further advance toward folkloric communal work for which the first continuing organization was created (even though it was limited to the Free State of Saxony and its teachers). It was supposed to make possible a continuing observation of the expressive forms of folk life, while the *Atlas* was conceived of from the very beginning as a one time undertaking. The supporters of this folkloric collecting activity are those folk-national keepers [*Volkstumswarte*] who are employed and obligated not only in every school district but also in every school, who for their part are again subject to the local folk-national keepers [*Kreisvolkstumswarte*] and thus to the central office in Dresden. The collected material for research, teaching, and education benefits all of those posts as well as the two Saxon universities. One year later (1934) the Deutsche Forschungsgemeinschaft [German Research Council], intending to place research on the essence and the development of the German folk on a broader foundation, brought into being the Reichsgemeinschaft für deutsche Volksforschung [Reich Community for German Folk Research], where prehistory, folklore, racial studies, folk speech, and settlement were supposed to be joined together in an inclusive working community. During this process the separation of "folk speech" from "folklore" came about through utilitarian considerations, which made the attaching of the department of "folk speech" to the *Deutscher Sprachatlas* [German Linguistic Atlas] seem desirable as a personal union. Even though the uniting of these departments into a tight working community, united in one research establishment, did not take place (with the exception of folklore and prehistory), still, in its two-year buildup of the Department of Folklore there was essential preliminary work on the old dream of a Reichsinstitut für deutsche Volkskunde.

IV. Preliminary Work for a Reichsinstitut für deutsche Volkskunde

It was clear to the representatives of folklore research for a long time that without such a central institute as the maternal household of all folkloric research in the Reich there was scarcely a satisfactory solution to all folkloric questions. The activity of all regional institutes, state offices, regional associations, and leagues with a folklore stamp can only receive through a Reichsinstitut its support and its assurance of life. Thus the Verband deutscher Vereine für Volkskunde called for such an institute before the world war, unfortunately without success, in a confidential memorandum printed in manuscript form. If the lack of interest of leading circles as well as the broader educated stratum appeared at that time as the greatest hindrance, all hesitation of this type has since disappeared, with the recognition of the meaning and the importance of folklore work by the state, the party and the folk. New dangers have arisen in the proximity and the confusion of equal or similarly directed folkloric material collections and archives on the part of the most varied posts and the associated wasting of strength, time, and money as well as the scaring off of willing staffs of helpers, often made shy through requests from various sides for the same purpose. I [Spamer] fear a final breakdown of these splintered folkloric efforts. Such concern will lose ground more surely the sooner one begins with the establishment of a Reichsinstitut für deutsche Volkskunde. No special difficulties should arise since such a Reichsinstitut can simply be created by assuming, gathering together and developing further already existing institutes. All the more so since the work carried out in two and a half years by the Reichsgemeinschaft für deutsche Volksforschung (Abteilung Volkskunde) [Reich Community for German Folk Research (Department of Folklore)] had at all times the development of such an institute in sight.

V. Tasks and Purpose of a Reichsinstitut für deutsche Volkskunde

At the founding of every scholarly institute there are three factors which have to be accounted for. First, this institute may not be the joining together of research undertakings which are methodologically and objectively at variance, as is often the case when gratification for numerous individual needs results in an embarrassing solution. This means in our case: the Reichsinstitut für deutsche Volkskunde should promote the *core* areas of folkloric research and keep itself free of the ballast of real or assumed neighboring disciplines whose overbearance would choke off the intellectual mother cell. Second: the shape of such an institute will be determined naturally, at least in the beginning, for the most part determined by already existing research holdings. Third: leaving out of the financial possibilities would not let such a beautiful plan grow beyond a useless memorandum which would end up in the wastepaper basket. Since, however, at this time the spirit is willing but the funds are weak, it is necessary to test thoroughly just how extreme parsimony can be united with the inner needs and necessities of such an institute. If, however, the means are lacking for continuing the most important works which have been taken on at the present within the scope of other institutions and are more or less quite advanced, then it seems more correct to shy away from the founding of such a Reichsinstitut rather than awaken hopes which cannot be fulfilled.

Beyond such general considerations it is necessary to clarify the purpose and the meaning of the Reichsinstitut. Here the desire of every one questioned will reflect differences; some will look more toward an institute *for* research, some toward a home base for individual research and researchers. But in our opinion the highest principle should be that such a central research place is primarily called upon to be a homeland and maternal household for German folklore research that is spread through the entire land. Even if the Reichsinstitut, in order to keep itself young and active, additionally takes on the organization of certain research, still its main task remains one of serving and giving. . . .

Translated from Adolf Spamer. *Erste Hinweise auf den Aufgabenkreis sowie die Aufbaumöglichkeiten eines Reichsinstituts für deutsche Volkskunde.* Unpublished manuscript of 1936. Excerpts. University Archives—Freiburg im Breisgau, Reg. Akten XVI/4/27: Institut für Volkskunde, Philosophische Fakultät.

Appendix III.3
Ultimate Goals of Research
(Conclusion to a Larger Work)
by John Meier

The ultimate goal of literary-folkloric as well as musical research in folk songs must be to work out the national peculiarities of a particular folk to distill out the pure German elements, and if possible, to clarify just where and how much race has had a deciding influence.

We can, however, only recognize precisely and with certainty the peculiarities of a national folksong when we compare our own folksong to those of other peoples. It is an effort which begins by considering the changes that a song or a song genre has undergone among the various peoples. Thus, in continuing the work of men like Uhland, Kestner, Bolte, Reifferscheid, etc., we have included appropriate non-German songs in abundance in the scholarly edition of German folk songs.[1] Here we wanted to bring together materials for a later comparative study. For these we have accomplished preliminary work in the aforementioned edition and even more strongly in the accompanying articles on the topic in the *Jahrbuch für Volkslied-forschung*.

We must be clear in our own minds that the ballad genre, with its form of oral style and its subject matter, is in many respects a common possession of the European community, and that in the Middle Ages Europe represents one rather homogeneous literary realm where these materials and motifs, as well as forms, diffused easily from one land to the next, from east to west as from west to east.

With the assimilation of songs, and in the course of their own further development, we see new formal and essential national elements appear and transform the original song. This we can clearly observe in German balladic song, e.g., that migrated into the Slavic region: *Swaten* [people in West Pakistan, in the land of Swat] make an appearance, the Turk plays a role, the clothing of the woman (veil) changes, the depiction of the environment (perhaps of the house) is transformed. The indigenous Nordic ballad adds to each verse a traditional and uniform refrain from a dance, which certainly was not originally there. It represents a product of Nordic development which is lacking in the ballads that were later taken over from the German in song form. Even within the German realm, such transformations in word and melody and in folksong forms are found. In the Bavarian-Austrian Alps, the *Schnaderhüpfl* [songs with four lines and one verse, often expressing pain or misery], surely was not developed during the Middle Ages as an improvised song to accompany a dance, but was developed recently, quickly suppressing and displacing almost all the lengthier songs of earlier times. These songs, as we can see by the transmission of numerous fragmentary stanzas, which came from the songs, had been widespread here much earlier. From this past unity with other German songs, a late and unique development results in both literary and musical form, one whose origins are probably to be explained through the racial peculiarity of the Bavarian-Austrian tribe. Additionally there also appear here and in yodeling environmental influences, since we find both restricted almost exclusively to the mountainous regions.

These differences and peculiarities must be explained, but such an interpretation is only possible through a most exacting familiarity with the factors being considered. The appearance of single-line stanzas, a formality of German Gottschee songs, can easily be recognized as Slovenian influence, as can much of the content material. But what about the music, which often moves us in a strange way? Do we have here in the German language island (Gottschee in Yugoslavia) a possible preservation of ancient German forms which have elsewhere mostly vanished, or is there evidence of Slovenian influence? For an informed answer it is also necessary to have a knowledge of German as well as a knowledge of the historical stratifications of European folk melodies and their regional importance. Only then can an answer be given with certainty. One sees from this one example, representative of many, how necessary a detailed knowledge of folk music of various peoples is for ascertaining pure German characteristics.

Only when we conduct comparisons of German folk song types and base this on a knowledge of the history and development of the song among the folk being studied will the results be certain and fruitful. Only then can a truly standard characterization of one's own song be reached. For the current age, this is easier than for the past, because the differences with songs of other peoples have become stronger.

It is almost more difficult to recognize the effect of racial elements on word and melody, even though they are certainly widespread. This is the case in Spanish folk ballads, where there are Gothic influences, as the most outstanding expert of the Spanish song, Menéndez Pidal, assumes. Here, however, there is still much to be accomplished, and it seems to be urgently necessary to undertake these steps on that unstable and slippery ground only after precise and far-reaching orientation.

These tasks demand, as preliminary work, quiet and self-sacrificing research on a single object. Only when this research has reached a specific stage can and may one proceed to establish from this detail a more complete view.

And still we must try to reach with all our means and all the energy at our disposal these ultimate goals of German folksong research: to sketch out the German folk song just for those unique, national peculiarities which belong to it alone, and also, if possible, to list the reflection of the racial basis in word and melody. May the task be ever so difficult: *sanctus patriae amor dat animum*! (the holy love for the Fatherland gives us strength!)

Translated from John Meier, "Volksliedsammlung und Volksliedforschung in Deutschland," *Deutsche Kultur im Leben der Völker* 15 (1940) 190–210; here 208–210.

Translations, Terminology, and Abbreviations

The following list of translations is intended to aid both the readers who know German and those who do not. It is quite extensive, covering not only the terms which appear in the text itself but also those which the individual authors refer to in their references. Many of the abbreviations refer to these same offices and institutions. The translations of the SS military ranks have been somewhat standardized, and we have utilized these existing equivalents in our work.

Translations of Terms

Academic Association of Germanists. Akademischer Verein der Germanisten
Academy for Scholarly Research and for the Cultivation of Germanness (German Academy). Akademie zur wissenschaftlichen Erforschung und zur Pflege des Deutschtums (Deutsche Akademie)
Academy of Sciences of the German Democratic Republic. Akademie der Wissenschaften der Deutschen Demokratischen Republik
accomplice. Mitläufer
Advanced School of the NSDAP. Hohe Schule der NSDAP
Advanced School under Preparation. Hohe Schule in Vorbereitung
advisory council. Beirat
Ancestral Inheritance Foundation Press. Ahnenerbe-Stiftung Verlag
assignments of importance to the war. Kriegswichtige Aufgaben
Atlas of German Folklore. Atlas der deutschen Volkskunde (ADV)
Baden Regional Institute for Folklore. Badische Landesstelle für Volkskunde
Battle Union for German Culture. Kampfbund für deutsche Kultur
battle unit, battle organization. Kampforganisation
Bavarian Association for Folk Art and Folklore. Bayerischer Verein für Volkskunst und Volkskunde
Bavarian Homeland Union. Bayerischer Heimatbund
Bavarian Regional Association for Homeland Protection. Bayerischer Landesverein für Heimatschutz
Berlin Academy for the Science of Judaism. Berliner Akademie für die Wissenschaft des Judentums

breeding for Nordic traits. Aufnordung

Breslau Jewish-Theological Seminary (Fraenckel Foundation). Breslauer Jüdisch-theologisches Seminar (Fraenckelscher Stiftung)

castle of order. Ordensburg

Catholic Action Group. Katholische Aktion

Central Archive of German Folk Narrative. Zentralarchiv der deutschen Volkserzählung (ZA)

Central Institute for Education and Instruction. Zentralinstitut für Erziehung und Unterricht

Central Institute for German Music Research. Zentralinstitut für deutsche Musikforschung

Central Library for the Advanced School. Zentralbibliothek der Hohen Schule

Central Office Director. Hauptamtsleiter

Central Office (Post) for German House Research. Hauptstelle der deutschen Hausforschung

Central Office (Post) for German Material Culture Research. Hauptstelle für deutsche Sachforschung

Central Office (Post) for Symbol Research. Hauptstelle für Sinnbildforschung

Central Office for Runic Research in the "Office of Ancestral Inheritance." Zentralstelle für Runenforschung beim "Ahnenerbe"

Central Word and Picture Archive. Zentrales Wort- und Bildarchiv

Circle of Leagues of German Homeland Museums. Ring der Verbände deutscher Heimatmuseen

Clinical Department for Foreign Practice, Family, and Inheritance Research. Klinische Außenabteilung für Außenpraxis, Familien- und Erbforschung

Commanding Branch for Immigration and Reemigration. Leitstelle für Ein- und Rückwanderung

Commission for Folklore. Kommission für Volkskunde

community. Gemeinschaft

compulsory dogma. Zwangsdogma

Cooperative Council for Aid to German Research. Notgemeinschaft der deutschen Wissenschaft

creating an exemplary model. typenschaffend

Cultivating Bureau for South German Folk Goods. Pflegamt für süddeutsches Volksgut

cultivation of the folk-nation, folk-national cultivation. Volkstumspflege

Cultural Chambers (cf. Reich Cultural Chambers). Kulturkammern (cf. Reichskulturkammern)

Cultural Commission Gottschee. Kulturkommission Gottschee

Cultural Commission South Tyrol. Kulturkommission Südtirol

Cultural Community. Kulturgemeinde

Cultural Office for Reich Youth Leadership. Kulturamt der Reichsjugendführung

custom and traits. Art und Sitte

defensive peasants. Wehrbauern

degenerate. entartet

Department for Folk and Antiquity Studies. Abteilung für Volks- und Altertumskunde

Division of Scholarship. Referat Wissenschaft

East Lands Picture Service. Ostlandbildstelle

eastern. Ostisch

Ethnic German Folklore. Auslandsdeutsche Volkskunde

Experimental Post for Folk-National Studies. Versuchsstelle für Volkstumskunde

External Institute. Außeninstitut, Außenstelle

folk and soil. Volk und Scholle

folk goods. Volksgut

folk man. Volksmensch

Folk Music Department. Abteilung Volksmusik

Folk-Nation and Homeland Office of the NS Community "Strength through Joy." Amt Volkstum und Heimat der NS-Gemeinschaft "Kraft durch Freude"

folk-nation keeper. Volkstumswart

folk-national. Volkstum

folk renewal. Volkserneuerung

folk root. volkhaft

folk-rootedness. Volkhaftigkeit

folk speech. Volkssprache

folk spirit. Volksgeist

Folklore Department. Abteilung Volkskunde

Folklore on a Racial Basis. Volkskunde auf rassischer Grundlage

Folkloric Stock Taking of German Archives. Volkskundliche Bestandsaufnahme der deutschen Archive

Folkloric Stock Taking of German Museums. Volkskundliche Bestandsaufnahme der deutschen Museen

Folkloric Stock Taking of German Picture Collections. Volkskundliche Bestandsaufnahme der deutschen Bildersammlungen

Führer principle. Führerprinzip

Führer's Commissioner for the Supervision of all Intellectual and World View Schooling and Education of the NSDAP. Beauftragter des Führers für die Überwachung der gesamten geistigen und weltanschaulichen Schulung und Erziehung der NSDAP

Gau. Gau (The German Reich was divided into more than forty party Gaus of the NSDAP, at the head of which was a Gau Leader)

Gau Leader. Gauleiter

Gau Research Office for Folklore. Gaufachstelle für Volkskunde

Gau Schooling Leader. Gauschulungsleiter

Gau Schooling Office. Gauschulungsamt

Gau Working Community for German Folklore. Gauarbeitsgemeinschaft für deutsche Volkskunde

General Trustee East. Generaltreuhänder Ost

German Academy (cf. Academy for Scholarly Research). Deutsche Akademie (cf. Akademie zur wissenschaftlichen Erforschung)

German Academy of Sciences, Berlin (GDR). Deutsche Akademie der Wissenschaften zu Berlin (DDR)

German Central Work Station for Folk and Cultural Landscape Research. Deutsche Mittelstelle für Volks- und Kulturbodenforschung

Germandom. Deutschtum

German Federal Archives, Koblenz (FRG). Bundesarchiv Koblenz (BRD)

German Folk Education Works. Deutsches Volksbildungswerk

German Folk-Nation. Deutsches Volkstum

German Folklore Meeting. Deutscher Volkskundetag

German Folklore Society. Deutsche Gesellschaft für Volkskunde (DGV)

German Folk Song Archive. Deutsches Volksliedarchiv (DVA)

German heritage. Deutschtum

German Institute for Foreign Studies. Deutsches Institut für Auslandskunde

German-Italian Commission for Evaluation. Deutsch-Italienische Kommission für Wertsetzung

German Linguistic Atlas. Deutscher Sprachatlas

German Research Council. Deutsche Forschungsgemeinschaft (DFG)

German Resettlement Trust Company. Deutsche Umsiedlungs-Treuhand-Gesellschaft (DUT)

German Workers' Front. Deutsche Arbeitsfront

German Youth Union. Bündische Jugend

Germanic. germanisch

Germanic Directive Posts. Germanische Leitstellen

Germanic Rebirth. Germanische Wiedererstehung

Germanic Scholarly Occupation, Germanic Scholarly Activity Plan. Germanischer Wissenschaftseinsatz

Germanic tribes. Germanen

Germanic Workers' Community Flanders. Germaansche Werkgemeenschap Vlaandern

Germanic Workers' Community Netherlands. Germaansche Werkgemeenschap Nederland

Germanness. Germanentum

goal-oriented rationality. Zweckrationalität

Guidelines for Planning Life Celebrations. Richtlinien für die Gestaltung der Lebensfeiern

Habilitation. Habilitation: postdoctoral study for title of professor

Hessian Folklore Society. Hessische Vereinigung für Volkskunde
high breeding, racial upgrading. Hochzucht
Holy Ancient Script of Mankind. Heilige Urschrift der Menschheit
homeland. Heimat
Homeland Troop. Heimatschar
honor concept. Ehrgedanke
Implementation Staff of Reich Leader Rosenberg. Einsatzstab Reichsleiter Rosenberg
indigenous. volksgeboren
indigenous stability. Bodenständigkeit
inferiority. Minderwertigkeit
Institute for Biology and Racial Studies. Institut für Biologie und Rassenlehre
Institute for Entomology. Institut für Entomologie
Institute for Folk-National Research. Institut für Volkstumsforschung
Institute for German Folklore. Institut für deutsche Volkskunde
Institute for Indo-Germanic Intellectual History. Institut für indogermanische Geistesgeschichte
Institute for National Socialist Folk Cultivation. Institut für nationalsozialistische Volkspflege
Institute for Overseas Research. Institut für Überseeforschung
Institute for Religious Studies. Institut für Religionswissenschaft
Institute for Research of Applied Military Scientific Goals. Institut für wehrwissenschaftliche Zweckforschung
Institute for Research on Bolshevism. Institut zur Erforschung des Bolschewismus
Institute for Research on the Jewish Question. Institut zur Erforschung der Judenfrage
Institute for Sorbian Folk Research. Institut für sorbische Volksforschung
Intermediate Post for Festival and Celebration Planning. Mittelstelle für Fest- und Feiergestaltung
Intermediate Post for Game Research. Mittelstelle für Spielforschung
Intermediate Branch for German Farm House Research. Mittelstelle für deutsche Bauernhausforschung
International Association for Folklore and Ethnology. Internationaler Verband für Volksforschung
Jewish Folklore Society. Gesellschaft für jüdische Volkskunde
Kurmark Regional Post for Folk Research. Landesstelle Kurmark für Volksforschung
League of German Societies for Folklore. Verband deutscher Vereine für Volkskunde
League of Socialist Working Youth. Verband der Sozialistischen Arbeiterjugend
legendry. Saggut
less tainted. minderbelastet

life celebrations. Lebensfeiern
Low German League for Folklore. Niederdeutscher Verband für Volkskunde
Main Lectureship for Folklore. Hauptlektorat Volkskunde
Main Office for Communal Politics. Hauptamt für Kommunalpolitik
Main Office for Security (cf. Reich Main Office for Security). Sicherheitshauptamt
    (cf. Reichssicherheitshauptamt)
Main Office for Supra-National Powers. Hauptamt Überstaatliche Mächte
Main Trust Office for the East. Haupttreuhandstelle Ost (HTO)
master race. Herrenmensch
Museum for Germanic Custom Studies. Museum für Germanische Trachtenkunde
myth studies. Mythenkunde
Mythus of the Twentieth Century: An Evaluation of the Soul-Spiritual Struggles
    of Our Age. Der Mythus des 20. Jahrhunderts. Eine Wertung der seelisch-
    geistigen Gestaltenkämpfe unserer Zeit
National Socialist. Nationalsozialist(isch), Nationalsozialismus (NS)
National Socialist German Workers Party. Nationalsozialistische Deutsche Arbeiter-
    partei (NSDAP)
new creation of the German peasantry. Neubildung deutschen Bauerntums
Nordic Meeting. Nordische Tagung
Nordic Society. Nordische Gesellschaft
NS Community "Strength through Joy." NS-Gemeinschaft "Kraft durch Freude"
NS Cultural Community. NS-Kulturgemeinde
NS Docent Camp. NS-Dozentenlager
NS Folk Welfare. NS-Volkswohlfahrt
NS Legal Aid Union. NS-Rechtwahrerbund
NS Student Union. NS-Studentenschaft
NS Teachers Union. NS-Lehrerbund (NSLB)
NS University Docent Union. NS-Dozentenbund
NS Women's Community. NS-Frauenschaft
NS Women's Work Service. NS-Frauenarbeitsdienst
Office for Folklore and Celebration Planning. Amt für Volkskunde und Feier-
    gestaltung
Office for Literary Promotion. Amt für Schrifttumspflege
Office for World View Information. Amt für weltanschauliche Information
Office of Ancestral Inheritance. Das Ahnenerbe
Office of Racial Politics of the NSDAP. Rassepolitisches Amt der NSDAP
Official German Immigration and Reemigration Bureau. Amtliche Deutsche Ein-
    und Rückwanderungsstelle (ADERST)
Official Party Testing Commission for the Protection of NS-Writing. Parteiamtliche
    Prüfungskommission zum Schutze des NS-Schrifttums
Ostmark. Austria
outpost. Aussenstelle
overtures. Anbiederung

patriotic folk drama. Thingspiel

Personal Staff of the Reichsführer SS (Office). Persönlicher Stab Reichsführer SS (Amt)

Pfohl Institute for Plant Preparation. Pfohl-Institut für Pflanzenpräparierung

Planning Office of the Advanced School. Aufbauamt der Hohen Schule

political coordination. Gleichschaltung

practical folk-national work. Volkstumsarbeit

Prehistory Department. Abteilung Vorgeschichte

primitive communal culture. Primitive Gemeinschaftskultur

Promotional Center for the Study of Inscriptions and Symbols. Pflegstätte für Schrift- und Sinnbildkunde

protective guard. Schutzstaffeln (SS)

pure German. völkisch

Pure German Picture Service. Völkischer Bilderdienst

Racial and Settlement Main Office of the SS. Rasse- und Siedlungshauptamt der SS

racial nativeness. Artechtheit

racial studies. Rassenkunde

racially alien. artfremd

racially pure. arteigen

racially related. artverwandt

rank. Stand

rebirth. Urständ

Refugee Associations. Vertriebenen-Verbände

Regional Association "Baden Homeland." Landesverein "Badische Heimat"

Regional Branch Southeast of the Ancestral Inheritance. Aussenstelle Südost des Ahnenerbes

Regional Institute for Folk Research and Folk-National Cultivation in the NS-Teachers Union of the Gau League Saxony. Landesstelle für Volksforschung und Volkstumspflege im NS-Lehrerbund des Gauverbandes Sachsen

Regional Institute Kurmark for German Folk Research. Landesstelle Kurmark für deutsche Volksforschung

Regional Research Office for Folklore in the Reich Union Folk-Nation and Homeland. Landesfachstelle für Volkskunde im Reichsbund Volkstum und Heimat

Regional Union for Folk-Nation and Homeland. Landschaftsbund Volkstum und Heimat

Reich Business Leader. Reichsgeschäftsführer

Reich Commissioner for Peasant Customs. Reichskommissar für bäuerliches Brauchtum

Reich Commissioner for Solidifying the German Folk Nation. Reichskommissar für die Festigung deutschen Volkstums

Reich Community for German Folk Research. Reichsgemeinschaft für deutsche Volksforschung

Reich Crystal Night. Reichskristallnacht
Reich Cultural Chambers. Reichskulturkammern
Reich Docent Union Leader. Reichsdozentenbundführer
Reich Educational Ministry. Reichserziehungsministerium (REM)
Reich Farm Leader. Reichsbauernführer
Reich Farmer Rank. Reichsnährstand
Reich Food Ministry. Reichsernährungsministerium
Reich Führer SS. Reichsführer SS (RFSS)
Reich Institute for German Folklore. Reichsinstitut für deutsche Volkskunde
Reich Institute for Pre- and Early History. Reichsinstitut für Vor- und Frühgeschichte
Reich Leader. Reichsleiter
Reich Leadership of the NSDAP. Reichsleitung der NSDAP
Reich Main Office for Security of the SS. Reichssicherheitshauptamt der SS
Reich Minister for the Occupied Eastern Regions. Reichsminister für die besetzten Ostgebiete
Reich Ministry for Science, Education, and Folk Training. Reichsministerium für Wissenschaft, Erziehung und Volksbildung (Reichserziehungsministerium, REM)
Reich Office Leader. Reichsamtsleiter
Reich Office for Instructional Film. Reichsstelle für den Unterrichtsfilm
Reich Office for Promotion of German Writing. Reichsstelle zur Förderung des deutschen Schrifttums
Reich Overview Office, Reich Overseeing Office. Reichsüberwachungsamt
Reich Party day. Reichsparteitag
Reich Professional Competition of German Students. Reichsberufswettkampf der deutschen Studenten
Reich Professional Group for Prehistory. Reichsfachgruppe für Vorgeschichte
Reich Propaganda Leadership. Reichspropagandaleitung
Reich Publication Chamber. Reichsschrifttumskammer
Reich Research Advisory Board. Reichsforschungsrat
Reich Schooling Teacher. Reichsschulungsbildner
Reich Treasurer of the NSDAP. Reichsschatzmeister der NSDAP
Reich Union for Chalk Formations and Cave Studies. Reichsbund für Karst- und Höhlenkunde
Reich Union Folk-Nation and Homeland. Reichsbund Volkstum und Heimat
Reich Union for Biology. Reichsbund für Biologie
Reich Union for German Prehistory. Reichsbund für deutsche Vorgeschichte
Reich Women's Core. Reichsfrauenschaft
Reich Work Führer. Reichsarbeitsführer
Reich Worker's Service. Reichsarbeitsdienst
Reich Working Community for German Folklore. Reichsarbeitsgemeinschaft für deutsche Volkskunde

Reich Youth Führer. Reichsjugendführer
Research and Teaching Community "The Office of Ancestral Inheritance." For-
schungs- und Lehrgemeinschaft "Das Ahnenerbe"
Research Institute for Ancient Intellectual History. Forschungsanstalt für Geis-
tesurgeschichte
Research Institute for German Folklore. Forschungsinstitut für deutsche Volkskunde
Research Post for Applied Geology. Forschungsstätte für angewandte Geologie
Research Post for Astronomy. Forschungsstätte für Astronomie
Research Post for Botany. Forschungsstätte für Botanik
Research Post for Chalk Formations and Cave Studies. Forschungsstätte für Karst-
und Höhlenkunde
Research Post for Dwelling Mound Studies. Forschungsstätte für Wurtenforschung
Research Post for Educational Science. Forschungsstelle für Erziehungswissen-
schaft
Research Post for Games and Sayings. Forschungsstelle Spiel und Spruch
Research Post for Geophysics. Forschungsstätte für Geophysik
Research Post for German Farmstead. Forschungsstelle Deutscher Bauernhof
Research Post for German Folk Speech. Forschungsstelle Deutsche Volkssprache
Research Post for Germanic Linguistics and Landscape Studies. Forschungsstätte
für germanische Sprachwissenschaft und Landschaftskunde
Research Post Gottschee. Forschungsstätte Gottschee
Research Post for House Signs and Kinship Symbols. Forschungsstätte für Haus-
marken und Sippenzeichen
Research Post for Indo-Germanic-German Music. Forschungsstätte für indoger-
manisch-deutsche Musik
Research Post for Mythology. Forschungsstelle Mythenkunde
Research Post for Natural Scientific Prehistory. Forschungsstätte für naturwissen-
schaftliche Vorgeschichte
Research Post for Peasant Handicrafts. Forschungsstelle Bäuerliches Handwerk
Research Post for Peasant Life Structures. Forschungsstelle Bäuerliche Lebensfor-
men
Research Post for Pedagogical Studies. Forschungsstelle für Erziehungswissenschaft
Research Post for the Study of Symbols. Forschungsstätte für Sinnbildkunde
Right for Racial Protection. Recht als Rasseschutz
Rosenberg Bureau, Rosenberg Office. Amt Rosenberg
Salvaging Action in Favor of German Cultural Goods. Bergungsaktion zugunsten
deutscher Kulturgüter
Salzburg Scholarly Weeks. Salzburger Wissenschaftswochen
Saxon League for Folklore. Sächsischer Verband für Volkskunde
Secret State Police. Geheime Staatspolizei (Gestapo)
Security Service of the SS. Sicherheitsdienst der SS (SD)
seizure of power. Machtergreifung

Service Branch of the Führer's Commissioner for the Supervision of all Intellectual and World View Schooling and Education of the NSDAP. Dienststelle des Beauftragten des Führers für die Überwachung der gesamten geistigen und weltanschaulichen Schulung und Erziehung der NSDAP

shock troop. Stoßtrupp

Special Staff for Folklore. Sonderstab Volkskunde

SS-Youth Corps. SS-Nachwuchskorps

Staff Office of the Reich Farm Leader. Stabsamt des Reichsbauernführers

stratum. Schicht

Strength through Joy (cf. NS-Community "Strength through Joy"). Kraft durch Freude (cf. NS-Gemeinschaft "Kraft durch Freude")

subhuman beings. Untermenschen

suborganizations of the Party. Gliederungen der Partei

sunken cultural property. gesunkenes Kulturgut

supranational. übervölkisch

tainted. belastet

Teaching and Research Community "The Office of Ancestral Inheritance." Lehr- und Forschungsgemeinschaft "Das Ahnenerbe"

Teaching and Research Post for Biology. Lehr- und Forschungsstätte für Biologie

Teaching and Research Post for Celtic Folk Research. Lehr- und Forschungsstätte für Keltische Volksforschung

Teaching and Research Post for Central Asia and Expeditions. Lehr- und Forschungsstätte für Innerasien und Expeditionen

Teaching and Research Post for Classical Antiquities. Lehr- und Forschungsstätte für Klassische Altertumskunde

Teaching and Research Post for Excavations. Lehr- und Forschungsstätte Ausgrabungen

Teaching and Research Post for Folk Medicine. Lehr- und Forschungsstätte für Volksmedizin

Teaching and Research Post for Folk Narrative, Fairy Tales and Legendry. Lehr- und Forschungsstätte für Volkserzählung, Märchen- und Sagenkunde

Teaching and Research Post for German Folk Research and Folklore. Lehr- und Forschungsstätte für deutsche Volksforschung und Volkskunde

Teaching and Research Post for Germanic Architecture. Lehr- und Forschungsstätte für germanisches Bauwesen

Teaching and Research Post for Germanic Cultural Science and Landscape Studies. Lehr- und Forschungsstätte für germanische Kulturwissenschaft und Landschaftskunde

Teaching and Research Post for Germanic-German Folklore. Lehr- und Forschungsstätte für germanisch-deutsche Volkskunde

Teaching and Research Post for Germanic Studies. Lehr- und Forschungsstätte für Germanenkunde

Teaching and Research Post for Indo-Germanic-Aryan Linguistics and Cultural Studies. Lehr- und Forschungsstätte für indogermanisch-arische Sprach- und Kulturwissenschaft

Teaching and Research Post for Indo-Germanic-Germanic Language and Cultural Studies. Lehr- und Forschungsstätte für indogermanisch-germanische Sprach- und Kulturwissenschaft

Teaching and Research Post for Indo-Germanic-Germanic Legal History. Lehr- und Forschungsstätte für indogermanisch-deutsche Rechtsgeschichte

Teaching and Research Post for Inscription and Symbol Studies. Lehr- und Forschungsstätte für Schrift- und Sinnbildkunde

Teaching and Research Post for Middle Latin. Lehr- und Forschungsstätte für Mittellatein

Teaching and Research Post for North African Cultural Studies. Lehr- und Forschungsstätte für nordafrikanische Kulturwissenschaft

Teaching and Research Post for Orientation and Landscape Symbols. Lehr- und Forschungsstätte für Ortung und Landschaftssinnbilder

Teaching and Research Post for Plant Genetics. Lehr- und Forschungsstätte für Pflanzengenetik

Teaching and Research Post for Prehistory. Lehr- und Forschungsstätte für Urgeschichte

Teaching and Research Post for Representative and Applied Natural History, "Haus der Natur." Lehr- und Forschungsstätte für darstellende und angewandte Naturkunde "Haus der Natur"

Teaching and Research Post for Runic and Symbol Studies. Lehr- und Forschungsstätte für Runen- und Sinnbildkunde

Teaching and Research Post for the Near East. Lehr- und Forschungsstätte für den vorderen Orient

Teaching and Research Post for the History of Indogermanic Belief. Lehr- und Forschungsstätte für indogermanische Glaubensgeschichte

Teaching Institute for Judaic Studies. Lehranstalt für die Wissenschaft des Judentums

Teaching Post for Celebration Planning. Lehrstätte für Feiergestaltung

Testing Commission for the Protection of NS-Publications. Prüfungskommission zum Schutze des NS-Schrifttums

Thousand Year Reich. Tausendjähriges Reich

Union for German Folklore. Bund für deutsche Volkskunde

Union for the German East. Bund deutscher Osten

Union of German Girls. Bund deutscher Mädchen

War Implementation by the Humanities. Kriegseinsatz der Geisteswissenschaften

western. Westisch

Winter Aid Work. Winterhilfswerk

Work Service, Workers' Service. Arbeitsdienst

Workers and Farmers College. Arbeiter- und Bauernfakultät (ABF)
Working Community for German Folklore. Arbeitsgemeinschaft für deutsche Volks-
    kunde
Working Community of Optants for Germany. Arbeitsgemeinschaft der Optanten
    für Deutschland (AdO)
Yiddish Scientific Institute. Jidishes Visnshaftlekhes Institut
young women's work service. Landjahr

Abbreviations

ABF	Arbeiter- und Bauernfakultät. Workers and Farmers College
ADERST	Amtliche Deutsche Ein- und Rückwanderungsstelle. Official German Immigration and Reemigration Bureau
AdO	Arbeitsgemeinschaft der Optanten für Deutschland. Working Community of Optants for Germany
ADV	Atlas der deutschen Volkskunde. Atlas of German Folklore
Archiv LA	Archiv der Badischen Landesstelle für Volkskunde, Freiburg i.Br. Archive of the Baden Regional Institute for Folklore, Freiburg im Breisgau
Archiv PH	Archiv der Philosophischen Fakultäten der Universität Freiburg i.Br. Archive of the Philosophical Faculty of the University of Freiburg im Breisgau
AVA	Allgemeines Verwaltungsarchiv, Wien. General Administrative Archives, Vienna
BA	Bundesarchiv Koblenz. German Federal Archives, Koblenz, BRD
BDC	Berlin Document Center, United States Mission
BDO	Bund deutscher Osten. Union for the German East
BRD	Bundesrepublik Deutschland. Federal Republic of Germany
DDR	Deutsche Demokratische Republik. German Democratic Republic
DFG	Deutsche Forschungsgemeinschaft. German Research Council
DGV	Deutsche Gesellschaft für Volkskunde. German Folklore Society
DUT	Deutsche Umsiedlungs-Treuhand-Gesellschaft. German Resettlement Trust Company
DVA	Deutsches Volksliedarchiv, Freiburg i.Br. German Folk Song Archive, Freiburg im Breisgau
Gestapo	Geheime Staatspolizei. Secret State Police

HTO	Haupttreuhandstelle Ost. Main Trust Office for the East
IfZ	Institut für Zeitgeschichte, München. Institute for Contemporary History, Munich
JNUL	The Jewish National and University Library, Jerusalem
KfdK	Kampfbund für deutsche Kultur. Battle Union for German Culture
LUI	Ludwig-Uhland-Institut, Zeitungsarchiv, Tübingen. Newspaper Archive of the Ludwig Uhland Institute, Tübingen
MEW	Marx-Engels Werke. Writings of Marx and Engels
NS	Nationalsozialist(isch), Nationalsozialismus. National Socialist, National Socialism
NSDAP	Nationalsozialistische Deutsche Arbeiterpartei. National Socialist German Workers Party
NSLB	Nationalsozialistischer Lehrerbund. NS Teachers Union
ÖBL	Österreichisches Biographisches Lexikon. Austrian Biographical Lexicon
PAG	Privatarchiv Geramb, Graz. Private Archive Geramb, Graz
PAL	Privatarchiv Lixfeld, Freiburg i.Br. Private Archive Lixfeld, Freiburg im Breisgau
REM	Reichsministerium für Wissenschaft, Erziehung und Volksbildung (Reichserziehungsministerium). Reich Ministry for Sciences, Education, and Folk Training (Reich Educational Ministry)
RFSS	Reichsführer SS. Reich Führer SS
SD	Sicherheitsdienst der SS. Security Service of the SS
SS	Schutzstaffeln. Protective Guard
StA Schwerin	Staatsarchiv Schwerin, Mecklenburg. State Archive Schwerin, Mecklenburg
UA Berlin	Universitätsarchiv der Humboldt-Universität zu Berlin
UA Freiburg	Universitätsarchiv Freiburg i.Br.
UA Göttingen	Universitätsarchiv Göttingen
UA Graz	Universitätsarchiv Graz
UA Greifswald	Universitätsarchiv Greifswald
UA Halle	Universitätsarchiv Halle-Wittenberg
UA Heidelberg	Universitätsarchiv Heidelberg
UA Jena	Universitätsarchiv Jena

UA Salzburg	Universitätsarchiv Salzburg
UA Wien	Universitätsarchiv Wien (Vienna)
VF	Vaterländische Front
YIWO	Jidishes Visnshaftlekes Institut. Yiddish Scientific Institute
ZA	Zentralarchiv der deutschen Volkserzählung. Central Archive of German Folk Narrative
ZA-AdW-DDR	Zentrales Archiv der Akademie der Wissenschaften der DDR, Berlin. Central Archive of the Academy of Sciences of the GDR, Berlin
ZStAP	Zentrales Staatsarchiv der DDR, Potsdam. Central State Archive of the GDR, Potsdam
ZStA Merseburg	Zentrales Staatsarchiv der DDR, Abteilung Merseburg. Central State Archive of the GDR, Department, Merseburg

Waffen SS Ranks* and U.S. Army Ranks

Commissioned

Reichsführer-SS	General of the Army
SS-Oberstgruppenführer	General
SS-Obergruppenführer	Lieutenant General
SS-Gruppenführer	Major General
SS-Brigadeführer	Brigadier General
SS-Oberführer	——
SS-Standartenführer	Colonel
SS-Obersturmbannführer	Lieutenant Colonel
SS-Sturmbannführer	Major
SS-Hauptsturmführer	Captain
SS-Obersturmführer	1st Lieutenant
SS-Untersturmführer	2nd Lieutenant

Noncommissioned

SS-Sturmscharführer	Sergeant Major
SS-Standarten-Oberjunker	——
SS-Hauptscharführer	Master Sergeant
SS-Oberscharführer	Technical Sergeant
SS-Standartenjunker	——
SS-Scharführer	Staff Sergeant
SS-Unterscharführer	Sergeant

Enlisted

SS-Rottenführer	——
SS-Sturmmann	Corporal

SS-Oberschütze	Private 1st Class
SS-Schütze	Private

Original: "Appendix I," in George H. Stein, *The Waffen SS: Hitler's Elite Guard at War 1939–1945*, p. 295. New York 1966. Cornell University Press.

*The ranks of the common SS given to NS scholars correspond as a rule to the ranks of the Waffen-SS, cf. Heiber 1966: 316–317.

Notes

FOREWORD BY JAMES R. DOW

1. Quoted in Brückner 1984c: 27.
2. Gerndt 1987; Dow 1987, 1988.
3. Bollmus 1987.
4. See Dow and Lixfeld 1991 and in press.
5. Lixfeld 1987a, 1991.
6. Indiana University Press (in press).
7. See our reference to this failure in Dow and Lixfeld 1991 and in the epilogue to Dow and Lixfeld in press.
8. Bausinger 1965 and Emmerich 1968.

INTRODUCTION

1. The "Third Reich" was clearly being associated through this slogan with the "First Reich," during which German kings from A.D. 800 to 1806 were called Roman kaisers, and with the "Second Reich," from 1871 to 1918 under the Hohenzollern kaisers.
2. Bausinger 1965; also published in Dow and Lixfeld in press.
3. Gerndt 1987.
4. According to Meier 1947: 27.
5. Associations, leagues, universities, etc. were "politically coordinated" after 1933, which means they were subjected to the authoritarian leadership principle (*Führerprinzip*) without democratic voting rights by their membership. These organizations in part carried out a "self-imposed political coordination" instead of the "political coordination" ordered from above; see Reimann 1984. "Political coordination" is also the term used for the annexation of organizations by National Socialist institutions.

1. BOURGEOIS-NATIONAL *VOLKSKUNDE* BETWEEN THE MONARCHY AND FASCISM

1. *Bericht der Notgemeinschaft* 12, 1933: 12.
2. Heiber 1966: 802.
3. *Bericht der Notgemeinschaft* 12, 1933: 7–8.
4. Meier 1947: 21; *Mitteilungen des Verbandes* 37, December 1928: 12–14.
5. Besprechung 1928: 3 (John Meier). I would like to thank Bernhard Oeschger, Freiburg im Breisgau, for his kind assistance in making this available.
6. Concerning the frequent use of the term *Deutung* (interpretation), cf. Besprechung 1928: 3 and 21 (Arthur Hübner).

7. See Besprechung 1928: 3 and Jacobeit 1965b: 132–142.

8. See Besprechung 1928: 7 (Theodor Frings) and frequently thereafter; in general, see Schöck 1970.

9. See Besprechung 1928: 21: "how then is it one of our best hopes that the adoption of the great central plan might become for each collaborator and helper, for every individual German landscape, a stimulus for the most lively and in-depth researching of their own lives . . . so that folkloric activities can be brought to thousands of individual people. The feeling for the meaning and the value of these things will become more general, stronger, and more lasting" (Arthur Hübner). Hübner 1930: 10: It is the specific goal of the questionnaire for the folklore *Atlas* "to awaken and strengthen folkloric interests in a broad area. For we do not want *Volkskunde* to be a cool, abstract science, but rather a force affecting life." Hübner 1930: 16: It was the distinct goal, that with the planned folklore *Atlas* . . . "a strong armification [*Rüstzeug*] for folk self-understanding should be created. This remains the highest goal of folklore work." In regard to the intended folklore feedback, see the section of this chapter entitled "A 1917 Proposal for a Central Institute for German Folklore" and John Meier's stated goals.

10. Meier 1947: 21. A substantially different viewpoint of the problematics is found in Grober-Glück 1988: 53–56. Concerning the research results of the *Atlas*, see Cox 1983.

11. Besprechung 1928: 3 (Arthur Hübner) and Hübner 1930: 16. The influences of the cultural-morphological school and of the German-language atlas on the *Atlas der deutschen Volkskunde* are repeatedly pointed out in Besprechung 1928.

12. See Röhr 1938. In regard to the problematics of the questionnaire technique, see Schenda 1970: 136–139; a critique of this is in Grober-Glück 1988: 61–63.

13. *Bericht der Notgemeinschaft* 12, 1933: 49–51; *Mitteilungen des Verbandes* 38, September 1929: 32.

14. *Bericht der Notgemeinschaft* 9, 1930: 193; cf. Wildhagen 1938: 16.

15. *Mitteilungen der Volkskundekommission* 1, February 1930: 5–14.

16. *Bericht der Notgemeinschaft* 9, 1930: 192; Röhr 1938: 74.

17. *Bericht der Notgemeinschaft* 11, 1932: 23.

18. Beitl 1934: 113.

19. Röhr 1938: 74.

20. *Bericht der Notgemeinschaft* 9, 1930: 217.

21. *Bericht der Notgemeinschaft* 9, 1930: 192; cf. *Mitteilungen des Verbandes* 38, September 1929: 32.

22. See *Bericht der Notgemeinschaft* 11, 1932: 23, and 12, 1933: 50; *Mitteilungen der Volkskundekommission* 4, July 1933: 54–55; Röhr 1938: 64, cf. 84.

23. See *Bericht der Notgemeinschaft* 9–12, 1930–1933; *Mitteilungen der Volkskundekommission* 1–4, 1930–1933.

24. See Seemann 1954; Holzapfel 1987a.

25. See Künzig 1934; Daxelmüller 1987c: VII–IX.

26. Dölker 1971: 84: Helmut Dölker, the successor of John Meier as chairman of the League of German Societies for Folklore, pursued the goal of "leading [the League] away from the 'authoritarian' leadership of John Meier and his personal method of conducting business, into more accessible paths."

27. *Mitteilungen des Verbandes* 37, December 1928: 14: "for the central office [of the ADV] is the seedbed of the Institute for German Folklore, its library will one day be the library of the Institute." See also Meier 1928a: 18.

28. Deutsches Volksliedarchiv Freiburg i.Br. (DVA). Bestand J 189. I would like to thank Otto Holzapfel for his kind assistance in locating the plan.

29. See Lixfeld 1987a.

30. Jacobeit 1965b: 111, 84–85.

31. Deutsches Volksliedarchiv (Bestand J 189). Main portion of the plan; cf. Jacobeit 1965b: 27–33.

32. DVA (Bestand J 189). Anlage D des Plans.

33. DVA (Bestand J 189). Printed in italics in the main portion of the plan.

34. DVA (Bestand J 189). Anlage D des Plans.

35. DVA (Bestand J 189). Anlage A des Plans.

36. DVA (Bestand J 189). Anlage B des Plans.

37. DVA (Bestand J 189). Anlage C.I. des Plans: "Folk-national Settlements, Construction Forms and their Decorations, Monuments, Household Items, Tools for Agriculture, Animal Breeding, Hunting and Fishing; Folk Art and Folk Industry, Food and Drink; Customs and Practices, Festivals and Games, Music and Dance; Folk Belief and Superstition; *Märchen*, Legends, Jests; Folk Riddles; Folk Drama; Colloquial Speech, Proverbs, Jokes, Formulas; Folk Gestures; Folk Speech: Dialect and Folk Names (Place Names, Field Names, Personal Names, Animal Names, Plant Names, etc.)."

38. DVA (Bestand J 189). Anlage B.II. des Plans.

39. See Jacobeit 1965b: 121–122.

40. DVA (Bestand J 189). Printed in italics in the main portion of the plan, and from which the previous citations were taken.

41. Meier 1926; concerning the German Academy, see Harvolk 1990.

42. See *Mitteilungen der Akademie* 1, 1925: 1–4; Schlicker 1977.

43. Meier 1926: 140.

44. According to another linguistic directive, the folkloric central institutes of the Nordic countries of Denmark, Norway, and Finland served as models; see Meier 1927: 3 and Seemann 1954: 17.

45. *Mitteilungen der Akademie* 1, 1925: 8–9.

46. Meier 1926: 142.

47. Meier 1926: 143.

48. Meier 1926: 140.

49. Meier 1926: 140–141.

50. Meier 1926: 141.

51. Riehl 1958: 34.

52. Schlicker 1977: 43.

53. Meier 1926: 141–142.

54. Meier 1926: 144.

55. Lauffer 1934: 1.

56. Abendroth 1984: 11.

57. Abendroth 1984: 21–22.

58. Abendroth 1984: 24.

59. Cf. Volkskunde an den Hochschulen 1986: 17.

60. von See 1970: 73 (emphasis added); see also Emmerich 1971: 132–161.

61. Nollau 1926; von See 1970: 74.

62. Nollau 1926, Einleitung: 1.

63. Nollau 1926, Einleitung: 3 (emphasis by Nollau).

64. Lauffer 1926.

65. Cf. Volkskunde an den Hochschulen 1986: 17.

66. Lauffer 1926: 25–36.

67. Lauffer 1926: 25 (emphasis added).

68. Lauffer 1926: 36.

69. Lauffer 1920.

70. Lauffer 1920: 9–10.
71. "Germanisches Erbe in . . . [Germanic Inheritance in]" experienced a broad renaissance during the Third Reich as a title for folklore studies; see Thiele 1939.
72. Tacitus 1959.
73. Lauffer 1920: 25; Felix Dahn was a co-worker of Wilhelm Heinrich Riehl.
74. Lauffer 1920: 27–28 (emphasis added).
75. See Lixfeld 1987b: 43–45.
76. See Scharfe 1986: 56 and 58, nn. 28 and 47.
77. Lauffer 1920: 46–47.
78. See Bausinger 1965: 183; also published in Dow and Lixfeld in press; Assion 1985: 225–226; also published in Dow and Lixfeld in press.
79. The list included Hanns (?) Bächthold-Stäubli, Basel; Hans Fehr, Bern; Eugen Fehrle, Heidelberg; Michael (or Arthur?) Haberlandt, Vienna; Adolf Helbok, Innsbruck; Otto Lehmann, Altona; Friedrich Lüers, Munich; Robert Mielke, Hermsdorf bei Berlin; Friedrich Panzer, Heidelberg; Wilhelm Peßler, Hannover; Paul Sartori, Dortmund; Adam Wrede, Cologne; Paul Zaunert, Wilhelmshöhe.
80. Including Richard Eichenauer, Josef Hanika, Rudolf Helm, Alfred Karasek-Langer, Walther Kuhn, Ernst Schwarz, Friedrich Sieber, Richard Wolfram.
81. Meier 1940: 208.
82. Naumann 1922: 2; cf. Dow and Lixfeld 1986: 9–10; Schmook 1983. For a critique of Naumann, see Spamer 1924, 1933a, 1933b, and 1933d and Strobach 1987, also published in the Dow and Lixfeld in press.
83. Naumann 1922: 5; cf. Schindler 1984: 32–36.
84. Naumann 1922: 3–4.
85. Cf. von See 1970: 53–56, Schindler 1984: 33.
86. Naumann 1922: 5.
87. Cf. Korff 1971; Peuckert 1931.
88. Meier 1928a: 20, cf. also 18–19; Meier 1958: 181.
89. Meier 1928a: 20, 1958: 181 (emphasis added).
90. Cf. *Schwäbische Heimat* 24, 1929: 46; *Mitteilungen des Verbandes* 37, December 1928: 12–13.
91. Deutsche Forschung 1928a, 1928b.
92. Deutsche Forschung 1928a: 73–74, 78–81, 107–108.
93. Schier 1932: VII–VIII.
94. Beitl 1934: 117–118.
95. Lauffer 1934: 1.
96. Lauffer 1934: 2. Concerning the thesis of German folk and cultural land, as well as the call for revisions in regard to east European countries, see Klessmann 1985: 354–370.
97. Lauffer 1934: 2.
98. Lauffer 1934: 2.
99. Lauffer 1934: 2.
100. Lauffer 1934: 3.
101. See Weber-Kellermann 1986, 1959.
102. Meier 1947: 26; see also the position taken by the Germanist Arthur Hübner: "*Volkskunde* is the science of prejudice, and thus it is also not completely innocent of prejudice, which sometimes would deny it the character of a science today. It is the science in which the effects of stronger words speak out, more so than in many others; exactly because *Volkskunde* calls forth through the strength of its materials the effects of that which belongs to the folk, that is why it draws in dilettantes to such a large degree." Hübner 1930: 2–3; cf. Jacobeit and Mohrmann 1982: 284–285.

103. *Mitteilungen des Verbandes* 45, June 1934: 25.
104. Meier 1947: 27.
105. Bausinger 1971a: 63: "If there is any place in scholarship where National Socialism must be looked upon not as an intrusion from the outside but rather as an inner consequence, then it is in *Volkskunde*."
106. Bausinger 1965: 198; also published in Dow and Lixfeld in press.
107. Meier 1947: 26; cf. *Mitteilungen des Verbandes* 45, June 1934: 25.
108. Cf. *Mitteilungen des Verbandes* 37, December 1928: 14.
109. *Schwäbische Heimat* 25, 1930: 58.
110. *Mitteilungen des Verbandes* 42, 1931: 16–18.
111. *Mitteilungen des Verbandes* 45, June 1934: 8, and 44, September 1933: 2. It can be assumed that Naumann was attacked soon after the seizure of power by the National Socialists; concerning the Weimar Folklore Meeting, see Strobach 1987: 24, also published in Dow and Lixfeld in press.
112. *Mitteilungen des Verbandes* 45, June 1934: 26–28.
113. Published as Schwietering 1933.
114. Published as Freudenthal 1934.
115. Cf. *Mitteilungen des Verbandes* 45, June 1934: 24–25.
116. Künzig 1933: 6; for his kind assistance in locating this document I would like to thank Berthold Hamelmann, Freiburg i.Br.
117. Künzig 1933: 2 (emphasis added by Künzig).
118. *Mitteilungen des Verbandes* 45, June 1934: 7.
119. *Mitteilungen des Verbandes* 45, June 1934: 7–8.
120. Cf. Reimann 1984: 38–52.
121. *Mitteilungen des Verbandes* 45, June 1934: 13–16; concerning Eugen Fehrle, see Assion 1985.
122. Cf. *Mitteldeutsche Blätter für Volkskunde* 8, 1933: 108–109; *Hessische Blätter für Volkskunde* 32, 1933: 155–156; *Oberdeutsche Zeitschrift für Volkskunde* 7, 1933: 1–2; *Zeitschrift des Vereins für rheinische und westfälische Volkskunde* 30, 1933: 1–2; *Niederdeutsche Zeitschrift für Volkskunde* 12, 1934: 1–4; *Mitteilungen der Schlesischen Gesellschaft für Volkskunde* 34, 1934: 68–84.
123. See Oesterle 1987; also published in Dow and Lixfeld in press.
124. Meier 1947: 25–26.
125. *Niederdeutsche Zeitschrift für Volkskunde* 11, 1933: 255; cf. *Mitteilungen der Schlesischen Gesellschaft für Volkskunde* 34, 1934: 376, 380.
126. Schewe 1934: IV.
127. *Niederdeutsche Zeitschrift für Volkskunde* 11, 1933: 255.
128. *Niederdeutsche Zeitschrift für Volkskunde* 11, 1933: 255.
129. Meier 1947: 26.
130. See *Mitteilungen des Verbandes* 45, 1934: 12–13; 47, March 1935: 19–21; 48, 1936: 9; 50, August 1937: 12, 16–20; 53, March 1939: 14–15.
131. Meier 1947: 26.
132. See Strobach 1987: 23–25; also published in Dow and Lixfeld in press.
133. *Niederdeutsche Zeitschrift für Volkskunde* 11, 1933: 255.
134. *Niederdeutsche Zeitschrift für Volkskunde* 11, 1933: 256.
135. Meier 1947: 26.
136. Meier 1947: 26; *Niederdeutsche Zeitschrift für Volkskunde* 11, 1933: 256.
137. *Niederdeutsche Zeitschrift für Volkskunde* 11, 1933: 255.
138. Meier 1947: 26.
139. Schewe 1934: IV.
140. See Oesterle 1987, 1988; also published in Dow and Lixfeld in press.

141. Heiber 1966: 802.
142. See chap. 3.

2. THE REICH COMMUNITY FOR GERMAN FOLK RESEARCH

1. Concerning the change of names, see Heiber 1966: 784–785.
2. Heiber 1966: 796–797.
3. Heiber 1966: 800; concerning the Kampfbund für Deutsche Kultur, see Brenner 1963: 7ff.
4. Heiber 1966: 797.
5. Heiber 1966: 800, cf. 792. The "Nordischer Ring" was a pure German cultural organization.
6. BDC Wildhagen, Eduard, born November 15, 1890. NSDAP membership number 1 668 634 as of April 1, 1933.
7. See Heiber 1966: 787.
8. Heiber 1966: 789–790; Wildhagen 1938: 10, 13.
9. Heiber 1966: 840.
10. Heiber 1966: 247.
11. Heiber 1966: 793.
12. Heiber 1966: 786.
13. Heiber 1966: 799; cf. 841.
14. Heiber 1966: 802–803.
15. Heiber 1966: 800.
16. Heiber 1966: 800.
17. UA Jena, Bestand U Abt. IV, No. 30. Biography of Matthes Ziegler in 1940. For the biography as well as other information from the University Archive in Jena, I want to thank Wolfgang Jacobeit, Berlin-Birkenwerder, and Reinhard Schmook, Wriezen an der Oder; cf. Lixfeld 1987a: 74, 81, n. 31.
18. Heiber 1966: 800.
19. Cf. Heiber 1966: 834, 779; 946: Ziegler, "resided as Rosenberg's representative in Wildhagen's Research Community and financed his research plans from there."
20. *Mitteilungen des Atlas der deutschen Volkskunde* 5, January 1935: 82.
21. Archive of the Landesstelle für Volkskunde, Freiburg i.Br. File "Atlas Zentrale," letter of the DFG president dated September 7, 1934, to the Landesstelle Baden des *Atlas der deutschen Volkskunde*, Heidelberg.
22. Archive of the Landesstelle für Volkskunde, Freiburg i.Br. File "Atlas Zentrale," letter of the DFG president dated September 7, 1934, to the Landesstelle Baden des *Atlas der deutschen Volkskunde*, Heidelberg.
23. Rosenberg 1934a; cf. Baumgärtner 1974: 42–81 and chap. 3 in this work.
24. Concerning the coined phrase, see Ponti 1950; concerning Rosenberg's role as chief ideologist, see Bollmus 1989.
25. Kater 1974: 21; cf. Biedermann 1944a: 1.
26. Cf. Bollmus 1970: 249.
27. UA Jena, Bestand U Abt. IV, No. 30. Biography of Matthes Ziegler of 1940; cf. Lixfeld 1987a: 74, 81, n. 31.
28. BDC Günther, Hans F. K., born February 16, 1891. NSDAP membership number 1 185 391 as of May 1, 1932.
29. See Stengel-von Rutkowski 1935a, 1935b, 1941.
30. See Reinerth 1932b.
31. Kater 1974: 22.
32. Kater 1974: 23; Ziegler 1934a.

33. Kater 1974: 23.
34. See, for example, Kater 1974: 140–142.
35. Kater 1974: 22.
36. Reinerth 1932a.
37. Concerning the later ideological involvement, see Rüdiger 1938a.
38. See, for example, Wildhagen 1938: 10, 13; Heiber 1966: 789.
39. *Mitteilungen des Verbandes* 37, December 1928: 14.
40. See Jacobeit and Mohrmann 1982.
41. See Weber-Kellermann 1984: 197–200; for additional citations I am indebted to Wolfgang Jacobeit.
42. Sokol 1985c: Thesis No. 2; I am indebted to Wolfgang Jacobeit and Thomas Scholze, Berlin/DDR, for making the unpublished study by Kristin Sokol available to me.
43. Jacobeit 1987: 303; also published in Dow and Lixfeld in press; cf. Sokol 1985b.
44. See Jacobeit 1965b: 112–125, esp. 120.
45. See Dow and Lixfeld 1986: 7–8.
46. Strobach 1987: 31–34; also published in Dow and Lixfeld in press.
47. Strobach 1987, Jacobeit 1987; both studies are published in Dow and Lixfeld in press.
48. See Ritz 1953; Sieber 1955; Steinitz 1955: 16–18; Beiträge zur sprachlichen Volksüberlieferung 1953; Bartel 1983; Burde-Schneidewind and Geissler 1984; Zippelius 1978; Weber-Kellermann 1969, 1984; Weber-Kellermann and Bimmer 1985: 103–113.
49. See Jacobeit 1987: 308; also published in Dow and Lixfeld in press.
50. Strobach 1973: 70; also published in Jacobeit and Mohrmann 1982: 293.
51. Strobach 1987: 25; also published in Dow and Lixfeld in press.
52. Sokol 1985a: 3–4.
53. Klemperer 1987: 121.
54. Twelfth entry in a series from the diaries of Victor Klemperer from 1936 to 1940, in the newspaper *Die Union*, Dresden, May 22, 1987. I am indebted to Wolfgang Jacobeit for making this material available to me.
55. Cf. Sokol 1985a: 1. Sokol speaks here about an "idealistically based voluntary self imposed political coordination with the fascist ideological apparatus." This is only partially correct, since Spamer did not represent the National Socialist ideology personally nor as a scholar.
56. Cf. BDC Spamer, Adolf, born April 10, 1883.
57. Sokol 1985b: 41–42; cf. Abendroth 1984: 21–22.
58. Cf. Myrdal 1971.
59. Weber-Kellermann 1984: 199–200.
60. Cf. Fritzsch 1936: 88, 90–95; Fritzsch 1956.
61. Spamer 1934a: 147.
62. In regard to the names and the places of the regional folk-national warders, see Fritzsch 1934: 153–154.
63. Spamer 1934a: 147.
64. Fritzsch 1934: 149.
65. Fritzsch 1934: 151.
66. Fritzsch 1934: 149, 152.
67. Aufbau der Landesstelle 1936: 25.
68. Fritzsch 1934: 153; Jacobeit 1987: 303, also published in the Dow and Lixfeld in press; BDC Spamer, Adolf, born April 10, 1883.
69. Fritzsch 1934: 149.
70. Fritzsch 1934: 152; Tagung 1934: 100–101.
71. Aufbau der Landesstelle 1936: 25.
72. *Mitteldeutsche Blätter für Volkskunde* 9, 1934: 153; Fritzsch 1936: 88.

73. *Mitteldeutsche Blätter für Volkskunde* 10, 1935: 60; Fritzsch 1935: 2. Concerning Spamer's leadership of the *Gau* Research Office meeting in Plauen i.V., see *Mitteldeutsche Blätter für Volkskunde* 10, 1935: 124–125. Concerning Spamer's lecture at this meeting, see Spamer 1935b: 97. Concerning the development of the Folk-Nation and Homeland Department of the NS-Cultural Community, see chap. 3 of this work.

74. Jacobeit and Mohrmann 1982: 282–286; Weber-Kellermann 1984: 201.

75. Cf. Jacobeit and Mohrmann 1982: 286–289.

76. Sokol 1985a: 3. Sokol refers here to the Archive of the Humboldt-Universität in Berlin (East), Sign. 163, Vol.1, p. 39; see also Heiber 1966: 802–804.

77. Sokol 1985a: 3 with a reference to the Archive of the Humboldt-Universität in Berlin (East), Sign. 163, Vol. 1, p. 44; what is meant here is the restructuring of the Technische Hochschule in Dresden, but the plans for developing the DFG Reich Community for German Folk Research in Berlin will certainly have been known by Spamer.

78. Heiber 1966: 802.

79. Jacobeit 1987: 315, n. 12; also published in Dow and Lixfeld in press.

80. Heiber 1966: 803.

81. Heiber 1966: 803–804.

82. Heiber (1966: 802–803) gained this insight through an analysis of the archives BA R 73/161, which in 1986–1987 could no longer be found in the Bundesarchiv Koblenz.

83. Vorschläge 1933: 94–150.

84. See *Mitteldeutsche Blätter für Volkskunde* 11, 1936: 89; Wildhagen 1938: 61.

85. Heiber 1966: 803.

86. Wildhagen 1938.

87. See *Mitteilungen des Atlas der deutschen Volkskunde* 5, January 1935: 83.

88. BA R 73/302. Letter of appointment by the DFG for Wilhelm Peßler dated August 29, 1934.

89. Files of the DGV in the DVA. File "Volkskundetag 1936 in Bremen," with a letter by Spamer to John Meier dated July 16, 1936.

90. BA R 73/302. Letter of Wildhagen to Peßler dated June 9, 1936.

91. Heiber 1966: 803.

92. Cf. Heiber 1966: 803, 141.

93. Cf. Assion 1985, also published in Dow and Lixfeld in press. Fehrle was an old Nazi of the NSDAP, membership number 729 466, who joined on December 1, 1931; see BDC Fehrle, Eugen, born August 7, 1880.

94. BA R 73/318. Letter by Spamer to Fehrle dated September 8, 1934.

95. BA R 73/318. Letter by Wildhagen to Fehrle dated January 2, 1935.

96. BA R 73/318. Letter by Wildhagen to Fehrle dated January 2, 1935.

97. BA R 73/318. Letter by Fehrle to Wildhagen dated January 22, 1935.

98. BA R 73/318. Memorandum by Fehrle dated January 13, 1935.

99. BA R 73/318. Letter by Fehrle to Wildhagen dated January 22, 1935.

100. Cf. Heiber 1966: 797 and repeatedly.

101. Heiber 1966: 787.

102. Heiber 1966: 780.

103. Cf. Bönisch, Gloistein, Gohde, Weinitschke and Wiese 1986; Grimm 1864a.

104. BA R 73/45. Postwar report by Eduard Wildhagen (October 1965), p. 19.

105. Heiber 1966: 786.

106. Heiber 1966: 802.

107. Cf. Wildhagen 1938: 13–15.

108. BA R 73/45. Postwar report by Eduard Wildhagen (October 1965), p. 13.

109. Cf. Beitl and Beitl 1982: 168.

110. Cf. Wildhagen 1938: 9–10, 13–15, addendum to the book 10–20.

111. BA R 73/318. Correspondence Wildhagen-Fehrle dated April 24, 1935, and April 29, 1935.
112. BA R 73/318. Correspondence Wildhagen-Fehrle dated December 18 and 23, 1935.
113. Beitl and Beitl 1982: 168.
114. Heiber 1966: 831–832.
115. BDC Bretschneider, Anneliese, born August 24, 1898. NSDAP membership number 1 277 168 as of August 1, 1932; see also her biography there.
116. BDC Beitl, Richard, born May 14, 1900. File Reichsschrifttumskammer.
117. Cf. Heiber 1966: 800.
118. Jacobeit 1965b: 138–142.
119. Jacobeit 1965b: 138.
120. Wildhagen 1938: 167.
121. Jacobeit 1965b: 139.
122. Beitl 1934: 117–118.
123. Lauffer 1934.
124. In chap. 1 of this study, see the treatment of the propaganda document by the Co-operative Council for Aid to German Research for the *Atlas*, Deutsche Forschung 1928a, 1928b.
125. Wildhagen 1938: 15.
126. Wildhagen 1938: 168.
127. Wildhagen 1938: 167–170.
128. Campbell 1937.
129. *Folk. Zeitschrift des Internationalen Verbandes für Volksforschung/Folk: The Journal of the International Association for Folklore and Ethnology* 1, 1937: 17–23.
130. *Folk* 1, 1937: 21; Bellmann 1937: 208.
131. Vorschläge 1933: 94–150.
132. *Mitteilungen des Atlas der deutschen Volkskunde* 5, January 1935: 81–96. Concerning the fifth questionnaire, see Grober-Glück 1988: 54, 62 and the negative criticism on the methodology by Cox 1988.
133. See Jacobeit 1987: 303; also published in Dow and Lixfeld in press.
134. *Mitteilungen des Atlas der deutschen Volkskunde* 5, January 1935: 84–85.
135. *Mitteilungen des Atlas der deutschen Volkskunde* 5, January 1935: 88.
136. *Mitteilungen des Atlas der deutschen Volkskunde* 5, January 1935: 88–89.
137. *Mitteilungen des Atlas der deutschen Volkskunde* 5, January 1935: 90–92.
138. *Mitteilungen des Atlas der deutschen Volkskunde* 5, January 1935: 91–92.
139. *Mitteilungen des Atlas der deutschen Volkskunde* 5, January 1935: 92–94.
140. *Mitteilungen des Atlas der deutschen Volkskunde* 5, January 1935: 95.
141. *Mitteilungen des Atlas der deutschen Volkskunde* 5, January 1935: 96.
142. Heiber (1966: 790) makes fun of what are in his opinion generally unusual questions by the ADV; the racial study and racial-soul study nature of the fifth questionnaire is also verified by Strobel 1936b: 920.
143. *Mitteilungen des Atlas der deutschen Volkskunde* 5, January 1935: 85.
144. Cf. Adolf Spamer's "Prelimary Remarks" in Vorschläge 1933: 94.
145. Cf. n. 54 in the autobiographical report by Victor Klemperer.
146. Fritzsch 1936: 88.
147. Spamer 1934a: 148.
148. Spamer 1935b: 99.
149. Spamer 1935b: 103.
150. Ziegler 1934a.
151. Spamer 1935b: 102.
152. Spamer 1935b: 103.
153. Spamer 1935b: 104.

154. Spamer 1936.
155. Cf. Heiber 1966: 842.
156. Cf. Heiber 1966: 804.
157. Spamer 1936: 145.
158. Spamer 1936: 146.
159. Cf. Spamer 1934a.
160. Cf. Thiele (ed.) 1939.
161. Cf. Kater 1974: 140.
162. Cf. Brednich 1983: 90–91, 1985 (also published in Dow and Lixfeld in press), 1987a.
163. As Brückner (1987c: 125) wants us to believe.
164. Cf. Spamer 1936: 145.
165. Reinerth 1932a: 256.
166. Spamer 1936: 149.
167. Spamer 1936: 146.
168. Reinerth 1932a: 257.
169. Spamer 1936: 145.
170. I want to thank Wolfgang Jacobeit for this information.
171. UA Freiburg i.Br., Reg. Akten XVI/4/27. The memorandum was handed in after the removal of DFG Vice-President Wildhagen (August 15, 1936) by the rector of the University of Freiburg i.Br., Friedrich Metz, who was also director of the Department of Settlement of the Reich Community for German Folk Research. Metz had the memorandum sent to John Meier on December 16, 1936, for his information.
172. UA Freiburg i.Br., Reg. Akten XVI/4/27. Memorandum by Adolf Spamer in 1936, pp. 16 and 9.
173. UA Freiburg i.Br., Reg. Akten XVI/4/27. Memorandum by Adolf Spamer in 1936, p. 4.
174. UA Freiburg i.Br., Reg. Akten XVI/4/27. Memorandum by Adolf Spamer in 1936, p. 6.
175. UA Freiburg i.Br., Reg. Akten XVI/4/27. Memorandum by Adolf Spamer in 1936, p. 8; cf. 14.
176. UA Freiburg i.Br., Reg. Akten XVI/4/27. Memorandum by Adolf Spamer in 1936, p. 7.
177. UA Freiburg i.Br., Reg. Akten XVI/4/27. Memorandum by Adolf Spamer in 1936, p. 12.
178. UA Freiburg i.Br., Reg. Akten XVI/4/27. Memorandum by Adolf Spamer in 1936, p. 6.
179. UA Freiburg i.Br., Reg. Akten XVI/4/27. Memorandum by Adolf Spamer in 1936, pp. 6–7, 17.
180. UA Freiburg i.Br., Reg. Akten XVI/4/27. Memorandum by Adolf Spamer in 1936, p. 2.
181. UA Freiburg i.Br., Reg. Akten XVI/4/27. Memorandum by Adolf Spamer in 1936, p. 2.
182. UA Freiburg i.Br., Reg. Akten XVI/4/27. Memorandum by Adolf Spamer in 1936, p. 12.
183. UA Freiburg i.Br., Reg. Akten XVI/4/27. Memorandum by Adolf Spamer in 1936, p. 13.
184. UA Freiburg i.Br., Reg. Akten XVI/4/27. Memorandum by Adolf Spamer in 1936, p. 2.
185. UA Freiburg i.Br., Reg. Akten XVI/4/27. Memorandum by Adolf Spamer in 1936, p. 13.
186. Bollmus 1970: 236.

187. Cf. Spamer 1935b: 99, 103.
188. Nationalsozialistische Bibliographie 1936–1943; concerning the Testing Commission, see Schier 1988: 143–144.
189. Heiber 1966: 804.
190. Heiber 1966: 804.
191. Spamer 1934–1935a.
192. Spamer 1934–1935b.
193. Ziegler 1934c.
194. Cf. Ziegler 1934c.
195. Cf. Ziegler 1935b: 1156.
196. Ziegler 1934c: 1165.
197. Harmjanz 1936a: 128, 133–134, 141ff.
198. Ziegler 1934c: 1165.
199. Deutsche Volkskunde im Schrifttum 1938.
200. Deutsche Volkskunde im Schrifttum 1938: 52, IV 61.
201. Deutsche Volkskunde im Schrifttum 1938: 52, IV 60.
202. Deutsche Volkskunde im Schrifttum 1938: 17, I 30.
203. Deutsche Volkskunde im Schrifttum 1938: 17–18, I 33.
204. Weber-Kellermann 1984: 202.
205. Weber-Kellermann 1984: 202.
206. Weber-Kellermann 1984: 202.
207. Deutsche Volkskunde im Schrifttum 1938: 17–18, I 30, I 33; 52, IV 60, IV 61.
208. Heiber 1966: 814–821.
209. Heiber 1966: 821–843, esp. 842.
210. Heiber 1966: 843.
211. UA Jena. Bestand U Abt. IV, No. 30, biography of Matthes Ziegler in 1940.
212. Heiber 1966: 804; the first delivery of maps by the ADV appeared in 1936, cf. Strobel 1936b.
213. Harmjanz 1936a: 128, 133–134, 141ff.
214. Jacobeit 1987: 303–304, also published in Dow and Lixfeld in press; Jacobeit and Mohrmann 1982: 289.
215. Weber-Kellermann 1984: 202.
216. Archive of the Philosophical Faculty of the University of Freiburg i.Br. File "Institut für Volkskunde," letter by the Dean to the Cultural and Educational Ministry in Karlsruhe dated February 7, 1942; letter by the Reich Educational Ministry (REM) to the Cultural and Educational Ministry in Karlsruhe dated March 28, 1942; letter by the Dean to the REM dated April 20, 1942.
217. Cf. Weber-Kellermann 1984: 203–205.
218. Strobach 1987: 32, also published in Dow and Lixfeld in press.
219. Wildhagen's organizational accomplishment and scholarly understanding for folk-national research were still attested in 1936 by Professors Hans F. K. Günther, Adolf Spamer, Eugen Fehrle, Friedrich Metz, Walther Mitzka, Wilhelm Peßler, and Ernst Bargheer in a *"geharnischten Demarche"* (unbridled statement) to the Reich Educational Ministry intended to ward off the removal of the DFG vice-president; see Heiber 1966: 840.
220. Sokol 1985a: 2; cf. Sokol 1985b: 2.
221. Heiber 1966: 841.
222. According to a statement by Matthes Ziegler, cf. Bollmus 1970: 94 and 283, n. 209; Heiber 1966: 834.
223. Bollmus 1970: 94.
224. Heiber 1966: 834.
225. Cf. Bollmus 1970: 94 and 283, n. 209.

3. FASCIST *VOLKSKUNDE* AND FOLK RENEWAL DURING THE THIRD REICH

1. Including the NS Community "Strength through Joy" in the German Workers' Movement, the Reich Youth Leadership, the Staff Office of the Reich Farm Leader, Reich Propaganda Leadership, the NS Teachers Union, NS Student Body, NS University Docent Union, Reich Women's Core, etc.

2. Concerning the person of Alfred Rosenberg, see Bollmus 1970: 17–20 and Baumgärtner 1977: 134–137.

3. Concerning the person of Heinrich Himmler and his closest coworkers in the SS Ancestral Inheritance, see Anka Oesterle's study in Dow and Lixfeld in press.

4. See Jeggle 1988a: 52–58, Lutz 1958, and chaps. 1 and 2 of this work.

5. Jeggle 1988a: 58.

6. Cf. Dow and Lixfeld 1986: 7–14.

7. Jeggle 1988a: 58.

8. See chap. 1 in this work.

9. See Jacobeit 1987, also published in Dow and Lixfeld in press.

10. Jeggle 1988a: 58.

11. BDC Schreiber, Georg, born January 5, 1882; Freckmann 1987; Bausinger 1965: 194–196, also published in Dow and Lixfeld in press.

12. Gilch 1986: 27; Bausinger 1965: 200–202, also published in Dow and Lixfeld in press.

13. BDC Peuckert, Will-Erich, born May 11, 1895; Daxelmüller 1987b: 153, also published in Dow and Lixfeld in press.

14. BDC Kriss, Rudolf, born March 5, 1903; see the study by Olaf Bockhorn published in Dow and Lixfeld in press; Kriss 1948.

15. Cf. Korff 1978: 43.

16. Cf. Gilch 1986: 27–29.

17. Gerndt 1987b: 18, also published in Dow and Lixfeld in press.

18. Weber-Kellermann and Bimmer 1985: 108.

19. Cf. Heiber 1966; Bollmus 1970; Kater 1974; Baumgärtner 1977.

20. Gerndt 1987b: 18, also published in Dow and Lixfeld in press.

21. Gerndt 1987b: 18.

22. Cf. Emmerich 1968; Emmerich 1971.

23. Gerndt 1987b: 18.

24. Jeggle 1988a: 61.

25. Bollmus 1987: 52.

26. Cf., for example, the comments on Georg Schreiber and Kurt Huber in Bausinger 1965: 194–196, 200–202, also published in Dow and Lixfeld in press.

27. Cf. Emmerich 1971: 11–12.

28. Emmerich 1971: 110–131; here 110.

29. Bollmus 1987: 54.

30. Peuckert 1948.

31. Bollmus 1987: 54.

32. Cf. Zmarzlick 1963.

33. Cf. Lixfeld 1987a: 70.

34. Cf. Emmerich 1971.

35. Rosenberg 1934a; concerning the concept of ideology, see Hunger 1984: 21–36, 364–399.

36. Cf. Petzold 1982a: 164–191.

37. Petzold 1982b: 192 and 198; cf. Bausinger 1971b: 62–63; Bollmus 1989.

38. Emmerich 1971: 108.
39. See, for example, Studien 1934 and 1935; Zipfel 1965: 54–60; Bollmus 1970: 20–23; Bausinger 1971b: 62–63; Baumgärtner 1977: 56–72; Petzold 1982b.
40. Cf. the doubts expressed by Bollmus 1970: 9.
41. Bollmus 1970: 21.
42. Bollmus 1970: 24.
43. See Brückner 1988d; the concept *Gläubige Wissenschaft* (scholarship of faith) was used by Catholic folk piety research, which saw *Volkskunde* as a religious task. See also Koren 1936.
44. See the enumeration in Baumgärtner 1977: 73–81.
45. Bollmus 1970: 17.
46. See, for example, Studien 1934 and 1935; Künneth 1935; Künneth 1947; Bollmus 1970: 17–26; Baumgärtner 1977: 56–72; Petzold 1982b.
47. Cf. also BA NS 8/22 (see text, appendix I.3).
48. Rosenberg 1934a: 3 (Introduction).
49. Rosenberg 1934a: 1 (Introduction).
50. Rosenberg 1934a: 1 (Introduction).
51. Rosenberg 1934a: 2 (Introduction).
52. Rosenberg 1934a: 1–2 (Introduction).
53. Cf. Rosenberg 1934a: 125–144 (1. Buch, II, 7); Emmerich 1971: 148.
54. Cf. Rosenberg 1934a: 2 (Introduction).
55. Rosenberg 1934a: 2 (Introduction).
56. Rosenberg 1934a: 2 (Introduction).
57. BA NS 8/22.
58. Cf. Rosenberg 1934a: 459–466 (3. Buch, I, 2); Daxelmüller 1987b; 154–158.
59. Rosenberg 1934a: 587 (3. Buch, IV, 4).
60. Rosenberg 1934a: 169 (1. Buch, II, 3).
61. Rosenberg 1934a: 169 (1. Buch, II, 3).
62. Cf. Baumgärtner 1977.
63. BA NS 8/22.
64. Rosenberg 1934a: 145 (1. Buch, II, 1).
65. Rosenberg 1934a: 146, 155 (1. Buch, II, 1–2).
66. Rosenberg 1934a: 156 (1. Buch, II, 2).
67. Rosenberg 1934a: 152 (1. Buch, II, 1).
68. Rosenberg 1934a: 155 (1. Buch, II, 1).
69. Rosenberg 1934a: 163–168; Zitat 166 (1. Buch, II, 2).
70. Cf. Rosenberg 1934a: 29, 121, 164 (1. Buch, I, 6; II, 2).
71. Rosenberg 1934a: 132–133 (1. Buch, I, 7).
72. Rosenberg 1934a: 141–142 (1. Buch, I, 7).
73. Rosenberg 1934a: 134–135 (1. Buch, I, 7).
74. BA NS 8/22.
75. Rosenberg 1934a: 684–685 (3. Buch, VII, 2); cf. Bollmus 1970: 238–239; Kater 1974: 49; Baumgärtner 1977: 70, 260.
76. Bollmus 1970: 24.
77. Rosenberg 1934a: 684 (3. Buch, VII, 2); concerning "organic truth," see also Baumgärtner 1977: 260.
78. Rosenberg 1934a: 684 (3. Buch, VII, 2).
79. Rosenberg 1934a: 684–685 (3. Buch, VII, 2).
80. Bollmus 1970: 24.
81. Emmerich 1971: 134; it seems however questionable whether this educated bourgeoisie was "unpolitical."

82. Emmerich 1971: 134; emphasis added by Emmerich.
83. BA NS 8/22.
84. Rosenberg 1934a: 169–170 (1. Buch, II, 3).
85. Cf. Volk und Gesundheit 1982.
86. Cf. Broszat 1984.
87. Rosenberg 1934a: 572 (3. Buch, IV, 3); emphasis added by Lixfeld.
88. Rosenberg 1934a: 574–575 (3. Buch, IV, 3).
89. Rosenberg 1934a: 578–579 (3. Buch, IV, 3).
90. Rosenberg 1934a: 580 (3. Buch, IV, 3).
91. Rosenberg 1934a: 169–179 (1. Buch, II, 3).
92. Rosenberg 1934a: 580 (3. Buch, IV, 4); 635 (3. Buch, V, 6).
93. Rosenberg 1934a: 635–636 (3. Buch, V, 6).
94. Rosenberg 1934a: 636 (3. Buch, V, 6).
95. Rosenberg 1934a: 602 (3. Buch, V, 1).
96. Cf. Rosenberg 1934a: 22–23 (1. Buch, I, 1); Künneth 1947: 135; emphasis added by Lixfeld.
97. Rosenberg 1934a: 701 (3. Buch, VII, 6).
98. Künneth 1935: 15.
99. Künneth 1935: 209.
100. Rosenberg 1934a: 602 (3. Buch, V, 1).
101. Rosenberg 1934a: 611 (3. Buch, V, 2).
102. Cf. Rosenberg 1934a: 386–387 (2. Buch, III, 5); 2 (Introduction).
103. Rosenberg 1934a: 614–615 (3. Buch, V, 2).
104. Rosenberg 1934a: 614 (3. Buch, V, 2).
105. Rosenberg 1934a: 616 (3. Buch, V, 3).
106. Rosenberg 1934a: 280 (2. Buch, I, 1).
107. Rosenberg 1934a: 617 (3. Buch, V, 3).
108. Rosenberg 1934a: 618–619 (3. Buch, V, 3).
109. Rosenberg 1934a: 450 (2. Buch, IV, 6).
110. Rosenberg 1934a: 1 (Introduction).
111. BA NS 8/22.
112. Rosenberg 1934a: 546 (3. Buch, III, 4); cf. Rosenberg 1934a: 485–486 (3. Buch, II, 2).
113. Rosenberg 1934a: 596 (3. Buch, IV, 5).
114. Cf. Rosenberg 1934a: 621 (3. Buch, V, 3).
115. Rosenberg 1934a: 3 (Introduction).
116. Rosenberg 1934a: 453 (3. Buch, I, 1).
117. Rosenberg 1934a: 599 (3. Buch, V, 1).
118. Rosenberg 1934a: 602–603 (3. Buch, V, 1).
119. Rosenberg 1934a: 685 (3. Buch, VII, 2).
120. Rosenberg 1934a: 2 (Introduction).
121. Rosenberg 1934a: 689, cf. 688 (3. Buch VII, 3).
122. Cf. Rosenberg 1934a: 131, 134, 141–142 (1. Buch, I, 7); 597–598 (3. Buch, IV, 5) and repeatedly.
123. Cf. Rosenberg 1934a: 614–615 (3. Buch, V, 2).
124. Cf. Rosenberg 1935b, 1937b, 1938a.
125. BA NS 8/22.
126. Rosenberg 1934a: 119 (1. Buch, I, 6).
127. Rosenberg 1934a: 120 (1. Buch, I, 6).
128. Bollmus 1970: 27; cf. Brenner 1963.
129. BA NS 8/122, Fol. 78–79 Rs., here Fol. 79: Aufruf des Kampfbundes für deutsche

Kultur (KfdK), München, January 1929; cf. *Nationalsozialistische Monatshefte* 2, Heft 11, 1931: 61–65.

130. See von See 1970: 73 and, in this study, the text to n. 60, chap. 1.

131. Deutsches Volksliedarchiv (DVA) J 189; see also the text to nn. 28ff., chap. 1.

132. Nollau 1926: Einleitung; cf. above in this present study, the text to nn. 61–63, chap. 1.

133. BA NS 8/122, Fol. 78.

134. BA NS 8/122, Fol. 78 Rs.

135. Bollmus 1970: 31–32, 37–38.

136. Bollmus 1970: 38; Kater 1974: 22; Reinerth 1932a.

137. BA NS 8/122, Fol. 79 Rs.; BDC Mielke, Robert, born December 12, 1963.

138. BDC Beitl, Richard, born May 14, 1900, Akte Reichsschrifttumskammer.

139. BDC Bretschneider, Anneliese, born August 24, 1898, files of the Reichsschrifttumskammer, Lebenslauf, p. 4.

140. *Die Sonne. Monatsschrift für nordische Weltanschauung und Lebensgestaltung* 10, 1933: 466–467; shortly after this the Battle Union for German Culture in Schleswig-Holstein tried to reintroduce women's costumes as everyday clothing; see *Die Sonne* 11, 1934: 44–45.

141. Bollmus 1970: 34, 39–46; cf. Brenner 1963: 32–34.

142. Bollmus 1970: 50.

143. BA NS 8/37, Fol. 35.

144. BA NS 8/123, Fol. 213–214.

145. BA NS 8/123, Fol. 211–212.

146. BDC Bretschneider, Anneliese, born August 24, 1898, files of the Reichsschrifttumskammer, Lebenslauf, p. 3.

147. Bollmus 1970: 47.

148. BDC Haverbeck, Werner, born October 28, 1909, NSDAP membership no. 142 009 as of August 1, 1929; cf. files of the Ahnenerbe, correspondence dated April 9 and 14, 1936.

149. Bollmus 1970: 50.

150. Bollmus 1970: 52.

151. Bollmus 1970: 54–60; concerning the assignment "in every form," see Kater 1974: 21; Biedermann 1944a: 1.

152. Bollmus 1970: 66–71; here 66–67.

153. Cf. Bausinger 1987a.

154. Cf. *Volkstum und Heimat* 3, Heft 1, January 1936; cf. in this study the section on the Reich Community for German Folk Research and the parallel regional development in Saxony, with the changes made by Adolf Spamer from the Regional Research Office for Folklore in the Reich Union Folk-Nation and Homeland into the *Gau* Research Office for Folklore in the Department of Folk-Nation and Homeland of the NS Cultural Community (*Gau* Saxony).

155. BA NS 15/91. G. U.: Auf dem Wege zur deutschen Volkskultur. "Volkstum und Heimat" in der NS-Kulturgemeinde. *Völkischer Beobachter*, Berlin, November 24, 1934.

156. Bausinger 1987a: 136.

157. Bollmus 1970: 101–102.

158. According to Heiber 1966: 834; concerning the Rosenberg Bureau in general cf. Bollmus 1970 and Baumgärtner 1977: 25–41.

159. Brückner 1986b: 190.

160. BDC Mackensen, Lutz, born June 15, 1901. NSDAP membership no. 3 391 290 as of November 1, 1933.

161. Cf. Brückner 1986b: 189–190.

162. UA Greifswald. Doctoral file no. 931, Lebenslauf Matthes Ziegler of 1936.

163. UA Greifswald. Doctoral file no. 931, Lebenslauf Matthes Ziegler of 1936.

164. Ziegler 1934–1940a-c.

165. UA Greifswald. Doctoral file no. 921, Lebenslauf Matthes Ziegler of 1936; cf. Ziegler 1937a: 10.

166. BDC Ziegler, Johann Matthäus, born June 11, 1911, SS-File, Lebenslauf of February 1, 1935.

167. UA Greifswald. Doctoral file no. 931, Lebenslauf Matthes Ziegler of 1936.

168. Brückner 1986b: 190.

169. Title page of the dissertation copy with a biography (= Brückner 1986b: 189–190) in the University Library Freiburg i.Br.; cf. Ziegler 1937a, Lixfeld 1987b.

170. Cf. Lixfeld 1987b.

171. BDC Kaiser, Karl, born September 23, 1906. NSDAP membership no. 4 104 926 as of May 1, 1937.

172. Cf. Kater 1975, 1984; Broszat 1958.

173. BA NS 8/141, Fol. 105; Bollmus 1970: 320, n. 246.

174. Brenner 1963: 18, 251, n. 29.

175. BDC Ziegler, Johann Matthäus, born June 11, 1911, SS-File, Lebenslauf of February 1, 1935.

176. UA Greifswald. Doctoral file no. 931, Lebenslauf Matthes Ziegler of 1936.

177. BDC Ziegler, Johann Matthäus, born June 11, 1911, SS-File, Lebenslauf of February 1, 1935.

178. BA NS 8/141, Fol. 105.

179. Concerning the Staff Office of Reich Farm Leader Darré and Darré's leadership of the Racial and Settlement Office of the SS as well as the transfer of the entire membership of Darré's Reich Farmers Rank into Heinrich Himmler's SS, see Kater 1974: 24–28.

180. BDC Ziegler, Johann Matthäus, born June 11, 1911, SS-File, Lebenslauf of February 1, 1935; Brückner 1988d: 36 presumes that Ziegler's *Namenbuch* appeared under the editorship of Erwin Metzner (Metzner 1934, 1939).

181. UA Greifswald. Doctoral file no. 931, Lebenslauf of 1936. According to the UA Jena, Bestand U Abt. IV, Nr.30, Lebenslauf von 1940, und BA NS 8/141, Fol. 103 and 105 the reappointment to the position of (main) editor of the *NS-Monatshefte* took place on April 1, 1934, but was not carried out until May 1, after an officially published (BA NS 8/128, Fol. 4) announcement in all journals and newspapers of the Central Publishing House NSDAP, Franz Eher Nachf., München.

182. UA Greifswald. Doctoral file no. 931, Lebenslauf Matthes Ziegler of 1936.

183. Kater 1974: 21.

184. BA NS 8/141, Fol. 103.

185. BA NS 8/141, Fol. 105.

186. BDC Ziegler, Johann Matthäus, born June 11, 1911, SS-File, Lebenslauf of February 1, 1935.

187. Bollmus 1970: 290, n. 51; concerning the competition between the SD Offices for World-View Research and Evaluation and Ziegler's Main Post or later office, see Bollmus 1970: 274, n. 49; to be sure, the SS member and Rosenberg collaborator Ziegler must have been transfered as of December 1934 at the order of the Reichsführer-SS from the Racial and Settlement Office of the SS into the Security Service of the SS (SD) and as of February 1935 carried the identification card of the SD; cf. BDC Ziegler, Johann Matthäus, born June 11, 1911. SS-File, letter by Ziegler dated July 2, 1935, to the Racial and Settlement Office of the SS.

188. BDC Ziegler (cf. above), SS-File, Lebenslauf of March 10, 1940.

189. BDC Ziegler (cf. above), Lebenslauf of February 1, 1935.

190. Rosenberg 1934a.

191. Ziegler 1934d.

192. Cf. Bollmus 1970: 290, n. 51.
193. Ziegler 1933.
194. BA NS 8/111, Fol. 201.
195. Ziegler 1933: 49.
196. Ziegler 1933: 61–63.
197. Bollmus 1970: 22.
198. Rosenberg 1934a: 114 (1. Buch, I, 5); cf. Bollmus 1970: 21.
199. Ziegler 1933: 49.
200. Bollmus 1970: 22.
201. Ziegler 1933: 62.
202. Ziegler 1933: 64.
203. Ziegler 1933: 64.
204. Ziegler 1933: 65.
205. Ziegler 1933: 65–66.
206. Bollmus 1970: 215.
207. Cf. Heilfurth 1937.
208. Cf. Ziegler 1935c, 1935d, 1935e, 1937b, 1937c, 1939c.
209. Cf. Bollmus 1970: 17–26.
210. *Nationalsozialistische Monatshefte* 13, Heft 152/153, 1942: 322; cf. Baumgärtner 1977: 260–265.
211. Cf. Ziegler 1935f.
212. Kater 1974: 141.
213. Cf. Bollmus 1970: 113–119.
214. Kater 1974.
215. Cf. Rosenberg 1935a, 1937a.
216. Lorenzen 1942.
217. Ziegler 1934c: 1166.
218. Ziegler 1935a: 675.
219. Ziegler 1935a: 675.
220. Ziegler 1935a: 679.
221. Ziegler 1935a: 676.
222. Ziegler 1935a: 680.
223. Ziegler 1935a: 678.
224. Naumann 1922; cf. Dow and Lixfeld 1986: 9–10.
225. Ziegler 1935a: 675.
226. Ziegler 1934a.
227. Ziegler 1934a: 715.
228. Bach 1937: 44.
229. Ziegler 1939a: 715.
230. Ziegler 1934a: 716–717.
231. Ziegler 1935a: 679.
232. Ziegler 1935a: 683.
233. Ziegler 1933: 63–66.
234. Ziegler 1935a: 683.
235. UA Jena. Bestand U Abt. IV, No. 30, Lebenslauf Matthes Ziegler of 1940.
236. Cf. Lüthi 1979: 4, 23, 64–65; Leopold Schmidt 1951: 133–137; cf. Bockhorn 1988, 1989.
237. Bollmus 1970: 273, n. 36; 308–309, n. 70.
238. Spieß 1934; cf. Spieß 1938a.
239. Ziegler 1934c: 1167.

240. Spamer 1934–1935b; Peßler 1934–1938; Haberlandt 1935.
241. Ziegler 1936a: 11, 1939a: 13.
242. Spieß 1934: 231.
243. Spieß 1938a: 381; Spieß 1934: 237.
244. Spieß 1934: 235, cf. 231–232.
245. Schultz 1924; cf. Lüthi 1979: 64.
246. Spieß 1933a.
247. Spieß 1938a: 382, 1934: 161, 167, 170.
248. Concerning National Socialist folktale research by Ziegler, see Lixfeld 1987b.
249. Leopold Schmidt 1951: 134.
250. Georg and Emma Hüsing 1932: I.
251. Georg and Emma Hüsing 1932: I.
252. Bublitz 1932.
253. Georg and Emma Hüsing 1932: III.
254. Konopath 1930: 425.
255. Konopath 1930: 426.
256. Cf. Bublitz 1932.
257. Cf. Lixfeld 1987b.
258. "Too quickly" was added in Ziegler 1936a: 13.
259. Ziegler 1939a: 16.
260. *Nationalsozialistische Monatshefte* 7, Heft 77, 1936: 774: "*Volkskunde* does not want to create a 'new religious system,' no 'new dogmatism,' it does however want to prepare with a fine sensitivity and drawing on the folk-nation the unified faith of the German folk."
261. Ziegler 1934a: 717.
262. In 1936 there were still three large groups: material culture, narrative and custom research/symbol studies, cf. Ziegler 1936a: 11–12. Ziegler had already recommended in 1934 the group "material culture" (cf. Ziegler 1934c: 1167) as an expansion of the division presented by von Spieß 1934, which he continually added to until 1939.
263. Ziegler 1939a: 13–14.
264. Settlement studies and material culture research, Ziegler 1939a: 13.
265. Narrative and legendary material research, Ziegler 1939a: 13.
266. Custom research and symbol studies, Ziegler 1939a: 13.
267. Folk speech/traditional communities, Ziegler 1939a: 14.
268. Ziegler 1939a: 14.
269. Ziegler 1939a: 15.
270. Ziegler 1939a: 15, cf. 5; cf. also the jewel metaphor in Rosenberg 1934a: 614 (3. Buch, V, 2).
271. Ziegler 1939a: 15–16, 1936a: 13.
272. Ziegler 1939a: 5; cf. Spieß 1934: 19–20, 236.
273. Ziegler 1937a: 6.
274. Emmerich 1971: 132–161.
275. Cf. Heilfurth 1937 and UA Jena. Bestand U Abt. IV, No. 30, Life History of Matthes Ziegler of 1940; concerning the name "Reichsarbeitsgemeinschaft," see, for example, *Deutsche Volkskunde* 1, 1939: 244.
276. See, for example, BA NS 8/170, Fol. 157–158, letter from Rosenberg to Rust dated March 6, 1937; BA NS 8/181, Fol. 11–12, letter from Rosenberg to Bormann dated June 28, 1939.
277. Ziegler 1939b: 8.
278. Ziegler 1939b: 8; concerning the inclusion of the Working Community into the Rosenberg Bureau, see, e.g., Der Reichsorganisationsleiter der NSDAP 1943: 312b.

279. BA NS 8/245, Fol. 1; BA NS 8/238, Fol. 5.

280. BA NS 8/128, Fol. 45–47; published in Kley 1937.

281. Ziegler 1938a: 6.

282. UA Jena. Bestand U Abt. IV, Nr.30, Life History of Matthes Ziegler of 1940.

283. Bollmus 1970: 60; cf. Bollmus 1989.

284. Bollmus 1970: 236.

285. BA NS 8/128, Fol. 45–47.

286. BDC Henschke, Karl-Heinrich, born October 16, 1910. NSDAP membership no. 5 804 535 as of May 1, 1937.

287. BDC Thiele, Ernst Otto, born February 23, 1902. NSDAP membership no. 1 278 325 as of August 1, 1932.

288. BDC Strobel, Hans, born November 28, 1911. NSDAP membership no. 387 719 as of December 1, 1930; concerning Strobel, see also Gajek 1986 and Brückner 1988f: 209.

289. Strobel 1934a; cf. Strobel 1938a: 195 Anmerkung 144.

290. BDC Haiding (Paganini), Karl, born July 3, 1906. NSDAP membership no. 332 498 as of June 1, 1933 (no. 26 787 as of 1923).

291. BDC Scheller, Theodor (Thilo), born December 9, 1897; BA NS 8/139, Fol. 74; concerning the Reich party celebrations, see Reimers 1979.

292. UA Jena. Bestand U Abt. IV, Nr. 30, Life History of Matthes Ziegler of 1940.

293. Cf. *Nationalsozialistische Monatshefte* 8, Heft 83, 1937: 164; *Germanen-Erbe* 2, 1937: 30.

294. *Volkstum und Heimat* 4, 1937: 61–62.

295. Cf. Martin 1983.

296. *Volk im Werden* 5, 1937: 103.

297. *NS Bildungswesen* 4, 1939: 45.

298. *Volk im Werden* 5, 1937: 381.

299. Cf. Heilfurth 1937.

300. BA NS 21/281. Report on the Second Meeting of the Working Community for German Folklore, dated October 22 1937.

301. BDC Kulke, Erich, born January 3, 1908. NSDAP membership no. 4 827 122 as of May 1, 1937.

302. These five working principles are also published in Kulke 1939a: 18; concerning the work of the National Socialist farm house research, see also Freckmann 1982, esp. 174–175, and 1985.

303. Deutsche Volkskunde im Schrifttum 1938.

304. BA NS 21/281. Report on the Second Meeting of the Working Community for German Folklore, dated October 22, 1937.

305. BA NS 21/293. From the Working Community for German Folklore. Sent together with an accompanying letter by the NSDAP, Reich Leadership, the Commissioner of the Führer . . . dated September 24, 1937 to Ancestral Inheritance, to Sievers.

306. BDC Bebermeyer, Gustav, born October 16, 1890. NSDAP membership no. 2 090 576 as of May 1, 1933; cf. Hesse and Schröter 1985; Jeggle 1988c.

307. BDC Diewerge, Heinz, born January 14, 1909. NSDAP membership no. 3 445 244 as of April 1, 1934.

308. BDC Fehrle, Eugen, born August 7, 1880. NSDAP membership no. 729 466 as of December 1, 1931; cf. Assion 1982, 1985, also published in Dow and Lixfeld in press.

309. BDC Fischer, Georg, born January 4, 1897. NSDAP membership no. 2 445 985 as of May 1, 1933.

310. BDC Freudenthal, Herbert Johann Wilhelm August, born July 9, 1894. NSDAP membership no. 2 731 981 as of May 1, 1933.

311. BDC Heilfurth, Gerhard Friedrich, born July 11, 1909. NSDAP membership no. 2 960 284 as of May 1, 1933.

312. BDC Kaiser, Karl, born September 23, 1906. NSDAP membership no. 4 104 926 as of May 1, 1937.

313. BDC Meyer, Gustav Friedrich, born February 28, 1878. NSLB-membership no. 307 739 as of September 20, 1934.

314. BDC Schier, Bruno, born February 17, 1902. Member of the Sudetendeutsche party no. 139 338 as of September 15, 1934; NSDAP membership no. 5 450 848 as of July 15, 1937.

315. BDC Wähler, Martin, born May 5, 1889. NSDAP membership no. 4 493 015 as of May 1, 1937.

316. Cf. Rothert 1937; L., H. 1937; Emil Lehmann 1937.

317. The Nordische Gesellschaft was under Rosenberg's Foreign Political Office in the Reich Leadership of the NSDAP; cf. Baumgärtner 1977: 17–19.

318. Strobel 1938b, 1937a.

319. Thiele 1938a.

320. Schier 1938a, 1937b.

321. Hanika 1938; BDC Hanika, Josef, born on October 30, 1900, member of the Sudetendeutsche party, no. 1 023 986 since January 1, 1938.

322. Fehrle 1938c.

323. Haberlandt 1938a; BDC Haberlandt, Arthur, born March 9, 1889.

324. Helm 1938; BDC Helm, Rudolf, born August 22, 1899. NSDAP membership no. 8 210 910 as of October 1, 1940.

325. Orend 1938a.

326. Siegfried Lehmann 1938; BDC Lehmann, Siegfried, born March 18, 1906, SS membership no. 291 028.

327. Plassmann 1938b; BDC Plassmann, Joseph Otto, born June 12, 1895. SS membership no. 278 272.

328. *Nationalsozialistische Monatshefte* 8, Heft 89, 1937: 749.

329. BA NS 21/281. Report on the Second Meeting of the Working Community for German Folklore, dated October 22, 1937.

330. Kulke 1939d; cf. Kulke 1939.

331. Kulke 1939f: 103.

332. See chap. 1.

333. Kulke 1939f: 102.

334. Kulke 1939f: 103.

335. Kulke 1939f: 103; Kulke is referring here to the law of July 14, 1933, concerning the rebuilding of German peasantry.

336. Cf. for example Söhrnsen-Petersen 1937.

337. Kulke 1941b: 129.

338. Kulke 1938b.

339. Kulke 1938c.

340. Plates in Lindner, Kulke, and Gutsmiedl 1938: 231.

341. Kulke 1938b: 219.

342. Kulke 1938b: 219.

343. Kulke 1938c.

344. BA NS 21/281. Report on the Second Meeting of the Working Community for German Folklore, dated October 22, 1937.

345. Kulke 1938c: 190.

346. Kulke 1938c: 188.

347. Cf. Kulke 1938c: 191.

348. Cf. Scharf 1985.

349. Kulke 1938c: pls. 5 and 6.

350. Kulke 1938c: 186.

351. Kulke 1938c: 187.

352. Kulke 1938c: 191–192.

353. Cf. Freckmann 1982, 1985.

354. Kulke 1938b: 219.

355. Cf. Kulke 1939e: 235, 237, 253, 256–262, 270–271, 277, 279–297.

356. Cf. Kulke 1938c: plates; Lindner, Kulke, and Gutsmiedl 1938: 231 and often.

357. *Deutsche Volkskunde*, Jahrgang 1, 1939–Jahrgang 6, Heft 1/2, 1944.

358. Cf. *Nationalsozialistische Monatshefte* 10, Heft 107, 1939: 166; concerning Fischer, see n. 309 and Alzheimer 1989.

359. UA Jena, GDR. Bestand U ABT. IV no. 30. Life history of Ziegler (1940).

360. BA NS 21/281. Report on the Second Meeting of the Working Community for German Folklore, dated October 22, 1937.

361. Ackermann 1970: 123.

362. Ackermann 1970: 122.

363. Cf. Ackermann 1970: 122, n. 131; cf. Bollmus 1987: 57.

364. See the chapter in this study on Rosenberg's *Mythus*.

365. See Ackermann 1970: 120–121 and the racist conception of the eternal law of life as struggle in the chapter in this study on the world-view *Volkskunde* of Ziegler.

366. Cf. Kater 1974: 21.

367. Cf. the differing statements, e.g., concerning Ziegler and Harmjanz in Kater 1974: 141 and Bollmus 1970: 217–218.

368. See the chapter in this study on the Reich Community for German Folk Research; concerning Darré's "blood and soil" ideology, see Corni 1989.

369. Cf. Kater 1974: 24–28.

370. Concerning Wolfram Sievers, see Kater 1974: 28–36 and Oesterle 1987, 1988.

371. BA NS 21/281. Letter from Ziegler to Sievers dated August 13, 1937.

372. BA NS 21/297. Letter from Strobel to Sievers dated September 15, 1936.

373. BA NS 21/281. Letter from Strobel to the Ancestral Inheritance dated September 20, 1937.

374. See the chapter in this study on the Reich Community for German Folk Research.

375. BA NS 21/281. Letter from Galke to the Ancestral Inheritance dated February 24, 1937.

376. Cf. Kater 1974: 37–43, 58.

377. Kater 1974: 64.

378. Kater 1974: 58, 65; concerning Herman Wirth and Walther Wüst, see Kater 1974: 11–16, 41–45, and Oesterle 1987, also published in Dow and Lixfeld in press.

379. BA NS 8/170, Fol. 159–161. Letter from Rosenberg to Rust dated January 5, 1937.

380. Cf. Lixfeld 1987b: 37, 53–55.

381. Cf. Heiber 1966: 843, 848.

382. See the chapter in this study on the destruction of the Department of Folklore.

383. Cf. also Röhr 1938: 69, 76–78; Scheidt-Lämke 1942; Hepding 1940.

384. BA NS 8/170, Fol. 159–161. Letter from Rosenberg to Rust dated January 5, 1937.

385. BA NS 8/170, Fol. 161.

386. Röhr 1938: 73, cf. 74.

387. Cf. Röhr 1938: 64–69, no. 118, 147–166.

388. Kaiser 1936; cf. Mackensen 1937c: Röhr 1938: 76–78.

389. Concerning this proverbial expression, see Röhrich 1973, Vol. I: 451–453.

390. Archive of the Baden Research Center for Volkskunde Freiburg i.Br. File "Atlas Zentrale." Letter from Erich Röhr to Eugen Fehrle dated July 2, 1937; BDC Harmjanz, Siegfried Elimar Heinrich, born May 22, 1904. NSDAP membership no. 245 176 as of May 1, 1930, or June 22, 1931. REM Personalakte, Fol. 37.

391. Heiber 1966: 804.

392. Cf. Strobel 1936b.

393. See the chapter in this study on the destruction of the Department of Folklore.

394. Harmjanz and Röhr 1937–1939; cf. Heiber 1966: 804–805.

395. BDC Röhr, Erich, born February 17, 1905. NSDAP membership no. 8 822 999 as of July 1, 1941; cf. Harmjanz 1943.

396. Cf. Oesterle 1987: 89.

397. Heiber 1966: 648.

398. Harmjanz 1936a.

399. Cf. Volkskunde an den Hochschulen 1986: 11, 23.

400. If I am seeing this correctly they limited themselves to the ADV maps published together with Röhr, cf. Harmjanz and Röhr 1937–1939, and Harmjanz 1937.

401. Heiber 1966: 647, 649.

402. Cf. Oesterle 1987: 89.

403. Heiber 1966: 648.

404. Cf. Bollmus 1970: 212–213; Kater 1974: 137.

405. Cf. Bollmus 1970: 214–215.

406. Bollmus 1970: 216.

407. Cf. BA NS 21/309. Letter from Walther Wüst to Himmler, dated April 2, 1939.

408. Cf. Heiber 1966: 650.

409. BA NS 8/170, Fol. 139–140 Rs. Letter from Rust to Rosenberg, dated March 10, 1938.

410. Harmjanz and Röhr 1937–1939.

411. Kaiser 1937a.

412. *Folk: Journal of the International Association for Folklore and Ethnology.* Editorial board Åke Campbell, Uppsala/ G. R. Gair, Edinburgh/Lutz Mackensen, Riga-Berlin/J. de Vries, Leiden. Jahrgang 1, 1937.

413. Cf. Schier 1988: 143–144.

414. BA NS 8/170, Fol. 139–140 Rs. Letter from Rust to Rosenberg, dated March 10, 1938.

415. UA Greifswald, DDR. No. 81, Personal file Karl Kaiser. Ordinance by the Reich Educational Minister "Wp Nr. Kaiser/v 37 (a)" dated March 10, 1938.

416. BDC Kaiser, Karl, born on September 23, 1906, card catalogue of the Rosenberg Bureau.

417. Cf. BA NS 8/170, Fol. 46.

418. Kaiser 1939a; concerning this publication, see the study by Daxelmüller 1987b, also published in Dow and Lixfeld in press.

419. Harmjanz 1939a.

420. UA Greifswald, DDR, presumably the personal file of Karl Kaiser. Letter from Henschke dated March 25, 1938.

421. BA NS 8/170, Fol. 121–126. Letter from Rosenberg to Rust, dated April 11, 1938.

422. Kaiser first became a docent at the University of Greifswald at the beginning of the Second World War. In 1940, at age thirty-four, he died as a soldier in France; see Scheidt-Lämke 1942.

423. BDC Kaiser, Karl, born September 23, 1906.

424. Cf. Bollmus 1970: 217, 320, n. 237a.

425. BA NS 8/170, Fol. 161.

426. BA NS 8/170, Fol. 121–126. Letter from Rosenberg to Rust dated April 11, 1938.

427. BA NS 8/170, Fol. 140–140 Rs.

428. BA NS 8/238, Fol. 11–23, here Fol. 12. Ziegler's report dated August 10, 1938, to Himmler concerning his discussion with Harmjanz on August 1, 1938, in Copenhagen.

429. BA NS 8/238, Fol. 13–14.

430. Cf. Kater 1974: 141.

431. BA NS 21/281. Report on the Second Meeting of the Working Community for German Folklore on October 22, 1937, pp. 1–2.

432. UA Jena, DDR. Bestand U Abt. IV Nr.30. Life History of Ziegler (1940).

433. Cf. Schier 1988: 142–143.

434. BA NS 8/238, Fol. 19.

435. BA NS 8/170, Fol. 161.

436. BDC Schier, Bruno, born December 17, 1902. Letter from Schier to the Reich treasurer of the NSDAP dated September 9, 1939.

437. See the chapter is this study on the Reich Working Community for German Folk Research.

438. BDC Diewerge, Heinz, born January 14, 1909. NSDAP membership no. 3 445 244 as of April 1, 1934.

439. Harmjanz 1936a.

440. Diewerge 1936.

441. Diewerge 1936: 966.

442. See the text to n. 303 above.

443. Deutsche Volkskunde im Schrifttum 1938.

444. BA NS 8/238, Fol. 16–17.

445. Deutsche Volkskunde im Schrifttum 1938: 5–8.

446. BA NS 8/238, Fol. 16.

447. See the chapter in this study on the destruction of the Department of Folklore.

448. Diewerge 1936.

449. Deutsche Volkskunde im Schrifttum 1938: 13, I/15.

450. Harmjanz 1936b.

451. Deutsche Volkskunde im Schrifttum 1938: 115, X/8.

452. Deutsche Volkskunde im Schrifttum 1938: 7.

453. Achterberg 1938: 539.

454. BA NS 8/238, Fol. 21–22.

455. Bollmus 1970: 216.

456. BA NS 8/238, Fol. 9–10. Report from Ziegler to SS-Gruppenführer Reinhard Heydrich, dated August 10, 1938.

457. BA NS 8/238, Fol. 9–10. Report from Ziegler to SS-Gruppenführer Reinhard Heydrich, dated August 10, 1938.

458. BA NS 8/238, Fol. 8. Ziegler's file note dated August 10, 1938, for Rosenberg.

459. Cf. Kater 1974: 139.

460. Cf. Bollmus 1970: 218.

461. BA NS 8/238, Fol. 11–23, here Fol. 12.

462. Cf. Jacobeit 1965a.

463. Cf. Schramka 1986.

464. BA NS 8/238, Fol. 14–16, 20–22.

465. BA NS 8/238, Fol. 23.

466. Cf. Bockhorn 1988: 66–77.
467. See the study by Bockhorn 1989, also published in Dow and Lixfeld in press.
468. See the chapter in this study on the world-view *Volkskunde* of Ziegler.
469. Ziegler 1936b.
470. BDC Höfler, Otto, born May 10, 1901. NSDAP membership no. 5 443 927 as of May 1, 1937; cf. Schramka 1986.
471. Höfler 1934.
472. Ziegler 1936b: 820–821.
473. Ziegler 1936b: 820, 822, 824.
474. Cf. Staubach 1974; Birkhan 1988.
475. Deutsche Volkskunde im Schrifttum 1938: 6–7.
476. Deutsche Volkskunde im Schrifttum 1938: 55, IV/72.
477. Deutsche Volkskunde im Schrifttum 1938: 56, IV/73.
478. Deutsche Volkskunde im Schrifttum 1938: 94, VI/69.
479. Deutsche Volkskunde im Schrifttum 1938: 43, IV/24.
480. Ziegler 1936b.
481. BDC Wolfram, Richard, born September 16, 1901. NSDAP membership no. 1 088 974 as of June 1, 1932.
482. Cf. Kater 1974: 83–84 and the study by Bockhorn 1989, also published in Dow and Lixfeld in press.
483. Kater 1974: 83.
484. Boberach 1984, vol. 2: 104–106, 268.
485. Boberach 1984, Vol. 2: 104.
486. Cf. Bollmus 1970: 218–220.
487. Rüdiger 1938b; cf. Thiele 1939.
488. Boberach 1984, Vol. 2: 105.
489. Boberach 1984, Vol. 2: 105.
490. Boberach 1984, Vol. 2: 268.
491. The listing follows for the most part BA NS 21/666. The Research and Teaching Community "Das Ahnenerbe." Development, Essence, Effect; BA NS 21/669. Ahnenerbe Working Report 1937/38; critical of this is Kater 1974: 110–113, esp. 112, n. 202.
492. BA NS 21/309. Wüst to Himmler on April 2, 1939.
493. Kater 1974: 95–96.
494. BA NS 21/669. Ahnenerbe Working Report 1937–1938: 3.
495. Cf. Jankuhn 1944; Kater 1974: 113–116.
496. Cf. Salzburger Wissenschaftswochen 1939; Kater 1974: 116–119, 143–144; Bollmus 1970: 227; the chapter "Reflection on the Question of Scholarship in the Office of Ancestral Inheritance" in Oesterle 1988, also published in Dow and Lixfeld in press.
497. Cf. Oesterle 1987: 86–88 and the chapter "John Meier and the SS-Ancestral Inheritance" in Oesterle 1988, also published in Dow and Lixfeld in press; in addition the letter from Meier to Süß dated April 22, 1944, published in Holzapfel 1989: 104–108; BA NS 21/777. Letter by Sievers to the curator of the Ancestral Inheritance dated April 22, 1939; BA NS 21/217. Letter by Sievers to Quellmalz dated March 28, 1942; Oesterle 1991: 158–159. In contrast Holzapfel 1989: 66–67 considers the possible takeover of the German Folk Song Archive by the SS Ancestral Inheritance to be idle speculation.
498. BA NS 21/11. Service logbook of Wolfram Sievers dated June 5, 1944. Cf. Oesterle as in n. 497.
499. Archive of the Philosophical Faculty of the University of Freiburg i.Br. File "Institut für Volkskunde," letter by the dean to the Cultural and Educational Ministry in Karlsruhe dated

February 7, 1942; letter by the Reich Educational Ministry (REM) to the Cultural and Educational Ministry in Karlsruhe dated March 28, 1942; letter by the dean to the REM dated April 20, 1942.

4. THE RISE AND FALL OF THE REICHSINSTITUT FÜR DEUTSCHE VOLKSKUNDE

1. Cf. Kater 1974: 145–146, 191–204 and BA NS 15/102. Führer decree of March 1, 1942.
2. Kater 1974: 193; cf. Bollmus 1970: 104–152; Hunger 1984: 441–442.
3. Cf. for example the chapter "The Ancestral Inheritance during the War in Regard to the Active Participation of Folklorists" in Oesterle 1988.
4. Cf. Kater 1974: 150–151.
5. Cf. Kater 1974: 159–170; Stuhlpfarrer 1985; Waibl 1985: 734–742. Peter Schwinn, Marburg an der Lahn, is preparing a study on the Cultural Commission South Tyrol and Olaf Bockhorn, Vienna, is preparing one on the Cultural Commission Gottschee.
6. Cf. the chapter "The Ancestral Inheritance during the War in Regard to the Active Participation of Folklorists" in Oesterle 1988; Schwinn 1989.
7. Concerning the SS concept, see Assion and Schwinn 1988: 233 in response to Grießmair 1988, and Schwinn 1989; concerning the Rosenbergian concept, see the chapter on the Predecessor of the Rosenberg Reich Institute in this study.
8. Cf. Kater 1974: 161, 401, n. 145.
9. See n. 6 above; Kater 1974: 170–190; cf. BDC Schneider, Hans Ernst, born December 15, 1909.
10. BA NS 19/1850. Memorandum [1944]. The Research and Teaching Community "The Ancestral Inheritance." Tasks and Structure: Blatt 5–6.
11. Kater 1974: 147.
12. Kater 1974: 149–154, here 154.
13. Kater 1974: 170–190, 294–296; Bollmus 1970: 145–152; Hunger 1984: 171–179; Baumgärtner 1977: 33–35; Brenner 1963: 142–153.
14. BA NS 15/102. Activity by the Implementation Staff of Reich Leader Rosenberg for the occupied regions (after September 30, 1942).
15. BA NS 15/102. Führer decree of March 1, 1942.
16. Brenner 1963: 240–241.
17. Cf. Kater 1974: 158, 295–296; Hunger 1984: 442–443.
18. BA NS 8/259, Fol. 123–124, here 124. First Service Discussion of the Working Group Leader of the Implementation Staff of Reich Leader Rosenberg December 18 and 19, 1941, in the house in Bellevuestr. 3.
19. BA NS 15/102. Activity by the Implementation Staff of Reich Leader Rosenberg for the occupied regions (after September 30, 1942).
20. Cf. Lorenzen 1942; Ruprecht 1943a, 1943b; Wolfgramm 1943, 1944b; Redlich 1942.
21. BA NS 8/245, Fol. 60–62.
22. BA NS 8/245, Fol. 60.
23. BA NS 8/245, Fol. 60–62.
24. BA NS 8/260, Fol. 28. File note for Rosenberg dated April 9, 1942; BA NS 8/260, Fol. 54–55. File note for Rosenberg dated January 4, 1943.
25. BA NS 8/260, Fol. 55.
26. BA NS 15/79. Office of Folklore on June 6, 1944, to the Central Office.
27. BA NS 30/152. Confidential report by Hans Strobel dated June 10, 1944, concerning the "Folklore Situation in the Eastern Lands."

28. BA NS 8/141, Fol. 109–110. Ziegler on June 6, 1941, to Rosenberg; cf. Bollmus 1970: 118–119 with assumptions about further reasons for Ziegler's leaving; the staff leader in the Rosenberg Bureau who had been drafted into a battle unit, Gotthard Urban, had already mentioned on April 19, 1941, in his parting letter to Rosenberg that the Office of World-View Information had "substantially fallen short of its previous accomplishments. This was no doubt because the Office Leader, Dr. Ziegler, was unsure for a considerable time about the objectives and the tasks of his office. . . . One might consider whether Dr. Ziegler, who is already active in a propaganda company . . . should be brought back and then compelled to take up his work just as systematically and efficiently as formerly," BA NS 8/140, Fol. 146–154, here 150; concerning the formation of positions by the political leaders of the Rosenberg Bureau, see Heiber 1966: 943–944.

29. BA NS 8/141, Fol. 11. Rosenberg on June 10, 1941, to Ziegler.

30. Ziegler 1939d; cf. Baumgärtner 1977: 84.

31. BA NS 8/238, Fol. 95–96. Klopfer on July 19, 1941, to Ziegler; BA NS 8/238, Fol. 94. Frank on July 30, 1941, to Rosenberg; BA NS 8/238, Fol. 97. Rosenberg Bureau on July 31, 1941, to Ziegler; unfortunately the memorandum by Ziegler could not be found.

32. BA NS 8/238, Fol. 98–99. Rosenberg on August 1, 1941, to Bormann.

33. BA NS 8/186, Fol. 132–133. Bormann on August 21, 1941, to Rosenberg; cf. also Bollmus 1970: 119 and Baumgärtner 1977: 39–40 with the statement about the editorship of the Rosenbergian "Handbuch der Romfrage," which Ziegler had taken up again at the end of 1943 and which Rosenberg took away from him when he was discharged on June 10, 1941, cf. BA NS 8/141, Fol. 111; concerning the "Handbuch der Romfrage," the first volume of which was published (Rosenberg 1940), cf. Baumgärtner 1977: 85–86.

34. BDC Ziegler, Matthes, born June 11, 1911. SS-Files. Until the end of 1944 and with the agreement of Himmler, Ziegler was active as the service leader in the Party Chancery of the NSDAP as well as honorary collaborator of the SD of the SS, and from the end of 1943 of the Rosenberg Bureau, cf. n. 33 above; toward the end of the war he was supposed to represent "as liaison officer all propaganda tasks of the SS" with the supreme commander of the Wehrmacht, cf. the brief note from SS-Standartenführer Gunter d'Alquen of November 1, 1944. In the regular SS Ziegler was Obersturmbannführer (Oberstleutnant) and as a reserve leader of the Waffen-SS he was Hauptsturmführer (Hauptmann) in the SS-Standarte Kurt Eggers.

35. BDC Strobel, Hans, born November 28, 1911; cf. Gajek 1986 and Brückner 1988f: 209.

36. Strobel 1934a.

37. BDC Strobel, Hans, born November 28, 1911. Life history in SS-Personal-file, SSO-Files, Files of the Reichskulturkammer.

38. BDC Strobel, Hans: SS-Personal-file, Files of the Reichskulturkammer.

39. BA NS 8/170, Fol. 159–161, here 161.

40. Deutsche Volkskunde im Schrifttum 1938; cf. Bollmus 1970: 215 and the chapter "Rosenberg's 'Brown' vs. Himmler's 'Black' *Volkskunde*" in this study.

41. Cf. the chapter on the Predecessor of the Rosenberg Reich Institute in this study.

42. BA NS 8/245, Fol. 1.

43. BA NS 8/245, Fol. 10.

44. BA NS 8/245, Fol. 1 and 57; BA NS 8/238, Fol. 5.

45. Cf. Baumgärtner 1977: 29; Bollmus 1970: 122; BA NS 8/128. Disposition by Rosenberg on April 22, 1942; BA NS 15/102. Main Offices and Offices of the Service Branch [1944]; before Hagemeyer, Strobel was the deputy leader of the Main Office for World-View Information, cf. BA NS 8/187, Fol. 201–210, here 203. Organization Plan of the Service Branch, 2.

46. Cf. BA NS 8/245; BA NS 8/140, Fol. 77. Letter of reference for Strobel by Rosenberg on November 23, 1941.

47. BA NS 8/245, Fol. 69. Appointed by Rosenberg on November 10, 1941.

48. BA NS 8/260, Fol. 28. File note for Rosenberg dated April 9, 1942; BA NS 8/260, Fol. 54–55. File note for Rosenberg dated January 4, 1943.

49. Cf. BA NS 15/20. Personnel list of August 8, 1944.

50. Ziegler 1933: 64; see nn. 202–203 in chap. 3.

51. See nn. 262–271 in chap. 3.

52. Strobel 1938a, 1938d, 1943a.

53. See the bibliography and Strobel 1943a.

54. Cf. BA NS 8/140, Fol. 77–77 *Rs.* Letter of reference of Strobel by Rosenberg on November 23, 1941.

55. Strobel 1939b.

56. Strobel 1939a; cf. Scheller 1939b.

57. Scheller and Strobel 1939.

58. BA NS 8/132. Fol. 28. Keyword—*Protokoll*: Record of the meeting by Ziegler and Bernatzky with the Reich leader on March 23, 1944, and n. 33 above.

59. BDC Strobel, Hans, born November 28, 1911, REM—Card catalog for the personnel files. Teaching assignments German *Volkskunde* 1934, 1938, 1939; concerning Adolf Spamer's unusual letter of reference in 1937 to the scholarship of Strobel, who on the one hand "has a certain tendency to quickly set forth theses and puts forth authoritative statements, where things are at least problematic and . . . need a careful weighing of all the possibilities," and on the other hand who can be singled out "already today as an obvious 'hope,' " cf. Jacobeit and Mohrmann 1982: 296–297, n. 19.

60. Strobel 1939a: 87.

61. Strobel 1943e: 44.

62. Strobel 1939b: 116–119.

63. Strobel 1939a: 87–88.

64. Scheller and Strobel 1939: 18.

65. Strobel 1943e: 44–54, 1939b: 120–126.

66. Scheller and Strobel 1939. *Calendar festivals* are Christmas, Mardi Gras, Spring Fest (Easter), May (Pentecost), Summer Solstice, Harvest (Kirwe), Advent. As *life festivals* the following are mentioned: baptism, wedding, funerals, memorials to the dead. To the *National Socialist* (political) *celebration year* belong the day of the seizure of power on January 30, the Day of National Work (May 1), the Reich Party Day (in Nürnberg), Harvest Thanksgiving, the day of the (unsuccessful) Hitler putsch in Munich on November 9. In addition the celebrations of the so-called *small festival year* are conducted, e.g., Mother's Day, the Day for Ethnic Germans, the Day for German Handwork, and the Offering Days for the Winter Aid Work, as well as Soup [Eintopf] Sundays.

67. Strobel 1939a: 87.

68. Scheller and Strobel 1939: 16.

69. Strobel 1943h: 222–223, 226–229; cf. the expanded version of this publication in Strobel 1943d.

70. Strobel 1938d: 24–39.

71. Scheller and Strobel 1939: 16; cf. Strobel 1939b: 113–114.

72. Strobel 1943e: 47–49, 50–51; concerning the celebration hall project of the Rosenbergian Working Community for German Folklore, see nn. 341–352 in chap. 3.

73. Strobel 1943e: 59.

74. Strobel 1938d: 28.

75. Strobel 1939a: 90; cf. Strobel 1943e: 43.

76. Strobel 1943h: 226, 1943d: 32.

77. Strobel 1943e: 54.

78. Concerning this term of Rosenberg's, see Baumgärtner 1977: 261.

79. BA NS 8/245, Fol. 23–24. File note by Thiele dated May 14, 1940.

80. Thiele 1940; cf. also the brief mention in *Die neue Gemeinschaft* 10, 1944: opposite 208.

81. Thiele 1940: 144.

82. Bollmus 1970: 117–118.

83. BA NS 8/183, Fol. 54–57. Bormann on February 22, 1940, to Rosenberg, printed in Poliakov and Wulf 1983: 201–205; BA NS 8/183, Fol. 43–45. Rosenberg on February 27, 1940, to Bormann.

84. Cf. Baumgärtner 1977.

85. Cf. for example the material collection on "De-Christianization of Youth" in Immer 1936.

86. BA NS 8/128, Fol. 102–103.

87. Cf. Baumgärtner 1977: 260–262, here 262.

88. Cf. the insistence on the missing rights to direct and the conclusions drawn from this of a marginal importance for Rosenberg and his Bureau in Bollmus 1970: 236–250 and the criticism of this interpretation in Baumgärtner 1977: 4, further the criticism of Baumgärtner in Bollmus 1980: 131; cf. also n. 116 of this chapter.

89. Cf. Bollmus 1970: 110; Baumgärtner 1977: 102.

90. BA NS 8/186, Fol. 129–131. Sketch of August 1941. Celebrations of the Reich and of the calendar were thus: Day of the Seizure of Power, Hero Memorial Day, Duty to Youth, Birthday of the Führer, National Celebration Day of the German Folk, Mother's Day, Summer Solstice, Harvest Thanksgiving, Memorial Day to the Fallen of the Movement on November 9, Fallen-Honor-Celebrations, Winter Solstice, and Advent.

91. Cf. the program examples in *Die neue Gemeinschaft* 10, 1944; 202–205; summarizations of NS celebrations in Gebhardt 1987b.

92. Cf. the program examples in *Idee und Tat* 1, 1944: 17–31; 2, 1944: 36–47; and 5, 1944; 40–53. The "preliminary work of the Folklore Working Community" did not in any way enter into the "World-View Celebration Hours" established by the Main Office for Art Cultivation of the Rosenberg Bureau, as Baumgärtner 1977: 101 incorrectly assumes. The programs of this kind of celebration did not reflect the celebration theory of *Mythus Volkskunde*.

93. BA NS 8/186, Fol. 126–128. Bormann on August 25, 1941, to Rosenberg.

94. BA NS 8/186, Fol. 125–126 *Rs.* Rosenberg on September 5, 1941, to Bormann.

95. BA NS 8/181, Fol. 106–108. Bormann on April 6, 1939, to Rosenberg.

96. BA NS 8/181, Fol. 90. Rosenberg Bureau on May 2, 1940, to Bormann; cf. the citations which differ somewhat in Bollmus 1970: 110.

97. BA NS 8/181, Fol. 11–12. Rosenberg on June 28, 1939, to Bormann.

98. Die Gestaltung der Lebensfeiern 1942. Just how unknown these guidelines are to recent folklore research can be seen in the suggestion made by Brückner (1989b: 83) that the *Gau* Schooling Office in Bayreuth published them as the competent collaboration or under the sole authorship of Friedrich Heinz Schmidt-Ebhausen.

99. Cf. *Mitteilungen zur weltanschaulichen Lage* 8/Nr. 4, April 15, 1942: 2.

100. Cf. *Mitteilungen zur weltanschaulichen Lage* 8/Nr. 4, April 15, 1942: 3.

101. Cf. the structuring examples in *Idee und Tat* 5, 1944: 54–56 (birthday celebration in the *Gau* Vienna) and in *Die neue Gemeinschaft* 10, 1944: 58–61 (birthday celebration in the *Gau* Kurhessen) and 62–63 (wedding celebration in the *Gau* Kurhessen); 8, 1942: 304–309 (funeral celebration with thoughts by Alfred Rosenberg and Edmund Mudrak about immortality); 10, 1944: 252–255 (funeral celebration in a village, by Kurth Speth). Concerning the collaboration on the journal *Die neue Gemeinschaft* as of 1942 in the Office of Folklore and Celebration Planning in the Main Cultural Office of the Reich Propaganda Leadership, see Bollmus 1970:

288, n. 30; Baumgärtner 1977: 102 nn. 255–256; and BA NS 8/245, Fol. 162–162 *Rs.* Letter by Strobel dated July 24, 1944, to Liese.

102. Die Gestaltung der Lebensfeiern 1942: 8–10.

103. Die Gestaltung der Lebensfeiern 1942: 4.

104. Die Gestaltung der Lebensfeiern 1942: 12. To these actions belonged, for example: festival or mourning parades; processions and lane formations; the German greeting at funerals; rising from the seat at celebratory happenings; bell ringing insofar as it is not called for in a confessional sense; symbolic customary actions, like tree planting, exchanging of rings, placing flowers into the grave of deceased, etc.

105. Die Gestaltung der Lebensfeiern 1942: 11–15.

106. Cf. Die Gestaltung der Lebensfeiern 1942: 15–18, 18–20, 20–24, the guidelines for the various celebrations.

107. Die Gestaltung der Lebensfeiern 1942: preface by Alfred Rosenberg.

108. *Mitteilungen zur weltanschaulichen Lage* 8/Nr. 6, June 15, 1942: 14–19, here 15–16.

109. *Mitteilungen zur weltanschaulichen Lage* 8/Nr. 6, June 15, 1942: 15–16; Scheller and Strobel 1939.

110. Die Gestaltung der Lebensfeiern 1942: 3–4.

111. Die Gestaltung der Lebensfeiern 1942: 6–7.

112. Die Gestaltung der Lebensfeiern 1942: 4.

113. See chap. 2, esp. nn. 180–185.

114. Cf. Strobel 1939a: 87; Scheller and Strobel 1939: 16.

115. BA NS 8/187, Fol. 136–136 *Rs.* Rosenberg on July 24, 1942, to Bormann; concerning the role of the *Gau* schooling leader as the deputy of Rosenberg, see Baumgärtner 1977: 94, 130–133; Bollmus 1970: 124.

116. The relatively low numbers given by Bollmus 1970: 113–114 for the *Gau* Thüringen in the first half of 1943 and the very low numbers for the SD in the SS on December 9, 1943, of "only 1% of all celebrations" in Hunger 1984: 132, are isolated cases and should be investigated in regard to all of the Reich *Gaus*. Bollmus and Hunger also represent the thesis of lacking competency in directing and thereby of the resulting marginal importance of the Rosenberg Bureau at the party and state level. Baumgärtner 1977: 4, 261–262 has already countered this generally troublesome thesis and has frequently offered convincing arguments, see n. 88 above on this; considerations on the reception of National Socialist life celebrations for the *Gau* Styria found in Brückner 1987b: 31–32, and which are based on Hoffer 1942, deal for the most part with the time before the publication of the guidelines of the Rosenberg Bureau in 1942.

117. *Mitteilungen zur weltanschaulichen Lage* 8/Nr. 4, April 15, 1942: 2.

118. *Mitteilungen zur weltanschaulichen Lage* 8/Nr. 4, April 15, 1942: 2.

119. Makeup of the Office of Folklore and Celebration Planning according to BA NS 15/102. Office of Folklore and Celebration Planning [1944]; BA NS 15/90. Appointment Plan for 1944, March 21, 1944; BA NS 15/102. Organization Plan of the Service Branch of Rosenberg of August 4, 1944: Leader Dr. Hans Strobel (h). *Main Post* Folklore and Scholarship—Dr. Karl Haiding (n); Post for Germanic Folklore—Dr. Edmund Mudrak (n); Post for Great German and Ethnic German Folklore—not occupied; Post for Folklore of Non-Germanic Peoples of Europe—not occupied. *Main Post* Political Folklore-Evaluation—Friedrich Kortkampf (h); Post of Archives and Libraries—Dr. Lieselotte Heil (h); Post for Schooling, Meetings—not occupied; Post for Printing and Publications—Dr. Rosemarein Roßbach (h). *Main Post* Folk-National Work—Dr. Erich Kulke (n); Post for Folk Belief and Custom—not occupied; Post for Games, Songs, Dance Music—not occupied; Post for Folk Art, Handwork, Home, Farmstead, Settlement—Richter(e). *Main Post* Celebration Planning—Theodor (Thilo) Scheller (n); Post for Cal-

endar Celebrations—Dr. Kurth Speth (e); Post for Life Celebrations—Kenntmann (e). *Main Post* for Folklore Defense—Dr. Karl Ruprecht (n); Post for Confessional Folklore—Dr. (Heinrich?) Müller (n). (h = hauptamtlich [full time], n = nebenamtlich [part time], e = ehrenamtlich [honorary]).

120. Concerning this phrase cf. Bollmus 1980: 138.

121. Baumgärtner 1977: 92, 124; Kater 1974: 280.

122. BA NS 8/245, Fol. 114–115, and BA NS 15/243, Fol. 251–253. Richard Wolfram was in second place on the appointment list for Posen and in third place were Gerhard Heilfurth and Alfred Karasek. Mudrak quickly received his *Habilitation* for this appointment in Posen. Since the *Habilitation* at German universities is as a rule required for a professorship, Matthes Ziegler was also interested and tried to accomplish this, as far as we know, in 1940 at the University of Jena. For unknown reasons he withdrew his application for *Habilitation*, which was supported by the Rosenberg Bureau and the NS Docent Union. For helpful research I am indebted to the University Archive in Jena as well as to Wolfgang Jacobeit and Reinhard Schmook, cf. BA NS 8/141, Fol. 97. *Gau* Docent Leader Jena on March 6, 1940, to Rosenberg, and UA Jena. File U Abt. IV, No. 30: NS-Dozentenbund, Gauleitung Thüringen, W-Z 1933–1945.

123. BA NS 8/130, Fol. 28–28 *Rs.* Rosenberg on July 16, 1942, to Bormann; BA NS 8/130, Fol. 99. Rosenberg on July 16, 1942, to Himmler. Copies of both letters, but without the enclosed materials, with the notation "Secret."

124. Concerning the SS Court Disposition, see BDC Harmjanz, Heinrich, born May 22, 1904. Ancestral Inheritance Files, Fol. 25; concerning the departure of Harmjanz from the Reich Educational Ministry, see BDC Harmjanz, Heinrich, born May 22, 1904. REM Personnel Files, Teil III, Fol. 151–152; concerning the discussion in the Rosenberg Bureau about the successor of Harmjanz in the ministry and concerning Rudolf Mentzel, see BA NS 8/131, Fol. 81–82, 93, 99–100, 109–110. Keyword—*Protokoll*: Record of the appointments with the Reich Leader on April 7, April 15, April 27, and April 30, 1943; see further Kater 1974: 288–289 and the detailed description of the "Harmjanz Affair" in Heiber 1966: 647–655.

125. Bollmus 1980: 132–135.

126. National Archives Washington EAP 99/340, Fol. 1138–1141: Primary plans for the establishment of the Advanced School, cited from Bollmus 1980: 131, who begins with the undated archival material of March 1, 1938.

127. National Archives Washington EAP 99/285. Rosenberg on August 12, 1940 to Rust, cited from Bollmus 1980: 125.

128. Bollmus 1980: 126.

129. Bollmus 1980: 143, cf. pages 143–149 concerning the question of the results for scholarship.

130. Cf. Bollmus 1980: 126, n. 2, last sentence.

131. BA NS 8/264, Fol. 92–93. File note by Alfred Baeumler on July 14, 1941, for the Reich leader. Re: the position of the directors of the outposts of the Advanced School.

132. Photographs of the model created by Professor Giesler in *Die Kunst im Dritten Reich* 3, 1939: 18–19; cf. Rosenberg 1939b.

133. BA NS 8/175, Fol. 45–65, here 60–61. The Advanced School of the NSDAP and its Tasks. Memorandum by Rosenberg for Hitler in 1937.

134. BA NS 8/175, Fol. 60–65, here 60.

135. BA NS 8/128, Fol. 153–161. Guidelines for the Building of the Advanced School, undated and anonymous.

136. BA NS 8/128, Fol. 154–155, here 155.

137. BA NS 8/128, Fol. 156.

138. BA NS 8/128, Fol. 156 and 161.

139. BA NS 8/182, Fol. 210–211; cf. BA NS 8/206, Fol. 168–170, 185–187 and Bollmus 1980: 131–136.

140. Poliakov and Wulf 1983: 131; cf. the critical comment in Bollmus 1980: 136–137 as well as the Führer's command published in the appendix.

141. Poliakov and Wulf 1983: 131; Bollmus 1980: 136–137.

142. BA NS 8/128, Fol. 80–83. Order concerning the preliminary work of the Advanced School dated June 26, 1940; a "Department for School and Camp-Education" remained unoccupied.

143. BA NS 8/128, Fol. 90. Order of November 1, 1940.

144. BA NS 8/128, Fol. 104. Order by Rosenberg on April 7, 1942.

145. BDC Baeumler, Alfred, born November 19, 1887, NSDAP membership no. 2 459 241 as of May 1, 1933; on August 13, 1942, Rosenberg named as his successor the leader of the Main Office for Scholarship, Walter Gross, and as the deputy of the latter Heinrich Härtle, cf. BA NS 8/128, Fol. 121 and Bollmus 1980: 144–145, n. 27.

146. BDC Wagner, Kurt, born June 29, 1911, NSDAP membership no. 907 370 as of February 1, 1932.

147. Cf. the bitter battle between Baeumler and Ziegler concerning unimportant questions, ZStA Potsdam 62 Di 1, Film 731, Aufn. 919–925. Baeumler on June 4 and June 23, 1937, to Ziegler. Ziegler on June 16, 1937, to Baeumler; concerning the collaborator factions who were fighting in the Rosenberg Bureau, see Heiber 1966: 943–944 and Ziegler's justification for leaving in n. 28 above.

148. Baeumler carried out a personally slanderous criticism of Edmund Mudrak and his appointment to the Reich University Posen, BA NS 8/245, Fol. 114–115. Strobel on January 6, 1944, to Rosenberg and on January 18, 1944, to Koeppen; ZStA Potsdam 62 Di 1, Film 730, Aufn. 1285–1286. Strobel's file note concerning the results of the discussion with Baeumler on January 18, 1944.

149. BA NS 8/265, Fol. 125. Order concerning the establishment of outposts of the Advanced School on October 30, 1940, cf. the sketch signed by Rosenberg BA NS 8/206, Fol. 152; special outposts were not named, and more detailed orders of implementation were to be put out in the near future.

150. BA NS 15/102. Main offices and offices of the Service Branch, p. 3. Institutes of the Advanced School [1944], cf. also the following notes. The Central Library contained and inventoried a large part of the libraries plundered by the Implementation Staff of Rosenberg, with whose help the establishment of outposts was made possible, cf. Bollmus 1970: 146, 151 and BA NS 8/267, Fol. 133–134 *Rs.* Yearly Report of the Central Library of the Advanced School 1943. Attachment 1.

151. ZStA Potsdam 62 Di 1, Film 732, Aufn. 470. Objectives and Building of the Institute, June 8, 1944.

152. Cf. also Bollmus 1980: 141–143.

153. BA NS 8/206, Fol. 147–151. Rosenberg on October 30, 1940, to Schwarz; Poliakov and Wulf 1983: 132–139; BA NS 8/202, Fol. 189–198; BA NS 8/265, Fol. 194–194 *Rs.*

154. BA NS 8/217, Fol. 141. File note by Leibbrandt on June 29, 1940. Re: Discussion with General Governor Reich Leader Frank. Advanced School.

155. BA NS 8/264, Fol. 67–69. File note by Scheidt on October 17, 1941, for Rosenberg.

156. Cf. Rüdiger 1939a.

157. BA NS 8/140, Fol. 146–186, here 156–157. Urban on April 19, 1941, to Rosenberg, Attachment 2; cf. Baumgärtner 1977: 82.

158. BA NS 8/184, Fol. 105–108. Rosenberg on June 25, 1940, to Bormann.

159. BA NS 15/102. Sketch by Wagner on August 12, 1944, for a letter of the Reich leader to the leader of the Party Chancery.

160. BA NS 8/264, Fol. 1.

161. BA NS 8/264, Fol. 15. Circular by Wagner on November 15, 1943.

162. Ziegler in Thiele 1939: 6.

163. ZStA Potsdam 62 Di 1 56/4, Fol. 11 and 10. Roth on February 11, 1939, to Ziegler. Ziegler on February 15, 1939, to Roth. In his answer Ziegler suggested Herbert Grabert of Tübingen for "religious studies with special emphasis on folklore," Josef Denner of Munich for "religious history with special emphasis on the religious history of the Aryans." For a chair for religious law within the law faculty he gave the address of Ministerial Councilor J. Roth, Berlin W.8, Leipziger Strasse 3 or Berlin NW.87, Cuxhavener Str. 2.

164. Kater 1974: 276; cf. Baumgärtner 1977: 112.

165. Cf. Bollmus 1980: 125–126, 139–143; Kater 1974: 275–280, 298–299; Losemann 1977b: 139–153.

166. Cf. Bollmus 1980: 142; Baumgärtner 1977: 40.

167. BA NS 8/264, Fol. 98–100. Memorandum by Brachmann of March 1940.

168. BA NS 8/265, Fol. 116–118. File note by Brachmann. Re: The establishment of a new faculty at the University of Munich, undated; cf. the comment of a possibly identical file note of August 23, 1940, in Bollmus 1980: 125–126, n. 2.

169. BA NS 15/243, Fol. 187. Rust on January 19, 1942, to Rosenberg.

170. BDC Ranke, Kurt, born April 14, 1908, NSDAP membership no. 1 048 574 as of March 1/April 1, 1932.

171. See Bollmus 1980: 144. According to Bollmus's research, Harder was won over by Alfred Baeumler; see p. 144, n. 27. Concerning Kurt Ranke's Munich candidacy, see also Losemann 1977: 152, 245–246, n. 80, and Kater 1974: 277.

172. BA NS 15/112. File note for the Reich leader by Dr. Wa. dated December 18, 1942; BDC Ranke, Kurt, born April 14, 1908. Reich education minister on May 31, 1943, to Rosenberg; concerning still other suggested chairs, see Losemann 1977: 143.

173. BA NS 15/243, Fol. 173–173 *Rs.* Rosenberg on March 11, 1943, to Rust.

174. Ranke 1944; cf. the *Habilitation* publication presented in 1938 to the University of Kiel, which however was not published until after the Second World War (Ranke 1951), as well as the publications by Ranke 1938 and Ranke 1939. Kurt Ranke was appointed in the postwar years to the University of Kiel and to the folklore chair at the University of Göttingen. He was the founder and the first president of the International Society for Folk-Narrative Research and a highly respected narrative researcher; see Moser-Rath 1985a and 1985b.

175. Concerning the confiscation of Schreiber's institutes, see the following notes and the chapter "University and Political Planning in the Ancestral Inheritance" in Oesterle 1988.

176. Cf. BA NS 8/181, Fol. 172. Bormann on February 4, 1939, to Rosenberg. That Ziegler conceived the Rosenberg letter of October 22, 1938, can be seen in the answer by Bormann of February 4, 1939, with a repeated file note by the Rosenberg Bureau. The vigorous public attacks by Rosenberg *Volkskunde* against Georg Schreiber, against so-called confessional *Volkskunde* and the Catholic Action, were not yet over; see, for example, Ruprecht 1937a and 1937b, Müller 1938a and 1938b, Rosenberg 1940: 34–40 (article "Aktion, Katholische").

177. BA NS 8/181, Fol. 172–172 *Rs.* Bormann on February 4, 1939, to Rosenberg. It is written by hand on the letter that was passed on to Ziegler.

178. Poliakov and Wulf 1983: 139; Rosenberg had offered to appoint the leader of the folklore outpost in Detmold-Münster at the suggestion of Himmler; see Kater 1974: 298.

179. BA NS 8/265, Fol. 190–193, here 192. File note by Scheidt on May 3, 1941, for Reich Leader Rosenberg. Re: Outpost Münster: Institute for Folklore.

180. BDC Scheller, Theodor (Thilo), born December 9, 1897. Scheller on July 29, 1939, to the deputy of Rosenberg (*Gau* schooling leader) in Franconia.

181. BA NS 8/206, Fol. 115–116. Report concerning further institute plans on January 28, 1941.

182. BA NS 8/169, Fol. 136. Rosenberg on July 2, 1940, to Frick; according to Baumgärtner (1977: 34), Himmler made the library available to his Ancestral Inheritance.

183. BA NS 8/265, Fol. 190–193.

184. BA NS 8/265, Fol. 193. Brachmann rose to the position of outpost leader without the *Habilitation* and completed his work later on the *Habilitation* at the University of Halle, with the help of Baeumler; see Baumgärtner 1977: 40, n. 159.

185. BA NS 8/265, Fol. 189–189 *Rs.*

186. BA NS 8/265, Fol. 189–189 *Rs.*

187. BA NS 8/265, Fol. 189–189 *Rs.* Concerning the German Academy, see Harvolk 1990; concerning Rosenberg's interest in it, see Kater 1974: 282.

188. See chaps. 1 and 2 in this study.

189. BA NS 8/264, Fol. 1. Existing and planned institutes of the Advanced School, undated, however from the beginning of the 1940s; cf. BA NS 8/207, Fol. 97–99. Rosenberg on September 30, 1942, to Schwarz, and BA NS 8/207, Fol. 93–93 *Rs.* Schwarz on October 21, 1942, to Rosenberg.

190. *Wiener Zeitschrift für Volkskunde* 49, 1944: 32. Report on the opening of the Institute for German Folklore in the Monastery Rein near Graz.

191. BA NS 8/128, Fol. 110, BA NS 8/137, Fol. 103, BA NS 8/264, Fol. 44. Similar to chartering orders by Rosenberg.

192. BA NS 8/206, Fol. 37–39. Rosenberg on December 12, 1941, to Schwarz. Monthly budget without salaries and only with expenses for the leader; BA NS 8/264, Fol. 50–57. File note by Scheidt of January 13, 1942, for Rosenberg and the sketches of the letters of appointment dated January 8, 1942, for Martin, Spieß, Haiding, Thiele, Kulke, Ruprecht, and Scheller; for the intermediate post "German costume," or rather the research post "costume and decoration," see Pesendorfer 1940: 90; BA NS 8/207, Fol. 97–99. Rosenberg on September 30, 1942, to Schwarz.

193. Cf. BDC Scheller, Theodor (Thilo), born December 9, 1897. Scheller on July 29, 1939, to the deputy of Rosenberg (*Gau* Schooling Leader) in Franconia.

194. BA NS 8/206, Fol. 37–39, here 38. Rosenberg on December 12, 1941, to Schwarz; cf. the sketch by Hans Strobel on October 8, 1941, for a letter by Rosenberg to Röver.

195. BA NS 8/264, Fol. 40. Order by Rosenberg on July 2, 1942.

196. BA NS 8/245, Fol. 72–76. Strobel on November 13, 1941, to Rosenberg. With the exception of the Teaching Post for Celebration Planning there was simply an expense account for the research post leaders whose salaries apparently were paid from other funds. War funds for four other research posts, whose work was impossible for the moment because of lacking personnel, were possibly to be transmitted later, cf. BA NS 8/245, Fol. 75.

197. Cf. BA NS 15/102. Offices and Main Offices of the Service Branch, page 4: Research Posts of the Institute for German Folklore [1944].

198. BA NS 8/207, Fol. 97–99, here 97. Rosenberg on September 30, 1942, to Schwarz; concerning Strobel's scholarly-political concept, see the article "Brauchtum" in Rosenberg 1940: 227–229, which Strobel wrote, see n. 58 above.

199. BA NS 8/245, Fol. 60–62.

200. BA NS 8/128, Fol. 110, BA NS 8/137, Fol. 103, BA NS 8/264, Fol. 44.

201. BA NS 8/264, Fol. 6. File note Dr. Wagner of December 15, 1943, for the personal referee of the Reich leader, Dr. Koeppen.

202. Cf. Beitl 1986.

203. Cf. for example Haiding 1943.

204. Haiding 1939c; cf. Moser-Rath 1985c.

205. BDC Haiding, Karl, born July 3, 1906. NSDAP membership no. 332 498 as of June 1, 1933 (no. 26 787 as of 1923). Life history on April 23, 1937. Incomplete list of publications as well as defective and misleading life history of Haiding in Hänsel and Walter 1981.

206. Cf. on this Brückner 1988e with several other undocumented contentions which could be disproven.

207. Cf. Bockhorn 1989, also published in Dow and Lixfeld in press and Haiding 1939c.

208. BDC Haiding, Karl, born July 3, 1906. Party Chancery correspondence.

209. BA NS 8/267, Fol. 33–34. Haiding on January 15 (February 15), 1944, to Rosenberg and the retroactive pay for Haiding dated February 4, 1944.

210. BA NS 8/207, Fol. 97–99. Rosenberg on September 30, 1942, to Schwarz.

211. BA NS 8/207, Fol. 97–99; BA NS 8/207, Fol. 93–93 *Rs.* Schwarz on October 21, 1942, to Rosenberg.

212. *Wiener Zeitschrift für Volkskunde* 49, 1944: 32. Report on the opening of the Institute for German Folklore in the Monastery Rein near Graz.

213. Concerning Erich Kulke's Research Post for Farmstead and Settlement, see Freckmann 1982 and 1985; see also the fund requests of the Planning Office of the Advanced School to the Reich treasurer of the NSDAP for the Institute for German Folklore and its research posts from December 1943 to March 1944 and from October to December 1944 in monthly sums of 23,200 to about 40,000 Reichsmark, BDC 0.386 (Hohe Schule). Fund requests of March 6, September 9, and November 11, 1944.

214. BA NS 8/245, Fol. 78–78 *Rs.* Strobel on January 5, 1942, to Rosenberg.

215. *Deutsche Volkskunde* 3, Heft 3/4, 1941 bis 6, Heft 1/2, 1944.

216. See n. 18 above.

217. BA NS 8/131, Fol. 67. Keyword—*Protokoll*: Record of the appointments with the Reich leader on March 31, 1943.

218. BA NS 8/131, Fol. 92. Keyword—*Protokoll*: Record of the appointments with the Reich leader on April 15, 1943.

219. BA NS 8/131, Fol. 102. Keyword—*Protokoll*: Record of the appointments with the Reich leader on April 28, 1943.

220. BA NS 8/264, Fol. 8–8 *Rs.* Haiding on November 5, 1943, to Rosenberg.

221. BA NS 8/131, Fol. 16. Keyword—*Protokoll*: Record of the appointments with the Reich Leader on March 10, 1943.

222. BA NS 8/267, Fol. 22–23. Martin on November 23, 1943, to Haiding; BA NS 267, Fol. 24. Haiding on December 2, 1943, to Martin; BA NS 8/267, Fol. 25. Martin on May 11, 1944, to Haiding; BA NS 8/267, Fol. 21. Haiding on June 28, 1944, to Rosenberg.

223. BA NS 8/264, Fol. 8–8 *Rs.* Haiding on November 5, 1943, to Rosenberg.

224. BA NS 8/264, Fol. 9–10.

225. BA NS 8/264, Fol. 7. Wagner on December 6, 1943, to Haiding.

226. BA NS 8/267, Fol. 28–28 *Rs.* Report on the work in April 1944, by Dr. Haiding; ZStA Potsdam 62 Di 1, Film 730, Aufn. 1223–1224. Haiding on September 19, 1944, to Strobel.

227. BA NS 8/267, Fol. 19–19 *Rs.* Haiding on August 20, 1944, to Koeppen.

228. BA NS 15/20. Bormann on September 16, 1944, to Rosenberg.

229. Cf. BA NS 15/102. Overview of the planned post approved by the Reich treasurer and the Reich Chancery and the posts occupied on August 8, 1944.

230. BA NS 15/102. Sketch for a letter of the Reich leader to the leader of the Party Chancery. Re: Planning of the post requirements in the area of the Advanced School, Dr. Wagner, Berlin, August 12, 1944.

231. BA NS 15/102. Personnel list of the establishments of the Advanced School after they were closed, November 1, 1944, and the list of the collaborators of the Advanced School who had been discharged. The remaining people were the honorary workers Prof. Karl von Spieß, Karl and Olga von Koeppen, Prof. Bernhard Martin, Prof. Gotthold Frotscher, Prof. Lutz Mackensen, and five librarians. In the way of folklore establishments there were in addition to the Central Institute seven research posts listed: Folk Custom, Myth Studies, German Folk Speech, Peasant Life Forms, Folk Art and Peasant Handwork, Games and Sayings, the German Farmstead.

232. ZStA Potsdam 62 Di 1, Film 730, Aufn. 1203. Strobel on October 31, 1944, to Rosenberg; also Aufn. 1202. Koeppen on November 4, 1944, to Strobel with the agreement of Rosenberg.

233. BA NS 8/267, Fol. 17. Haiding on December 22, 1944, to Rosenberg.

234. See in n. 73, chap. 1, the confessional path by the bourgeois-national folklore scholar Otto Lauffer on the ideology of the Germanic "*Götterdämmerung.*"

APPENDIX I.9

The editor would like to thank Fred Schwink (University of Texas) for making the first draft of the translation of this document.

1. Ziegler 1934a.
2. Naumann 1929.
3. Ziegler 1935a.
4. Spamer 1934–35; Peßler 1934–38; Haberlandt 1935. The first and until now only attempt at an organic presentation of the essence and the breadth of German *Volkskunde* has been carried out by Dr. Karl von Spieß (Spieß 1934).
5. Ed. note: The *Reichsarbeitsdienst* [Reich Worker's Service] was a male job service, and every young man had to spend a certain amount of time working with others, in a quasi-military setting, including agriculture.
6. Ed. note: The *Landjahr* was a job service for young girls who worked with farmers and in agriculture.
7. Revised and expanded reprint of Ziegler 1936a.

APPENDIX III.3

1. *Deutsche Volkslieder mit ihren Melodien. Balladen.* Band 1–5. 1935–1939.

BIBLIOGRAPHY

Abendroth, Wolfgang. 1984. "Die deutschen Professoren und die Weimarer Republik." In Tröger 1984: 11-25.

Abschied. 1970. *Abschied vom Volksleben*. Untersuchungen des Ludwig-Uhland-Instituts der Universität Tübingen. Vol. 27. Tübingen.

Achterberg, Eberhard. 1938. "Deutsche Volkskunde im Schrifttum." *Nationalsozialistische Monatshefte* 9, Heft 99: 538-540.

Ackermann, Josef. 1970. *Heinrich Himmler als Ideologe*. Göttingen, Zürich and Frankfurt.

Ackermann, Josef. 1989. "Heinrich Himmler - 'Reichsführer SS.'" In Smelser and Zitelmann 1989: 115-133.

Acker-Sutter, Rotraut (ed.). 1984. *Heimat als Erbe und Auftrag. Beiträge zur Volkskunde und Kulturgeschichte. Festschrift für Kurt Conrad, Direktor des Salzburger Freilichtmuseums, zum 65. Geburtstag*. Salzburg.

Alkemeyer, Thomas. 1988. "Gewalt und Opfer im Ritual der Olympischen Spiele 1936." In Gebauer 1988: 44-79.

Althaus, Hans-Joachim; Hildegard Canzik-Lindemaier; Kathrin Hoffmann-Curtius; and Ulrich Rebstock. (eds.). 1988. *Der Krieg in den Köpfen. Beiträge zum Tübinger Friedenskongreß "Krieg-Kultur-Wissenschaft."* Untersuchungen des Ludwig-Uhland-Instituts der Universität Tübingen. Vol. 73. Tübingen.

Alzheimer, Heidrun. 1989. "Georg Fischer - Ein Nationalökonom und Lehrerbildner als Volkskundler. Oder: Über die Schwierigkeiten, etwas von gestern zu erfahren." *Jahrbuch für Volkskunde* N.S. 12: 51-65.

Art. 1986. *Art. Folklore, Theatre, Music*. Proceedings of the Ninth World Congress of Jewish Studies. Division D. Vol. 2. Jerusalem.

Assion, Peter. 1982. "Fehrle, Eugen." In Ottnad 1982: 112-114.

Assion, Peter. 1984a. "Volkskunde in Baden. Versuch einer Standortbestimmung." *Badische Heimat* 64: 463-490.

Assion, Peter. 1984b. "Aspects of Empirical Research into the Culture of Big Cities. 24th German Folklore Congress in Berlin (Sept. 26-30, 1983). *Zeitschrift für Volkskunde* 80: 81-86.

Assion, Peter. 1985. "'Was Mythos unseres Volkes ist.' Zum Werden und Wirken des NS-Volkskundlers Eugen Fehrle." *Zeitschrift für Volkskunde* 81: 220-244.

Assion, Peter. 1987. "Künzig, Johannes." In Ottnad 1987: 174-177.

Assion, Peter; and Peter Schwinn. 1988. "Migration, Politik und Volkskunde. Zur Tätigkeit des SS-Ahnenerbes in Südtirol." In Greverus, Köstlin and Schilling 1988: 221-226.

Aufbau der Landesstelle. 1936. "Aufbau der Landesstelle für Volksforschung und Volkstumspflege Sachsen." *Mitteldeutsche Blätter für Volkskunde* 11: 23-26.

Bach, Adolf. 1937. *Deutsche Volkskunde. Ihre Wege, Ergebnisse und Aufgaben. Eine Einführung*. Leipzig.

Bachmann, Manfred. 1983. "Ein Brief aus dem 'anderen Deutschland.' Zur Erinnerung an den Volkskundler Adolf Spamer - Forscher, Lehrer, Humanist." *Union* (Dresden) vom 14.4.1983.

Bächthold-Stäubli, Hanns; and Eduard Hoffmann-Krayer (eds.). 1927-1942. *Handwörterbuch des deutschen Aberglaubens*. Vols. 1-10. Berlin and Leipzig.

Bächtold-Stäubli, Hanns; and Eduard Hoffmann-Krayer (eds.). 1987. *Handwörterbuch des deutschen Aberglaubens*. Mit einem Vorwort von Christoph Daxelmüller. Vol. 1. Unveränderter photomechanischer Nachdruck der Ausgabe 1927-1942. Berlin.

Bargheer, Ernst; and Herbert Freudenthal (eds.). 1934. *Volkskunde-Arbeit. Zielsetzungen und Gehalte. Otto Lauffer zum 70. Geburtstage*. Berlin and Leipzig.

Bartel, Horst. 1983. "Ein humanistischer Volkskundler. Zum 100. Geburtstag von Adolf Spamer." *Spektrum. Monatszeitschrift der Akademie der Wissenschaften der DDR* 1983, Heft 3: 29.

Barthes, Roland. 1964. *Mythen des Alltags*. Edition Suhrkamp. Vol. 92. Frankfurt am Main.

Bauer, Ingolf; Edgar Harvolk; and Wolfgang A. Mayer (eds.). 1989. *Forschungen zur historischen Volkskultur. Festschrift für Torsten Gebhard zum 80. Geburtstag*. München.

Baumgärtner, Raimund. 1977. *Weltanschauungskampf im Dritten Reich. Die Auseinandersetzung der Kirchen mit Alfred Rosenberg*. Veröffentlichungen der Kommission für Zeitgeschichte. Series B. Vol. 22. Mainz.

Baumhauer, Joachim Friedrich. 1988. "Regional - national - nationalsozialistisch. Wandlungen des Nationalgefühls in einem niedersächsischen Dorf." In Lehmann and Kuntz 1988: 197-218.

Bausinger, Hermann. 1965. "Volksideologie und Volksforschung. Zur nationalsozialistischen Volkskunde." *Zeitschrift für Volkskunde* 61: 177-204.

Bausinger, Hermann. 1971a. *Volkskunde. Von der Altertumsforschung zur Kulturanalyse*. Darmstadt.

Bausinger, Hermann. 1971b. "Konsequentes Extrem: Völkische Wissenschaft." In Bausinger 1971a: 61-73.

Bausinger, Hermann. 1982. "Zwischen Grün und Braun. Volkstumsideologie und Heimatpflege nach dem Ersten Weltkrieg." In Cancik 1982b: 215-229.

Bausinger, Hermann. 1987a. "Volkskunde und Volkstumsarbeit im Nationalsozialismus." In Gerndt 1987: 131-141.

Bausinger, Hermann. 1988a. "Volkskunde in den Vorlesungsverzeichnissen der Universität Tübingen. Anmerkungen zur Vor-Geschichte des LUI." *Tübinger Korrespondenzblatt* 33: 35-38.

Becker, Winfried. 1989. "Begriffe und Erscheinungsformen des Widerstands gegen den Nationalsozialismus." *Jahrbuch für Volkskunde* N.S. 12: 11-41.

Beitl, Klaus. 1986. "Karl Haiding †." *Österreichische Zeitschrift für Volkskunde* 89: 47.

Beitl, Klaus (ed.). 1990. *Atlas der deutschen Volkskunde. Kleine Geschichten eines großen Forschungsunternehmens. Aus den "Erinnerungen eines Westpreußen" (1968) von Reinhold Knopf und aus dem Nachlaßarchiv von Richard Beitl*. Veröffentlichungen zur Volkskunde und Kulturgeschichte. Vol. 41. Würzburg.

Beitl, Richard. 1934. "Die volkserzieherische Bedeutung des Atlas der deutschen Volkskunde." *Deutsche Volkserziehung* 3: 112-118.
Beitl, Richard. 1955. *Wörterbuch der deutschen Volkskunde.* Begründet von Oswald A. Erich und Richard Beitl. Second Edition. Kröners Taschenausgabe. Vol. 127. Stuttgart.
Beitl, Richard; and Klaus Beitl. 1974. *Wörterbuch der deutschen Volkskunde.* Begründet von Oswald A. Erich und Richard Beitl. Third Edition. Kröners Taschenausgabe. Vol. 127. Stuttgart.
Beitl, Richard; and Klaus Beitl. 1982. "Lebenslauf von Richard Beitl." *Österreichische Zeitschrift für Volkskunde* 85: 166-172.
Beiträge zur sprachlichen Volksüberlieferung. 1953. *Beiträge zur sprachlichen Volksüberlieferung.* Deutsche Akademie der Wissenschaften zu Berlin. Veröffentlichungen der Kommission für Volkskunde. Vol. 2. Berlin/DDR.
Bellmann, Herbert. 1937. "Deutsche volkskundliche Organisationen." *Folk. Zeitschrift des Internationalen Verbandes für Volksforschung* 1: 205-210.
Bergmann, Klaus. 1970. *Agrarromantik und Großstadtfeindschaft.* Marburger Abhandlungen zur politischen Wissenschaft. Vol. 20. Meisenheim am Glan.
Bericht. 1937. *Bericht. Weltkongress für Freizeit und Erholung Hamburg/ Vom 23. bis 30. Juli 1936/ Berlin.* Bearbeitet im Internationalen Zentral-Büro "Freude und Arbeit" Berlin. Hamburg.
Bericht der Notgemeinschaft. 1930-1950. *Bericht der Notgemeinschaft der Deutschen Wissenschaft (Deutsche Forschungsgemeinschaft)* umfassend ihre Tätigkeit (9.) vom 1.4.1929 bis zum 31.3.1930; (10.) vom 1.4.1930 bis zum 31.3.1931; (11.) vom 1.4.1931 bis zum 31.3.1932; (12.) vom 1.4.1932 bis zum 31.3.1933; vom 1.3.1949 bis zum 31.3.1950. Berlin.
Berning, Cornelia. 1960. 1961. 1962. 1963. "Die Sprache des Nationalsozialismus." *Zeitschrift für deutsche Wortforschung* 16: 71-118, 178-188; 17: 83-121, 171-182; 18: 108-118, 160-172; 19: 92-112.
Besch, Werner; Ulrich Knoop; Wolfgang Putschke; and Herbert Ernst Wiegand (eds.). 1983. *Dialektologie. Ein Handbuch zur deutschen und allgemeinen Dialektforschung.* Vol. 2. Berlin, New York.
Besprechung. 1928. *Besprechung über den Plan eines Atlas der Deutschen Volkskunde am 16. und 17. Juni 1928 in der Notgemeinschaft der Deutschen Wissenschaft, Berlin C 2, im Schloß.* Manuskriptdruck. Archiv der Landesstelle für Volkskunde Freiburg im Breisgau, Aktenordner "Atlas Zentrale."
Biedermann, Otto. 1944a. "Der Auftrag des Reichsleiters Rosenberg." *Nationalsozialistische Monatshefte* 15, Heft 161: 1-6.
Biedermann, Otto. 1944b. "Idee und Tat. 10 Jahre Kampf und Arbeit der Dienststelle Rosenberg." *Der deutsche Erzieher* 1944: 8-10.
Bimmer, Andreas C.; Gitta Böth; Annemie Schenk; Harald Schäfer; and Dorothea Zeh (eds.). 1978. *Brauch, Familie, Arbeitsleben. Schriften von Ingeborg Weber-Kellermann.* Marburger Studien zur vergleichenden Ethnosoziologie. Vol. 10. Marburg: Marburger Studienkreis für Europäische Ethnologie e.V.
Birkhan, Helmut. 1988. "Otto Höfler. Nachruf." *Almanach der Österreichischen Akademie der Wissenschaften* 138: 384-406.

Boberach, Heinz (ed.). 1984. *Meldungen aus dem Reich 1938-1945. Die geheimen Lageberichte des Sicherheitsdienstes der SS.* Vol. 1-17. Herrsching.

Bockhorn, Olaf. 1987. "Wiener Volkskunde 1938-1945." In Gerndt 1987: 229-237.

Bockhorn, Olaf. 1988. "Zur Geschichte der Volkskunde an der Universität Wien. Von den Anfängen bis 1939." In Lehmann and Kuntz 1988: 63-83.

Bockhorn, Olaf. 1989. "Der Kampf um die 'Ostmark.' Ein Beitrag zur Geschichte der nationalsozialistischen Volkskunde in Österreich." In Heiß, Mattl, Meissl, Saurer and Stuhlpfarrer 1989: 17-38.

Bockhorn, Olaf; and Helmut Paul Fielhauer (eds.). 1982. *Kulturelles Erbe und Aneignung. Festschrift für Richard Wolfram zum 80. Geburtstag.* Veröffentlichungen des Instituts für Volkskunde der Universität Wien. Vol. 9. Wien.

Bockhorn, Olaf; Eberhart, Helmut; and Wolfdieter Zupfer (eds.). 1989. *Auf der Suche nach der verlorenen Kultur. Arbeiterkultur zwischen Museum und Realität. Beiträge der 4. Arbeitstagung der Kommission "Arbeiterkultur" in der Deutschen Gesellschaft für Volkskunde in Steyr vom 30.4. - 2.5. 1987.* Beiträge zur Volkskunde und Kulturanalyse. Vol. 3. Wien.

Bockhorn, Olaf; and Gertraud Liesenfeld (eds.). 1989. *Volkskunde in der Hanuschgasse. Forschung - Lehre - Praxis. 25 Jahre Institut für Volkskunde der Universität Wien.* Veröffentlichungen des Instituts für Volkskunde der Universität Wien. Vol. 13. Wien.

Bollmus, Reinhard. 1970. *Das Amt Rosenberg und seine Gegner. Zum Machtkampf im nationalsozialistischen Herrschaftssystem.* Studien zur Zeitgeschichte. Stuttgart.

Bollmus, Reinhard. 1980. "Zum Projekt einer nationalsozialistischen Alternativ-Universität: Alfred Rosenberg's 'Hohe Schule.'" In Heinemann 1980. Vol. 2: 125-152.

Bollmus, Reinhard. 1987. "Zwei Volkskunden im Dritten Reich. Überlegungen eines Historikers." In Gerndt 1987: 49-60.

Bollmus, Reinhard. 1989. "Alfred Rosenberg - 'Chefideologe' des Nationalsozialismus?" In Smelser and Zitelmann 1989: 223-235.

Bönisch, Brigitte; Asta Gloistein; Claudia Gohde; Ulrike Weinitschke; and Magret Wiese. 1986. "Die Göttinger Sieben." In Brednich 1986: 67-82.

Borst, Otto (ed.). 1988. *Das Dritte Reich in Baden und Württemberg.* Stuttgarter Symposion. Vol.1. Stuttgart.

Bracher, Karl Dietrich. 1966. "Die Gleichschaltung der deutschen Universität." In Nationalsozialismus und die deutsche Universität 1966: 126-142.

Bracher, Karl Dietrich. 1971. *Die Auflösung der Weimarer Republik.* Fifth Edition. Villingen.

Brednich, Rolf Wilhelm. 1981. "Sonnensymbolik?" *Anno-Journal* Juli 1981: 48-50.

Brednich, Rolf Wilhelm. 1983. "Die volkskundliche Forschung an der Universität Göttingen 1782-1982." In Brückner and Beitl 1983: 77-94.

Brednich, Rolf Wilhelm. 1985. "Das Weigelsche Sinnbildarchiv in Göttingen. Ein Beitrag zur Geschichte und Ideologiekritik der nationalsozialistischen Volkskunde." *Zeitschrift für Volkskunde* 81: 22-38.

Brednich, Rolf Wilhelm. 1987a. "Die Volkskunde an der Universität Göttingen 1938-1945." In Gerndt 1987: 109-117.

Brednich, Rolf Wilhelm. 1987b. "Volkskunde - die völkische Wissenschaft von Blut und Boden." In Die Universität Göttingen 1987: 313-320.

Brednich, Rolf Wilhelm (ed.). 1986. *Die Brüder Grimm in Göttingen 1829-1837*. Schriftenreihe der Volkskundlichen Kommission für Niedersachsen e.V. Vol. 1. Göttingen.

Brednich, Rolf Wilhelm (ed.). 1988. *Grundriss der Volkskunde. Einführung in die Forschungsfelder der Europäischen Ethnologie*. Ethnologische Paperbacks. Berlin.

Brenke, Annemarie. 1938. "Trachtenpflege und Trachtenerneuerung in Deutschland." In Thiele 1938: 64-75.

Brenner, Hildegard. 1963. *Die Kunstpolitik des Nationalsozialismus*. Rowohlts deutsche Enzyklopädie. Vol. 167/168. Reinbek bei Hamburg.

Bringéus, Nils-Arvid; Uwe Meiners; Ruth-E. Mohrmann; Dietmar Sauermann; and Hinrich Siuts (eds.). 1988. *Wandel der Volkskultur in Europa. Festschrift für Günter Wiegelmann zum 60. Geburtstag*. Vol. 1. Beiträge zur Volkskultur in Nordwestdeutschland. Vol. 60/I. Münster.

Broszat, Martin. 1958. "Die völkische Ideologie und der Nationalsozialismus." *Deutsche Rundschau* 84: 53-68.

Broszat, Martin. 1960. *Der Nationalsozialismus. Weltanschauung, Programmatik und Wirklichkeit*. Schriftenreihe der Niedersächsischen Landeszentrale für Politische Bildung. Zeitgeschichte. Vol 8. Hannover.

Broszat, Martin. 1984. "Nationalsozialistische Konzentrationslager 1933-1945. Schriftliches Sachverständigen-Gutachten für den Auschwitz-Prozeß, vor dem Schwurgericht Frankfurt a.M. am 21. Februar 1964 mündlich vorgetragen." In Buchheim, Broszat, Jacobsen and Krausnick 1984. Vol. 2: 9-133.

Bruckbauer, Maria. 1989. "Verordnete Kultur - Überlegungen zur Volksmusik in Bayern während der NS-Zeit." *Bayerisches Jahrbuch für Volkskunde* 1989: 82-91.

Brückner, Wolfgang. 1986a. "Frömmigkeitsforschung im Schnittpunkt der Disziplinen. Über methodische Vorteile und ideologische Vor-Urteile in den Kulturwissenschaften." In Brückner, Korff and Scharfe 1986: 5-37.

Brückner, Wolfgang. 1986b. "'Volkskunde und Nationalsozialismus.' Zum Beispiel Matthes Ziegler." *Bayerische Blätter für Volkskunde* 13: 189-192.

Brückner, Wolfgang. 1987a. "Geschichte der Volkskunde. Versuch einer Annäherung für Franzosen." In Chiva and Jeggle 1987: 105-127.

Brückner, Wolfgang. 1987b. "Nachträge und Anfragen zum Nationalsozialismus." *Bayerische Blätter für Volkskunde* 14: 28-32.

Brückner, Wolfgang. 1987c. "Volkskunde." In Buddensieg, Düwell and Sembach 1987: 123-127.

Brückner, Wolfgang. 1987d. "Volkskunst und Realienforschung." In Harvolk 1987: 113-139.

Brückner, Wolfgang. 1987e. "Volkskunde in Bayern als gegenwärtige Aufgabe." In Harvolk 1987: 549-559.

Brückner, Wolfgang. 1988a. "Berlin und die Volkskunde." *Bayerische Blätter für Volkskunde* 15: 1-18.

Brückner, Wolfgang. 1988b. "1988: Ein Jahr der NS-Forschung." *Bayerische Blätter für Volkskunde* 15: 19-23.

Brückner, Wolfgang. 1988c. "Volkskunde-Syndrome. Von Nestbeschmutzern und Fakelore-Fabrikanten." *Bayerische Blätter für Volkskunde* 15: 23-25.

Brückner, Wolfgang. 1988d. "Volkskunde als gläubige Wissenschaft. Zum protestantischen Aspekt der ideologischen Wurzeln deutscher Volkskultur-Konzepte." In Bringéus, Meiners, Mohrmann, Sauermann, and Siuts 1988. Vol.1: 17-42.

Brückner, Wolfgang. 1988e. "Bildgebrauch und Kreuzzug gegen Bauern im 13. Jahrhundert. Oder die Nazis in Stedingen." *Bayerische Blätter für Volkskunde* 15: 91-97.

Brückner, Wolfgang. 1988f. "Görres-Tagung in Bayreuth 1988." *Bayerische Blätter für Volkskunde* 15: 207-213.

Brückner, Wolfgang. 1989a. "Fünfzig Jahre nach der Unterdrückung des Jahrbuchs. Zur Geschichte der Sektion Volkskunde." *Jahrbuch für Volkskunde* N.S. 12: 7-8.

Brückner, Wolfgang. 1989b. "Friedrich Heinz Schmidt-Ebhausen. Volkskundedozent der Hochschule für Lehrerbildung Bayreuth im Dritten Reich." *Jahrbuch für Volkskunde* N.S. 12: 67-84.

Brückner, Wolfgang (ed.). 1971. *Falkensteiner Protokolle.* Frankfurt am Main.

Brückner, Wolfgang; and Klaus Beitl (eds.). 1983. *Volkskunde als akademische Disziplin. Studien zur Institutionenausbildung. Referate eines wissenschaftsgeschichtlichen Symposions vom 8.-10. Oktober 1982 in Würzburg.* Österreichische Akademie der Wissenschaften. Philosophisch-Historische Klasse. Sitzungsberichte. Vol. 414. Mitteilungen des Instituts für Gegenwartsvolkskunde. Vol. 12. Wien.

Brückner, Wolfgang; Gottfried Korff; and Martin Scharfe. 1986. *Volksfrömmigkeitsforschung.* Ethnologia Bavarica. Vol. 13. Würzburg and München.

Bublitz, Ernst. 1932. "Der Laich." *Die Sonne* 9: 526.

Buchheim, Hans; Martin Broszat; Hans-Adolf Jacobsen; and Helmut Krausnick (eds.). 1984. *Anatomie des SS-Staates. Gutachten des Instituts für Zeitgeschichte.* Vol. 1-2. Deutscher Taschenbuch Verlag. Vol. 2915-2916. Fourth Edition. München.

Buddensieg, Tilmann; Kurt Düwell; Klaus-Jürgen Sembach. (eds.). 1987. *Wissenschaften in Berlin: Begleitband zur Ausstellung "Der Kongress Denkt" vom 14. Juni - 1. November 1987 in der wiedereröffneten Kongresshalle Berlin.* Vol. 2. Disziplinen. Berlin (West).

Burckhardt-Sebass, Christine. 1988. "Echt - gepflegt - organisiert? Hoffmann-Krayers Gedanken zur Volkskultur." *Kieler Blätter zur Volkskunde* 20: 49-60.

Burde-Schneidewind, Gisela; and Friedemar Geissler. 1984. "Erinnerungen an den Hochschullehrer Adolf Spamer anläßlich seines 100. Geburtstages am 10. 4. 1983." *Jahrbuch für Volkskunde und Kulturgeschichte* 27: 156-160.

Campbell, Åke. 1937. "Historical Notes on the International Association for Folklore and Ethnology." *Folk. Zeitschrift des Internationalen Verbandes für Volksforschung* 1: 7-11.

Cancik, Hubert. 1982a. "Antike Volkskunde 1936." *Der altsprachliche Unterricht* 24: 80-99.

Cancik, Hubert (ed.). 1982b. *Religions- und Geistesgeschichte der Weimarer Republik*. Düsseldorf.

Cavazza, Stefano. 1987. "Volkskunde und Faschismus in Italien." In Gerndt 1987: 39-48.

Cecil, Robert. 1972. *The Myth of the Master Race: Alfred Rosenberg and Nazi Ideology*. London.

Chamberlain, Houston Stewart. 1899. *Die Grundlagen des neunzehnten Jahrhunderts*. Vol. 1-2. München.

Chamberlain, Houston Stewart. 1901. *Die Grundlagen des neunzehnten Jahrhunderts*. Third Edition. Vol. 1-2. München.

Chamberlain, Houston Stewart. 1909. *Immanuel Kant. Die Persönlichkeit als Einführung in das Werk*. Second Edition. München.

Chiva, Isac; and Utz Jeggle (eds.). 1987. *Deutsche Volkskunde - Französische Ethnologie. Zwei Standortbestimmungen*. Frankfurt am Main, New York and Paris.

Conte, Edouard. 1987. "Wilhelm Schmidt: Des letzten Kaisers Beichtvater und das 'neudeutsche Heidentum.'" In Gerndt 1987: 261-278.

Corni, Gustavo. 1989. "Richard Walther Darré - Der 'Blut-und-Boden'-Ideologe." In Smelser and Zitelmann 1989: 15-27.

Cox, Heinrich L. 1983. "Wechselseitige Beziehungen zwischen Dialektologie und thematischer Kartographie in der deutschen Volkskunde." In Besch, Knoop, Putschke and Wiegand 1983: 1579-1597.

Cox, Heinrich L. 1988. "Adolf Spamers Versuch, Stereotypen sowie geschlechts-, alters- und berufsspezifische Verhaltensmuster mittels Fernbefragung zu erkunden." In Gerndt 1988a: 114-120.

Dahle, Wendula. 1969. *Der Einsatz einer Wissenschaft. Eine sprachinhaltliche Analyse militärischer Terminologie in der Germanistik 1933-1945*. Bonn.

Darré, R. Walter. 1928. *Das Bauerntum als Lebensquell der Nordischen Rasse*. München.

Darré, R. Walter. 1929. *Das Bauerntum als Lebensquell der Nordischen Rasse*. München.

Darré, R. Walter. 1933. *Das Bauerntum als Lebensquell der Nordischen Rasse*. Second Edition. München.

Darré, Walther. n.d. *80 Merksätze und Leitsprüche über Zucht und Sitte aus Schriften und Reden*. Second Edition. Goslar.

Daxelmüller, Christoph. 1983. "Jüdische Volkskunde in Deutschland vor 1933." In Brückner and Beitl 1983: 117-142.

Daxelmüller, Christoph. 1986. "Max Grunwald and the Origin and Conditions of Jewish Folklore at Hamburg." In Art 1986: 73-80.

Daxelmüller, Christoph. 1987a. "Die deutschsprachige Volkskunde und die Juden. Zur Geschichte und den Folgen einer kulturellen Ausklammerung." *Zeitschrift für Volkskunde* 83: 1-20.

Daxelmüller, Christoph. 1987b. "Nationalsozialistisches Kulturverständnis und das Ende der jüdischen Volkskunde." In Gerndt 1987: 149-167.

Daxelmüller, Christoph. 1987c. "Vorwort." In Bächtold-Stäubli and Hoffmann-Krayer 1987: V-XL.

Daxelmüller, Christoph. 1988a. "Vergessene Geschichte. Die 'Gesellschaft für jüdische Volkskunde' in Hamburg." In Lehmann and Kuntz 1988: 11-31.

Dehnert, Walter. 1987. "Volkskundlicher Film und Filmanalyse. Ansätze zur Annäherung." In Husmann 1987: 201-227.

Dehnert, Walter. 1989. "Volkskunde an der Albert-Ludwigs-Universität bis 1945." *Beiträge zur Volkskunde in Baden-Württemberg* 3: 145-165.

Der deutsche Mensch. 1935. *Der deutsche Mensch. Fünf Vorträge von Hans Naumann, Willy Andreas, Adolf Feulner, Gerhard Fricke, Erich Rothacker.* Stuttgart and Berlin.

Der Fall. 1929. *Der Fall Herman Wirth oder Das Schicksal des Schöpfertums.* Jena.

Der Reichsorganisationsleiter der NSDAP. 1943. *Organisationsbuch der NSDAP.* Seventh edition. München: Zentralverlag der NSDAP., Franz Eher Nachf.

Deutsche Forschung. 1928a. *Deutsche Forschung. Aus der Arbeit der Notgemeinschaft der Deutschen Wissenschaft.* Vol. 2: Deutsche Volkskunde. Berlin.

Deutsche Forschung. 1928b. *Deutsche Forschung. Aus der Arbeit der Notgemeinschaft der Deutschen Wissenschaft (Deutsche Forschungsgemeinschaft).* Vol. 6: Deutsche Volkskunde. Berlin.

Deutsche Volkskunde. Deutsche Volkskunde. Vierteljahresschrift der "Arbeitsgemeinschaft für Deutsche Volkskunde." Hauptschriftleiter: Reichsamtsleiter Dr. Mattes Ziegler und Prof. Dr. Georg Fischer. Verantwortlicher Schriftleiter: Dr. Ernst Otto Thiele. [Ab 3. Jahrgang, 3./4. Heft 1941: Kriegsschriftleiter: Dr. Karl Haiding]. München: Hoheneichen-Verlag. 1. Jahrgang 1939 - 6. Jahrgang, Heft 1./2., 1944.

Deutsche Volkskunde im Schrifttum. 1938. *Deutsche Volkskunde im Schrifttum. Ein Leitfaden für die Schulungs- und Erziehungsarbeit der NSDAP.* Herausgegeben von der parteiamtlichen "Arbeitsgemeinschaft für Deutsche Volkskunde" in Verbindung mit dem Amt Schrifttumspflege beim Beauftragten des Führers für die gesamte geistige und weltanschauliche Erziehung der NSDAP. Berlin.

Die Gestaltung der Lebensfeiern. 1942. *Die Gestaltung der Lebensfeiern. Richtlinien. Nur für den Dienstgebrauch.* Herausgegeben vom Beauftragten des Führers für die Überwachung der gesamten geistigen und weltanschaulichen Schulung und Erziehung der NSDAP. Bearbeitet vom Amt Volkskunde und Feiergestaltung. Berlin. 26 pp.

Die Universität Göttingen. 1987. *Die Universität Göttingen unter dem Nationalsozialismus. Das verdrängte Kapitel ihrer 250-jährigen Geschichte.* München.

Diewerge, Heinz. 1936. Review of Harmjanz 1936a. *Nationalsozialistische Monatshefte* 7, Heft 79: 963-966.

Dirks, Walter. 1988. "Die beiden Kriege und die deutsche Identität." In Althaus et alii 1988: 173-183.

Dittmar, Jürgen. 1987. "Seemann, Erich." In Ottnad 1987: 256-257.

Dölker, Helmut. 1971. "Nachruf Friedrich Heinz Schmidt-Ebhausen 1902-1971." *Zeitschrift für Volkskunde* 67: 84-85.

Dow, James R. 1987. "German *Volkskunde* and National Socialism." *Journal of American Folklore* 100 (397): 300-304.

Dow, James R. 1988. Review of Gerndt 1987. *Journal of American Folklore* 101: 358-360.

Dow, James R. 1989. "Zur amerikanischen Volkskunde. Standortbestimmung der heutigen Theorie und Praxis. Mit einem Beispiel aus der Feldforschung bei deutschsprechenden Amerikanern (Amische Alter Ordnung)." *Österreichische Zeitschrift für Volkskunde* 92: 1-23.

Dow, James R. 1990. "Review of Gerndt 1988b." *The German Quarterly* 63: 293-295.

Dow, James R. 1992. "Austrian *Volkskunde*: A Contemporary Sampler." *Journal of American Folklore* 105: 368-373.

Dow, James R.; and Hannjost Lixfeld. 1991. "National Socialist Folklore and Overcoming the Past in the Federal Republic of Germany." *Asian Folklore Studies* L-1: 117-153.

Dow, James R.; and Hannjost Lixfeld (eds.). 1986. *German Volkskunde. A Decade of Theoretical Confrontation, Debate, and Reorientation (1967-1977)*. Folklore Studies in Translation. Bloomington, Indiana.

Dow, James R.; and Hannjost Lixfeld (eds.). In Press. *The Nazification of an Academic Discipline. German Folklore in the Third Reich*. Folklore Studies in Translation. Bloomington, Indiana.

Dülmen, Richard van; and Norbert Schindler (eds.). 1984. *Volkskultur. Zur Wiederentdeckung des vergessenen Alltags (16.-20. Jahrhundert)*. Fischer Taschenbuch. Vol. 3460. Frankfurt am Main.

Dümling, Albrecht; and Peter Girth (eds.). 1988. *Entartete Musik. Zur Düsseldorfer Ausstellung von 1938. Eine kommentierte Rekonstruktion*. Düsseldorf.

Eberhart, Helmut. 1983. "Die Entwicklung des Faches Volkskunde an der Karl-Franzens-Universität Graz." In Brückner and Beitl 1983: 36-50.

Eberhart, Helmut. 1984. "Die Volkskunde an der Universität Salzburg. Ein Beitrag zur Institutionengeschichte." In Acker-Sutter 1984: 99-119.

Eberhart, Helmut. 1985. "Zwischen Realität und Romantik. Die Viktor-Geramb-Fotosammlung am Institut für Volkskunde in Graz." *Zeitschrift für Volkskunde* 81: 1-21.

Eberhart, Helmut. 1987. "Folklore and National Socialism. Symposium of the German Folklore Society in Munich (Oct. 22-25, 1986)." *Zeitschrift für Volkskunde* 83: 74-79.

Ehalt, Hubert Ch. (ed.). 1984. *Geschichte von unten. Fragestellung, Methoden und Projekte einer Geschichte des Alltags*. Wien, Köln and Graz.

Eichberg, Henning; Michael Dultz et alii. 1977. *Massenspiele, NS-Thingspiel, Arbeiterweihespiel und olympisches Zeremoniell*. Stuttgart and Bad Cannstadt.

Emmerich, Wolfgang. 1968. *Germanistische Volkstumsideologie. Genese und Kritik der Volksforschung im Dritten Reich*. Volksleben. Vol. 20. Tübingen.

Emmerich, Wolfgang. 1971. *Zur Kritik der Volkstumsideologie*. Edition Suhrkamp. Vol. 502. Frankfurt am Main.

Engelhardt, Ingeborg. 1938. "Neuer deutscher Schmuck." In Thiele 1938: 185-191.

Erb, Rainer; and Michael Schmidt (eds.). 1987. *Antisemitismus und Jüdische Geschichte. Studien zu Ehren von Herbert A. Strauss.* Berlin.

Erich, Oswald A.; and Richard Beitl. 1936. *Wörterbuch der deutschen Volkskunde.* Unter besonderer Mitarbeit von Otto Bramm, Anneliese Bretschneider, Wilhelm Hansen, Nikola Michailow und Wolfgang Schuchardt. Kröners Taschenausgabe. Vol. 127/128. Leipzig.

Ericksen, Robert P. 1968. *Theologen unter Hitler. Das Bündnis zwischen evangelischer Dogmatik und Nationalsozialismus. Aus dem Amerikanischen von Annegret Lösch.* München and Wien.

Erixon, Sigurd. 1937. "Geschichte und heutige Aufgaben der Bauernhausforschung." In Thiele 1937: 1-20.

Faust, Anselm. 1980. "Professoren für die NSDAP. Zum politischen Verhalten der Hochschullehrer 1932/33." In Heinemann 1980, Vol. 2: 31-49.

Fehrle, Eugen. 1938a. "Zur Entwicklung des Sinnbildes." *Oberdeutsche Zeitschrift für Volkskunde* 12: 165.

Fehrle, Eugen. 1938b. "Sudetenland - Deutsches Land." *Oberdeutsche Zeitschrift für Volkskunde* 12: 73.

Fehrle, Eugen. 1938c. "Die Brautkrone." In Thiele 1938: 76-81.

Fehrle, Eugen. 1939a. "Die volkskundliche Lehrschau der Universität Heidelberg." *Badische Heimat* 26: 293-312.

Fehrle, Eugen. 1939b. "Böhmen und Mähren." *Oberdeutsche Zeitschrift für Volkskunde* 13: 1-2.

Fehrle, Eugen. 1940a. *Die Eligiussage.* Frankfurt.

Fielhauer, Helmut Paul. 1984a. "Volkskunde als demokratische Kulturgeschichtsschreibung." In Ehalt 1984: 59-79.

Fielhauer, Helmut Paul (ed.). 1968. *Volkskunde und Volkskultur. Festschrift für Richard Wolfram.* Veröffentlichungen des Instituts für Volkskunde der Universität Wien. Vol. 2. Wien.

Fischer, Eugen. 1935. "Hans F. K. Günther. Der Rassen-Günther." *Mein Heimatland* 22: 219-221.

Flitner, Andreas (ed.). 1965. *Deutsches Geistesleben und Nationalsozialismus. Eine Vortragsreihe der Universität Tübingen mit einem Nachwort von Hermann Diem.* Tübingen.

Frank, Walter. 1937. *Deutsche Wissenschaft und Judenfrage. Rede zur Eröffnung der Forschungsabteilung Judenfrage des Reichsinstituts für Geschichte des neuen Deutschlands gehalten am 19. November 1936 in der großen Aula der Universität München.* Schriften des Reichsinstituts für Geschichte des neuen Deutschlands. Vol. 18. Hamburg.

Freckmann, Klaus. 1982. "Hausforschung im Dritten Reich." *Zeitschrift für Volkskunde* 78: 169-186.

Freckmann, Klaus. 1985. "Zur Foto- und Plandokumentation in der Hausforschung der 30er und 40er Jahre. Das Beispiel des ehemaligen 'Bauernhofbüros' Berlin/Münster." *Zeitschrift für Volkskunde* 81: 40-50.

Freckmann, Klaus. 1987. "Aufklärung und Verklärung - Positionen im Werk Georg Schreibers." In Gerndt 1987: 283-295.

Frenzel, Walter; Fritz Karg; and Adolf Spamer (eds.). 1933. *Grundriss der Sächsischen Volkskunde.* Vols. 1-2. Leipzig.

Freudenthal, Herbert. 1934. "Volkskunde und Nationalerziehung. Zur Geschichte ihrer Beziehungen." In Bargheer and Freudenthal 1934: 7-22.

Freudenthal, Herbert. 1935. *Deutsche Wissenschaft im Kampf um das Volk. Zur volkserzieherischen Sendung der Volkskunde*. Berlin and Leipzig.

Freudenthal, Herbert. 1955. *Die Wissenschaftstheorie der deutschen Volkskunde*. Hannover.

Fritzsch, Karl Ewald. 1934. "Die Landesstelle für Volksforschung und Volkstumspflege im NSLB. Sachsen. Ihr Aufbau, ihre Arbeitsweise und ersten Ergebnisse." *Mitteldeutsche Blätter für Volkskunde* 9: 148-154.

Fritzsch, Karl Ewald. 1935. "An die Erforscher, Pfleger und Künder des deutschen Volkstums!" *Mitteldeutsche Blätter für Volkskunde* 10: 1-3.

Fritzsch, Karl Ewald. 1936. "Adolf Spamer - zehn Jahre in Dresden (1926-1936)." *Mitteldeutsche Blätter für Volkskunde* 11: 87-95.

Fritzsch, Karl-Ewald. 1956. "Volkskundliche Staatsarbeiten, vergeben durch Adolf Spamer 1926-1935 an der kulturwissenschaftlichen Abteilung der Technischen Hochschule Dresden." *Deutsches Jahrbuch für Volkskunde* 2: 245-251.

Fünfzig Jahre Verband. 1954. *Fünfzig Jahre Verband der Vereine für Volkskunde 1904-1954*. Stuttgart.

Gajek, Esther. 1986. "Die Inszenierung von 'Volksgemeinschaft.' Zum volkskundlichen Beitrag zur nationalsozialistischen Feiergestaltung." In Volkskunde im Dritten Reich 1986: 17-23.

Gebauer, Gunter (ed.). 1988. *Körper- und Einbildungskraft. Inszenierungen des Helden im Sport*. Reihe Historische Anthropologie. Vol. 2. Berlin.

Gebhardt, Winfried. 1987a. *Fest, Feier und Alltag. Über die gesellschaftliche Wirklichkeit des Menschen und ihre Deutung*. Europäische Hochschulschriften. Reihe 22. Vol. 143. Frankfurt am Main, Bern, New York and Paris.

Gebhardt, Winfried. 1987b. "Nationalsozialistische Feiern." In Gebhardt 1987a: 146-155.

Gerndt, Helge. 1987a. "Vorwort." In Gerndt 1987: 8.

Gerndt, Helge. 1987b. "Volkskunde und Nationalsozialismus. Thesen zu einer notwendigen Auseinandersetzung." In Gerndt 1987: 11-21.

Gerndt, Helge (ed.). 1987. *Volkskunde und Nationalsozialismus. Referate und Diskussionen einer Tagung der Deutschen Gesellschaft für Volkskunde. München, 23. bis 25. Oktober 1986*. Münchner Beiträge zur Volkskunde. Vol.7. München.

Gerndt, Helge (ed.). 1988a. *Stereotypvorstellungen im Alltagsleben. Beiträge zum Themenkreis Fremdbilder - Selbstbilder - Identität. Festschrift für Georg R. Schroubek zum 65. Geburtstag*. Münchner Beiträge zur Volkskunde. Vol. 8. München.

Gerndt, Helge (ed.). 1988b. *Fach und Begriff "Volkskunde" in der Diskussion*. Wege der Forschung. Vol. 641. Darmstadt.

Ghirardini, Claudia. 1986. "'Heim ins Reich.' Untersuchungen über das Deutschtum im Ausland - Volkskunde im Dienst der Machtpolitik." In Volkskunde im Dritten Reich 1986: 31-36.

Gilbert, G.M. 1962. *Nürnberger Tagebuch*. Fischer Bücherei. Vol. 447/448. Frankfurt am Main.

Gilch, Eva. 1986. "'Volkskunde' an der Ludwig-Maximilians-Universität in den Jahren 1933-1945." In Gilch, Schramka and Prütting 1986: 11-39.

Gilch, Eva; Carmen Schramka; and Hildegunde Prütting. 1986. *Volkskunde an der Münchner Universität 1933-1945*. Münchner Beiträge zur Volkskunde. Vol. 6. München.

Giordano, Ralph. 1987. *Die zweite Schuld oder Von der Last Deutscher zu sein*. Hamburg.

Gläubige Wissenschaft. 1936. "Gläubige Wissenschaft." *Wille und Macht* 4/22: 8-12.

Goetze, Alfred; Wilhelm Horn; and Friedrich Maurer (eds.). 1934. *Germanische Philologie. Festschrift für Otto Behagel*. Germanische Bibliothek. 1. Abteilung. 1. Reihe. Vol. 19. Heidelberg.

Gotto, Klaus; and Konrad Repgen (eds.). 1980. *Kirche, Katholiken und National-sozialismus*. Topos-Taschenbücher. Vol. 96. Mainz.

Greverus, Ina-Maria; Konrad Köstlin; and Heinz Schilling (eds.). 1988. *Kultur-kontakt, Kulturkonflikt. Zur Erfahrung des Fremden. 26. Deutscher Volkskundekongreß in Frankfurt vom 28. September bis 2. Oktober 1987*. Vol. 1-2. Notizen. Die Schriftenreihe des Instituts für Kulturanthropologie und Europäische Ethnologie der Universität Frankfurt am Main. Vol.28. Frankfurt am Main: Institut für Kulturanthropologie und Europäische Ethnologie.

Grießmair, Hans. 1988. "Die Option in Südtirol 1939. Volkskunde als Hilfs-wissenschaft zur Umsiedlung." In Greverus, Köstlin and Schilling 1988. Vol. 1: 219-220.

Grimm, Jacob. 1864a. "Über meine Entlassung." In Grimm 1864b: 25-52.

Grimm, Jacob. 1864b. *Kleinere Schriften*. Vol. 1. Berlin.

Grober-Glück, Gerda. 1988. "Zum Abschluß des Atlas der deutschen Volkskunde - Neue Folge. Ein Beitrag zur Wissenschaftsgeschichte der Volkskunde." In Bringéus et al. 1988: 53-70.

Gröhsl, Margit. 1957. "Wissenschaftliche Arbeiten von Prof. Karl von Spieß." *Mitteilungen der Anthropologischen Gesellschaft in Wien* 87: 78-82.

Guggenberger, Eduard. 1985/1986. "Ariosophie: Wandlungen und Verkleidun-gen." *Zeitgeschichte* 13, Heft 9/10: 303-310.

Günther, Hans F.K. 1922. *Rassenkunde des deutschen Volkes*. München.

Günther, Hans F.K. 1924. *Deutsche Rassenbilder*. München.

Günther, Hans F.K. 1929. *Rassenkunde Europas*. Third Edition. München.

Günther, Hans F.K. 1930. *Rassenkunde des jüdischen Volkes*. Second Edition. München.

Günther, Hans F.K. 1933. *Kleine Rassenkunde des deutschen Volkes*. Third Edition. München.

Günther, Hans F.K.. 1934. *Die Verstädterung. Ihre Gefahren für Volk und Staat vom Standpunkt der Lebenserforschung und Geschichtswissenschaft*. Leipzig and Berlin.

Haberlandt, Arthur. 1933. "Lebenskreise als ein Forschungsziel der Volkskunde. Ein Beitrag zur Methodenlehre." In Steller 1933: 377-392.

Haberlandt, Arthur. 1935. *Die deutsche Volkskunde. Eine Grundlegung nach Geschichte und Methode im Rahmen der Geisteswissenschaften.* Volk. Vol. 1. Halle/Saale.

Haberlandt, Arthur. 1938a. "Textilkunst bei Germanen und Indogermanen." In Thiele 1938: 117-125.

Haberlandt, Arthur. 1938b. "Der Verein für Volkskunde an der Zeitenwende." *Wiener Zeitschrift für Volkskunde* 43: 50-52.

Haberlandt, Arthur. 1939. "Germanisches Erbe im Donauraum." In Thiele 1939: 84-90.

Haiding, Karl. 1939a. "Erzähler des Dorfes." *Deutsche Volkskunde* 1: 48-57.

Haiding, Karl. 1939b. "Germanisches Erbe in Volkstanz und Volksspiel." In Thiele 1939: 138-163.

Haiding, Karl. 1939c. *Kinderspiel und Volksüberlieferung.* Deutsche Volkskunde. Schriftenreihe der Arbeitsgemeinschaft für deutsche Volkskunde. Gruppe: Spiel, Lied und Tanz. München.

Haiding, Karl. 1943. "Der Mythus unseres Jahrhunderts und die deutsche Volkskunde." *Deutsche Volkskunde* 5: 169-170.

Hanika, Josef. 1938. "Gestalttypen in den europäischen Kopftrachten." In Thiele 1938: 53-63.

Hanika, Josef. 1939. "Neugestaltung der Trachten im Sudentengau." *Deutsche Volkskunde* 1: 234-240.

Hänsel, Volker; and Sepp Walter (eds.). 1981. *Volkskundliches aus dem steirischen Ennsbereich. Festschrift für Karl Haiding zum 75. Geburtstag.* Schriftenreihe des Landschaftsmuseums Schloß Trautenfels am Steiermärkischen Landesmuseum Joanneum. Vol. 1. Liezen.

Harmening, Dieter. 1989. "Himmlers Hexenkartei. Ein Lagebericht zu ihrer Erforschung." *Jahrbuch für Volkskunde* N.S. 12: 99-112.

Harmjanz, Heinrich. 1936a. *Volk, Mensch, Ding. Erkenntniskritische Untersuchungen zur volkskundlichen Begriffsbildung.* Schriften der Albertus-Universität. Geisteswissenschaftliche Reihe. Vol. 1. Königsberg in Preußen und Berlin.

Harmjanz, Heinrich. 1936b. *Volkskunde und Siedlungsgeschichte Altpreußens.* Berlin.

Harmjanz, Heinrich. 1937. "Der Atlas er deutschen Volkskunde." *Deutsche Wissenschaft, Erziehung und Volksbildung* 23: 225.228.

Harmjanz, Heinrich. 1939a. Review of Kaiser 1939a. *Germanien* 11: 380-381.

Harmjanz, Heinrich. 1943. "Erich Röhr zum Gedächtnis." *Volkswerk* 1943: 231-234.

Harmjanz, Heinrich; and Erich Röhr (eds.). 1937-1939. *Atlas der deutschen Volkskunde. Lieferung 1-5 (Karte 1-99).* Herausgegeben mit Unterstützung der Deutschen Forschungsgemeinschaft. Leipzig.

Hart, Franz Theodor. 1939. *Alfred Rosenberg. Der Mann und sein Werk.* Fourth Edition. München and Berlin.

Harvolk, Edgar. 1989. "'Volkserziehung' durch 'Volkserkenntnis.' Zur 'angewandten Volkskunde' der Jahre 1934-1938." In Bauer, Harvolk and Mayer 1989: 339-354.

Harvolk, Edgar. 1990. *Eichenzweig und Hakenkreuz. Die Deutsche Akademie in München (1924-1962) und ihre volkskundliche Sektion.* Münchner Beiträge zur Volkskunde. Vol. 11. München.

Harvolk, Edgar (ed.). 1987. *Wege der Volkskunde in Bayern. Ein Handbuch.* Veröffentlichungen zur Volkskunde und Kulturgeschichte. Vol. 25. Beiträge zur Volkstumsforschung. Vol. 23. München and Würzburg.

Haug, Wolfgang Fritz. 1967. *Der hilflose Antifaschismus. Zur Kritik der Vorlesungsreihen über Wissenschaft und NS an deutschen Universitäten.* First Edition. Edition Suhrkamp. Vol. 236. Frankfurt am Main.

Haug, Wolfgang Fritz. 1977. *Der hilflose Antifaschismus. Zur Kritik der Vorlesungsreihen über Wissenschaft und NS an deutschen Universitäten.* Fourth Edition. Kleine Bibliothek. Vol. 79. Köln.

Hauschild, Thomas. 1987. "Völkerkunde im 'Dritten Reich.'" In Gerndt 1987: 245-259.

Heiber, Helmut. 1966. *Walter Frank und sein Reichsinstitut für Geschichte des neuen Deutschlands.* Quellen und Darstellungen zur Zeitgeschichte. Vol. 13. Stuttgart.

Heiber, Helmut (ed.). 1968. *Reichsführer! ... Briefe an und von Himmler.* Stuttgart.

Heilfurth, Gerhard. 1937. "Die Arbeitsgemeinschaft für deutsche Volkskunde." *Mitteldeutsche Blätter für Volkskunde* 12: 110-111.

Heilfurth, Gerhard. 1961. *Volkskunde jenseits der Ideologien. Zum Problemstand des Faches im Blickfeld empirischer Forschung.* Schriften der Philipps-Universität Marburg. Vol. 9. Marburg.

Heilfurth, Gerhard. 1962a. "Volkskunde jenseits der Ideologien. Zum Problemstand des Faches im Blickfeld empirischer Forschung." *Hessische Blätter für Volkskunde* 53: 9-28.

Heilfurth, Gerhard. 1989. ["Erinnerungen 1936"]. In Holzapfel 1989: 161-167.

Heinemann, Manfred (ed.). 1980. *Erziehung und Schulung im Dritten Reich. Teil 1: Kindergarten, Schule, Jugend, Berufserziehung. Teil 2: Hochschule, Erwachsenenbildung.* Veröffentlichungen der Historischen Kommission der Deutschen Gesellschaft für Erziehungswissenschaft. Vol. 4, 1-2. Stuttgart.

Heiß, Gernot; Siegfried Mattl; Sebastian Meissl; Edith Saurer; and Karl Stuhlpfarrer (eds.). 1989. *Willfährige Wissenschaft. Die Universität Wien 1938-1945.* Österreichische Texte zur Gesellschaftskritik. Vol 43. Wien.

Helbok, Adolf. (1964). *Erinnerungen. Ein lebenslanges Ringen um volksnahe Geschichtsforschung.* Fritz Ranzi und Margit Gröhsl (eds.) im Auftrag seiner Innsbrucker, Berliner und Leipziger Schüler. Innsbruck. n.d.

Helbok, Adolf. 1964. *Von der Frühzeit bis zur Reformation.* Deutsche Volksgeschichte. Wesenszüge und Leistungen des deutschen Volkes. Vol. 1. Tübingen.

Helm, Rudolf. 1938. "Germanische Schmuckformen in der deutschen Bauerntracht." In Thiele 1938: 135-144.

Hepding, Hugo. 1940. "Karl Kaiser †." *Hessische Blätter für Volkskunde* 37: 134-139.

Herrmann, Ferdinand; and Wolfgang Treutlein (eds.). 1940. *Brauch und Sinnbild. Eugen Fehrle zum 60. Geburtstag gewidmet von seinen Schülern und Freunden.* Karlsruhe.

Hesse, Wolfgang; and Christian Schröter. 1985. "Sammeln als Wissenschaft. Fotografie und Film im 'Institut für deutsche Volkskunde Tübingen' 1933-1945." *Zeitschrift für Volkskunde* 81: 51-75.

Hitler, Adolf. 1933. *Mein Kampf.* Seventeenth Edition. München.

Hoffer, Heinrich. 1942. "Standesamtliche Lebensfeiern." *Deutsche Volkskunde* 4: 114-117.

Höfler, Otto. 1934. *Kultische Geheimbünde der Germanen.* Vol. 1. Frankfurt am Main.

Höfler, Otto. 1937a. *Das germanische Kontinuitätsproblem.* Hamburg.

Höfler, Otto. 1937b. "Antwort." *Oberdeutsche Zeitschrift für Volkskunde* 11: 97-102.

Höfler, Otto. 1937c. "Rudolf Much †." *Wörter und Sachen* 18: VII-XV.

Höfler, Otto. 1973. *Verwandlungskulte, Volkssagen und Mythen.* Österreichische Akademie der Wissenschaften. Philosophisch-Historische Klasse. Sitzungsberichte. Vol. 279/2. Wien.

Hofstaetter, Walther; and Franz Schnabel (eds.). 1929. *Grundzüge der Deutschkunde.* Vol.2. Leipzig.

Holzapfel, Otto. 1987a. "John Meier." In Ottnad 1987: 203-204.

Holzapfel, Otto. 1987b. "Das Deutsche Volksliedarchiv im Drittem Reich." In Gerndt 1987: 95-102.

Holzapfel, Otto. 1989. *Das Deutsche Volksliedarchiv Freiburg i. Br.* Studien zur Volksliedforschung. Vol. 3. Bern, Frankfurt am Main, New York and Paris.

Horkheimer, Max. 1967. *Zur Kritik der instrumentellen Vernunft.* Ed. by A. Schmidt. Frankfurt am Main.

Huber, Kurt. 1959. *Volkslied und Volkstanz. Aufsätze zur Volksliedkunde des bajuwarischen Raumes.* Ettal.

Hübner, Arthur. 1930. "Der Atlas der deutschen Volkskunde." *Zeitschrift für Volkskunde* 39: 1-16.

Hübner, Arthur. 1934. *Herman Wirth und die Ura-Linda-Chronik.* Berlin and Leipzig.

Huck, Gerhard (ed.). 1980. *Sozialgeschichte der Freizeit. Untersuchungen zum Wandel der Alltagskultur in Deutschland.* Wuppertal.

Hunger, Ulrich. 1984. *Die Runenkunde im Dritten Reich. Ein Beitrag zur Wissenschafts- und Ideologiegeschichte des Nationalsozialismus.* Europäische Hochschulschriften. Reihe 3. Vol. 227. Frankfurt am Main, Bern, New York and Nancy.

Hüsing, Georg. 1927. *Die deutschen Hochgezeiten.* Wien.

Hüsing, Georg. 1931. "Einführung in die Weltgeschichte." *Bausteine zur Geschichte, Völkerkunde und Mythenkunde* 1: 3-56.

Hüsing, Georg and Emma. 1932. *Deutsche Laiche und Lieder.* Wien: Eichendorff-Haus. Knyrim, Schier und Stöhr.

Husmann, Rolf (ed.). 1987. *Mit der Kamera in fremden Kulturen. Aspekte des Films in Ethnologie und Volkskunde.* Interdisziplinäre Reihe. Vol. 1. Emsdetten.

Immer, Karl. 1936. *Entchristlichung der Jugend. Eine Materialsammlung. Der Bekenntnissynode der Deutschen Evangelischen Kirche vorgelegt.* Wuppertal-Barmen: Verlag 'Unter dem Wort" e.V.

Jacobeit, Wolfgang. 1965a. Comment to Helbok (1964). *Deutsches Jahrbuch für Volkskunde* 11: 399-401.

Jacobeit, Wolfgang. 1965b. *Bäuerliche Arbeit und Wirtschaft. Ein Beitrag zur Wissenschaftsgeschichte der deutschen Volkskunde.* Veröffentlichungen des Instituts für deutsche Volkskunde. Vol. 39. Berlin.

Jacobeit, Wolfgang. 1987. "Die Auseinandersetzung mit der NS-Zeit in der DDR-Volkskunde." In Gerndt 1987: 301-318.

Jacobeit, Wolfgang; and Ute Mohrmann. 1982. "Zur Geschichte der volkskundlichen Lehre unter Adolf Spamer an der Berliner Universität (1933-1945)." *Ethnographisch-Archäologische Zeitschrift* 23: 283-298.

Jacobeit, Wolfgang; Hannjost Lixfeld; Olaf Bockhorn; in Zusammenarbeit mit James R. Dow. In Press. *Völkische Wissenschaft. Gestalten und Tendenzen in der deutschen und österreichischen Volkskunde in der ersten Hälfte des 20. Jahrhunderts*, Böhlau Verlag: Wien.

Jankuhn, Herbert (ed.). 1944. Forschungs- und Lehrgemeinschaft "Das Ahnenerbe." *Jahrestagungen. Bericht über die Kieler Tagung 1939.* Neumünster.

Jeggle, Utz. 1986. "In stolzer Trauer. Umgangsformen mit dem Kriegstod während des 2. Weltkriegs." In Jeggle, Kaschuba, Korff, Scharfe, and Warneken 1986: 242-259.

Jeggle, Utz. 1987. "Nationalsozialismus." In Erb and Schmidt 1987: 495-514.

Jeggle, Utz. 1988a. "Volkskunde im 20. Jahrhundert." In Brednich 1988: 51-71.

Jeggle, Utz. 1988b. "Kontinuität in der Lebensgeschichte von Nazis." *Schweizerisches Archiv für Volkskunde* 84: 201-211.

Jeggle, Utz. 1988c. "Bebermeyer. Institutsdirektor. Eine persönliche Vignette." In Nationalsozialismus im Landkreis Tübingen 1988: 61-62.

Jeggle, Utz. 1988d. "L'ethnologie de l'Allemagne sous le régime nazi. Un regard sur la Volkskunde deux générations aprés." *Ethnologie française* 18/2: 114-119.

Jeggle, Utz; and Gottfried Korff. 1972. "Zur Sendung Wolfgang Brückners." *Tübinger Korrespondenzblatt* 6: 1-8.

Jeggle, Utz; Wolfgang Kaschuba; Gottfried Korff; Martin Scharfe; and Bernd Jürgen Warneken (eds.). 1986. *Tübinger Beiträge zur Volkskultur.* Untersuchungen des Ludwig-Uhland-Instituts der Universität Tübingen. Vol. 69. Tübingen.

John, Eckhard. 1984. "Vom Deutschtum in der Musik." *Zwischentöne* 2 (Der diskrete Charme der Theorie. Musikwissenschaft in Freiburg 1919-1984): 5-33.

John, Eckhard. 1987. "Die andere Seite der Freiburger Musikwissenschaft." *Zwischentöne* 10 (Musik im NS-Staat und Exil): 5-12.

John, Eckhard. 1988. "Vom Deutschtum in der Musik." In Dümling and Girth 1988: 49-55.

John, Eckhard; Bernd Martin; Marc Mück; and Hugo Ott (eds.). 1991. *Die Freiburger Universität in der Zeit des Nationalsozialismus.* Freiburg i. Br. und Würzburg.

Kaiser, Karl. 1936. *Atlas der pommerschen Volkskunde. Textband. Kartenmappe: 5 + 44 Karten in doppelter Ausführung*. Veröffentlichungen des Volkskundlichen Archivs für Pommern. Vol. 4-5. Greifswald.

Kaiser, Karl. 1937a. "Pommern im Lichte der volkstumsgeographischen Forschung." *Folk* 1, Heft 2: 147-167.

Kaiser, Karl (ed.). 1939a. *Lesebuch zur Geschichte der Deutschen Volkskunde. Volkskundliche Texte*. Vol. 10. Dresden.

Kamenetzky, Christa. 1972. "Folklore as a Political Tool in Nazi Germany." *Journal of American Folklore* 85: 221-235.

Kamenetzky, Christa. 1977. "Folktale and Ideology in the Third Reich." *Journal of American Folklore* 90: 168-178.

Kater, Michael. 1971. "Die Artamanen - Völkische Jugend in der Weimarer Republik." *Historische Zeitschrift* 213: 577-638.

Kater, Michael H. 1974. *Das "Ahnenerbe" der SS 1935-1945. Ein Beitrag zur Kulturpolitik des Dritten Reiches*. Stuttgart.

Kater, Michael H. 1975. *Studentenschaft und Rechtsradikalismus in Deutschland 1918-1933. Eine sozialgeschichtliche Studie zur Bildungskrise in der Weimarer Republik*. Hamburg.

Kater, Michael H. 1981. "Die nationalsozialistische Machtergreifung an den deutschen Hochschulen. Zum politischen Verhalten akademischer Lehrer bis 1939." In Vogel, Simon and Podlech 1981: 49-75.

Kater, Michael H. 1984. "Die Studenten auf dem Weg in den Nationalsozialismus." In Tröger 1984: 26-37.

Kinkelin, Wilhelm. 1939. "Der Bauernhof als Gesittungsgrundlage des Volkes." In Kulke 1939: 9-16.

Klagges, Dietrich. 1939. "Zum deutschen Volkskundetag in Braunschweig." In Thiele 1939: 10-13.

Klemperer, Victor. 1987. LTI. *Notizbuch eines Philologen*. Röderberg-Taschenbuch. Vol. 35. Fourth Edition. Köln.

Klessman, Christoph. 1985. "Osteuropaforschung und Lebensraumpolitik im Dritten Reich." In Lundgreen 1985: 350-383.

Kley, Hans. 1937. "Errichtung einer Arbeitsgemeinschaft für deutsche Volkskunde." *Nationalsozialistische Monatshefte* 8, Heft 83: 164.

Knoch, Peter; and Thomas Leeb (eds.). 1984. *Heimat oder Region? Grundzüge einer Didaktik der Regionalgeschichte*. Geschichte lehren und lernen. Frankfurt am Main, Berlin and München.

Kogon, Eugen. 1989. *Der SS-Staat. Das System der deutschen Konzentrationslager*. Heyne Sachbuch. Vol. 19/9. München.

Kohlmann, Theodor; and Hermann Bausinger (eds.). 1985. *Großstadt. Aspekte empirischer Kulturforschung. 24. Deutscher Volkskunde-Kongress in Berlin vom 26. bis 30. September 1983*. Staatliche Museen Preussischer Kulturbesitz. Schriften des Museums für Deutsche Volkskunde Berlin. Vol. 13. Berlin.

Könenkamp, Wolf-Dieter. 1988a. "Volkskunde und Statistik. Eine wissenschaftsgeschichtliche Korrektur." *Zeitschrift für Volkskunde* 84: 1-25.

Könenkamp, Wolf-Dieter. 1988b. "Natur und Nationalcharakter. Die Entwicklung der Ethnographie und die frühe Volkskunde." *Ethnologia Europaea* 18: 25-52.

Konopath, Marie Adelheid. 1930. "Neunter Bundestag der 'Adler und Falken' in Koblenz." *Die Sonne* 7: 425-426.

Koren, Hanns. 1936. *Volkskunde als gläubige Wissenschaft*. Second Edition. Texte und Arbeiten zur religiösen Volkskunde. Vol. 1. Salzburg and Leipzig.

Korff, Gottfried. 1971. "Bemerkungen zur Arbeitervolkskunde." *Tübinger Korrespondenzblatt* 2: 3-8.

Korff, Gottfried. 1978. "Didaktik des Alltags. Hinweise zur Geschichte der Bildungskonzeption kulturhistorischer Museen." In Kuhn and Schneider 1978: 32-48.

Köstlin, Konrad. 1973. "Relikte: Die Gleichzeitigkeit des Ungleichzeitigen." *Kieler Blätter zur Volkskunde* 5: 135-157.

Köstlin, Konrad; Rosemarie Pohl-Weber; and Rainer Alsheimer (eds.). 1987. *Kinderkultur. 25. Deutscher Volkskundekongreß in Bremen vom 7. bis 12. Oktober 1985*. Hefte des Focke-Museums. Vol. 73. Bremen.

Krause, Wolfgang. 1935. Comment to Weigel 1935. *Historische Zeitschrift* 52: 552-556.

Kriss, Rudolf. 1948. *Im Zeichen des Ungeistes. Erinnerungen an die Jahre 1933-1945*. München-Pasing.

Krömer, Wolfram; and Osmund Menghin (eds.). 1983. *Die Geisteswissenschaften stellen sich vor*. Veröffentlichungen der Universität Innsbruck. Vol. 137. Innsbruck.

Kuczynski, Jürgen. 1982a. *Geschichte des Alltags des deutschen Volkes*. Vol. 5: 1918-1945. Köln.

Kuczynski, Jürgen. 1982b. "Die faschistische Diktatur." In Kuczynski 1982a; 48-85.

Kuczynski, Jürgen. 1982c. "Terror und Ideologien." In Kuczynski 1982a: 78-85.

Kuhn, Annette; and Gerhard Schneider (eds.) 1978. *Geschichte lernen im Museum*. Geschichtsdidaktik. Vol.4. Düsseldorf.

Kuhn, Walter. 1982. "Eine Jugend für die Sprachinselforschung. Erinnerungen." *Jahrbuch der Schlesischen Friedrich-Wilhelms-Universität zu Breslau* 23: 225-278.

Kulke, Erich. 1938a. "Haus und Hof des deutschen Bauern." In Lindner, Kulke and Gutsmiedl (1938): 7-11.

Kulke, Erich. 1938b. "Das neue, heimatgebundene Bauen." In Lindner, Kulke and Gutsmiedl (1938): 216-231.

Kulke, Erich. 1938c. "Das Dorfhaus. Eine Zukunftsaufgabe des dörflichen Gemeinschaftslebens." *Odal* 7: 186-192 (einschließlich 8 Abbildungen).

Kulke, Erich. 1939a. "Die Arbeitsgrundlagen der 'Mittelstelle deutscher Bauernhof.' (Auszug aus dem am 17. März 1938 anläßlich der Bauernhofforschertagung gehaltenen Vortrag)." In Kulke 1939: 17-26.

Kulke, Erich. 1939b. "Bauernhofformen in der Mark Brandenburg." In Kulke 1939: 140-141.

Kulke, Erich. 1939c. "Die Laubenhäuser des Oderranddorfes Zäckerick." In Kulke 1939: 142-153.

Kulke, Erich. 1939d. "Vorwort." In Kulke 1939: 7.

Kulke, Erich. 1939e. *Die Laube als ostgermanisches Baumerkmal unter besonderer Berücksichtigung der Bauernhöfe an der unteren Oder.* Deutsche Volkskunde. Schriftenreihe der Arbeitsgemeinschaft für Deutsche Volkskunde. Gruppe: Haus und Hof. München: Hoheneichen-Verlag.

Kulke, Erich. 1939f. "Baupflege gegen Landflucht. Zur 2. Reichsarbeitstagung der 'Mittelstelle deutscher Bauernhof.'" *Neues Bauerntum* 31: 102-103.

Kulke, Erich. (1941a.) *Die Land-Baufibel.* Ed by Arbeitskreis Baugestaltung in der Fachgruppe Bauwesen des NSBDT mit der Arbeitsgemeinschaft Heimat und Haus und dem Reichsamt für das Landvolk. München and Berlin: Verlag Georg D.W. Callwey/Alfred Metzner Verlag, n.d.

Kulke, Erich. 1941b. "Deutsches Siedlungsgut im Osten." *Odal* 10: 125-129.

Kulke, Erich (ed.). (1939). *Vom deutschen Bauernhof. Vorträge der ersten Arbeitstagung der "Mittelstelle deutscher Bauernhof" in der Arbeitsgemeinschaft für Deutsche Volkskunde.* Deutsche Volkskunde. Schriftenreihe der Arbeitsgemeinschaft für Deutsche Volkskunde. Gruppe: Haus und Hof. München: Hoheneichen-Verlag, n.d.

Kummer, Bernhard. 1935. *Midgards Untergang. Germanischer Kult und Glaube in den letzten heidnischen Jahrhunderten.* Leipzig.

Künneth, Walter. 1935. *Antwort auf den Mythus. Die Entscheidung zwischen dem nordischen Mythus und dem biblischen Christus.* Third Edition. Berlin.

Künneth, Walter. 1947. Der große Abfall. *Eine geschichtstheologische Untersuchung der Begegnung zwischen Nationalsozialismus und Christentum.* Hamburg.

Künzig, Johannes. 1933. "Deutsche Volkskunde und Nationalerziehung." *Der Alemanne* Nr. 311 A vom 8.11.1933: 6.

Künzig, Johannes. 1934. "Verzeichnis der von John Meier 1886-1934 veröffentlichten Schriften." In Seemann and Schewe 1934: 307-314.

L., H. 1937. "2. Nordischer wissenschaftlicher Kongreß 'Tracht und Schmuck' in Lübeck 30. August bis 4. September 1937." *Rasse* 4: 438-439.

Lauffer, Otto. 1920. *Deutsche Sitte.* Deutschkundliche Bücherei. Leipzig.

Lauffer, Otto. 1926. "Die Entwicklungsstufen der germanischen Kultur. Umwelt und Volksbrauch in altgermanischer Zeit." In Nollau 1926: 17-155.

Lauffer, Otto. 1934. "Die Volkskunde und der deutsche Osten." *Geistige Arbeit* 1/No. 6: 1-3.

Lauterbach, Burkhart. 1986. "Schlußgedanken: Ungereimtheiten - Fragen." In Volkskunde im Dritten Reich 1986: 37-39.

Lehmann, Albrecht; and Andreas Kuntz (eds.). 1988. *Sichtweisen der Volkskunde. Zur Geschichte und Forschungspraxis einer Disziplin. Gerhard Lutz zum 60. Geburtstag.* Lebensformen. Vol. 3. Berlin and Hamburg.

Lehmann, Emil. 1937. "Tracht und Schmuck (Der zweite Nordische wissenschaftliche Kongreß in Lübeck 1937)." *Mitteldeutsche Blätter für Volkskunde* 12: 224-228.

Lehmann, Siegfried. 1938. "Sinnbild an Tracht und Schmuck." In Thiele 1938: 192-200.

Lindner, Werner. 1938. "Heimatpflege." In Lindner, Kulke and Gutsmiedl (1938): 25-89.

Lindner, Werner; Erich Kulke and Franz Gutsmiedl (eds.). (1938). *Das Dorf. Seine Pflege und Gestaltung.* Die landschaftlichen Grundlagen des deutschen Bauschaffens. Buchreihe der Arbeitsgemeinschaft Heimat und Haus. Vol. 1. München.

Lipp, Wolfgang (ed.). 1984. *Industriegesellschaft und Regionalkultur.* Schriftenreihe der Hochschule für Politik München. Vol. 6. Köln, Berlin, Bonn and München.

Lixfeld, Hannjost. 1987a. "Die Deutsche Forschungsgemeinschaft und die Dachverbände der deutschen Volkskunde im Dritten Reich." In Gerndt 1987: 69-82.

Lixfeld, Hannjost. 1987b. "Matthes Ziegler und die Erzählforschung des Amts Rosenberg. Ein Beitrag zur Ideologie der nationalsozialistischen Volkskunde." *Rheinisches Jahrbuch für Volkskunde* 26 [1985/1986; erschienen 1987]: 37-59.

Lixfeld, Hannjost. 1989. "John Meier und sein 'Reichsinstitut für deutsche Volkskunde.' Zur volkskundlichen Fachgeschichte zwischen Monarchie und Faschismus." *Beiträge zur Volkskunde in Baden-Württemberg* 3: 102-144.

Lixfeld, Hannjost. 1991. "The *Deutsche Forschungsgemeinschaft* and the Umbrella Organizations of German *Volkskunde* during the Third Reich." *Asian Folklore Studies* L-1: 95-116.

Lorenzen, Hans. 1942. "Zur bolschewistischen Volkskunde." *Deutsche Volkskunde* 4: 51-53.

Losemann, Volker. 1977a. *Nationalsozialismus und Antike. Studien zur Entwicklung des Faches Alte Geschichte 1933-1945.* Historische Perspektiven. Vol. 7. First Edition. Hamburg.

Losemann, Volker. 1977b. "Richard Harder und die 'Hohe Schule' Alfred Rosenbergs." In Losemann 1977a: 139-174.

Losemann, Volker. 1980. "Programme deutscher Althistoriker in der Machtergreifungsphase." *Quaderni di Storia* 11: 35-105.

Lundgreen, Peter (ed.). 1985. *Wissenschaft im Dritten Reich.* Edition Suhrkamp. Vol. 1306. Frankfurt am Main.

Lüthi, Max. 1979. *Märchen.* Seventh Edition. Sammlung Metzler. Vol. 16. Stuttgart.

Lutz, Gerhard. 1983. "Das Amt Rosenberg und die Volkskunde." In Brückner and Beitl 1983: 161-171.

Lutz, Gerhard (ed.). 1958. *Volkskunde. Ein Handbuch zur Geschichte ihrer Probleme.* Berlin.

Mackensen, Lutz. 1937a. *Volkskunde in der Entscheidung. Versuch einer Standortbestimmung.* Philosophie und Geschichte. Eine Sammlung von Vorträgen und Schriften aus dem Gebiet der Philosophie und Geschichte. Vol. 63. Tübingen.

Mackensen, Lutz. 1937b. *Volkskunde der deutschen Frühzeit.* Leipzig.

Mackensen, Lutz. 1937c. Review of Kaiser 1936. *Folk* 1: 224-225.

Mackensen, Lutz (ed.). 1930-1933. *Handwörterbuch des deutschen Märchens.* Herausgegeben unter besonderer Mitwirkung von Johannes Bolte und Mitarbeit zahlreicher Fachgenossen. Vol. 1. Handwörterbücher zur deutschen Volkskunde, Abteilung II, Märchen. Berlin and Leipzig.

Mackensen, Lutz (ed.). 1934-1940. *Handwörterbuch des deutschen Märchens*. Herausgegeben unter Mitarbeit zahlreicher Fachgenossen. Vol. 2. Handwörterbücher zur deutschen Volkskunde, Abteilung II, Märchen. Berlin.

Markmiller, Fritz. 1984. "Beobachtungen zum Fest- und Brauchwesen während der NS-Zeit. Teil 1: Dokumentation des Fallbeispiels Stadt Dingolfing und Umgebung im Jahr 1933. Aufgrund und im Spiegel der Lokalpresse." *Der Storchenturm. Geschichtsblätter für die Landkreise um Dingolfing, Landau und Vilsbiburg* 19, Heft 38: 1-114.

Markmiller, Fritz. 1986/1987. "Beobachtungen zum Fest- und Brauchwesen während der NS-Zeit. Teil 2: Fest- und Feiergestaltung während der NS-Zeit. Im Spiegel der Lokalpresse Dingolfing 1933-1937. *Der Storchenturm. Geschichtsblätter für die Landkreise um Dingolfing, Landau und Vilsbiburg* 21/22, Doppelheft 42/43: 1-262.

Martin, Peter. 1983. "Volkskundliches im Reichsberufswettkampf der deutschen Studenten 1935-1941." In Brückner and Beitl 1983: 174-188.

Meier, John. 1926. "Goethe, Freiherr vom Stein und die deutsche Volkskunde. Vergangenheit, Gegenwart und Zukunft." *Mitteilungen der Akademie zur wissenschaftlichen Erforschung und zur Pflege des Deutschtums/ Deutsche Akademie* 4: 129-144.

Meier, John. 1928a. "Wege und Ziele der deutschen Volkskundeforschung." In Deutsche Forschung 1928a: 7-35.

Meier, John. 1928b. "Wege und Ziele der deutschen Volkskundeforschung." In Deutsche Forschung 1928b: 15-43.

Meier, John. 1940. "Volksliedsammlung und Volksliedforschung in Deutschland." *Deutsche Kultur im Leben der Völker* 15: 190-210.

Meier, John. 1947. *Der Verband deutscher Vereine für Volkskunde. Sein Werden und Wirken 1904-1944*. Lahr (Baden).

Meier, John. 1958. "Wege und Ziele der deutschen Volkskundeforschung." In Lutz 1958: 180-185.

Meier, John (ed.). 1927. *Nordische Volkskundeforschung. Vier Vorträge von Kaarle Krohn, Reidar Th. Christiansen, C.W. von Sydow, Henrik Ussing*. Im Auftrage des Verbandes deutscher Vereine für Volkskunde herausgegeben. Leipzig.

Metzner, Erwin. 1934. *Die deutschen Vornamen. Mit einem Vorwort von Reichsbauernführer Walther Darré*. Goslar: Blut und Boden Verlag.

Metzner, Erwin. 1939. *Die deutschen Vornamen. Mit einem Vorwort von Reichsbauernführer Walther Darré*. Second Edition. Goslar: Blut und Boden Verlag.

Mieder, Wolfgang. 1982. "Proverbs in Nazi Germany. The Promulgation of Anti-Semitism and Stereotypes through Folklore." *Journal of American Folklore* 95: 435-464.

Mitteilungen der Akademie. Mitteilungen der Akademie zur wissenschaftlichen Erforschung und zur Pflege des Deutschtums/ Deutsche Akademie. München: Verlag Dr. C. Wolf & Sohn. 1. Jahrgang 1929 - 12. Jahrgang 1937.

Mitteilungen der Volkskundekommission. 1930-1933. *Mitteilungen der Volks-kundekommission* (Notgemeinschaft der Deutschen Wissenschaft - Deutsche Gemeinschaft zur Erhaltung und Förderung der Forschung) 1-4. Berlin.

Mitteilungen des Atlas der deutschen Volkskunde. 1935. *Mitteilungen des Atlas der deutschen Volkskunde zum V. Fragebogen*. Deutsche Forschungsgemein-schaft - Notgemeinschaft der Deutschen Wissenschaft 5. Berlin.

Mitteilungen des Verbandes. 1928-1952. *Mitteilungen des Verbandes deutscher Vereine für Volkskunde* 37-60. Freiburg im Breisgau.

Mohr, Klaus. 1986. "Der deutsche Arbeiter: 'Pfeiler des Volkstums' oder 'Biologischer Flugsand.' Der Betrag der Volkskunde zur NS-Arbeiterpoli-tik." In Volkskunde im Dritten Reich 1986: 26-30.

Mohrmann, Ute. 1989. Review of Gerndt 1987. *Jahrbuch für Volkskunde und Kulturgeschichte* 32: 223-227.

Moser, Josef. 1989. "Arbeit im Faschismus.   Aspekte nationalsozialistischer Herrschaft in der industriellen Arbeitswelt unter besonderer Berücksichti-gung Oberösterreichs." In Bockhorn, Eberhart and Zupfer 1989: 247-274.

Moser-Rath, Elfriede. 1981. "Märcheninterpretation im Dritten Reich." In Ranke 1981: 551-553.

Moser-Rath, Elfriede. 1985a. "Zum Gedenken an Prof. Dr. Kurt Ranke." *Österreichische Zeitschrift für Volkskunde* 88: 271-272.

Moser-Rath, Elfriede. 1985b. "Zum Gedenken an Kurt Ranke." *Fabula* 26: 1-2.

Moser-Rath, Elfriede. 1985c. "Karl Haiding (1906-1985)." *Fabula* 26: 342-343.

Mudrak, Edmund. 1938a. "Deutsche Volkskunde - eine politische Wissenschaft." In Spieß and Mudrak 1938: 3-11.

Mudrak, Edmund. 1938b. "Deutsche Volkskunde - eine politische Wissenschaft." *Geist der Zeit* 16: 371-379.

Mudrak, Edmund. 1939a. *Die deutsche Heldensage*. Jahrbuch für historische Volkskunde. Vol. 7. Berlin.

Mudrak, Edmund. 1942a. Comment to Viergutz 1942. *Deutsche Volkskunde* 4: 143-144.

Müller, Hans. 1963. *Katholische Kirche und Nationalsozialismus. Dokumente 1930-1935. Mit einer Einleitung von Kurt Sontheimer*. München.

Müller, Heinrich. 1938a. "Das deutsche Volkstum im Angriff der Katholischen Aktion der Gegenwart." *Nationalsozialistische Monatshefte* 9, Heft 95: 98-112.

Müller, Heinrich. 1938b. "Die katholische Aktion in der praktischen Volkstums-arbeit." *Nationalsozialistische Monatshefte* 9, Heft 105: 1094-1095.

Muller, Jerry Z. 1986. "Enttäuschung und Zweideutigkeit. Zur Geschichte rechter Sozialwissenschaftler im 'Dritten Reich'." *Geschichte und Gesellschaft* 12: 289-316.

Myrdal, Gunnar. 1971. *Objektivität in der Sozialforschung*. Edition Suhrkamp. Vol. 508. Frankfurt am Main.

Nationalsozialismus im Landkreis Tübingen. 1988. *Nationalsozialismus im Landkreis Tübingen. Eine Heimatkunde*. Ed. by Projektgruppe "Heimatkun-de des Nationalsozialismus." Ludwig-Uhland-Institut für Empirische Kulturwissenschaft der Universität Tübingen. Tübingen: Tübinger Ver-einigung für Volkskunde.

Nationalsozialismus und die deutsche Universität. 1966. *Nationalsozialismus und die deutsche Universität. Universitätstage 1966.* Veröffentlichung der Freien Universität Berlin. Berlin.

Nationalsozialistische Bibliographie. 1936-1943. *Nationalsozialistische Bibliographie. Monatshefte der Parteiamtlichen Prüfungskommission zum Schutze des Ns. Schrifttums.* Reichsleiter Philipp Bouhler (ed.). Berlin: Zentralverlag der NSDAP., Franz Eher Nachf. GmbH. Jahrgang 1 - Jahrgang 8.

Naumann, Hans. 1921. *Primitive Gemeinschaftskultur. Beiträge zur Volkskunde und Mythologie.* Jena.

Naumann, Hans. 1922. *Grundzüge der deutschen Volkskunde.* Wissenschaft und Bildung. Einzeldarstellungen aus allen Gebieten des Wissens. Vol.181. Leipzig.

Naumann, Hans. 1929. *Grundzüge der deutschen Volkskunde.* Second edition. Leipzig.

Naumann, Hans. 1932. *Deutsche Nation in Gefahr.* Stuttgart.

Naumann, Hans. 1935a. *Deutsche Volkskunde in Grundzügen.* Third Edition. Leipzig.

Naumann, Hans. 1935b. "Der germanisch-deutsche Mensch des frühen Mittelalters." In Der deutsche Mensch 1935: 9-34.

Neumeister, Andreas. 1986. "'Der neue deutsche Lehrer will die Jugend ganz!' (Freudenthal). Der Beitrag der Volkskunde zur nationalpolitischen Schulerziehung." In Volkskunde im Dritten Reich 1986: 10-16.

Neuss, Wilhelm. 1947. *Kampf gegen den Mythus des 20. Jahrhunderts. Ein Gedenkblatt an Clemens August Kardinal Graf Galen.* Dokumente zur Zeitgeschichte. Vol.4. Neuss.

Nierhaus, Rolf. 1940. "Abschied vom 'Königssprung.'" *Volk und Vorzeit. Volkstümliche Hefte für oberrheinische Ur- und Frühgeschichte* 2: 87-89.

Nollau, Hermann (ed.). 1926. *Germanische Wiedererstehung. Ein Werk über die germanischen Grundlagen unserer Gesittung.* Unter Mitwirkung von Klaudius Bojunga, Albrecht Haupt, Karl Helm, Andreas Heusler, Otto Lauffer, Friedrich von der Leyen, Josef Müller-Blattau, Claudius Freiherr von Schwerin. Heidelberg.

Oesterle, Angelika. 1988. *John Meier - Eine Biographie im Schatten des Nationalsozialismus.* Maschinenschriftliche Magisterarbeit. Tübingen: Ludwig-Uhland-Institut für empirische Kulturwissenschaft.

Oesterle, Anka. 1987. "John Meier und das SS-Ahnenerbe." In Gerndt 1987: 83-93.

Oestele, Anka. 1991. "Letzte Autonomieversuche: Der Volkskundler John Meier. Strategie und Taktik des Verbandes deutscher Vereine für Volkskunde 1933-1945." In John, Martin, Mück and Ott 1991: 151-162.

Orend, Misch. 1938a. "Der Schmuck der Siebenbürger Sachsen." In Thiele 1938: 166-184.

Ott, Hugo. 1985. "Martin Heidegger und die Universität Freiburg nach 1945. Ein Beispiel für die Auseinandersetzung mit der politischen Vergangenheit." *Historisches Jahrbuch im Auftrag der Görres-Gesellschaft* 105: 95-128.

Ott, Hugo. 1987. "Alfred Rosenbergs Großkundgebung auf dem Freiburger Münsterplatz am 16. Oktober 1937. Ein Beitrag zum nationalsozialistischen Alltag." *Freiburger Diözesan-Archiv* 107 /3. Folge: 39: 303-319.

Ott, Hugo. 1988a. "Universitäten und Hochschulen." In Borst 1988: 137-148.

Ottnad, Bernd (ed.). 1982-1987. *Badische Biographien*. Neue Folge. Im Auftrag der Kommission für geschichtliche Landeskunde in Baden-Württemberg herausgegeben. Vol. 1-2. Stuttgart.

Pesendorfer, Gertrud. 1940. "Zur Trachtenarbeit." *Deutsche Volkskunde* 2: 90-97. 4 Abbildungen.

Peßler, Wilhelm. 1927. *Das Heimat-Museum im deutschen Sprachgebiet als Spiegel deutscher Kultur*. München.

Peßler, Wilhelm. 1934a. "Der Volkskunde Wert und Wesen, Wirkung und Weite." In Peßler 1934-1938. Vol. 1: 3-7.

Peßler, Wilhelm. 1937. "Das niedersächsische Bauernhaus, ein Denkmal germanischer Kultur." In Thiele 1937: 52-57.

Peßler, Wilhelm. 1938. "Von den neuen Räumen des Niedersächsischen Volkstumsmuseums der Hauptstadt Hannover." *Die Kunde* 6: 166-172.

Peßler, Wilhelm (ed.). 1934-1938. *Handbuch der deutschen Volkskunde*. Vol.1-3. Potsdam.

Petzold, Joachim. 1978. *Konservative Theoretiker des deutschen Faschismus. Jungkonservative Ideologen in der Weimarer Republik als geistige Wegbereiter der faschistischen Diktatur*. Berlin.

Petzold, Joachim. 1982a. *Die Demagogie des Hitlerfaschismus. Die politische Funktion der Naziideologie auf dem Wege zur faschistischen Diktatur*. Berlin.

Petzold, Joachim. 1982b. "Alfred Rosenbergs 'Mythus des 20. Jahrhunderts.'" In Petzold 1982a: 192-216.

Peuckert, Will-Erich. 1931. *Volkskunde des Proletariats. I. Aufgang der proletarischen Kultur*. Schriften des Volkskundlichen Seminars der Pädagogischen Akademie Breslau. Vol. 1. Frankfurt am Main.

Peuckert, Will-Erich. 1931/1932. "Jude, Jüdin." In Bächthold-Stäubli and Hoffmann-Krayer 1927-1942. Vol. 6: 809.

Peuckert, Will-Erich. 1948. "Zur Situation der Volkskunde." *Die Nachbarn. Jahrbuch für vergleichende Volkskunde* 1: 130-135.

Pfister, Friedrich. 1940. "Bild und Sinnbild." In Herrmann and Treutlein 1940: 34-49.

Phleps, Hermann. 1937. "Handwerk und Hausbau." In Thiele 1937: 77-91.

Plaßmann, Joseph Otto. 1938a. "Deutschösterreichs germanische Sendung." *Germanien* 10: 99-102.

Plaßmann, Joseph Otto. 1938b. "Der Schmuck im nordischen Volksglauben." In Thiele 1938: 201-211.

Plaßmann, Joseph Otto. (1939). "Germanenkunde als europäischer Beitrag." In Salzburger Wissenschaftswochen 1939: 3 Seiten ohne Seitenzählung.

Plaßmann, Joseph Otto; and Gilbert Trathnigg. 1939a. "Vorwort." In Plaßmann and Trathnigg 1939: 7-8.

Plaßmann, Joseph Otto; and Gilbert Trathnigg (eds.). 1939. *Deutsches Land kehrt heim. Ostmark und Sudetenland als germanischer Volksboden.* Deutsches Ahnenerbe. Reihe C: Volkstümliche Schriften. Vol. 3. Berlin.

Poliakov, Léon; and Joseph Wulf. 1983. *Das Dritte Reich und seine Denker.* Ullstein Buch. Vol. 33038. Frankfurt am Main, Berlin, Wien.

Ponti, Zita. 1950. *Critical Analysis of the Implementation of Rosenbergian National Socialism in the Field of the History of Culture by Professor Hans Naumann.* Ph.D. dissertation. University of Maryland.

Populus revisus. 1966. *Populus revisus. Beiträge zur Erforschung der Gegenwart.* Volksleben. Vol. 14. Tübingen.

Prütting, Hildegunde. 1986. "Die Zerstörung des volkskundlichen Seminars. Zwei kommentierte Briefe vom Juli 1944." In Gilch, Schramka and Prütting 1986: 65-76.

Ranke, Friedrich. 1936. "Märchenforschung. Ein Literaturbericht (1920-1934)." *Deutsche Vierteljahrsschrift für Literaturwissenschaft und Geistesgeschichte* 14: 246-304.

Ranke, Kurt. 1938. *Auszug aus 'Indogermanische Totenverehrung.'* Bd.1: *Der dreißigste Tag im Totenkult der Indogermanen.* Kiel.

Ranke, Kurt. 1939. "Der dreißigste Tag im Totenkult der Indogermanen." *Zeitschrift für Deutschkunde* 53: 5-17.

Ranke, Kurt. 1944. "Die Toten in Recht und Brauch der Lebenden." In Jankuhn 1944: 35-44.

Ranke, Kurt. 1951. *Indogermanische Totenverehrung.* Bd.1: *Der dreißigste und vierzigste Tag im Totenkult der Indogermanen.* Folklore Fellows Communications. Vol. 140. Helsinki.

Ranke, Kurt (ed.). 1981. *Enzyklopädie des Märchens. Handwörterbuch zur historischen und vergleichenden Erzählforschung.* Vol. 3. Berlin and New York.

Redlich, Friedrich Alexander. 1942. "Volkskunst und Brauchtum der Völker im Ostland." *Nationalsozialistische Monatshefte* 13, Heft 142: 40-45.

Reif, Sieglinde. 1986. "Irrationales Argumentieren. Das Beispiel nationalsozialistischer Sinnbildforschung." In Volkskunde im Dritten Reich 1986: 4-9.

Reimann, Bruno W. 1984. "Die 'Selbstgleichschaltung' der Universitäten 1933." In Tröger 1984: 38-52.

Reimers, Karl Friedrich. 1979. "Der Reichsparteitag als Instrument totaler Propaganda. Appell, Feier, Kult, Magie." *Zeitschrift für Volkskunde* 75: 216-228.

Reimers, Karl Friedrich. 1987. "'Hände am Werk - ein Lied von deutscher Arbeit' (1935). Volkskundliche 'Ästhetikreferenzen' im nationalsozialistischen Dokumentarfilm. Ein Hinweis." In Gerndt 1987: 219-224.

Reinerth, Hans. 1932a. "Die deutsche Vorgeschichte im Dritten Reich." *Nationalsozialistische Monatshefte* 3, Heft 27: 256-259.

Reinerth, Hans. 1932b. "Gustav Kossinna †." *Nationalsozialistische Monatshefte* 3, Heft 27: 259-261.

Reinerth, Hans (ed.). 1937. *Haus und Hof der Germanen in vor- und frühgeschichtlicher Zeit.* Haus und Hof im nordischen Raum. Im Auftrage der Nordischen Gesellschaft ed. by Alexander Funkenberg. Vol.1. Leipzig.

Reischle, Hermann. 1936. "Volkstum als Erbe. Vortrag auf der Reichstagung der NS-Kulturgemeinde München." *Nationalsozialistische Monatshefte* 7, Heft 77: 683-694.

Reischle, Hermann. 1939a. "Das germanische Erbe im deutschen Bauerntum." In Thiele 1939: 14-33.

Riehl, Wilhelm Heinrich. 1958. "Die Volkskunde als Wissenschaft." In Lutz 1958: 23-37.

Riehl, Wilhelm Heinrich; and Adolf Spamer. 1935. *Die Volkskunde als Wissenschaft. Mit einem Verlagsbericht: "Zwölf Jahre Arbeit für die deutsche Volkskunde" und einem Anhang: "Der Wilhelm-Heinrich-Riehl-Preis der Deutschen Volkskunde."* Berlin and Leipzig.

Ringer, Fritz K. 1969. *The Decline of the German Mandarins. The German Academic Community, 1890-1933.* Cambridge, Mass.: Harvard University Press.

Ringer, Fritz K. 1983. *Die Gelehrten. Der Niedergang der deutschen Mandarine 1890-1933.* Stuttgart.

Ringshausen, Friedrich. 1938. "Geleitwort." *Volk und Scholle* 16: 1.

Ritz, Joseph Maria. 1953. "Adolf Spamer (1883-1953)." *Zeitschrift für Volkskunde* 50: 303-305.

Röhr, Erich. 1938. "Das Schrifttum über den Atlas der deutschen Volkskunde (Von der Aussendung der ersten Fragebogen bis zum Erscheinen der ersten Kartenlieferung)." *Zeitschrift für Volkskunde* 47: 52-86.

Röhr, Erich. 1939. "Deutsche Volkskunstforschung. Zum Schrifttum der Jahre 1937 und 1938." *Zeitschrift für Volkskunde* 48: 228-232.

Röhrich, Lutz. 1973. *Lexikon der sprichwörtlichen Redensarten.* Vol.1-2. Freiburg, Basel and Wien.

Rosenberg, Alfred. 1930a. *Wege, Grundsätze und Ziele der NSDAP. Das Programm der Bewegung, erweitert durch das Agrarprogramm.* München.

Rosenberg, Alfred. 1932. *Der Mythus des 20. Jahrhunderts. Eine Wertung der seelisch-geistigen Gestaltenkämpfe unserer Zeit.* Fourth edition. München.

Rosenberg, Alfred. 1934a. *Der Mythus des 20. Jahrhunderts. Eine Wertung der seelisch-geistigen Gestaltenkämpfe unserer Zeit.* 27.-28. Auflage. München.

Rosenberg, Alfred. 1935a. *Der Bolschewismus als Aktion einer fremden Rasse.* München.

Rosenberg, Alfred. 1935b. "Freiheit der Wissenschaft." *Volk im Werden* 3: 69-80.

Rosenberg, Alfred. 1937a. *Pest in Rußland. Der Bolschewismus, seine Häupter, Handlanger und Opfer.* Gekürzte Ausgabe. Georg Leibbrandt (ed.). München.

Rosenberg, Alfred. 1937b. "Die Freiheit der wissenschaftlichen Forschung." *Die Sonne* 14: 284-286.

Rosenberg, Alfred. 1938a. *Der Kampf um die Freiheit der Forschung.* Schriften der Hallischen Wissenschaftlichen Gesellschaft. Vol. 1. Halle/Saale.

Rosenberg, Alfred. 1939a. "Zum Geleit." *Deutsche Volkskunde* 1: 3.

Rosenberg, Alfred. 1939b. "Die Hohe Schule am Chiemsee." *Die Kunst im Dritten Reich* 3: 17-19.

Rosenberg, Alfred (ed.). 1940. *Handbuch der Romfrage. Unter Mitwirkung einer Arbeitsgemeinschaft von Forschern und Politikern.* Vol. 1. A-K. München.

Roth, Martin. 1987. "Heimatmuseum und nationalpolitische Erziehung." In Gerndt 1987: 185-199.

Roth, Martin. 1989. "Xenophobie und Rassismus in Museen und Ausstellungen." *Zeitschrift für Volkskunde* 85: 48-66.

Rothert, L. 1937. "2. Nordischer Wissenschaftlicher Kongreß 'Tracht und Schmuck' in Lübeck vom 30. August bis 4. September 1937." *Germanen-Erbe* 2: 292-296.

Rothfeder, Herbert Phillips. 1963. *A Study of Alfred Rosenberg's Organisation for National Socialist Ideology.* Ph.D. Thesis Michigan (Microfilm).

Rüdiger, Karlheinz. 1938a. "Die fünfte Reichstagung für deutsche Vorgeschichte." *Nationalsozialistische Monatshefte* 9, Heft 104: 1011-1012.

Rüdiger, Karlheinz. 1938b. "Der erste nationalsozialistische deutsche Volks-kundetag in Braunschweig." *Nationalsozialistische Monatshefte* 9, Heft 104: 1012-1013.

Rüdiger, Karlheinz. 1939a. "Politische Wissenschaft im Aufbau. Zum Ausbau des Hoheneichen-Verlages als weltanschaulich-wissenschaftlicher Verlag der NSDAP." *Nationalsozialistische Monatshefte* 10, Heft 113: 722-724.

Rüdiger, Karlheinz. 1939b. "Institut der NSDAP zur Erforschung der Judenfrage." *Nationalsozialistische Monatshefte* 10, Heft 114: 74.

Ruprecht, Karl. 1937a. "Deutsches Volkstum und konfessionelle Volkskunde." *Nationalsozialistische Monatshefte* 8, Heft 92: 962-969.

Ruprecht, Karl. 1937b. "Nationalsozialistische oder liberale Volkskunde?" *Nationalsozialistische Monatshefte* 8, Heft 88: 632-634.

Ruprecht, Karl. 1943a. "Bolschewismus und Volkstum im Spiegel der 'Sowjetlo-re.'" *Deutsche Volkskunde* 5: 1-4.

Ruprecht, Karl. 1943b. "Bolschewismus und Volkskultur." *Nationalsozialistische Monatshefte* 14, Heft 158: 370-376.

Salzburger Wissenschaftswochen. 1939. *Salzburger Wissenschaftswochen 23. August bis 2. September 1939. Veranstaltet vom Reichsministerium für Wissenschaft, Erziehung und Volksbildung sowie von der Forschungs- und Lehrgemeinschaft "Das Ahnenerbe." Festschrift. Verzeichnis der Vorlesungen. Verzeichnis der Dozenten.* Ed. by Generalsekretariat der "Salzburger Wissenschaftswochen." Leipzig.

Scharf, Helmut. 1985. "Die Feldherrnhalle in München. Ein Beitrag zur Rezeption durch die Nationalsozialisten." In Schuchard and Claussen 1985: 151-156.

Scharfe, Martin. 1984. "Einschwörung auf den völkisch-germanischen Kulturbe-griff." In Tröger 1984: 105-115.

Scharfe, Martin. 1986. "A Critique of the Canon." In Dow and Lixfeld 1986: 54-61.

Scharfe, Martin. 1987a. "Der Spiegel-'Analytiker' Wolfgang Brückner als Fachhistoriker? Eine Polemik gegen den Würzburger Polemiker." *Hessische Blätter für Volks- und Kulturforschung* 21: 146-148.

Scheel, Klaus. 1979. "Faschistische Kulturpropaganda im zweiten Weltkrieg. Ihr Einsatz zur Irreführung des deutschen Volkes während der ersten Kriegs-jahre (1939-1941)." *Jahrbuch für Volkskunde und Kulturgeschichte* 22: 99-119.

Scheffler, Jürgen. 1989. "'Lemgo, das Hexennest.' Folkloristik, NS-Vermarktung und lokale Geschichtsdarstellung." *Jahrbuch für Volkskunde* N.S. 12: 113-132.

Scheidt-Lämke, Dora. 1942. "Karl Kaiser zum Gedächtnis." *Deutsche Volkskunde* 4: 3-9.

Scheller, Thilo. 1939a. "Die Heimholung des Feuers. Ein neues Weihnachtsbrauchtum." *Deutsche Volkskunde* 1: 293-297.

Scheller, Thilo. 1939b. "Das nationalsozialistische Feierjahr." *Deutsche Volkskunde* 1: 155-157.

Scheller, Thilo; and Hans Strobel. 1939. "Gedanken zur Feiergestaltung." *Deutsche Volkskunde* 1: 16-19, 91-92.

Schenda, Rudolf. 1970. "Einheitlich - Urtümlich - Noch heute. Probleme der volkskundlichen Befragung." In Abschied 1970: 124-154.

Schenda, Rudolf. 1975. Review of Beitl and Beitl 1974. *Tribus* (Stuttgart) 24: 188-189.

Schewe, Harry. 1934. "Hochverehrter, lieber Herr Professor!" In Seemann and Schewe 1934: III-V.

Schier, Barbara. 1988. "Volkskundliche Verlage im Dritten Reich vor dem Hintergrund nationalsozialistischer Kulturpolitik." *Bayerisches Jahrbuch für Volkskunde* 1988: 138-173.

Schier, Barbara. 1990. "Hexenwahn und Hexenverfolgung. Rezeption und politische Zurichtung eines kulturwissenschaftlichen Themas im Dritten Reich. *Bayerisches Jahrbuch für Volkskunde 1990*: 43-115.

Schier, Bruno. 1932. *Hauslandschaften und Kulturbewegungen im östlichen Mitteleuropa.* Beiträge zur sudetendeutschen Volkskunde. Vol. 21. Reichenberg.

Schier, Bruno. 1934a. "Das deutsche Haus." In Spamer 1934-1935a. Vol. 1: 477-534.

Schier, Bruno. 1937a. "Die germanischen Grundlagen der deutschen Volkskultur." *Mitteilungen des Verbandes* 50, August 1937: 19-20.

Schier, Bruno. 1937b. "Vorgeschichtliche Elemente in den europäischen Volkstrachten." *Nationalsozialistische Monatshefte* 8, Heft 92: 985-995.

Schier, Bruno. 1937c. "Der germanische Einfluß auf den Hausbau Osteuropas." In Thiele 1937: 21-34.

Schier, Bruno. 1938a. "Vorgeschichtliche Elemente in den europäischen Volkstrachten." In Thiele 1938: 1-17.

Schier, Bruno. 1939a. "Die Gliederung der deutschen Haus- und Hofformen." In Kulke 1939: 27-44.

Schier, Bruno. 1939b. "Von der bäuerlichen Baukunst des Egerlandes." In Kulke 1939: 114-120.

Schier, Bruno. 1939c. "Germanisches Erbe in Siedlung und Hausbau." In Thiele 1939: 57-83.

Schindler, Norbert. 1984. "Spuren in der Geschichte der 'anderen' Zivilisation. Probleme und Perspektiven einer historischen Volkskulturforschung." In Dülmen and Schindler 1984: 13-77.

Schlicker, Wolfgang. 1977. "Die 'Akademie zur wissenschaftlichen Erforschung und Pflege des Deutschtums (Deutsche Akademie).' Eine Institution imperialistischer Auslandskulturpolitik in der Zeit der Weimarer Republik und des Faschismus." *Jahrbuch für Volkskunde und Kulturgeschichte* 20 (N.S. 5): 43-66.

Schmidt, Friedrich Heinz. 1954. "Der Verband der Vereine für Volkskunde bis 1954." In Fünfzig Jahre Verband 1954: 27-31.

Schmidt, Leopold. 1951. *Geschichte der österreichischen Volkskunde*. Buchreihe der Österreichischen Zeitschrift für Volkskunde. N.S.. Vol.2. Wien.

Schmidt, Leopold. 1957. "Karl Spieß †." *Österreichische Zeitschrift für Volkskunde* 60: 335-338.

Schmidt-Ebhausen, Friedrich-Heinz. 1963. *Forschungen zur Volkskunde im deutschen Südwesten*. Veröffentlichungen des Staatl. Amtes für Denkmalspflege Stuttgart. Reihe C: Volkskunde. Vol. 2. Stuttgart.

Schmitt, Heinz. 1987. "Theorie und Praxis der nationalsozialistischen Trachtenpflege." In Gerndt 1987: 205-213.

Schmitt, Heinz. 1988. *Volkstracht in Baden: Ihre Rolle in Kunst, Staat, Wirtschaft und Gesellschaft seit zwei Jahrhunderten*. Bildbände Heimatkunde/Landesgeschichte. Karlsruhe.

Schmook, Reinhard. 1983. *Anmerkungen zur Bedeutung Hans Naumanns und seiner Schriften in der Wissenschaftsgeschichte der deutschen Volkskunde*. Diplomarbeit. Humboldt-Universität zu Berlin, Sektion Geschichte, Fachrichtung Ethnographie. Maschinenschrift. Berlin (Ost).

Schmook, Reinhard. 1988. *Der Germanist Hans Naumann in seiner Bedeutung für die Volkskunde*. Ph. D. Thesis. Bereich Ethnographie der Humboldt-Universität zu Berlin. Berlin (Ost).

Schöck, Gustav. 1970. "Sammeln und Retten. Anmerkungen zu zwei Prinzipien volkskundlicher Empirie." In Abschied 1970: 85-104.

Schöck, Inge. 1978. *Hexenglaube in der Gegenwart. Empirische Untersuchungen in Südwestdeutschland*. Untersuchungen des Ludwig-Uhland-Instituts der Universität Tübingen. Vol. 45. Tübingen.

Scholze, Thomas. 1988. *Die Großstadt als Problemfeld volkskundlicher Gegenwartsforschung. Studien zur Wissenschaftsgeschichte der bürgerlich-deutschen Volkskunde im 20. Jahrhundert (1918-1988)*. Ph. D. Thesis. Bereich Ethnographie der Humboldt-Universität zu Berlin. Berlin (Ost).

Schramka, Carmen. 1986. "Mundartenkunde und Germanische Religionsgeschichte. Zur Tätigkeit von Otto Maußer und Otto Höfler." In Gilch, Schramka and Prütting 1986: 41-64.

Schreiber, Georg. 1949. *Zwischen Demokratie und Diktatur. Persönliche Erinnerungen an die Politik und Kultur des Reiches (1919-1944)*. Regensberg-Münster.

Schreiber, Georg. 1950. "Volkskunde einst und jetzt. Zur literarischen Widerstandsbewegung." In Tack 1950: 275-317.

Schroeder, Leopold von. 1914-1916. *Arische Religion*. Vol.1: *Einleitung. Der Altarische Himmelsgott. Das Höchste Gute Wesen*. Vol.2: *Naturverehrung und Lebensfeste*. Leipzig.

Schroubek, Georg. 1983. "Wissenschaftsgeschichte und regionale Besonderheiten der Volkskunde an der Deutschen Prager Universität bis 1934." In Brückner and Beitl 1983: 51-62.

Schubert, Günter. 1961. *Die Anfänge der nationalsozialistischen Außenpolitik 1919-1923.* Ph.D. Thesis. Berlin (West).

Schuchard, Jutta; and Horst Claussen (eds.). 1985. *Vergänglichkeit und Denkmal. Beiträge zur Sepulkralkultur.* Schriften des Arbeitskreises selbständiger Kulturinstitute. Vol. 4. Bonn.

Schultz, Wolfgang. 1924. *Zeitrechnung und Weltordnung in ihren übereinstimmenden Grundzügen bei den Indern, Iraniern, Hellenen, Italikern, Kelten, Germanen, Litauern, Slawen.* Mannus-Bibliothek. Vol. 35. Leipzig.

Schwebe, Joachim. 1985. "Das Zentralarchiv der deutschen Volkserzählung in Marburg." *Hessische Blätter für Volks- und Kulturforschung* N.S. 18: 187-190.

Schwietering, Julius. 1933. "Die sozialpolitische Aufgabe der deutschen Volkskunde." *Oberdeutsche Zeitschrift für Volkskunde* 7: 3-11.

Schwinn, Peter. 1989. "Auf Germanensuche in Südtirol. Zu einer volkskundlichen Enquête des SS-Ahnenerbes." *Jahrbuch für Volkskunde* N.S. 12: 85-98.

See, Klaus von. 1970. *Deutsche Germanen-Ideologie. Vom Humanismus bis zur Gegenwart.* Frankfurt am Main.

Seemann, Erich. 1954. *John Meier (1864-1953). Sein Leben, Forschen und Wirken.* Freiburger Universitätsreden. Neue Folge. Vol. 17. Freiburg im Breisgau.

Seemann, Erich; and Harry Schewe (eds.). 1934. *Volkskundliche Gaben. John Meier zum siebzigsten Geburtstag dargebracht.* Berlin and Leipzig.

Seraphim, Hans-Günther (ed.). 1956. *Das politische Tagebuch Alfred Rosenbergs aus den Jahren 1934/35 und 1939/40.* Göttingen.

Sieber, Friedrich. 1955. "Adolf Spamer †" *Deutsches Jahrbuch für Volkskunde* 1: 249-251.

Smelser, Ronald; and Rainer Zitelmann (eds.). 1989. *Die braune Elite. 22 biographische Skizzen.* Darmstadt.

Söhrnsen-Petersen. 1937. "Die Bedeutung des 'Hermann-Göring-Kooges' für die Pflege der Hausbautradition in der Gegenwart." In Thiele 1937: 102-105.

Sokol, Kristin. 1985a. *Vorstudie zur Diplomarbeit* Sokol 1985b: 2.1. Zur wissenschaftspolitischen Situation der volkskundlichen Disziplin und zur ideologischen Haltung Adolf Spamers in der ersten Hälfte der 30er Jahre. Spamers Berufung nach Berlin; 2.2 Spamers Leitung der Abteilung Volkskunde in der Reichsgemeinschaft für Deutsche Volksforschung; 2.3. Die Tätigkeit Adolf Spamers als Hochschullehrer an der Friedrich-Wilhelms-Universität. Maschinenschrift. Berlin (Ost).

Sokol, Kristin. 1985b. *Zum wissenschaftlichen Werk Adolf Spamers. Ein Beitrag zur Wissenschaftsgeschichte der deutschen Volkskunde.* Diplomarbeit zur Erlangung des akademischen Grades für Ethnographie (Diplomethnograph) vorgelegt der Sektion Geschichte der Humboldt-Universität zu Berlin, Bereich Ethnographie. Maschinenschrift. Berlin (Ost).

Sokol, Kristin. 1985c. *Thesen zur Diplomarbeit,* Sokol 1985b. Maschinenschrift. Berlin (Ost).

Sontheimer, Kurt. 1962. *Antidemokratisches Denken in der Weimarer Republik. Die politischen Ideen des deutschen Nationalismus zwischen 1918 und 1933.* München.

Spamer, Adolf. 1924. "Um die Prinzipien der Volkskunde. Anmerkungen zu Hans Naumanns Grundzügen der deutschen Volkskunde." *Hessische Blätter für Volkskunde* 23: 67-108.

Spamer, Adolf. 1934a. "Die Lehrerschaft und die Volkskunde." *Mitteldeutsche Blätter für Volkskunde* 9: 145-148.

Spamer, Adolf. 1934b. "Sitte und Brauch." In Peßler 1934-1938. Vol.2: 33-256.

Spamer, Adolf. 1935a. "Die Volkskunde als Gegenwartswissenschaft. Ein Vortrag 1932." In Riehl and Spamer 1935: 77-85.

Spamer, Adolf. 1935b. "Stand und Aufgaben der deutschen Volksforschung." *Mitteldeutsche Blätter für Volkskunde* 10: 97-105.

Spamer, Adolf. 1936. "Aufgaben und Arbeiten der 'Abteilung Volkskunde' in der 'Reichsgemeinschaft der deutschen Volksforschung.'" *Niederdeutsche Zeitschrift für Volkskunde* 14: 145-154.

Spamer, Adolf. (ed.). 1934-1935a. *Die deutsche Volkskunde.* Vols. 1-2. First Edition. Leipzig and Berlin.

Spamer, Adolf. (ed.). 1934-1935b. *Die deutsche Volkskunde.* Vols. 1-2. Second Edition. Das Deutsche Volk. Vols. 3-4. Leipzig and Berlin.

Spieß, Karl von. 1911. *Der Mythos als Grundlage der Bauernkunst.* Programm des Staats-Obergymnasiums in Wiener-Neustadt.

Spieß, Karl von. 1925. *Bauernkunst, ihre Art und ihr Sinn. Grundlinien einer Geschichte der unpersönlichen Kunst.* First Edition. Wien.

Spieß, Karl von. 1933a. "Das arische Fest." *Bausteine zur Geschichte, Völkerkunde und Mythenkunde* 3: 1-64.

Spieß, Karl von. 1934. *Deutsche Volkskunde als Erschließerin deutscher Kultur.* Berlin.

Spieß, Karl von. 1935. *Bauernkunst, ihre Art und ihr Sinn.* Wien.

Spieß, Karl von. 1938a. "Deutsche Volkskunde - Deutsche Bildung - Deutsche Erneuerung." *Geist der Zeit* 16: 379-388.

Spieß, Karl von. 1938b. "Deutsche Volkskunde - Deutsche Bildung - Deutsche Erneuerung." In Spieß and Mudrak 1938: 11-20.

Spieß, Karl von. 1939a. "Germanisches Erbe in der deutschen Volkskunst." In Thiele 1939: 34-56.

Spieß, Karl von. 1941a. Comment to Fehrle 1940a. *Deutsche Volkskunde* 3: 215-216.

Spieß, Karl von; and Edmund Mudrak. 1938. *Deutsche Volkskunde als politische Wissenschaft. Zwei Aufsätze.* Berlin.

Staubach, Nikolaus. 1974. Review of Höfler 1973. *Fabula* 15: 268-272.

Steglich, Hans. 1934. "Von der Volksforschung zur praktischen Volkstumspflege." *Mitteldeutsche Blätter für Volkskunde* 9: 154-160.

Stein, George H. 1966. *The Waffen SS: Hitler's Elite Guard at War 1939-1945.* New York: Cornell University Press.

Stein, Mary Beth. 1987. "Coming to Terms with the Past: The Depiction of *Volkskunde* in the Third Reich since 1945." *Journal of Folklore Research* 24: 157-185.

Steinitz, Wolfgang. 1955. *Die volkskundliche Arbeit in der Deutschen Demokratischen Republik.* Second Edition. Kleine Beiträge zur Volkskunstforschung. Vol. 1. Leipzig.

Steinitz, Wolfgang. 1954-1962. *Deutsche Volkslieder demokratischen Charakters aus sechs Jahrhunderten.* Vol. 1-2. Deutsche Akademie der Wissenschaften zu Berlin. Veröffentlichungen des Instituts für deutsche Volkskunde. Vol. 4, I-II. Berlin.

Steinitz, Wolfgang. 1959. "Zum 100. Geburtstag Richard Wossidlos." *Deutsches Jahrbuch für Volkskunde* 5: 3-7.

Steller, Walther (ed.). 1933. *Festschrift Theodor Siebs zum 70. Geburtstag 26. August 1932.* Breslau.

Stemmermann, Paul Hans. 1939. "War der sog. 'Königssprung' der Germanen möglich?" *Volk und Vorzeit. Volkstümliche Hefte für oberrheinische Ur- und Frühgeschichte* 1: 86-88.

Stengel-von Rutkowski, Lothar. 1935a. "Hans F.K. Günther, der Programmatiker des Nordischen Gedankens." *Nationalsozialistische Monatshefte* 6, Heft 68: 962-998.

Stengel-von Rutkowski, Lothar. 1935b. "Hans F.K. Günther, der Programmatiker des Nordischen Gedankens." *Nationalsozialistische Monatshefte* 6, Heft 69: 1099-1114.

Stengel-von Rutkowski, Lothar. 1941. "Hans F.K. Günther 50 Jahre alt." *Nationalsozialistische Monatshefte* 12, Heft 132: 263-265.

Stief, Werner. 1938. *Heidnische Sinnbilder an christlichen Kirchen und auf Werken der Volkskunst. Der "Lebensbaum" und sein Gestaltwandel im Jahreslauf.* Deutsches Ahnenerbe. Reihe C. Vol. 8. Leipzig.

Strobach, Hermann. 1973. "Positionen und Grenzen der 'kritischen Volkskunde' in der BRD. Bemerkungen zu Wolfgang Emmerichs Faschismuskritik." *Jahrbuch für Volkskunde und Kulturgeschichte* 16: 45-91.

Strobach, Hermann. 1981a. "Mißbrauch der Volksdichtung durch den deutschen Faschismus." In Strobach 1981: 159-166.

Strobach, Hermann. 1987. "'...aber wann beginnt der Vorkrieg?' Anmerkungen zum Thema Volkskunde und Faschismus (vor und um 1933)." In Gerndt 1987: 23-38.

Strobach, Hermann; Rudolf Weinhold; and Bernhard Weissel. 1974. "Volkskundliche Forschungen in der Deutschen Demokratischen Republik. Bilanz und Ausblick." *Jahrbuch für Volkskunde und Kulturgeschichte* 17: 9-39.

Strobach, Hermann (ed.). 1981. *Geschichte der deutschen Volksdichtung.* Berlin.

Strobel, Hans. 1933-1934. "Lebendiges Erbe." *Der Türmer* 36/2: 505-511.

Strobel, Hans. 1934a. *Die Flurnamen von Heinersreuth. Ein Beitrag zur ostfränkischen Volkskunde.* Fränkische Forschungen. Vol. 4. Erlangen.

Strobel, Hans. 1934b. "Sitte als Recht." *Völkische Kultur* 2: 425-428.

Strobel, Hans. 1934c. "Östliche Agrarrevolution und Bauernpolitik." *Völkische Kultur* 2: 333-335.

Strobel, Hans. 1934d. "Deutsches Bauernschicksal im Spiegel der deutschen Dichtung." *Nationalsozialistische Monatshefte* 5, Heft 49: 369-371.

Strobel, Hans. 1934e. "Eine ostfränkische Kirchweih und ihre Sinndeutung." *Nationalsozialistische Monatshefte* 5, Heft 53: 729-734.

Strobel, Hans. 1934-1935a. "Eindruck vom 2. Reichsbauerntag." *Der Türmer* 37/1: 361-364.

Strobel, Hans. 1934-1935b. "Der Baum als Sinnbild des Lebens." *Der Türmer* 37/2: 260.

Strobel, Hans. 1935b. "Der Bückeberg." *Der Schulungsbrief* 2: 332-334.

Strobel, Hans. 1936a. "Weihnachtsbrauchtum." *Nationalsozialistiche Monatshefte* 7, Heft 81: 1078-1088.

Strobel, Hans. 1936b. "Atlas der deutschen Volkskunde. Gedanken zur ersten Kartenlieferung." *Nationalsozialistische Monatshefte* 7, Heft 79: 917-920.

Strobel, Hans. 1936c. "Neue Brauchtumskunde." *Das Thüringer Fähnlein. Monatshefte für die mitteldeutsche Heimat* 5: 589-593.

Strobel, Hans. 1936d. *Brauchtum und Sitte des deutschen Volkes.* Schriften zur politischen Bildung. Reihe 7. Heft 16. Langensalza.

Strobel, Hans. 1936e. "Weihnachtsbrauchtum." *Nationalsozialistische Monatshefte* 7, Heft 81: 1078-1088.

Strobel, Hans (Pseudonym: Hasso Volker). 1936f. "Germanisches Erbe im deutschen Weihnachtsbrauchtum." *Wille und Macht* 4, Heft 1: 33-38.

Strobel, Hans. 1936/1937. "Die bäuerliche Hausweberei." *Odal* 5: 126-130.

Strobel, Hans. 1937a. "Tracht und Mode. (Nach einem Vortrag des Verfassers auf dem 2. Nordischen Wissenschaftlichen Kongreß 'Tracht und Schmuck', Lübeck 1937)." *Nationalsozialistische Monatshefte* 8, Heft 92: 970-984.

Strobel, Hans. 1937b. "Volksbrauch und Kirchen." *Volk im Werden* 5: 519-535.

Strobel, Hans. 1937c. "Brauchtum der Fasnächte." *Nationalsozialistische Monatshefte* 8, Heft 83: 132-144.

Strobel, Hans. 1937d. "Fasnächte - Gestalten und Gestaltung." *Die Spielschar* 2: 52-57.

Strobel, Hans. 1937e. "Jahr und Leben." *Die Spielschar* 2: 373-376.

Strobel, Hans. 1937/1938. "Der 'primitive' Bauer." *Odal* 6: 169-170.

Strobel, Hans. 1938a. *Bauernbrauch im Jahreslauf.* Deutsches Ahnenerbe. Hrsg. von der Gemeinschaft "Das Ahnenerbe" e.V., Berlin. Abteilung 2: Fachwissenschaftliche Untersuchungen. Vol. 1. Leipzig.

Strobel, Hans. 1938b. "Tracht und Mode." In Thiele 1938: 28-43.

Strobel, Hans. 1938c. "Zur Erforschung des germanischen Erbgutes im deutschen Volksbrauch." *Rasse* 5: 401-408.

Strobel, Hans. 1938d. *Volksbrauch und Weltanschauung.* Forschungen zur deutschen Weltanschauungskunde und Glaubensgeschichte. Vol. 2. Stuttgart and Berlin.

Strobel, Hans. 1938e. "Ganz Frankreich an der Seine! Ein Gang durch das 'Centre regional' der Pariser Weltausstellung." *Odal* 7: 26-35.

Strobel, Hans. 1938f. Review of Ziegler 1937a. *Odal* 7: 249-250.

Strobel, Hans. 1939a. "Altes Brauchtum in unseren Feiern. Auszug aus einem Vortrag auf der 1. Arbeitswoche für Feiergestaltung der Arbeitsgemeinschaft für Deutsche Volkskunde vom 13. bis 18. März in Berlin." *Deutsche Volkskunde* 1: 87-90.

Strobel, Hans. 1939b. "Germanisches Erbe im deutschen Brauchtum." In Thiele 1939: 112-137.

Strobel, Hans. 1939c. "Wohngesittung aus bäuerlicher Haltung." *Odal* 8: 101-106.

Strobel, Hans. 1939d. "Erntezeit - Erntedank." *Odal* 8: 709-711.

Strobel, Hans. 1939e. "Wie die letzten Indianer?" *Deutsche Volkskunde* 1: 182-185.

Strobel, Hans. 1939f. "Volkskunde im Dienste der Volkstumsarbeit." *Mitteldeutsche Blätter für Volkskunde* 14: 1-9.

Strobel, Hans. 1939g. Volkstumsarbeit ohne Wissenschaft?" *Nationalsozialistische Monatshefte* 10, Heft 106: 69-72.

Strobel, Hans. 1943a. *Erbe und Erneuerung. Volkskundliche Beiträge zu weltanschaulichen Fragen unserer Zeit.* Schriftenreihe zur weltanschaulichen Schulungsarbeit der NSDAP. Vol. 36. Nur für den Dienstgebrauch! München: Zentralverlag der NSDAP., Franz Eher Nachf. GmbH.

Strobel, Hans. 1943b. "Bauerntumskunde als Grundlage deutscher Volkskunde." In Strobel 1943a: 3-11.

Strobel, Hans. 1943c. "Volkskunde und Volkskultur." In Strobel 1943a: 12-22.

Strobel, Hans. 1943d. "Volkstumswerte in der nationalsozialistischen Feiergestaltung." In Strobel 1943a: 22-41.

Strobel, Hans. 1943e. "Zur deutschen Lebensgestaltung." In Strobel 1943a: 41-62.

Strobel, Hans. 1943f. "Gefallenenehrung in der Familie." *Die neue Gemeinschaft* 9: 184-185.

Strobel, Hans. 1943g. "Volkskunde und Volkskultur." *Deutsche Volkskunde* 5: 172-176.

Strobel, Hans. 1943h. "Volkstum und nationalsozialistische Feiergestaltung." *Nationalsozialistische Monatshefte* 14, Heft 157: 220-231.

Strobel, Hans. 1943i. "Dr. Claus Padel zum Gedenken." *Deutsche Volkskunde* 5: 113-114.

Strobel, Hans. 1943k. "Haltung und Handlung." *Idee und Tat* 1: 32-33.

Strobel, Hans. 1943l. "Partei oder Familie." *Idee und Tat* 1: 33-36.

Strobel, Hans. 1943m. "Verordnung oder Erziehung?" *Idee und Tat* 1: 41-42.

Strobel, Hans. 1943n. "Feiergut - Feiergerät." *Die neue Gemeinschaft* 9: 240-243.

Strobel, Hans. 1944a. "Die Hochzeitsfeier als nationalsozialistische 'Lebensfeier.'" *Deutsche Volkskunde* 6: 12-15.

Strobel, Hans. 1944b. "Bauernglaube." *Nationalsozialistische Monatshefte* 15, 2. Doppelheft: 173-175.

Strobel, Hans. 1944c. "Über die Tiefenangst." *Idee und Tat* 2: 22-24.

Strobel, Hans. 1944d. "Die Verpflichtungsfeier." *Idee und Tat* 2: 25-28.

Strobel, Hans. 1944e. "Märchen in unserer Zeit?" *Idee und Tat* 2: 28-25.

Strobel, Hans. 1944f. "Kult oder Brauchtum?" *Idee und Tat* 2: 35.

Strobel, Hans. 1944g. "Zur Sprachregelung in der Volkskunde." *Idee und Tat* 5: 56-58.

Strobel, Hans. 1944h. "Weihnachten unter Waffen, Weihnachten der Bewährung." *Idee und Tat* 6: 5-7.

Strobel, Hans. 1944i. "Alte oder neue Weihnachtslieder?" *Idee und Tat* 6: 14-19.

Strobel, Hans. 1944k. "Weihnachten oder Julfest?" *Idee und Tat* 6: 32.

Studien. 1934 and 1935. "Studien zum Mythus des 20. Jahrhunderts." [Von Wilhelm Neuss und einer Anzahl von Mitarbeitern]. *Kirchlicher Anzeiger für die Erzdiözese Köln. Amtliche Beilage.* Köln (1. August 1934. 4.-5. Neudruck "August" bzw. "Herbst" 1935).

Stuhlpfarrer, Karl. 1985. *Umsiedlung Südtirol 1939-1940.* Vol.1-2. Wien and München.

Tacitus, Publius Cornelius. 1959. *Germania.* Herausgegeben, übersetzt und mit Erläuterungen versehen von Eugen Fehrle. Fünfte überarbeitete Auflage besorgt von Richard Hünnerkopf. Heidelberg.

Tack, Wilhelm (ed.). 1950. *Festgabe für Alois Fuchs zum 70. Geburtstag.* Paderborn.

Tagung. 1934. "Tagung der Kreisvolkstumswarte des Gaues Sachsen in Kamenz." *Mitteldeutsche Blätter für Volkskunde* 9: 99-102.

Thiele, Ernst Otto. 1937a. "Das märkische Vorhallenhaus." In Thiele 1937: 58-68.

Thiele, Ernst Otto. 1937b. "Das Osterwasser im märkischen Brauchtum." *Germanen-Erbe* 2: 84-88.

Thiele, Ernst Otto. 1938a. "Der Wocken, ein nordisch-germanisches Spinngerät." In Thiele 1938: 94-116.

Thiele, Ernst Otto. 1939a. "Germanisches Erbe in Darstellungen auf bäuerlichem Sachgut." In Thiele 1939: 91-102.

Thiele, Ernst Otto. 1940. "Der Brixentaler Flurritt." *Deutsche Volkskunde* 2: 134-144.

Thiele, Ernst-Otto (ed.). 1937. *Haus und Hof der Germanen in geschichtlicher Zeit.* Haus und Hof im nordischen Raum. Im Auftrage der Nordischen Gesellschaft ed. by Alexander Funkenberg. Vol.2. Leipzig.

Thiele, Ernst-Otto (ed.). 1938. *Tracht und Schmuck der Germanen in Geschichte und Gegenwart.* Tracht und Schmuck im nordischen Raum. Im Auftrage der Nordischen Gesellschaft ed. by Alexander Funkenberg. Vol. 2. Leipzig.

Thiele, Ernst Otto (ed.). 1939. *Das germanische Erbe in der deutschen Volkskultur. Die Vorträge des 1. Deutschen Volkskundetages zu Braunschweig, Herbst 1938.* Deutsche Volkskunde. Schriftenreihe der Arbeitsgemeinschaft für Deutsche Volkskunde. Vol. 1. München.

Tréfois, Clemens. 1937a. "Der Hausbau am Westrand des germanischen Siedlungsraumes." In Thiele 1937: 35-51.

Tröger, Jörg (ed.). 1984. *Hochschule und Wissenschaft im Dritten Reich.* Frankfurt am Main and New York.

Trümpy, Hans. 1987. "'Volkscharakter' und 'Rasse.' Zwei fatale Schlagworte der NS-Volkskunde." In Gerndt 1987: 169-177.

Uhland, Ludwig. 1865-1873. *Schriften zur Geschichte der Dichtung und Sage.* Ed. by F. Pfeifer. Stuttgart.

Veit, Ulrich. 1984. "Gustav Kosinna und V. Gordon Childe. Ansätze zu einer theoretischen Grundlegung der Vorgeschichte." *Saeculum* 35: 326-364.

Verhey, Hans. 1950. "Wilhelm Peßler, 70 Jahre." *Neues Archiv für Niedersachsen* 4, Heft 15: 1-8.

Viergutz, Rudolf F. 1942. *Von der Weisheit unserer Volksmärchen.* Berlin.

Vogel, Hans Jochen; Simon, Helmut; and Podlech, Adalbert (eds.). 1981. *Die Freiheit des Anderen. Festschrift für Martin Hirsch.* Baden-Baden.

Volkskunde an den Hochschulen. 1986. *Volkskunde an den Hochschulen im Dritten Reich. Eine vorläufige Datensammlung.* Bearbeitet von Esther Gajek. Als Manuskript vervielfältigt. Institut für deutsche und vergleichende Volkskunde. München.

Volkskunde im Dritten Reich. 1986. *Volkskunde im Dritten Reich. Diskussions-anstöße*. Begleitheft zu einer Ausstellung anläßlich der Tagung "Volkskunde und Nationalsozialismus" im Institut für deutsche und vergleichende Volkskunde an der Ludwig-Maximilians-Universität München, 23.-25. Oktober 1986. Als Manuskript vervielfältigt. München.

Volkskunde und Nationalsozialismus. 1986. *Volkskunde und Nationalsozialismus. Tagungshinweise. Programm. Kurzfassungen der Referate*. Vervielfältigtes Manuskript. Institut für deutsche und vergleichende Volkskunde. München.

Volkskundliche Gaben. 1934. *Volkskundliche Gaben. John Meier zum 70. Geburtstag dargebracht*. Berlin and Leipzig.

Volk und Gesundheit. 1982. *Volk und Gesundheit. Heilen und Vernichten im Nationalsozialismus. Begleitbuch zur gleichnamigen Ausstellung im Ludwig-Uhland-Institut für Empirische Kulturwissenschaft der Universität Tübingen*. Ed. by Projektgruppe "Volk und Gesundheit." Tübingen: Tübinger Vereinigung für Volkskunde e.V.

Vorländer, Herwart. 1984. "Heimat und Heimaterziehung im Nationalsozialismus." In Knoch and Leeb 1984: 30-43.

Vorländer, Herwart. 1986. "NS-Volkswohlfahrt und Winterhilfswerk des deutschen Volkes." *Vierteljahrshefte für Zeitgeschichte* 34: 341-380.

Vorschläge. 1933. *Vorschläge für 150 Fragen zum Abschluß des Frageplanes des Atlas der Deutschen Volkskunde*. Deutsche Forschung. Aus der Arbeit der Notgemeinschaft der Deutschen Wissenschaft. Vol. 19. Berlin.

Voßkamp, Wilhelm. 1985. "Kontinuität und Diskontinuität. Zur deutschen Literaturwissenschaft im Dritten Reich." In Lundgreen 1985: 140-162.

Waibl, Gunther. 1985. *Photographie und Geschichte. Sozialgeschichte der Photographie in Südtirol 1919-1945*. Ph.D. Thesis. Wien.

Weber-Kellermann, Ingeborg. 1959. "Zur Frage der interethnischen Beziehungen in der 'Sprachinselvolkskunde.'" *Österreichische Zeitschrift für Volkskunde* 62: 19-47.

Weber-Kellermann, Ingeborg. 1969. *Deutsche Volkskunde zwischen Germanistik und Sozialwissenschaften*. Sammlung Metzler. Vol. 79. Stuttgart.

Weber-Kellermann, Ingeborg. 1984. "Zum Gedenken an Adolf Spamer zu seinem 100. Geburtstag am 10. April 1983." *Hessische Blätter für Volks- und Kulturforschung* 16: 197-206.

Weber-Kellermann, Ingeborg. 1986. "Problems of Interethnic Research in Southeast Europe. A Consideration of Method." In Dow and Lixfeld 1986: 172-183.

Weber-Kellermann, Ingeborg; and Andreas C. Bimmer. 1985. *Einführung in die Volkskunde/Europäische Ethnologie. Eine Wissenschaftsgeschichte*. 2. erweiterte und ergänzte Auflage von "Deutsche Volkskunde zwischen Germanistik und Sozialwissenschaften." Sammlung Metzler. Vol. 79. Stuttgart.

Weigel, Karl Theodor. 1934. *Lebendige Vorzeit rechts und links der Landstraße*. Berlin.

Weigel, Karl Theodor. 1935. *Runen und Sinnbilder*. Berlin.

Weigel, Karl Theodor. 1936. "Runen am deutschen Hause." *Nationalsozialistische Monatshefte* 7, Hefte 71 und 79: 163-165, 900-904.

Weigel, Karl Theodor. 1937. "Sinnbilder am Hause." In Thiele 1937: 111-123.

Weigel, Karl Theodor. 1939a. *Germanisches Glaubensgut in Runen und Sinnbildern.* München.

Weigel, Karl Theodor. 1939b. "Sinnbilder als germanisches Erbgut." In Thiele 1939: 103-111.

Weigel, Karl Theodor. 1941. *Sinnbilder in Niedersachsen.* Hildesheim.

Weigel, Karl Theodor. 1943. *Beiträge zur Sinnbildforschung.* Berlin.

Weiser, Lily. 1927. *Altgermanische Jünglingsweihen und Männerbünde. Ein Beitrag zur deutschen und nordischen Altertums- und Volkskunde.* Bausteine zur Volkskunde und Religionswissenschaft. Vol. 1. Bühl.

Weiss, Richard. 1946. *Volkskunde der Schweiz. Grundriss.* Erlenbach-Zürich.

Werner-Künzig, Waltraut. 1977. *Johannes Künzig zum 80. Geburtstag. Freiburg.*

Weyer, Johannes. 1984. "Die Forschungsstelle für das Volkstum im Ruhrgebiet (1935-1941): Ein Beispiel für Soziologie im Faschismus." *Soziale Welt* 35: 124-145.

Wildhagen, Eduard. 1938. *Der Atlas der deutschen Volkskunde. I. Grundlagen.* Als Manuskript gedruckt. Berlin.

Wimmer, Erich. 1987a. "Die Errichtung der Volkskundlichen Abteilung am Seminar für deutsche Philologie (1936) und die Volkskunde an der Hochschule für Lehrerbildung in Würzburg." In Gerndt 1987: 119-126.

Wimmer, Erich. 1987b. *Organisationsformen volkskundlicher Sammlung und Forschung und volkskundliche Institutionen in Bayern.* Augsburger Reader. Vol. 5. Augsburg.

Wimmer, Erich. 1987c. "Volkskunde und Nationalsozialismus. Arbeitstagung der Deutschen Gesellschaft für Volkskunde vom 23.-25. Oktober 1986 in München." *Bayerische Blätter für Volkskunde* 14: 26-28.

Wippermann, Wolfgang. 1989. *Faschismustheorien. Zum Stand der gegenwärtigen Diskussion.* Erträge der Forschung. Vol. 17. Fifth Edition. Darmstadt.

Wirth, Herman. 1931-1936. *Die Heilige Urschrift der Menschheit.* Vol. 1-2. Leipzig.

Wirth, Herman. 1933. *Die Ura Linda Chronik.* Leipzig.

Wolf, Christa. 1983. *Kassandra. Vier Vorlesungen. Eine Erzählung.* Berlin.

Wolfgramm, Eberhard. 1943. "Kaukasische Sagen in Sowjetischer Umbildung." *Deutsche Volkskunde* 5: 114-122.

Wolfgramm, Eberhard. 1944a. "Verwandelte Volkssänger. Ein Beitrag zur sowjetischen Kulturpolitik." *Deutsche Volkskunde* 6: 1-6.

Wolfgramm, Eberhard. 1944b. "Verwandelte Volkssänger. Ein Beitrag zur sowjetischen Kulturpolitik." *Deutsche Volksforschung in Böhmen und Mähren* 3: 42-51.

Wolfram, Richard. 1936-1937. *Schwerttanz und Männerbund.* Lieferungen 1-3. Kassel.

Wolfram, Richard. 1938a. "Volkskundliches aus dem Waldviertel." *Germanien* 10: 121-125.

Wolfram, Richard. 1938b. "Tänze der Germanen." *Germanien* 10: 156-160.

Wolfram, Richard. 1938c. "Deutsches Brauchtum im Böhmerwald." *Germanien* 10: 355-360.

Wolfram, Richard. 1944. "Die Sinnbilder in der Volkskunde." In Jankuhn 1944: 17-34.

Wolfram, Richard. 1947. "Das Radmähen, ein unscheinbarer Volksbrauch und eine Fülle von Fragen." *Schweizerisches Archiv für Volkskunde* 44: 270-278.

Wolfram, Richard. 1987. *Südtiroler Volksschauspiele und Spielbräuche*. Österreichische Akademie der Wissenschaften. Philosophisch-Historische Klasse. Sitzungsberichte. Vol. 480. Wien.

Wrede, Adam. 1936. *Deutsche Volkskunde auf germanischer Grundlage*. Osterwieck/Harz and Berlin.

Wüst, Walther. 1942. *Indogermanisches Bekenntnis*. Berlin-Dahlem: Ahnenerbe-Stiftung Verlag.

Zentner, Kurt. 1966. *Illustrierte Geschichte des Widerstandes in Deutschland und Europa, 1933-1945*. (Mitarbeit Gerd Schreiber). München.

Ziegler, Matthäus. 1957. *Engel und Dämon im Lichte der Bibel mit Einschluß des ausserkanonischen Schrifttums*. Lehre und Symbol. Vol. 7. Zürich.

Ziegler, Matthes. 1933. *Kirche und Reich im Ringen der jungen Generation*. Reden und Aufsätze zum nordischen Gedanken. Vol. 6. Leipzig.

Ziegler, Matthes. 1934-1940a. "Familienleben." In Mackensen 1934-1940: 47-51.

Ziegler, Matthes. 1934-1940b. "Frau." In Mackensen 1934-1940: 211-215.

Ziegler, Matthes. 1934-1940c. "Geschwister." In Mackensen 1934-1940: 588-596.

Ziegler, Matthes. 1934a. "Volkskunde auf rassischer Grundlage." *Nationalsozialistische Monatshefte* 5, Heft 53: 711-717.

Ziegler, Matthes. 1934b. "Die 1. Tagung des Reichsbundes für deutsche Vorgeschichte." *Nationalsozialistische Monatshefte* 5, Heft 56: 1067-1068.

Ziegler, Matthes. 1934c. "Deutsche Volkskunde" [Sammelrezension]. *Nationalsozialistische Monatshefte* 5, Heft 57: 1165-1168.

Ziegler, Matthes. 1934d. "Friedrich Hölderlin. Sein Künstlertum und seine Frömmigkeit." *Nationalsozialistische Monatshefte* 5, Heft 47: 155-163.

Ziegler, Matthes. 1935a. "Kirchliche oder religiöse Volkskunde?" *Nationalsozialistische Monatshefte* 6, Heft 65: 674-685.

Ziegler, Matthes. 1935b. "Volkskunde" [Sammelbesprechung]. *Nationalsozialistische Monatshefte* 6, Heft 69: 1156-1159.

Ziegler, Matthes. 1935c. "Bedenkliche Theologie." *Nationalsozialistische Monatshefte* 6, Heft 59: 177-181.

Ziegler, Matthes. 1935d. "Aus der Arbeit der katholischen Aktion." *Nationalsozialistische Monatshefte* 6, Heft 60: 276-278.

Ziegler, Matthes. 1935e. "Christentum und Judentum." *Nationalsozialistische Monatshefte* 6, Heft 60: 279-281.

Ziegler, Matthes. 1935f. "Alfred Rosenberg antwortet!" *Nationalsozialistische Monatshefte* 6, Heft 61: 290-297.

Ziegler, Matthes. 1936a. *Volkskunde auf rassischer Grundlage. Voraussetzungen und Aufgaben*. Nationalsozialistische Wissenschaft. Schriftenreihe der N.S. Monatshefte. Vol. 4. München.

Ziegler, Matthes. 1936b. "Germanische Religionsforschung im Weltanschauungskampf. Bemerkungen zum neuesten germanenkundlichen Schrifttum." *Nationalsozialistische Monatshefte* 7, Heft 78: 819-824.

Ziegler, Matthes. 1937a. *Die Frau in Märchen*. Deutsches Ahnenerbe. 2.Abteilung: Fachwissenschaftliche Untersuchungen. Vol. 2. Leipzig.

Ziegler, Matthes. 1937b. "Zur Weltkirchenkonferenz in Oxford, Juli 1937." *Nationalsozialistische Monatshefte* 8, Heft 87: 506-514.

Ziegler, Matthes. 1937c. *Der Protestantismus zwischen Rom und Moskau*. Second Edition. München.

Ziegler, Matthes. 1938a. "Zur Einführung." In Deutsche Volkskunde im Schrifttum 1938: 5-8.

Ziegler, Matthes. 1938b. "Von den innern Kräften der deutschen Geschichte." *Nationalsozialistische Monatshefte* 9, Heft 100: 592-595.

Ziegler, Matthes. 1938c. "Weltanschauung und Staatstreue." *Nationalsozialistische Monatshefte* 9, Heft 102: 754-756.

Ziegler, Matthes. 1939a. *Volkskunde auf rassischer Grundlage. Voraussetzungen und Aufgaben*. Deutsches Volkstum. Eine Schriftenreihe über deutsche Volkskunde für die Schulungs- und Erziehungsarbeit der NSDAP. Hrsg. vom Beauftragten des Führers für die Überwachung der gesamten geistigen und weltanschaulichen Schulung und Erziehung der NSDAP in Verbindung mit der "Arbeitsgemeinschaft für Deutsche Volkskunde." München.

Ziegler, Matthes. 1939b. "Die Aufgaben der Arbeitsgemeinschaft für Deutsche Volkskunde. Eröffnungsrede zum 1. Deutschen Volkskundetag in Braunschweig, Sept. 1938." In Thiele 1939: 7-10.

Ziegler, Matthes. 1939c. *Illusion oder Wirklichkeit? Offenbarungsdenken und mythischer Glaube*. München.

Ziegler, Matthes. 1939d. *Soldatenglaube, Soldatenehre. Ein deutsches Brevier für Hitler-Soldaten*. Nordland-Bücherei. Vol. 10. Berlin.

Ziegler, Matthes. 1939e. "Einführung." *Deutsche Volkskunde* 1: 5.

Ziegler, Matthes. 1940a. "Die Aufgaben des Handbuches." In Rosenberg 1940: VIII-XI.

Ziegler, Matthes. 1940b. *Aberglaube. Eine volkskundliche Wert- und Begriffsbestimmung*. Stubenrauchs deutsche Grundrisse. Die Schwarze Reihe: Deutsche Kultur. Vol. 3/4. Berlin.

Zipfel, Friedrich. 1965. *Kirchenkampf in Deutschland 1933-1945. Religionsverfolgung und Selbstbehauptung der Kirchen in der nationalsozialistischen Zeit*. Mit einer Einleitung von Hans Herzfeld. Veröffentlichungen der Historischen Kommission zu Berlin beim Friedrich-Meinecke-Institut der Freien Universität Berlin. Vol. 11. Publikationen der Forschungsgruppe Berliner Widerstand beim Senator für Inneres von Berlin. Vol.1. Berlin (West).

Zippelius, Adelhart. 1978. "Ingeborg Weber-Kellermann zum 26.6.1978." In Bimmer, Böth et alii 1978: 199-207.

Zischka, Johannes. 1986. *Die NS-Rassenideologie. Machttaktisches Instrument oder handlungsbestimmendes Ideal?* Europäische Hochschulschriften. Reihe 3. Vol. 274. Frankfurt am Main.

Zitelmann, Rainer. 1987. *Hitler. Selbstverständnis eines Revolutionärs*. Hamburg, Leamington Spa and New York.

Zmarzlick, Hans Günther. 1963. "Der Sozialdarwinismus in Deutschland." *Vierteljahreshefte für Zeitgeschichte* 11: 246-273.

Zur Geschichte von Volkskunde. 1964. *Zur Geschichte von Volkskunde und Mundartforschung in Württemberg. Helmut Dölker zum 60. Geburtstag.* Volksleben. Vol. 6. Tübingen.

Zwernemann, Jürgen. 1980. *Hundert Jahre Hamburgisches Museum für Völkerkunde.* Hamburg.

Name Index

HANNJOST LIXFELD, Akademischer Oberrat in the Department of Folklore at the University of Freiburg im Breisgau, is the co-editor of *German* Volkskunde: *A Decade of Theoretical Confrontation, Debate, and Reorientation (1967–1977)*. He has published numerous studies on narratives, especially on the joke and the *Schwank*, as well as on folk song, community research and on German *Volkskunde* during the Third Reich.

JAMES R. DOW, Professor of German and Chair of the Department of Foreign Languages and Literatures at Iowa State University, is the co-editor of *German* Volkskunde: *A Decade of Theoretical Confrontation, Debate, and Reorientation (1967–1977), Language and Ethnicity, Sprachminoritäten—Minoritätensprachen*, and several studies on German folklore during the Third Reich.